EYEWITNESS TRAVEL

ALASKA

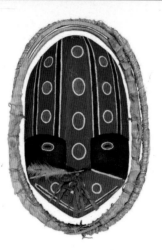

EYEWITNESS TRAVEL

ALASKA

Main Contributor **Deanna Swaney**

DK

LONDON, NEW YORK,
MELBOURNE, MUNICH AND DELHI
www.dk.com

Managing Editor Aruna Ghose
Art Editor Priyanka Thakur
Project Editor Ankita Awasthi
Project Designer Mathew Kurien
Editor Arundhti Bhanot
Designer Baishakhee Sengupta
Senior Cartographer Uma Bhattacharya
Cartographer Alok Pathak
Senior Picture Researcher Taiyaba Khatoon
Picture Researcher Sumita Khatwani
DTP Coordinator Shailesh Sharma
DTP Designers Vinod Harish, Azeem Siddiqui

Contributors
Deanna Swaney, Eric Amrine

Photographers
Nigel Hicks, Andrew Holligan

Illustrators
Arun Pottirayil, Madhav Raman, T. Gautam Trivedi

Printed and bound in China

15 16 17 18 10 9 8 7 6 5 4 3 2 1

First published in Great Britain in 2006
by Dorling Kindersley Limited,
80 Strand, London WC2R 0RL

Reprinted with revisions 2008, 2010, 2012, 2015

MIX
Paper from
responsible sources
FSC
www.fsc.org   FSC™ C018179

Front cover main image: The Taiga (Boreal forest) in fall, Denali National Park

◀ Fireweed on the shore of Bear Glacier Lake, Kenai Fjords National Park

Steller sea lion rookery on the Chiswell
Islands, Kenai Fjords National Park

Contents

How to Use this Guide **6**

Introducing
Alaska

The New Eddystone Rock, Behm Canal,
Misty Fiords National Monument

Kayaking in the calm waters off Whittier,
Prince William Sound

Survival Guide

Alaska Area By Area

Handwoven
Aleut basket

Travelers' Needs

The Beaver Clan House in Saxman Totem
park, near Ketchikan

Following the Gold Rush trail on the White
Pass and Yukon Route Railway

The historical town of Kennicott in the Eastern Interior

HOW TO USE THIS GUIDE

This guide helps you get the most from your visit to Alaska with expert recommendations and detailed practical information. The first section, *Introducing Alaska,* maps the state and sets it in its historical and cultural context. *Alaska Area by Area* focuses first on Alaska's largest city, Anchorage, then on the state's main regions, with all the major towns and important sights described and illustrated in rich detail. Restaurant and hotel recommendations and information about cruising the coastlines, hiking in the interior, and other outdoor activities can be found in *Travelers' Needs.* The *Survival Guide* contains practical tips on everything, from transport around the country to the Alaskan word for "Great!"

Anchorage

The first section of *Alaska Area by Area* concentrates on the vibrant, culturally rich city of Anchorage and its municipality, from the sights and bustle of the historic center to places of interest in the wider city and the rural communities, historical attractions, and many areas of outstanding natural beauty in the surrounding landscape.

Colored thumb tabs continue through the extent of each section.

1 Introduction The city's geographical setting and economic life are described, as well as its historical development and features of interest to the visitor.

A country map shows the city's location in Alaska.

2 City Map For easy reference, the sights are numbered and located on a map. The main streets, bus stations and railway stations, parking areas, and civic buildings are also shown.

Sights at a Glance lists the city's sights by category, from historic buildings to hip neighborhoods, parks and outlying wilderness areas, museums, theaters, and other visitor attractions.

3 Detailed Information All the sights in the city are described individually. Addresses, telephone numbers, opening hours, admission charges, and information on how to get there are given for each sight. The key to symbols is shown on the back flap.

Each area of Alaska is identified by color-coded thumb tabs.

1 Introduction
An overview of the history and characteristics of each region.

Country maps show the location and area of the region covered in the section.

Alaska Region by Region

In the chapters that follow the section on Anchorage, the state is divided into seven main regions. The map on the inside front cover shows these regional divisions. The most interesting places to visit are given on the Regional Map at the beginning of each chapter.

2 Regional Map This shows the main road network and gives an illustrated overview of the whole region. Interesting places to visit are numbered and there are useful tips on getting around.

Practical information at the start of each entry includes a map reference relating to the road map that appears on the inside back cover.

3 Detailed Information All the important towns and other places to visit are dealt with individually. They are listed in order, following the numbering given on the Regional Map. Each entry also contains practical information such as map references, addresses, telephone numbers, and opening times.

Story boxes explore some of the region's historical and cultural topics in detail.

The Visitors' Checklist provides a summary of the practical information you need to plan your visit.

4 Alaska's Top Sights These are given two or more full pages. All the important features of interest are highlighted.

Expanded maps and other illustrations make orientation easy.

INTRODUCING ALASKA

DISCOVERING ALASKA

The following tours have been created to take in a number of Alaska's highlights. In an area as vast and rugged as Alaska, some long-distance journeys are needed to reach more remote locations such as the Arctic; however, the itineraries are designed to keep travel time and distance realistic. To begin with, there are two three-day city tours, covering the most popular city, Anchorage, and its neighbor Seward. These tours can be taken on their own or combined to form a seven- or ten-day tour taking in the scenic Kenai Peninsula. The Kenai tour is followed by two seven-day itineraries encompassing the wildest and most scenic parts of the state: the far north and Arctic, and the Gold Rush Territory to the east. Pick, choose, and combine at your leisure.

Aurora borealis
A winter trip to Alaska can be made magical by the appearance of the aurora borealis, or Northern Lights.

0 kilometers   300
0 miles   300

Prudhoe B

Colville

Wisen

Coldfoot

Arctic Circle — Koyukak River

Arctic Circle Sign

Koyukuk

Yukon River and
Trans-Alaska Pipeline

Yukon   Arctic Circle Trading Post

Fairbanks

*See Kenai Peninsula
inset map*

Anchorage

A Week in the Far North and Arctic

- Experience the pristine wilderness of Alaska's far northern territory.

- Cross the line to get your official Arctic Circle Certificate.

- Visit a working oldfield, try your hand at panning for gold, and hear stories of survival in this harshest of climates.

- Watch a dog sled team train, and visit a Native village to meet with the elders.

- Chase the Northern Lights to catch their mesmerising dance across the sky.

The Trans-Alaska Pipeline
An astonishing feat of engineering, the pipeline crosses some of the most barren landscapes of North America, carrying the "black gold."

A Week in Gold Rush Territory

- Tour the mighty Mendenhall Glacier, and hike along rainforest trails beside waterfalls and streams.
- Learn how thousands of prospectors staked their lives on dreams of gold.
- Ride the Alaska Marine Highway for the scenic cruise of a lifetime.
- Follow the prospecting trail on the White Pass railroad north to Canada's Yukon, site of the first big North American gold rush.
- Visit Native galleries for high-quality arts and crafts.
- Learn about the extraordinary blending of Russian and American cultures in one of Alaska's most beautiful towns.
- Catch your own salmon or halibut; eat it fresh, or have it shipped home.

The Yukon Route A narrow-gauge railway follows the gold rush trail over the awesome White Pass summit.

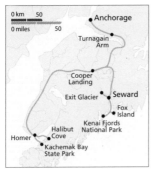

Key

— Far North and Arctic tour
— Gold Rush Territory tour
— Kenai Peninsula tour

Outdoor Adventures in the Kenai Peninsula

- Take cruises and hikes to get close up to glaciers.
- Meet harbor seals, sea lions, and a giant octopus at Alaska's superb SeaLife Center.
- Make a helicopter trip to try your hand at dog-mushing.
- Practice your skills at fishing or sea-kayaking.
- Spot wildlife with the help of experienced guides on a river float trip.
- Browse local art galleries and see craftsmen at work; shop for unique souvenirs.

Glacial majesty Tour boats sail thrillingly close to the ice face, while everyone hopes to see the spectacle of the glacier calving.

3 Days in Anchorage

Anchorage is a year-round destination with once-in-a-lifetime experiences. It's the most-visited city in Alaska.

- **Arriving** Ted Stevens Anchorage International Airport is just 15 minutes' drive from downtown. Rent a car at the airport, or take the excellent bus or shuttle services into the city.

- **Getting around** Downtown Anchorage is easily explored on foot, but a car is convenient for further afield.

Day 1
Morning A few days in the state's largest city gives you enough time to enjoy the main sights. Spend your first morning visiting the **Anchorage Museum** *(see pp72–3)* to get grounded in the city's history and its connection to Native American tribes, gold miners, and modern pioneers. Stop for a leisurely lunch downtown in the area along 5th and 6th Streets, where brewpubs, fine restaurants and casual cafés cluster.

Afternoon Lace up your boots for a hike or rent a bike to enjoy the **Tony Knowles Coastal Trail** *(see pp78–9)*, a gentle, paved trail that winds 11 miles (18 km) from downtown through pristine forests and streams. End the day with a drink at one of the pubs overlooking **Lake Hood** *(see p79)*.

Day 2
Morning Take a city trolley tour to get an overview of the city, or book a flightseeing tour for a bird's-eye view of the entire city and the top of Mount McKinley. If visiting on a summer weekend stop in at the **Anchorage Market** *(see p74)* and have lunch in the Eat Local section, with Alaska-grown produce, seafood, and meats. Or, in winter, shop where the locals do at the **5th Avenue Mall** *(see p93)*, with major national stores and shops showcasing Alaskan products.

Afternoon Take a shuttle bus or drive to the excellent **Alaska Zoo** *(see p80)* to see and learn more about the state's wildlife, including grizzly bears and mighty moose. Another option is a salmon-fishing cruise, where you're guaranteed to land a delicious fish, prepared at the dock ready for eating or shipping back home. End the day with live theater or music at the **Center for Performing Arts** *(see p94)*.

Day 3
Morning Pay a visit to the **Alaska Native Heritage Center** *(see pp76–7)*, a famous educational and cultural center that celebrates the arts and traditions of the state's 11 major native cultural groups. Be sure to visit the six full-sized Native dwellings built on the shores of Lake Tiulana. Watch Native artists demonstrating their work.

Afternoon Take a small-boat cruise through Prince William Sound, during which you'll glide past hundreds of glaciers, very likely spot black bears on the shore, and view myriad species of seabirds.

3 Days in Seward

Located on the southern coast, Seward is home to one of Alaska's oldest communities and is surrounded by spectacular scenery.

- **Arriving** Seward is a short flight from Anchorage, but the 120-mile (190-km) drive from Anchorage south to Seward is magnificent, taking you along the dramatic coastline of Turnagain Arm.

- **Moving on** Drive back to Anchorage, or to Cooper Landing to extend the trip. Or, fly back to Anchorage from Kenai Municipal Airport.

Day 1
Morning After your trip from Anchorage, head for one of the many casual restaurants on the **waterfront** *(see p102)* for an early lunch of freshly caught salmon or other fish. Stretch your legs with a stroll around the downtown historic district to visit some of the quaint shops and art galleries.

Afternoon Book a helicopter for a flight to a dog camp at the top of one of the nearby glaciers. Glide across the snow and glacial ice with a team of working dogs, play with husky puppies, and hear trail stories from your Alaskan musher. Dine at your hotel.

Day 2
Take a day-cruise into **Kenai Fjords National Park** *(see pp106–7)*, where you'll view wildlife, see tidewater glaciers; and enjoy a sumptuous buffet ashore at Fox Island, in the private Fox Island Lodge. National Park rangers give a presentation on the area's wildlife, which includes many different types of whales, seals, sea lions, otters, and porpoises.

The Tony Knowles Coastal Trail, popular with walkers, joggers, and cyclists

For practical information on getting around Alaska's cities see pp280–91

The icy tongue of Exit Glacier, spilling down from the Harding icefield west of Seward

Day 3
Morning Take a hike around **Exit Glacier** (see p103) for some of the best, most expansive views of this mammoth icefield. Alternately, visit the birds, marine mammals, and other residents at the **Alaska SeaLife Center** (see pp104–5), Alaska's only public aquarium and a world-class marine research and wildlife rescue center.

Afternoon Back to Anchorage, or drive on to Cooper Landing; see Day 3 of the Kenai Peninsula tour (below).

Outdoor Adventures in the Kenai Peninsula

- **Duration** 7 days
- **Airports** Ted Stevens Anchorage International Airport, Kenai Municipal Airport
- **Transport** Renting a car allows you to stop as often as you like to view the scenery and wildlife. Tour buses also offer frequent trips and options.

Days 1 and 2: Seward
Arriving from Anchorage, select two days from the 3-day Seward tour (see facing page and above).

Day 3: Cooper Landing
Make your way to **Cooper Landing** (see p100), at the confluence of Kenai Lake and the Kenai River, and fuel up with lunch at your hotel when you arrive. Spend the afternoon with expert guides on a float trip through the turquoise waters of the Upper Kenai River, passing through scenic wilderness and viewing wildlife. Dinner in Cooper Landing, perhaps at a roadhouse overlooking the river.

Day 4: Homer
Pack a lunch and make tracks for **Homer** (see pp112–13) along the Kenai Spur Highway, with sweeping views of Cook Inlet, mountains, and volcanoes. Visit the Alaska Islands and Oceans Visitor Center (and pick up a Hiking Trails Map) as you come into town. Take an afternoon stroll along the **Homer Spit** (see p113), a long narrow finger of land jutting into Kachemak Bay, pausing at the shops, galleries and pubs to enjoy the life of this artisan community. Select one of the restaurants for dinner.

Day 5: Homer
Three excellent options for an all-day excursion all involve fun on Kachemak Bay: a boat cruise to fish for halibut, with lunch provided on board; a boat cruise to **Halibut Cove** (see p113), with lunch and dinner provided; or sea-kayaking along coast, with lunch provided.

Days 6: Homer
Visit the **Pratt Museum** (see p112), which specializes in early homesteading, Native Alaskan traditions, and local art, or the contemporary **Bunnell Strett Arts Center** (see p112), then lunch nearby. Afterwards, take a water taxi to **Kachemak Bay State Park** (see p113) and enjoy an easy 3.5 mile (6 km) hike on the Grewingk Lake Glacier Trail, above the forest to the foot of a glacier. Dinner at your hotel.

Day 7: Homer back to Anchorage
Breakfast in town (and pack a box lunch) before making a leisurely return journey to Anchorage, stopping along the spectacular **Turnagain Arm** (see pp84–5). See birds returning to nest as the lights of the city approach, then head back to your Anchorage hotel for a final dinner.

The Harrington Cabin, reconstructing life on a 1940s homestead, at Homer's Pratt Museum

A Week in the Far North and Arctic

- **Airports** Ted Stevens Anchorage International Airport is the departure point for an early morning flight to Fairbanks, your base for venturing into the Arctic.

- **Transport** In Fairbanks, several tour companies offer tours along the famous Dalton Highway, the only highway in the US to cross the mighty Yukon River and to connect the highway system to the Arctic Ocean.

Day 1: Prudhoe Bay
Arrive in **Fairbanks** (see pp174–8) and take a small plane north to **Prudhoe Bay** (see p224). Visit the Prudhoe Bay oil fields, with lunch at a restaurant that caters to the rough-and-ready oilfield workers. Get a taste of the rest of your adventure by dipping your toe in the frigid waters of the Arctic Ocean. Overnight at Prudhoe Bay; there's only two hotels to choose from.

Day 2: Coldfoot
Breakfast in Prudhoe Bay, and pack or buy a lunch. Take the tour bus along the **Dalton Highway** (see pp222–3) to rustic Coldfoot, where you can visit a

Discovery III, a sternwheeler riverboat, makes daily trips from Fairbanks in summer

dog sled team in training or take a hike in the silent, pristine wilderness. Dine simply at your lodgings in Coldfoot.

Day 3: Coldfoot
From Coldfoot, in summer take a scenic float down the Middle Fork of the Koyukak River, stopping along the shore for a barbecue lunch. If it's winter, take a short bus trip to a viewing station for your best chance to glimpse the aurora borealis, or Northern Lights. Overnight in Coldfoot.

Day 4: Wiseman
Visit the nearby historic gold-mining town of **Wiseman** (see p222), the only community that

is occupied year-round along the Dalton Highway. Return to Fairbanks via small plane.

Day 5: Fairbanks
Enjoy a **Riverboat Discovery** (see p175) river cruise with lunch aboard a sternwheeler. See a dog sledding presentation and learn about life at an Athabascan Indian village.

Day 6: Arctic Circle
From Fairbanks, take an all-day guided excursion by small plane and bus to cross the Arctic Circle and get that all-important official Arctic Circle Certificate. Take a walk on the spongy tundra, laced with veins of ice. View the mighty **Yukon River** (see pp174–8) and the **Trans-Alaska Pipeline** (see pp174–8) and visit the Arctic Circle Trading Post for mementoes of your trip.

Day 7: Fairbanks
Back in Fairbanks for more of its attractions. Take a vintage train ride to try your hand at panning for gold at **Gold Dredge No. 8** (see p178). Visit the **University of Alaska Museum of the North** (see p175), one of the top 10 attractions in the state; don't miss Blue Babe, the mummified Ice Age bison. Return to Anchorage on an evening flight or the following morning.

Arctic winters in Alaska offer the chance to see the mesmerising, rippling spectacle of the aurora borealis

For practical information on traveling around Alaska see pp280–91

Native arts and artifacts on display at the Alaska State Museum

A Week in Gold Rush Territory

- **Getting there** Juneau has an international airport, or, from Anchorage, take a tour bus, plane, or train.
- **Transport** The itinerary is planned around internal flights, ferries, and guided day trips and tours.

Day 1: Juneau
Make your first port of call from **Juneau** (see pp142–3) the **Mendenhall Glacier** (see p45), calling into the Visitor Center for an interpretive talk then hiking through the rainforest. You'll pass by waterfalls and streams, with views of the base of the glacier itself. Have a light lunch and spend the remaining daylight hours strolling and shopping for Native art and limited-edition local designer goods in the Mendenhall Valley shopping districts or downtown on South Franklin Street.

Day 2: Juneau
Visit the newly expanded and relocated **Alaska State Museum** (see p142) for a broad overview of Native art and culture, as well as state history. The **Last Chance Mining Museum** (see p143) celebrates the city's mining history. Have a lunch of fresh seafood in one of the downtown restaurants just a few blocks from the docks. In the afternoon, ride the **Mount Roberts Tramway** (see p143) from almost sea level to 1,800 ft (550 m) up Mount Roberts, for a wide-angle view of downtown and the Gastineau Channel.

Day 3: Ketchikan
Take the short flight to **Ketchikan** (see pp128–9) in time for a lunch of fresh fish by the cruise ship docks, or a brew at the Arctic Bar, a local favorite for almost 80 years. Explore the arty district around Mission, Main, Front, and Creek Streets, perhaps picking up some original art and finding somewhere for dinner.

Day 4: Ketchikan to Skagway
Take the **Alaska Marine Highway** (see pp290–91) to Skagway; grab a recliner in the lounge or the heated solarium, and watch the stunning scenery drift past, catch up on a book, or chat to your fellow passengers. It's a 22-hour trip; if that's an adventure too far, travel by air instead (you'll probably need to transfer in Juneau).

Day 5: Skagway
In **Skagway** (see pp150–51) it's hard to escape the town's Gold Rush history, so dive right in. Top attraction is the scenic, sometimes hair-raising Summit Tour on the narrow-gauge **White Pass and Yukon Route Railroad** (see pp153), following the trail of the prospectors.

Day 6: Sitka
Take a small plane from Skagway to **Sitka** (see pp140–41) to explore this Baranof Island city, the 19th-century hub of Russian-American culture. Tour the city's historic buildings and learn about the Tlingit people at **Sitka National Historical Park** (see p141). Stay overnight; Sitka has some excellent hotels and restaurants.

Day 7: Sitka to Juneau
With its access to the open ocean as well as inland waters, Sitka offers excellent sport-fishing opportunities. Take a trip with a local charter captain and wait for the tug of a fish on your line. Return to Juneau for a final dinner on the waterfront.

Creek Street has a notorious past as Ketchikan's former red-light district (see p128)

Putting Alaska on the Map

Flanked by the Arctic and Pacific Oceans, separated from Russia by the Bering Strait, and bordered by Canada in the east, Alaska lies across the Arctic Circle. Covering over 586,400 sq miles (1.5 million sq km) and with just 710,000 people, it is the largest and least densely populated US state. Almost half of all Alaskans live in Anchorage, while the rest are concentrated around Fairbanks, Southeast Alaska, the Mat-Su Valley, and the Kenai Peninsula. The spectacular landscape, dotted with national parks, is dominated by glaciers, rugged mountain ranges, island chains, broad river valleys, and wide coastal plains.

Key

- ━━━ Alaska highway
- ━━━ Highway
- ┈┈┈ Minor road
- ┄┄┄ Railroad
- ━━━ International border

| 0 kilometers | 200 |
| 0 miles | 200 |

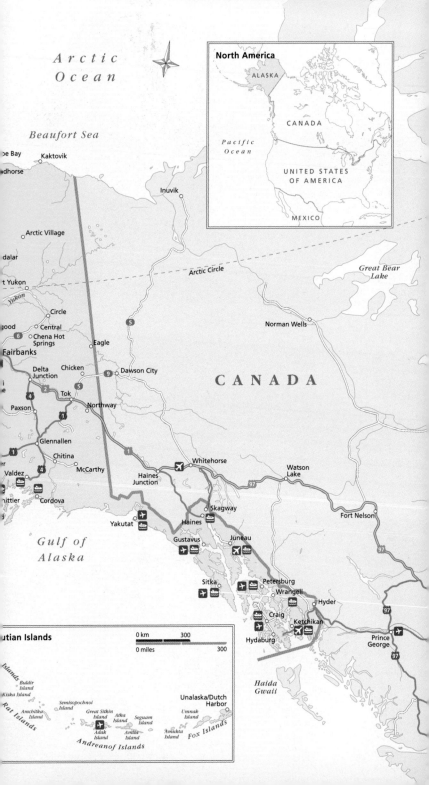

Arctic Ocean

Beaufort Sea

North America

ALASKA

CANADA

Pacific Ocean

UNITED STATES OF AMERICA

MEXICO

oe Bay
Kaktovik
adhorse

Inuvik

Arctic Village
dalar

Great Bear Lake

t Yukon

Arctic Circle

Yukon

Circle

good   Central
6   Chena Hot
        Springs   Eagle

Norman Wells

Fairbanks

Delta   Chicken
Junction   Dawson City

2   Tok   5   9

4   Northway

Paxson   **CANADA**

1

Glennallen

Chitina

Valdez   4   McCarthy

hittier   Cordova

Whitehorse

Watson
Lake

Gulf of Alaska   Haines
                         Junction

Yakutat   Fort Nelson

                    Haines   Skagway

            Gustavus   Juneau
97

            Sitka   Petersburg
                         Wrangell

                              Hyder
                    Craig
            Hydaburg   Ketchikan   97

utian Islands   Prince
                                       George
        0 km   300   97

        0 miles   300

                    Haida Gwaii

Islands
    Buldir
    Island
Kiska Island

    Semisopochnoi
    Island
Amchitka   Great Sitkin Atka   Unalaska/Dutch
Island   Island   Island   Seguam   Harbor
Rat Islands   Adak   Amlia Island Umnak
                    Island Island   Island   Amukta
                                                     Island   Fox Islands
        Andreanof Islands

A PORTRAIT OF ALASKA

Dominated by thundering glaciers, vast forests, wild rivers, and island-studded seas and fjords, Alaska is undoubtedly one of America's most scenic states. The magnificence of the land, wildlife-viewing opportunities, an almost unmatched range of outdoor activities, and the chance to explore the state's Russian and Native heritage, all combine to draw visitors to Alaska.

Detached from the rest of the country by Canada's Yukon Territory and British Columbia, Alaska is the largest state in the US. While its monumental size can at times seem overwhelming, no one could fail to appreciate the grandeur of the land.

Evidence of Alaska's Native heritage abounds in towns and villages, where many indigenous groups keep their age-old traditions alive. Museums across the state are filled with Native artifacts and ceremonial objects, but the best place for an overview of these diverse cultures is the Alaska Native Heritage Center in Anchorage.

Remnants of Alaska's Russian past are also still in evidence. In the 18th century,

Russian Orthodox clergy followed Russian trappers to Alaska and converted many locals to the Orthodox faith. Several large communities have at least one Russian Orthodox church, and the cities of Kodiak, Sitka, and Unalaska retain especially strong Russian influences.

The state offers an incredible variety of outdoor activities, including white-water rafting and wildlife viewing in the summer, and skiing and dog sledding in the winter. It is also one of the top cruise destinations in the world, with spectacular trips in the Gulf of Alaska and through the quiet channels of the Inside Passage.

Traditional crosses and domes of St. Innocent Russian Orthodox Cathedral in Anchorage

◀ Carved and painted totem pole, characteristic of many Alaskan Native cultures

Serene landscape of the Chugach National Forest along the Seward Highway

The Land and Ecology

Alaska's wilderness landscapes and diverse wildlife have long provided both resources and inspiration for those fortunate enough to experience them. The impact of humans reaches back many thousands of years to when the first Native peoples are said to have arrived via the Bering land bridge. Roaming across the landscape in search of resources, these semi-nomadic hunter-gatherers lived largely in harmony with the environment.

When the Russians arrived in the 18th century, however, their interest in sea otter and seal pelts sparked drastic declines in populations of those marine mammals, which have only recently begun to return in large numbers. The Russians were followed by Gold Rush prospectors, who trailed the Interior rivers in search of gold. Large-scale dredging along these watercourses left mountains of tailings, or mining residue, that remain as unsightly scars across the landscape.

After the discovery of oil on the North Slope in the 1970s, the Trans-Alaska Pipeline was built amid widespread concern that it would alter the ecology along its corridor. As a result of extensive environmental impact studies, the pipeline was designed to allow caribou to migrate freely beneath it or over it, and drilling companies were required to follow strict drilling and cleanup guidelines.

Today, Alaska has the largest population of bears, moose, wolves, and bald eagles in the US, and also supports species, such as musk ox and caribou, that are found in no other US state. The prolific wildlife is due not only to Alaska's relative remoteness, but also to the fact that it has more protected or semi-protected habitat than any other state.

However, Alaska faces several prominent ecological issues, from the possibility that an enormous gold mine will be developed on the Bristol Bay Watershed to the aerial hunting of

Caribou on the autumn tundra, Denali National Park

wolves. Global warming also ignites passions. Scientists report that human-created greenhouse gases, especially in Arctic regions, have caused rapid changes. Alaska faces dramatic changes as rising sea levels erode coastal villages, glaciers continue to recede, ocean acidification threatens fish and crab populations, and insect infestations and forest fires become more devastating. Polar bears and walruses also face a bleak future as the sea ice melts.

The Economy

Historically, Alaska's economy revolved around timber, fishing, and mining, but that changed in the 1960s when oil was discovered at Prudhoe Bay. Even with the closure of most sawmills, commercial fishing and seafood processing remain viable industries. The most prominent export is salmon, and Alaska provides one of the world's last wild stocks of salmon. However, competition with cheaper farmed salmon from Chile, Norway, Scotland, and other places led to declines in the market in the 1990s. Since then, prices have rebounded as consumers have come to appreciate the advantages of wild Alaskan salmon over farmed fish. On the mining front, the zinc mine near Kotzebue and a large gold mine near Fairbanks are also proving

Alaska Pipeline with the backdrop of the Alaska Range

profitable. In addition, both tourism and government agencies provide major sources of employment.

Government and Politics

In general, Alaskan politics are far more conservative than most other US states. Due to its small population of around 735,000, Alaska is represented in the US Congress by the usual two senators but only one representative. It also has a state governor and lieutenant governor, and a bicameral legislature. Unlike other states, Alaska has no county governments, but is instead organized into boroughs and municipalities.

Cruise ship *Carnival Spirit* docked at the marina in Seward

Yup'ik dancer performing at the Anchorage Native Heritage Center

Alaska's position as the crossroads between North America and Asia makes it a militarily strategic site for the US. During World War II, the Aleutian Islands were attacked by Japanese forces and even today, Alaska is considered a first line of defense against potential troubles from the west. Anchorage and Fairbanks have army and air force bases, and there are military installations across the state.

Politically, the most sensitive issues involve resource exploitation. One very vocal group of mostly younger people view the land as a wilderness to be preserved, while others who arrived in the earlier, more rough-and-ready days can be opportunists who see vast wealth to exploit. Conflicts between these two groups frequently escalate into national debate.

People and Society

On the whole, Alaskans are friendly and genuinely welcome visitors with great pride in their home state. While typically American in most respects, Alaskans are usually younger and live a somewhat more rugged life. Beyond the major cities, most people are accustomed to the remoteness, extreme cold, and high retail prices. Alaska has more hunting licenses per capita and more subsistence hunters living off the land than any other state. More Alaskans own snow-machines (the local term for snowmobiles) and all-terrain vehicles than other Americans, and about one in 50 residents is a private pilot.

All but about 30 percent of today's Alaskans are transplanted from elsewhere and are in the state by choice. Many have come for economic opportunities or with the military, but a majority

Colorful buildings in downtown Juneau in Southeast Alaska

have moved here because of a perceived sense of individual freedom that is becoming increasingly rare in most of the Lower 48 (the contiguous US states).

Demographically, about 15 percent of Alaskans are of Native heritage, while the rest are mainly of European descent. Over 18 percent of the population is African-American, Hispanic, Asian, or Pacific Islander, and minority numbers are increasing, especially in Anchorage. Most of the Native population lives in rural Alaska off the road system, while other minorities live primarily in Juneau, Anchorage, Fairbanks, and other large towns. Significant numbers of Asians, mainly Koreans and Filipinos, work as temporary laborers on fishing boats and in canneries along the Gulf of Alaska, and every summer, the cruising and tourist industry employs hundreds of seasonal workers.

Most Alaskans tend to hole up during the cold, dark months of winter, preferring to work on indoor projects and plan for the summer, although this hibernation is usually broken up by forays into the outdoors to ski, ice-fish, buzz around on snowmachines, or go mushing (dog sledding). In the

Kayaking in glacial waters in Southeast Alaska

endless daylight of summer, however, Alaskans go into overdrive, packing in as many activities as possible before the season winds down, the days shorten and winter returns. While summer visitors would be forgiven for assuming that all Alaskans are hyperactive, there is so much to see and do that it is almost impossible not to join them in their infectious round-the-clock summer spirit.

Fly fishing in the clear blue waters of the Kenai River

Alaska's Native Cultures

Alaska's Native peoples have long enjoyed rich cultures based upon deep spiritual values derived from their relationship to the plants, animals, and climate of their natural environments. There is no single "Native" culture or way of life, as each group has its own traditions and arts that were initially linked to the environment they lived in and the available resources *(see pp26–7)*. While few Natives now strictly follow traditional ways, many have a renewed interest in preserving their heritage, both through material arts and the revival of Native languages. Evidence of this resurgence is seen in Native villages and cultural centers, where visitors can meet Native Alaskans and explore their traditions, art, and crafts.

Summer visitors to Kotzebue participating in a blanket toss

Traditional housing included Aleut semi-subterranean shelters, such as this *ulax* replica at the Alaska Native Heritage Center *(see pp76–7)*.

The raven is honored in the colorful stylized motif that graces the front of this clan house.

The colors used were significant. Red represented valor, blue stood for the sea and sky, and white signified space and peace.

Clan Houses

These community dwellings, such as this Tlingit Raven clan house in Totem Bight State Historical Park (see p129), housed up to 50 people in one large room. Each family had its own space, but shared a single fireplace and stored its belongings beneath the planked flooring.

Doorways were small to conserve heat, and those passing through needed to stoop down to enter.

Whaling is an annual springtime event for Inupiat and St. Lawrence Island Yup'ik peoples, who set out in traditional sealskin boats called *umiaqs* as soon as ice conditions permit. The skins need to be changed every other year to remain watertight.

Igloos (structures constructed of blocks of ice) were historically built by Inuit hunters and mountain climbers as temporary shelters. The word itself simply means "house."

Dancing, as in this Inupiat performance, is usually accompanied by chanting and drumming and is used to celebrate festive events and ceremonial rituals.

Drumming and drum-making, using caribou hide or sealskin, are spiritually rooted Inupiat traditions. Here, a Kotzebue elder beats a drum while chanting in the Inupiat language.

The main house pole shows Duk-toothl, a legendary man of the Raven clan, who wears a weasel skin hat.

Totem pole raisings are festive events for the Tlingit, Haida, and Tsimshian peoples of Southeast Alaska. Historically, such events were commemorated by potlatches, or gifting feasts. Here, Tsimshian celebrants lift a pole into place at a gathering of three clans in Metlakatla.

Soapstone carving is prominent among the Inupiat and Yup'ik, who use soft black soapstone to create figurines of hunters, dancers, and animals. They also make scrimshaw, intricate designs carved on ivory or whalebone.

Each eye of the raven in this design has been expanded to depict a complete face.

Athabaskan beaded boots are traditionally worn by women for dancing on festive occasions. The designs are usually intricate and demonstrate great skill.

Aleut baskets, such as this one at the Anchorage Museum of History and Art, are tightly woven of Aleutian Island grasses.

Tlingit masks feature human-like visages, depicting interaction between humans and supernatural beings, or animals, that represent individual clans, such as Beaver or Wolf.

Native Art and Crafts

Every Native group celebrates its cultural heritage in arts and crafts that utilize locally available media. Thus, the Inupiat used walrus ivory for scrimshaw, while Aleuts are skilled at basket-weaving. Historically, all Native art either had a practical or ceremonial use. Today, while much of the art still serves traditional purposes, works are also sold in shops across Alaska. They may also be purchased directly from the artists.

Native Peoples of Alaska

Some anthropologists believe that the first Native peoples migrated to Alaska 30,000 to 12,000 years ago during the Ice Age that lowered sea levels and created a land bridge across the Bering Strait. These hunter-gatherers, ancestors of modern-day Indian peoples, were followed by the Inuit and Aleut peoples, who arrived by boat starting around 8,000 years ago, after the disappearance of the land bridge. There are, however, other theories that dispute this. Today, about 15 percent of Alaska's population claims Native descent. The Inuit or Eskimo include the Inupiat, Alutiiq, Aleut, Yup'ik, while the Indians include the Tsimshian, Athabaskan, Eyak, Tlingit, and Haida. While the term "Eskimo" ("eaters of raw meat" in Athabaskan) is generally not considered offensive in Alaska, Native Alaskans usually refer to themselves as members of a particular group, or collectively as Natives.

Key

- Athabaskan
- Tlingit
- Haida
- Tsimshian
- Inupiat
- Yup'ik
- Aleut and Alutiiq

Athabaskan

Historically, the Athabaskans occupied the vast taiga forests of the Interior, which are characterized by a harsh climate. Largely a hunting and gathering society, the Athabaskans spent summers in riverside tent camps, collecting and drying fish and game for the cold season. In winter, they lived in houses made of sod and wood. Their clothing was made primarily of caribou or moose hide, colorfully decorated with porcupine quills and, after the arrival of the Europeans, with traded goods such as beads. Modern Athabaskans live mainly in the Interior, many in Fairbanks, where they enjoy an urban lifestyle but also make efforts to demonstrate their traditional ways to visitors.

Athabaskan family with pelts from the winter catch

Tlingit

Alaska's Tlingit (pronounced KLINK-it), a Northwest Coast culture, have long inhabited Southeast Alaska. Historically, the Tlingit were a seafaring people, and their traders traveled as far as present-day Washington State in huge ocean-going canoes hewn from single cedar logs. Traditional Tlingit society had no central government, but each village had a stratified society that included high-ranking families, commoners, and slaves captured from neighboring tribes. Like the Haida, Tsimshian, and other Northwest Coast cultures, the Tlingit carved totem poles (see p129) to commemorate the culture unique to their respective clans. Pole-raisings and memorial ceremonies were accompanied by grand feasts called potlatches. Currently, the art of totem carving is re-emerging across Southeast Alaska, and other Tlingit arts are enjoying widespread popularity.

Tlingit dancer dressed in traditional style

Haida

The Haida share many cultural traditions with the Tlingit, including clan structures and totem pole carving. Expert sailors, they were known for their decorative ceremonial canoes. They traditionally depended on salmon and sea mammals for their subsistence. In the late 19th century, as many as 10,000 Haida lived in far southern Alaska, but by the 1890s, their numbers had been decimated by diseases brought in by Western explorers. Today, the Alaskan Haida population is about 2,000, but many more claim partial Haida descent. While they are now centered on Hydaburg on Prince of Wales Island, people of Haida descent live across southern Alaska.

Haida man in a bark hat and button cloak

Tsimshian

Alaska's Tsimshian are descendants of 823 people who left Canada with Anglican missionary, Father Duncan, after local authorities denied their land claims. Settling in an abandoned Tlingit settlement on Annette Island, which they named Metlakatla after their village in British Columbia, they set up a model Protestant Christian community of white houses and well-appointed churches. The Tsimshian were the only Alaskan Native group that rejected the Alaska Native Claims Settlement Act of 1971 *(see p60)*. As a result, they are the only Native group to retain sovereignty over their land, with Annette Island being Alaska's only official Indian Reservation.

Tsimshian drummers at a ceremony

Inupiat men returning with a caribou caught in Kobuk Valley National Park

Inupiat

The Inupiat (plural Inupiaq) mainly occupy areas along the Arctic Ocean coast and on the North Slope. Prior to European contact and influence, distinct Inupiat groups of extended families occupied home territories between Norton Sound on the Bering Strait and the Canadian border. Some groups were settled, but others traveled great distances to cooperatively hunt seals, whales, caribou, and other game animals. The Inupiat had no chiefs, but each family was headed by an *umialik*, who managed food and other family needs. Women were responsible for gathering plants and berries, skinning animals, drying *muktuk* (whale blubber), meat, and fish, and preparing food. While conflicts existed between groups, peaceful interaction did occur, especially during trade fairs at the end of each hunting season, which drew participants from as far away as Siberia. While some Inupiat today work for Native corporations or government agencies, many rural residents still make a livelihood from subsistence hunting, fishing, and gathering.

Yup'ik

The Yup'ik traditionally lived on the broad, marshy plains of the Yukon-Kuskokwim Delta, as well as on the Bering Sea coast and parts of the Seward Peninsula. Due to the milder and more vege-tated environment, the Yup'ik made more use of wood, vegeta-bles, and land animals than the Inupiat. With summer hunting camps, they also had permanent villages, where men lived in *qasgiqs*, or communal houses, and women and children in sod dwellings called *enet*. Lacking the resources Europeans wanted, the Yup'ik first encountered Westerners much later than the Aleut, Alutiiq, and Inupiat. In recent years, many Yup'ik have moved to towns, especially Bethel, but some still practice subsistence hunting or spend the summers working in family fish camps.

Yup'ik family beneath an *umiaq*, a traditional skin boat

Alutiiq woman in a beaded headdress

Aleut (Unangax̂) and Alutiiq (Sugpiaq)

Both the Aleut and Alutiiq live in Southwest Alaska, the former in the Aleutian Islands and the latter from Prince William Sound to Kodiak Island and the Alaska Peninsula. The difference in their languages, however, suggests that they have entirely separate origins. Despite Southwest Alaska's stormy climate, both groups had a maritime hunting culture, using *baidarkas* (skin boats) to chase seals, otters, and whales. Early Russian otter hunters often killed or enslaved them and also introduced foreign diseases. The Russian Orthodox clergy that followed converted large numbers to the church, which remains a strong spiritual force for both groups. During World War II, entire villages were transferred to evacuation centers in Southeast Alaska to keep them from being taken prisoner by the Japanese. Aleut people often prefer the name Unangax̂ and Alutiiq call themselves Sugpiaq.

Volcanoes and Earthquakes

Alaska lies on the geologically active Pacific Ring of Fire, where tectonic shifts can result in earthquakes and volcanic eruptions. One of the earth's tectonic plates is sliding under another, causing major geological changes. The entire southern Alaskan region is geologically dynamic; it is the site of about 8 percent of all the world's earthquakes and boasts dozens of active volcanoes. The second strongest earthquake in recorded history struck Southcentral Alaska in 1964, and in 1912, Novarupta exploded in what was the second most powerful volcanic eruption ever recorded.

Locator map

━ Aleutian Megathrust

— Subduction zone

Great Sitkin (1987), a 5,742-ft (1,740-m) volcano, is a vent inside the caldera of an older shield volcano on the well-glaciated Great Sitkin Island, which is covered in a layer of dark pumice 20 ft (6 m) thick.

Mount Cleveland (2010), a symmetrical 5,675-ft (1,730-m) cone on Chuginadak Island, is one of the Aleutians' most active volcanoes. This dramatic peak is a prominent feature of the beautiful Islands of Four Mountains.

Bearing Sea

Kiska *(1962)*
Little Sitkin
Tanaga *(1914)*
Kanaga *(1996)*
Korovin *(2006)*
Carlisle *(1987)*
Bogoslof *(1992)*
Makushin *(1995)*
Okmok *(2008)*
Amukta *(1997)*
Vsevidof *(1957)*
Ur
Rat Islands
The Aleutian Megathrust is a very active fault line that is responsible for the numerous earthquakes in southern Alaska.
Gareloi *(1996)*
Adak
Andreanof Islands
Atka
Seguam *(1993)*
Yunaska *(1937)*
Kagamil *(1929)*
Nikolski
Fox Islan
Aleutian Trench

Tectonic Activity

The distinctive chain of islands and peaks that makes up the Aleutian Islands is the result of plate tectonics – the movement of the interlocking plates of the earth's crust that ride on the molten material (magma) in the mantle. At the subduction zone, the oceanic Pacific plate is being forced under the continental North American plate, creating the Aleutian Trench. North of this zone, fractures in the continental plate allow magma from below to migrate upward. When the pressure increases, the magma bursts through the crust in dramatic volcanic activity.

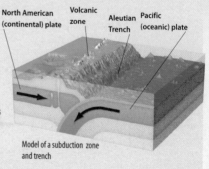

North American (continental) plate
Volcanic zone
Aleutian Trench
Pacific (oceanic) plate

Model of a subduction zone and trench

Mount Augustine (2005) currently rises 4,025 ft (1,207 m) above the waters of lower Cook Inlet. In early 2005, its dramatic eruptions created ash clouds up to 7 miles (11 km) high, disrupting aviation and shipping.

Novarupta (1912) was the site of a cataclysmic eruption. For two years, dust in the upper atmosphere darkened skies throughout the northern hemisphere.

Spurr *(1992)*

Redoubt *(2009)*

Anchorage

Katmai *(1912)*

Kenai Peninsula

Mount Wrangell *(1930)*

Iliamna *(1953)*

Dillingham

King Salmon

Fourpeaked *(2006)*

Trident *(1953-63)*

Mageik

Kodica

Martin

Kodiak Island

Peulik

Ukinrek *(1977)*

Chiginagak *(1971)*

Aniakchak *(1931)*

Bristol Bay

Alaska Peninsula

Gulf of Alaska

k *(1796)* Dutton

ischer

Cold Bay

Isanotski

Mount Pavlof

Shishaldin *(2004)* *(2007)*

Westdahl *(1991)*

Sand Point

0 km   200

0 miles   200

Aleutian Trench

The Aleutian Trench marks the zone where the Pacific plate slides beneath the North American plate.

Pacific Ocean

Kodiak's waterfront destroyed by the tsunami after the 1964 earthquake

The 1964 Earthquake

On Good Friday, March 27, 1964, the second strongest earthquake in recorded history, measuring 9.2 on the Richter scale, hit Southcentral Alaska. Much of Anchorage, which rested on alluvial silt, collapsed into the cracks in the earth. Dramatic damage occurred along 4th Avenue, where a bluff slumped and the land slipped downhill. Around Valdez, the land sank about 4 ft (1.2 m) and destroyed the town, while the resulting tsunami destroyed much of Valdez, Seward, and Kodiak.

Mount Veniaminof (2008) features a volcanic vent surrounded by a crater about 20 miles (32 km) in circumference that contains a glacier. This very active volcano has erupted several times in the early 21st century.

Alaska's Glaciers

Much of Alaska's spectacular landscape has been shaped by 5,000 major and countless minor glaciers that scraped downhill from icefields in the coastal mountains, gouging out steep-sided valleys. As glaciers melted, valleys that were below sea level were filled by seawater to create long, narrow fjords. Although glaciers continue to reshape the landscape, most of these rivers of ice – the earth's largest reservoir of freshwater – are currently receding, and scientific research points to human-caused warming of the planet as the primary reason.

Crevasses develop when stresses on the flowing ice cause large cracks in glaciers. The largest crevasses are found on steep sections of rapidly flowing ice.

Outlet Glaciers, such as Mendenhall Glacier near Juneau, spill down steeply from icefields, creating ravines that serve as outlets for the icefield. They often flow into lakes created by the glacier's terminal moraine, a ridge of debris at the foot of the glacier.

Glacial Changes

As glaciers flow downhill, friction against the rock melts the bottom ice, forming a "slide" so the glacier can surge ahead. Increasing air temperatures can cause melting at glacier faces, but can also cause surging, as higher temperatures mean more snowfall, and therefore, pressure, on parent icefields. Tidewater glaciers flowing into warming seas tend to recede due to higher water temperatures.

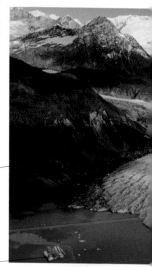

Lateral moraines are strips of ground rock on the edges of glaciers.

Bergy bits are large chunks of glacier ice or small icebergs, rising up to 13 ft (4 m) out of the water.

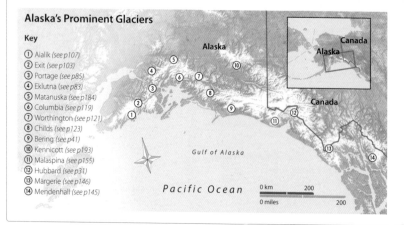

Alaska's Prominent Glaciers

Key

1. Aialik *(see p107)*
2. Exit *(see p103)*
3. Portage *(see p85)*
4. Eklutna *(see p83)*
5. Matanuska *(see p184)*
6. Columbia *(see p119)*
7. Worthington *(see p121)*
8. Childs *(see p123)*
9. Bering *(see p41)*
10. Kennicott *(see p193)*
11. Malaspina *(see p155)*
12. Hubbard *(see p31)*
13. Margerie *(see p146)*
14. Mendenhall *(see p145)*

Alaska

Canada

Alaska

Canada

Gulf of Alaska

Pacific Ocean

0 km 200
0 miles 200

Valley Glaciers are created when the weight of an icecap is great enough to make its edges flow downhill, creating rivers of ice that grind away underlying rock to form valleys. Valley glaciers are sub-divided into outlet, tidewater, and piedmont glaciers.

Hanging glaciers in high mountain valleys may eventually become tributaries of a main valley glacier.

Medial moraines are wide, dark strips of debris and ground rock in the middle of valley or tidewater glaciers.

Icefields, including the Juneau, Harding, and Bagley Icefields, are formed between high mountains when snow compresses into ice under the weight of additional snowfall. Liquid water beneath glaciers and shallow portions of icefields is revealed in deep wells called *moulins*, French for "mills." Peaks rising from icefields are called *nunataks*.

Growler ice is a small chunk of floating ice that releases trapped air as it melts, making a growling noise.

Hubbard Glacier

Located near the town of Yukutat, Hubbard Glacier is North America's largest tidewater glacier, and one of the only advancing glaciers in Alaska. In 1986, it rammed across the mouth of Russell Fjord in just a few days, turning the fjord into a lake and trapping marine life on the wrong side of the ice wall. While the fjord has since reopened, the glacier still occasionally surges and may eventually seal off the fjord.

Fjords, such as Prince William Sound's College Fjord, are narrow submarine valleys flanked by steep, glacier-carved walls that may erode into gentler slopes over time.

Landscape and Wildlife

With its range of landforms and wild country, Alaska naturally supports a wealth of wildlife, not only in the mountains and forests, but also on the barren tundra, in the surrounding seas, and even in the cities and towns. In fact, Anchorage has a healthy moose population, and bears are occasionally sighted in city parks. Perhaps the most reliable wildlife viewing venue is Denali National Park. Visitors to the park's interior are typically treated to sightings of grizzlies, moose, caribou, Dall sheep, and a host of birds and smaller animals. A wealth of marine mammals – sea lions, sea otters, seals, and whales – abound in the Gulf of Alaska, Bering Sea, and the Arctic Ocean. Sightings are practically guaranteed on Inside Passage cruises, and on day cruises and ferry trips in Southeast Alaska, Prince William Sound, and the Kenai Fjords.

Orcas are often seen in the Gulf of Alaska and its sheltered bays, where visitors can also spot other marine mammals such as seals and otters.

Temperate Rainforest

The islands of the eastern Gulf Coast and Southeast Alaska form the world's largest expanse of temperate rainforest *(see p131)*. Conifers such as Western hemlock and Sitka spruce dominate, but there is also muskeg or spongy bog, composed of sphagnum moss, peat, and ground cover.

Taiga and Boreal Forest

The boreal forest *(see p161)*, which covers most of the Alaskan mainland, ranges from mixed birch to black and white spruce woodland. Low-lying, poorly drained areas are typified by taiga, characterized by bog dominated by spindly black spruce.

Black bears are the most common and widely distributed of North America's three species of bears *(see p111)*. At about 5 ft (2 m) in length, they are the smallest. They range in color from black to almost white.

Lynx are the only wild cats native to Alaska. They are distinguished by long tufts on the tip of each ear and have unusually large paws that act as snowshoes in very deep snow and aid in winter hunting.

Sitka black-tailed deer are native to the Southeast, whose old-growth forests provide optimal foraging and habitat.

Moose, the largest member of the deer family, can weigh up to 1,500 lb (675 kg). Besides pondweed, they feed on willow, birch, and aspen twigs.

Rocky Coastlines

In many places along the coast of the Gulf of Alaska and the Bering Sea, the land rises from the sea in rocky beaches and high cliffs that are frequently pummeled by storms and pounding waves. The seas, rich in plankton and fish, support both nesting birds and marine mammals, such as sea otters, seals, sea lions, and walruses. Below the high-tide line, seaweed beds and tide pools provide a habitat for mollusks and soft-bodied creatures such as octopuses and jellyfish.

Northern fur seals haul out on the Pribilof Islands to breed and bear pups. About 700,000 – half of the world population of northern fur seals – gather here every summer. Over the last decade the population has declined sharply.

Walruses, with their distinctive coarse whiskers and ivory tusks, are seen mainly on rocky Bering Sea beaches, where males break their journey northward to their breeding grounds around the Arctic Ocean.

High Mountains and Icefields

The alpine areas of Alaska are found in the high mountain ranges that arc along the southern coast of the state and in the peripheral ranges crossing the Interior and Arctic regions. The southern ranges are capped by extensive icefields that give rise to the valley glaciers that carve intermontane valleys and fjords.

Arctic Tundra

Most of Arctic and Western Alaska is covered with Arctic tundra (see p225), which ranges from rolling expanses covered by low shrubs and miniature grasses to spongy tussocks and vast open plains. Despite the harsh climate, the shallow soils support a diversity of plant life including flowers, berries, and lichen.

Dall sheep inhabit alpine meadows and steep slopes, fleeing to rocky crags to escape pursuers. These herbivores are rarely found below the timberline.

Musk oxen, hunted to extinction in Alaska, were reintroduced from Greenland in the 1930s. *Qiviut*, their soft, warm underhair, is spun into fiber.

Hoary marmots burrow on alpine slopes and use high-pitched whistles as alarm signals. These rodents hibernate for seven months.

Caribou in Alaska number about a million individuals. Herds of up to 400,000 migrate annually between summer and winter ranges that can be up to 250 miles (400 km) apart.

Birds of Alaska

From enormous trumpeter swans to tiny hummingbirds, Alaska's bird life is varied and prolific, with 437 identified species and over 60 incidental visitors. Bald eagles can be spotted in old-growth timber, while sandpipers and peeps scurry around at the water's edge. Countless migratory birds summer in Alaska, and loons, snow geese, and herons can be seen at lakes and ponds across the state. On the remote Pribilofs, red-legged kittiwakes, puffins, crested auklets, and many others nest on the storm-battered sea cliffs.

Bird-watching is popular on coastal cruises, such as this tour at Glacier Bay.

Cliff-nesters

Many Alaskan seabirds nest on sea cliffs to protect their nests and hatchlings from predators. The best places to see nesting gannets, fulmars, petrels, cormorants, puffins, kittiwakes, and other cliff-nesting birds include Glacier Bay, Kenai Fjords National Park, and the Pribilof Islands.

Thick-billed murres inhabit large cliff colonies, but do not build nests, instead laying their eggs on bare rock.

Glaucous gulls, among the world's largest gulls, live on the Pribilof Islands *(see pp216–17)* and on the western and northern coasts, from the Yukon-Kuskokwim Delta to Canada's northern regions. The similar, but smaller, glaucous-winged gull breeds along Alaska's southern coasts.

Black-billed magpies have a lustrous green iridescence on their wings and tails. They can be seen in open country, but need birch, cotton-woods, or shrubs for nesting.

Winter Birds

Most nesting and migratory birds in Alaska go south in winter, but Steller's jays, magpies, ravens, and ptarmigan are year-round residents. The availability of food in towns has changed the migratory patterns of ducks and geese and it is often possible to see them in mid-winter in the Southeast. Chickadees, nut-hatches, and other small birds that winter in Alaska can also be seen around bird-feeders in the south.

The raven has long been revered by indigenous peoples as the creator of the world and bringer of daylight. These intelligent corvids especially like to raid urban garbage bags.

The willow ptarmigan, the official state bird, is seen all year round. Its plumage, brilliant white in winter, becomes a mottled brown in summer to blend in with the forest floor.

Freshwater birds

During the spring and summer mating season, Alaska's lakes and muskeg attract ducks, snow geese, trumpeter and tundra swans, blue herons, loons, and several species of grebes. Sandhill cranes, which perform an elaborate mating dance, can easily be seen in Creamer's Field in Fairbanks (see p174).

Horned puffins are excellent swimmers, spending the winters offshore and nesting in rock clefts in the summer.

Arctic terns, frequently observed swooping over lakes throughout Alaska, migrate 25,000 miles (40,000 km) each year between their Arctic breeding grounds and their wintering grounds in Antarctica. Usually smaller than gulls, they will attack anything – even a human – that approaches their chicks.

Red-legged kittiwakes, found in the Pribilof Islands, build cliff nests made of mud, grass, and kelp.

The red-throated loon, much rarer than the iconic common loon, is one of Alaska's five loon species. Their haunting calls are signature sounds of the North American wilderness.

Trumpeter swans, with wingspans of up to 7 ft (2 m), are the world's largest waterbirds. Surprisingly efficient flyers, they migrate at altitudes up to 10,000 ft (3,000 m) at speeds of up to 60 mph (100 kph). They are most readily seen in their nesting grounds on the Copper River Delta *(see p123)*.

Snowy owls are perhaps the most spectacular summer birds on the Arctic coast. Diving from the sky with outstretched talons, these birds can drive away even an advancing caribou.

Raptors

Alaska is home to a variety of raptors, not the least of which is the US national bird, the magnificent bald eagle. Denali National Park (see pp166–9) and other parts of the Interior also have a healthy population of golden eagles. Other common raptors include merlins, red-tailed hawks, harriers, ospreys, and numerous species of owls.

Bald eagles, although established across the Lower 48, are found in their greatest numbers in Alaska. From October to December, thousands of eagles gather along the Chilkat River, but they can also be readily spotted almost anywhere in southern Alaska from late spring to early fall.

Russian Culture in Alaska

While modern Alaska is tied ideologically to mainstream USA and traditionally to its own Native cultures, there are also remnants of 18th- and 19th-century Russian colonization. The distinctive crosses and onion-domed spires of Orthodox churches across Alaska attest to the fact that the colonizers were not just concerned with trade, but also brought with them their religious convictions, converting many Native Alaskans to their faith. Today, most Southwest Alaska villages still have a Russian Orthodox majority population.

Russian Big Diomede (right) and the US island of Little Diomede (left) lie in the Bering Strait.

A Russian priest and settlers gather with Native Tlingit people in traditional dress in this photograph taken in Sitka circa 1900.

Icons include All Saints of Alaska: Innocent, Herman, Jakov, Juvenali, and Peter the Aleut.

Deacon doors in this chapel have icons of St. Stephen (left) and St. Lawrence (right).

Alexander Baranov (1747–1819) is honored with this statue in Sitka, where he once lived. Attracted to Alaska by the fur trade, he became the manager of the Russian-American Company in 1790 and the first Colonial Governor of Russian America in 1799.

The analogian displays icons for worshipers, who may not approach the iconostasis.

Old Believers

In 1652, Patriarch Nikon of Moscow ordered reforms to traditional Orthodoxy and excommunicated any dissidents. Many of the dispossessed, calling themselves Old Believers, fled to Siberia to escape persecution. In 1945, to escape the Soviet system, many migrated to Brazil and eventually to the USA. In the late 1960s, one group established several villages around Nikolaevsk, which are modern Alaska's only Russian settlements. Currently, about 2,000 Old Believers, who still speak Old Russian, live largely by fishing and farming.

Old Believer women working in the fields near Nikolaevsk

The New Archangel Dancers of Sitka perform Russian folk songs and dances to promote Alaska's Russian heritage.

The Holy Assumption of the Virgin Mary Russian Orthodox Church, in Kenai, was completed in 1895. A distinctive crown-shaped cupola marks this National Historic Landmark.

The iconostasis separates the church from the altar and symbolizes separation between the human world and the Divine. Only men may pass this wall.

The Russian Bishop's House is the oldest intact Russian building in Sitka. Built in 1842 by the Russian American Company as the Bishop's residence, it also functioned as an orphanage, school, and seminary.

The altar, behind the iconostasis, is where the priest celebrates the Holy Liturgy.

St. Nicholas Russian Orthodox Church (1893) was founded for Juneau's mostly Tlingit Orthodox community.

Orthodox Interiors

The interiors of Russian Orthodox churches are simple in layout, but are lavishly decorated with rich colors and beautiful, vibrant icons, as seen here in the chapel at St. Herman's Theological Seminary in Kodiak. In most Orthodox churches there are no pews, as worshipers are expected to stand in deference to Christ's suffering.

St. Michael's Russian Orthodox Cathedral, in Sitka, was begun in 1844 when the original cornerstone was laid by Bishop Veniaminov. Destroyed by fire in 1966, the church was rebuilt and reconsecrated by 1976.

Spirit houses grace the churchyard behind St. Nicholas Russian Orthodox Church in the tiny Athabaskan village of Eklutna. Each of these structures is a gravesite and is decorated according to individual family traditions.

Cruising the Inside Passage

First time and repeat passengers fill cruise ships every year to sail the Inside Passage and experience some of the most breathtaking vistas this sliver of Alaska can offer. The Inside Passage is usually remote, remarkable, and ultimately rewarding in rain or shine. Majestic tidewater glaciers, gouged-out valleys, and impenetrable forests compete for views of whales, bears, and eagles. Along with bustling ports of call, cruising here makes perfect sense. Cruise ships call on quaint fishing outposts, hidden coves, and small cities that dot the coastline – many in places inaccessible except by boat or floatplane.

Tracy Arm twists into the mainland from Stephens Passage and rewards with a blanket of icebergs, created by the calving Sawyer Glaciers.

Locator

— Area of main map

Skagway, a slice of Gold Rush mining history, nestles at the end of narrow Taiya Inlet.

⑦ Skagway

⑥ Haines

Haines sits in a gorgeous location on the Chilkat Peninsula, below the Fairweather Range.

Juneau ⑤

• Gustavus

To the Gulf Route (see pp40–41)

Hoonah is a quietly fascinating Tlingit settlement along Icy Strait where humpback whales are frequently sighted.

Sitka ④

Juneau, the nation's smallest state capital, boasts a vibrant tourist economy that caters to cruise ship passengers.

Glacier Bay *(see pp146–7)* is almost entirely water-access only. Cruise ships easily bring their passengers within camera range of some of the park's 12 spectacular tidewater glaciers.

PORTS OF CALL

Sitka's mix of Russian and Tlingit culture makes it a fascinating port of call and its protected location within a verdant valley is stunning. Most sights are within walking distance of the docks.

Petersburg lies at the north end of the Wrangell Narrows, a barely navigable passage lined with dense forests, hunting and fishing lodges, and homes for rugged vacationers. The town retains its strong Norwegian influence and remains less explored than Ketchikan or Juneau.

Planning a Cruise

Cruises either sail a round trip through the Inside Passage from a port to the south (often Seattle or Vancouver), or cruise one way, adding on the Gulf Route and starting or ending at Anchorage.
Consider splashing out on a cabin with a balcony, or at least with a window, for great views.
Take memory cards, and batteries for your camera.
For more information on booking and planning see pp256–63.

0 km   50
0 miles   50

Wrangell is a laid-back town at the mouth of the Sitkine River. The totems at Chief Shakes Island are a highlight.

Misty Fiords National Monument *(see p130)* is on the itinerary of many smaller ships, which conduct slow tours of its placid waters. This protected area is a wonderland of bottomless fjords and granite escarpments laced with waterfalls.

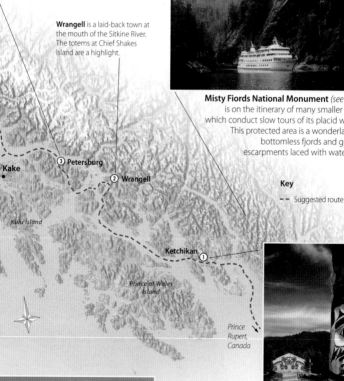

Kake

Kulu Island

③ Petersburg

② Wrangell

Ketchikan ①

Prince of Wales Island

Prince Rupert, Canada

Key

- - Suggested route

Frederick Sound is the widest body of water in the Inside Passage and serves as a nutrient-rich feeding ground for Pacific Ocean humpback whales. They rise above the water with jaws gaping during feeding.

Ketchikan welcomes more than 900,000 cruise ship visitors every season. Many visitors head to Tlingit presentations at Saxman Village and Totem Park.

Cruising the Gulf Route

Vast seascapes and endless mountain ranges are the great attraction of a Gulf of Alaska cruise. The shoreline has relatively few conventional or convenient cruise destinations; instead of ports, the wildernesses of national parks and nature refuges line up one after another. Mammoth calving glaciers, such as the Hubbard, are top of the itinerary on all cruise lines and many passengers tack on a multi-day trip north from Seward to Denali *(see pp166–9)*. Most ships transit the Gulf's wild expanse between Whittier or Seward and Juneau during the night, so stargazing might be the best prescription.

College Fjord *(see p119)* snakes towards the pinnacles of the Chugach Range, dazzling at every turn. The dense network of tidewater glaciers were named for Ivy League schools.

Whittier has become an important port of call, as it is so close to Anchorage and on Passage Canal, an inlet just off beautiful Prince William Sound.

ALASKA **CANADA**

The Gulf Route

The Inside Passage *see pp38–39*

Locator

— Area of main map

• **Anchorage**

Cook Inlet

③ **Whittier**

Prin
Willi
Sou

④ **Seward**

Montague Island

Seward is the beginning or end point for some cruises sailing the Gulf of Alaska. Nestled between mountains and the sea, this attractive city has plenty of charm.

0 km   50

0 miles   50

PORTS OF CALL

① **Cordova** *see p122*
② **Valdez** *see pp120–21*
③ **Whittier** *see p118*
④ **Seward** *see pp102–5*

Prince William Sound's fragile environment has made a partial recovery since 1989's disastrous Exxon Valdez oil spill *(see p121)*. Wildlife sightings are practically guaranteed.

Valdez, a coastal port between the two flanks of the vast Chugach National Forest, is notable for being at the end of the famed Trans-Alaska Pipeline. Large cruise ships do not stop here.

Planning a Cruise

Cruises through the Gulf of Alaska are usually part of a one-way trip from either Vancouver or Seattle to Anchorage and also include the Inside Passage.
Ships dock in Seward or Whittier and passengers travel to or from Anchorage via train or bus.
A tour to Denali will take at least three nights; the train trip is spectacular *(see pp286–7).*
For more information on booking and planning see pp256–63.

Hubbard Glacier *(see p31)*, Alaska's longest tidewater glacier, stretches across 6 miles (10 km) of Yakutat Bay's headwaters. Massive columns of ancient ice tumble from the glacier's face with the sound of thunder followed by a dull splash.

Key

-- - Suggested route

① Cordova

• Alaganik

• Cape Yakatage

Kayak Island

Malaspina Glacier, at 1,500 square miles (3,890 sq km), is the largest piedmont glacier in North America. It was named for the 18th-century Spanish explorer, Alejandro Malaspina.

Icy Bay was formed within the last century when four tidewater glaciers retreated. Its icy waters provide spectacularly isolated sea kayaking.

Bering Glacier dramatically surges forward up to 328 ft (100 m) per day about every 20 years, sometimes filling the lake at its foot with calving icebergs.

Yakutat *(see p155)*, a tiny Tlingit town on the route to Hubbard Glacier, boasts one of the most dramatic coastal locations on the continent.

To the Inside Passage (see pp38–9)

Cordova, inaccessible by road and rail, is an occasional port of call for small ships. Originally the terminus of the Copper River and Northwestern Railway *(see p187)*, which served the copper mines at Kennicott, today it is a pleasant fishing town.

Dog Sledding

The Native peoples of Alaska's northern regions have long relied on dog sleds as essential survival tools in the winter, using them while hunting, trading, or moving camp. As other people moved to Alaska, dog sleds continued to play an important role, delivering medicine, food, and mail. While the practical use of dog sleds has now been replaced by snowmachines, dog sledding, locally called "mushing," is popular as a recreational activity and is the official state sport.

Historical image of Alaskan mail carriers delivering mail via dog sled

Dog sleds are built on wooden or aluminum runners, with an area in the front to carry freight, passengers, or tired or injured dogs.

Wheel dogs, at the very back, help in steering the sled.

Alaskans traditionally made sleds of wood, bone, sinew, and rawhide, but modern sleds are made of wood, steel, plastics, Kevlar, and aluminum. Here, Inupiat elder Don Smith works on a sled in his workshop in Kiana, near Kotzebue.

Mushers either stand on the runners of the sled or jog behind or alongside.

The Sled Team

For mushers, dog sledding is as much an art form as a sport. In the harsh winter wilderness, the close interplay of human and dog is symbiotic: for the musher, the dog team is a faithful lifeline in an exposed environment, while for the dogs, the musher is a trusted companion who supplies sustenance. The dogs are directed not by reins, but by the musher's spoken commands to the lead dogs, who guide the others accordingly.

Sled Dogs

Malamutes, Siberians, Samoyeds, and other purebred huskies are popularly associated with dog sledding, but are rarely used as sled dogs. Most mushers prefer mixed-breed dogs that are bred for speed and endurance.

Wind-resistant kennels provide shelter for sled dogs at home. On the trail, they sleep outdoors on hay, eating meat and fish for energy and warmth. Bred for Alaskan winters, they perform best at about -29° C (-20° F).

Dog team transport, when the dogs are not running, is in mobile kennels mounted on the back of pick-up trucks.

Denali Park Rangers use sleds to patrol the park in winter, but summer visitors can watch demonstrations of dog sleds adapted for use on trails.

Alaska's Dog Sled Races

Dog sled races feature in winter festivals all over Alaska, but the best-known mushing event is the famed Iditarod. Other popular races include the Yukon Quest, Glennallen's Copper Basin 300, which is a qualifier for the Iditarod, and the World Championship Sled Dog Races. Racers come from all over the world to serve apprenticeships with established mushers and learn how to care for the dogs and cope with the elements.

Team dogs follow the swing dogs and provide a steady pulling action.

Lead dogs, in the front, follow the musher's commands.

Swing dogs back up the lead dogs and assist in steering.

The Yukon Quest is one of Alaska's major dog sled races. The 1,000-mile (1,600-km) race follows a Gold Rush and historic mail delivery route between Whitehorse, Canada, and Fairbanks, Alaska.

The World Championship Sled Dog Races take place on a short track around Anchorage during the Anchorage Fur Rendezvous. This weekend event focuses more on speed and strategy than on endurance, which is the main factor in long-distance mushing.

The Last Great Race on Earth

Dog sled team pulling out of the Iditarod starting line

Historically, the Athabaskans called their hunting grounds Haiditarod, "the distant place." In 1910, the derivation Iditarod was given to the rough trail between Seward and Nome. In 1925, dog teams transported life-saving diphtheria serum to epidemic-stricken Nome along a portion of this trail. To commemorate this feat, a dog sled race between Anchorage and Nome was initiated in 1973 by legendary musher Joe Redington, affectionately known as the "Father of the Iditarod." Held in early March, this annual event begins with a ceremonial start in Anchorage and restarts the next day from Willow. Each year, the race follows one of two alternating courses. The leaders usually complete the 1,100-mile (1,760-km) run in about nine days.

Sportfishing in Alaska

Sportfishing is Alaska's most popular sport, and Alaskans fish regularly while outsiders often make it their main reason to visit the state. Some visit in the hopes of shipping home a crate of frozen fish, but for most the real attraction is the opportunity to spend some solitary time outdoors. However, anglers in the best fishing areas may find themselves up against hordes of competing fishermen. Remote sites and wilderness lodges offer more serene experiences. Those whose chief objective is to catch fish will find lakes and streams so prolific that success is practically guaranteed, even when several anglers are competing.

Catch-and-release fishing is a popular pastime that also maintains breeding stocks.

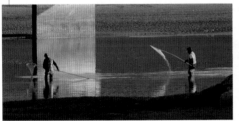

Dipnetting is a favored way of catching Copper River red salmon and the small and greasy hooligan (eulachon) in Turnagain Arm *(see pp84–5)*. Only Alaska residents are permitted to use dipnets.

Fly Fishing

Fly fishing, which involves the use of a long, light rod, an artificial fly made of fur, feathers, or yarn, and a heavy line that helps to place the fly accurately, is used primarily to catch salmon and trout in smaller lakes, rivers, and streams. The most rewarding fly fishing is found in wilderness waterways accessed by bush plane.

Special Fishing Tours

Anglers in Alaska can choose from a range of sportfishing packages, which typically include transportation, tackle, food, and accommodation. Tours range from deep-sea fishing charters to superb fishing adventures at remote lodges that are approachable only by floatplane.

Charter fishing tours involve chartering a boat with a guide for half a day or a full day. Sportfishing vessels can travel far from shore to find the best sportfishing grounds for enthusiastic anglers looking for a good catch.

Fly-in fishing, a quintessential Alaskan experience, involves a floatplane flight to a remote lake for some quiet angling.

Combat fishing is common in Kenai Peninsula rivers when the salmon are running. Competing anglers stand elbow-to-elbow, trying to land one of the thousands of fish going upstream.

Tips for Anglers

Fishing licenses: non-residents pay $20 per day, $35 for 3 days, $55 for a week, $80 for 2 weeks, and $145 for a year. Licenses can be bought at tackle or grocery stores across Alaska, or purchased in advance at
🆆 **adfg.alaska.gov**
Best fishing sites: the Kenai River, Bristol Bay, Homer Spit, Seward, and Kodiak offer the best salmon fishing. Halibut are found along the Kenai Peninsula, Kodiak Island, and Southeast Alaska. Lakes and streams across Alaska have great trout fishing.

Waterproof waders made of a synthetic rubber are essential gear for anglers in Alaska.

Deep-sea fishing for the huge halibut known as "barn doors" is especially popular around Homer and Deep Creek on the Kenai Peninsula.

Alaskan Sportfish

Alaska offers keen anglers excellent fishing opportunities, and a wide variety of game fish are available in the state's waterways and along the coasts. Salmon is the most popular catch, but halibut, trout, and grayling are also highly prized.

King (chinook) salmon, the largest of all Pacific salmon, are relatively common in Bristol Bay and the Kenai River.

Arctic grayling, a game fish, is found in clear, cold streams in the Interior between April and September.

Halibut, which occasionally weigh over 300 lb (135 kg), are found in the Gulf of Alaska, especially around Homer.

Red (sockeye) salmon run from May to mid-August in Southwest, Southcentral, and Western Alaska.

Rainbow trout, found in rivers from Southeast Alaska to the Kuskokwim Delta, are best fished in spring and fall.

Arctic char are found in clear, fresh waters in Interior and Southern Alaska between May and September.

ALASKA THROUGH THE YEAR

Alaskans are festive types and nearly every town and village has evolved its own celebrations. Events that are not music- or sports-related typically focus on a local commodity, historic or ethnic event, some sort of novelty, or a natural phenomenon, such as events based around the midnight sun or sea ice. The atmosphere ranges from the elegant formality of the Sitka Summer Music Festival to uninhibited revelry at the Talkeetna Bluegrass Festival. Summer festivals are often boisterous, round-the-clock affairs, while winter events give people the opportunity to get out of the house during the darkest days of the year. On Alaska Day and the Fourth of July, the entire state joins in the festivities, usually with displays of fireworks, but some communities often stage large celebrations that draw people from across the state.

Bird's-eye view of the rides at the Alaska State Fair

Spring

In the spring, as the days grow longer, the ice is starting to break up, the birds are beginning to return, and Alaskans are gearing up for summer activity. Some communities try to get a jump on the excitement by staging early festivities, but the weather can be unpredictable, with snow possible in April and May.

April
Alaska Folk Festival *(mid-Apr)*, Juneau. This weeklong festival features the hottest folk and bluegrass performers from around Alaska and the Northwest. Participants can also attend free dance work-shops at the festival.
Alyeska Spring Carnival *(3rd week)*, Girdwood. This popular spring festival is the ski resort's finale for the season, with a freestyle competition, kids' games, and the Slush Cup, where skiers and snowboarders attempt to cross an icy pond at full speed. Most end up very wet and cold.

May
Copper River Delta Shorebird Festival *(1st week)*, Cordova. The return of shorebirds to the Copper River Delta is marked with three days of bird-related activities, including talks and the Great Cordova Birder's Challenge.
Kachemak Bay Shorebird Festival *(1st full weekend)*, Homer. Birding trips, music, kayaking, and

Musicians performing at the Sitka Summer Music Festival

bird-oriented activities honoring 100,000 shorebirds on the beaches of Kachemak Bay.
Little Norway Festival *(weekend nearest May 17)*, Petersburg. A vibrant celebration of the town's Norwegian roots, including a traditional *bunader* dress competition, parade, and Norwegian delicacies.
Great Alaska Craftbeer and Homebrew Festival *(3rd weekend)*, Haines. This competition between home- and microbrewers is an excellent opportunity to taste some unusual beers.
Crab Festival *(Memorial Day weekend)*, Kodiak. The end of the crabbing season is marked with music, festivities, and races, including one in which teams wearing heavy survival suits swim out to boats in the harbor.

Summer

Summer is understandably the favorite season of most Alaskans, and communities organize an explosion of festivities designed for both locals and tourists. Attendees can plan on partying late into the midnight brightness.

June
Sitka Summer Music Festival *(three weeks in Jun)*, Sitka. This popular event attracts international classical musicians every summer. Book chamber music performances in advance.
Copper River Wild Salmon Festival *(2nd week)*, Cordova. This event commemorates the famous Copper River reds with a dance, a salmon banquet, and

a marathon race along the Copper River Highway.

Midnight Sun Festival *(Jun 21)*, Fairbanks. The festival features live music, a classic auto show, and the Alaska Goldpanners Midnight Sun Baseball Game, played by natural light at midnight.

Nalukataq *(late Jun)*, Barrow. An early summer festival that celebrates the end, and hopefully the successes, of the spring whaling season with Inuit games, a feast, and a blanket toss.

Alaska Highland Games *(last weekend)*, Eagle River near Anchorage. Visitors can see the hammer toss, stone and caber throws, eat haggis, and listen to bagpipe music.

Elmendorf Open House and Air Show *(last weekend)*, Anchorage. Featuring ear-splitting maneuvers by the Air Force Thunderbirds, this is an unmissable summer event at Elmendorf Air Force Base.

July

Independence Day *(Jul 4)*, across Alaska. While there are statewide celebrations, Seward has the biggest event with its Mount Marathon race. Seldovia and Skagway are also popular venues.

Girdwood Forest Fair *(1st weekend)*, Girdwood. This very

Athlete participating in the high kick event, World Eskimo-Indian Olympics in Fairbanks

popular festival takes place about an hour south of Anchorage in the resort town of Girdwood. Food and craft booths cover the grounds, and partygoers dance to bands on two stages. Campsites are available.

World Eskimo-Indian Olympics *(mid-Jul)*, Fairbanks. This Native event includes an array of traditional games, including the kneel jump, toe kick, blanket toss, ear pull, and greased pole walk.

Alaska Bearpaw Festival *(mid-Jul)*, Eagle River near Anchorage. On offer are bear-oriented events, including a parade, a teddy bear picnic, Miss Bear Paw Pageant, and a 300-yard

(270-m) dash called Running with the Bears.

Fairbanks Golden Days *(3rd week)*. An air show and a host of citywide activities are part of this event, which ends with a grand parade featuring a junk truck and a "hoosegow" (jail) wagon.

Deltana Fair *(last weekend)*, Delta Junction. A carnival, rodeo, and outhouse and mud bog races are on offer at this agricultural fair.

Southeast Alaska State Fair *(4th week)*, Haines. This fair features a farmers' market, a lumberjack show, pig races, a dog show, and live music.

August

Talkeetna Bluegrass Festival *(1st weekend)*, Mile 102, Parks Highway. This festival is a Woodstock-style campout, with non-stop partying. Despite the name, bluegrass music is conspicuously absent, while rock, folk, and blues predominate.

Blueberry Festival *(1st weekend)*, Ketchikan. The humble blueberry is honored with pie-eating contests, art exhibitions, folk music, food stalls, and even a slug race.

Seward Silver Salmon Derby *(mid-Aug)*, Seward. Alaska's most famous salmon derby offers a $10,000 grand prize and a total purse of $100,000.

Crowds at the Fourth of July parade in downtown Seward

Bald eagles crowding cottonwood trees in the fall, Haines

Fall

As tourists and seasonal workers leave, birch trees turn yellow, the air fills with the scent of woodsmoke, and over half the state's population ends up at the Alaska State Fair. With winter approaching, the frenetic activity of summer begins to wind down, with one last burst of excitement on Alaska Day.

September
Alaska State Fair *(Aug–Sep)*, Palmer. This extremely popular 11-day event attracts visitors from all over the state with agricultural exhibits (including gargantuan vegetables), livestock auctions, art, food and retail booths, rides, music and theater performances, lumberjack shows, and other daily events.
Kodiak State Fair and Rodeo *(1st weekend)*, Kodiak. Stock-car racing, a rodeo, and live music are the highlights of this small fair.
Labor Day *(1st Mon)*, across Alaska. Although this is celebrated statewide, Nome hosts the quirkiest events, including a Rubber Duck Race and a Bathtub Race.
Klondike Trail of '98 International Road Relay *(early Sep)*, Skagway to Whitehorse. This demanding relay attracts up to 150 teams of 10 runners each, who race along the 110-mile (176-km) Klondike Highway between Skagway and Whitehorse, Canada, following the 1890s Gold Rush trail.

October
Alaska Day *(Oct 18)*, across Alaska. Celebrated statewide, this day marks Russia's handing over of Alaska to the US in 1867. Sitka has one of the largest festivals, featuring wonderful Russian costumes and dances, a parade, and a re-enactment of the flag-raising ceremony.

November
Alaska Bald Eagle Festival *(2nd week)*, Haines. Live music, photography workshops, and lectures fête the phenomenal return of the bald eagles to the Chilkat Valley in the fall.
Carrs/Safeway Great Alaska Shoot-Out *(Thanksgiving weekend)*, Anchorage. The University of Alaska Anchorage hosts top basketball teams in one of the largest pre-season tournaments in the US.

Winter

In early winter, Christmas preparations dominate, and Alaska's snow and cold provide a quintessential holiday atmosphere. After New Year, those who haven't migrated to warmer climes participate in winter festivities, including ice-sculpture contests, indoor sports, dog sled races, and ski events.

Taking an icy dip in the Polar Bear Jump-Off, Seward

December

Wilderness Woman *(1st weekend)*, Talkeetna. Pitting women against each other in order to gain the favor of Talkeetna's single men, this competition includes snowmachine driving, wood chopping, and providing a sandwich and beer to a bachelor watching TV. It winds up with a Bachelor Auction.

Colony Christmas *(2nd weekend)*, Palmer. Old-fashioned Christmas festival echoing the Matanuska Valley Colony of the 1940s with reindeer sleigh rides, fireworks, caroling, and food.

January

Russian Orthodox Christmas *(Jan 7)*, across Alaska. Russian Orthodox communities mark Christmas with both solemn commemorations and joyous celebration. Traditions include "starring," in which carolers carry a decorated star from house to house singing religious carols called *koyadki*.

Polar Bear Jump-Off *(3rd weekend)*, Seward. People jump into icy Resurrection Bay dressed up in costumes.

February

Iceworm Festival *(1st weekend)*, Cordova. Iceworms, small, thin worms that actually do inhabit glacial ice, are the inspiration for this wacky winter event. A 150-ft (45-m) long iceworm is paraded through the streets, and there is a carnival, dress-up competition, talent show, and the crowning of Miss Iceworm.

Yukon Quest International Sled Dog Race *(early Feb)*, Whitehorse to Fairbanks or vice versa. The race follows a route along the Yukon river and over the wild mountains between Fairbanks and whitehorse.

Anchorage Fur Rendezvous *(Feb–Mar)*, Anchorage. Originally meant to bring fur trappers and buyers together, "Fur Rondy"

World Ice Art Championship, Fairbanks

features a snow sculpture competition, the World Championship Sled Dog Races, and a run with the reindeer.

Nenana Ice Classic *(Feb–Apr)*, Nenana. Bets are laid on the exact minute that the ice breaks up on the Nenana River, with all correct entries splitting the purse.

March

Iditarod Trail Sled Dog Race *(early Mar)*, Anchorage to Nome. This classic race is ceremonially flagged off from Anchorage and restarts in Willow the next day, arriving in Nome nine days later.

World Ice Art Championship *(early Mar)*, Fairbanks. Huge blocks of ice are sculpted into artistic forms. Dozens of teams, including participants from China, Japan, and Russia, take part in this impressive contest.

Bering Sea Ice Golf Classic *(at the end of the Iditarod race)*, Nome. Golf on the frozen Bering Sea, with orange golf balls and painted greens.

Pillar Mountain Golf Classic *(late Mar)*, Kodiak. A one-hole, par 70 golf game played up the slopes of 1,400-ft (424-m) Pillar Mountain, with the aim of hitting the ball into a bucket at the summit.

Team starting off in the Iditarod Trail Sled Dog Race

The Climate of Alaska

Alaska's wide range of climates can be divided into six major zones. The Southeast experiences mild winters and cool, rainy summers. Shielded from the Gulf of Alaska by mountains, the region around Cook Inlet has longer, colder winters and shorter, warmer summers than elsewhere around the Gulf. The Aleutians have year-round stormy, blustery weather. The coldest winter temperatures are found in the Interior, where -40° C (-40° F) or lower is not uncommon, although the summer more than compensates with sunny days up to 32° C (90° F). Arctic winters are not as cold as those in the Interior, but snow can linger until July. The alpine climate is dictated by terrain and altitude.

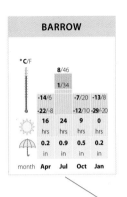

Climate Zones

- Arctic (cold dry): Short, cool summer and long, cold winter.
- Interior (cold to hot): Extremely cold winters and warm summers.
- Southcentral (cold to warm): Variable winter, warm summer.
- Alpine (variable): Weather depends on terrain and altitude.
- Bering Sea (mild and stormy): Year-round blustery conditions.
- Southeast Maritime (cool wet): Cool rainy summer, mild winter.

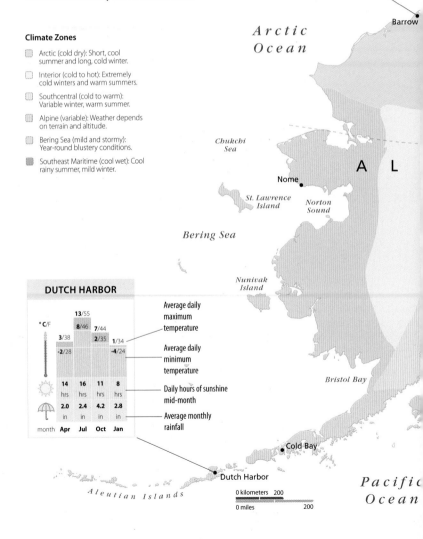

FAIRBANKS

°C/F			
	23/73		
6/42	**11**/52		
-7/20		**0**/32	
		-8/17	**-18**/-2
			-28/-19
15 hrs	20 hrs	10 hrs	5 hrs
0.2 in	1.8 in	0.8 in	0.6 in
month Apr	Jul	Oct	Jan

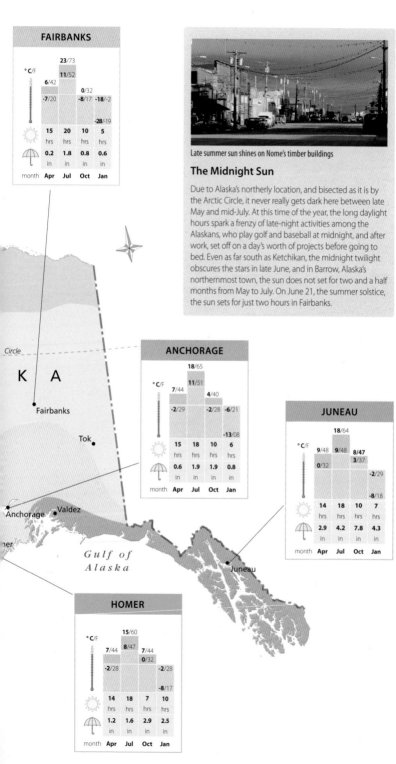

Late summer sun shines on Nome's timber buildings

The Midnight Sun

Due to Alaska's northerly location, and bisected as it is by the Arctic Circle, it never really gets dark here between late May and mid-July. At this time of the year, the long daylight hours spark a frenzy of late-night activities among the Alaskans, who play golf and baseball at midnight, and after work, set off on a day's worth of projects before going to bed. Even as far south as Ketchikan, the midnight twilight obscures the stars in late June, and in Barrow, Alaska's northernmost town, the sun does not set for two and a half months from May to July. On June 21, the summer solstice, the sun sets for just two hours in Fairbanks.

Circle

K   A

● Fairbanks

Tok ●

Anchorage ● Valdez

Gulf of Alaska

Juneau ●

ANCHORAGE

°C/F			
	18/65		
7/44	**11**/51		
-2/29		**4**/40	
		-2/28	**-6**/21
			-13/08
15 hrs	18 hrs	10 hrs	6 hrs
0.6 in	1.9 in	1.9 in	0.8 in
month Apr	Jul	Oct	Jan

JUNEAU

°C/F			
		18/64	
9/48	**9**/48	**8**/47	
0/32		**3**/37	
			-2/29
			-8/18
14 hrs	18 hrs	10 hrs	7 hrs
2.9 in	4.2 in	7.8 in	4.3 in
month Apr	Jul	Oct	Jan

HOMER

°C/F			
	15/60		
7/44	**8**/47	**7**/44	
-2/28		**0**/32	**-2**/28
			-8/17
14 hrs	18 hrs	7 hrs	10 hrs
1.2 in	1.6 in	2.9 in	2.5 in
month Apr	Jul	Oct	Jan

THE HISTORY OF ALASKA

Known to the Aleut peoples as Alaxsxag, "The Great Land," Alaska has been defined by cycles of prosperity and stagnation. Russian traders in the 18th century were followed by Gold Rush prospectors in the 1890s who struggled north with dreams of fantastic wealth. The discovery of North Slope oil in the 1960s led to a new boom that not only drew people to Alaska and rejuvenated its economy, but continues to affect the state and its fortunes today.

During the Pleistocene era, between 1.8 million and 11,000 years ago, the growth of continental ice sheets caused sea levels to drop temporarily and expose shallow sea floors. The sea floor between Asia and North America formed a land bridge known as Beringia. This relatively dry and ice-free area provided access across open tundra to Alaska. As a result, the Alaskan Interior became a migration corridor from Central Asia to other parts of the North American continent. This led some anthropologists to believe that Alaska was the point of entry for some of the first people to set foot on the continent.

However, timelines differ between researchers. Some believe that the first groups of hunter-gatherers arrived from Siberia as recently as 12,000 years ago, but other evidence suggests that the first migration may have taken place as early as 30,000 to 25,000 years ago. Despite such discrepancies, it is generally thought that this early migration brought the ancestors of the modern Athabaskan, Tlingit, Haida, and Tsimshian peoples, who are still

resident across Alaska. By about 15,000 years ago, most of the continental ice covering Alaska had melted, closing off the Bering land bridge but opening up migration routes deeper into the continent. Although opinions vary, modern scientific thought suggests that most contemporary Native groups across the Americas are descended from these Central Asian migrants.

It is estimated that the first Inuit peoples arrived in western Alaska by *umiaq* (skin boat) after the ice had melted. Some researchers date this to 8,000 years ago, while others claim it was as recent as 4,500 years ago. These hunters, familiar with Arctic coastal conditions, followed a maritime hunting culture along the Bering Sea and Arctic Ocean coasts. Over the next few thousand years, they spread farther southeast to the Cook Inlet region and east through northern Canada as far as Greenland. The Aleut settled in Southwest Alaska, as evidenced by the remains of their ancient *barabaras* or *ulax* (semi-subterranean sod dwellings).

Inuit stone harpoon blade

30,000 BC	20,000 BC	10,000 BC	AD 1	AD 1000
30,000–12,000 BC First settlers cross the Bering land bridge to Alaska		**10,000 BC–AD 1000** At least 5,000 sites of human habitation across Alaska		**1000–1700** First Inuit settlers arrive in upper Cook Inlet region
23,000–7,500 BC Wisconsin Ice Age and migrations east and south	**8,000–4,500 BC** Inuit and Aleut migration to Alaska from Asia by *umiaq* (skin boat)	**2,500–1,500 BC** Inuit migrations into Canada and as far as Greenland		**1700** Dena'ina Athabaskans begin settling around upper Cook Inlet

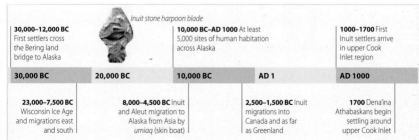

◄ Painting depicting the signing of the Alaska Treaty of Cessation, March 30, 1867

Color engraving dated between 1820 and 1840 depicting Alaska during Captain Cook's 1778 voyage

European Explorers and the Russian Era

It is possible that the first European to sight Alaska was the Spaniard Bartolomeo de Fonte, who is said to have sailed up the Inside Passage in 1640. Semyon Dezhnev, the first Russian in the region, saw the Bering Strait in 1648 and reported that a "great land" existed to the east. He was followed in 1728 by Vitus Bering, a Dane sailing for Tsar Peter the Great. Sailing through the Bering Strait, he claimed the land for the Russian Empire. In 1741, Bering set out on another voyage, with Alexei Chirikov as the commander of the second vessel. Chirikov landed on Prince of Wales Island in Southeast Alaska, paving the way for the eventual establishment of Russian America. Bering did not survive the journey, but his crew returned with sea otter pelts. Their success inspired many hunters and traders, known as *promyshleniki*, who headed for Alaska, exploiting not only the land's natural wealth, but also the labor of the Aleuts.

By 1772, a Russian settlement at Unalaska was harvesting the prized sea otter pelts throughout the Aleutians. Two years later, Spanish captain Juan Perez reported a Russian presence on Prince of Wales Island. In 1778, on his third and final voyage, British captain James Cook sailed the *Resolution* up the Southeast Alaskan coast and through Cook Inlet to the site of present-day Anchorage in his unsuccessful attempt to find the Northwest Passage to Europe.

To discourage British interest in the region, merchant and head of the Russian-American Company, Grigory Shelikov, established the first permanent Russian community at Three Saints Bay on Kodiak Island in 1784. Eight years later, he was granted a fur monopoly by Tsarina Catherine II. Over the next decade, both George Vancouver, who had been one of Cook's lieutenants, and Alejandro Malaspina of Spain, explored the Southeast and the Gulf of Alaska for their respective countries. Despite their efforts, Russian influence

1725 Bering explores the area east of the Russian mainland

Vitus Bering

1733 On Bering's second expedition, Georg Wilhelm Steller conducts nature studies in Alaska

1764 Clashes between Russians and Aleuts

1781 Grigory Shelikov establishes Russian-American fur trading company

1720

1740

1760

1780

1728 Bering sails through Bering Strait, but does not land in Alaska

1741 Alexei Chirikov reaches Prince of Wales Island; Bering dies on Bering Island in the Komandorski Islands

1772 Russian settlement established at Unalaska

1784 Shelikov sets up a town on Kodiak Island

in the region continued to expand, and at one stage the colony extended as far south as Fort Bragg in northern California.

Under the directorship of former sales representative Alexander Baranov, the Russian-American Company was granted a trade monopoly by Tsar Paul I in 1799. He was also authorized to make Sitka the seat of colonial government. Just two years later, the Russian fort at Sitka was attacked and destroyed by Tlingit protesting their forced allegiance to the tsar. Despite the defeat, the Russians returned in 1804 and Sitka was rebuilt as a veritable stockade. In 1824, Russia, Britain, and the United States signed a treaty forming the boundaries of Russian America and British Canada roughly along Alaska's current boundaries.

William H Seward, US Secretary of State

The Sale of Alaska

By the 1830s, the Russian population of Sitka had grown to around 1,300, with Baranov emerging as the most powerful man in the North Pacific region. At the same time, overhunting of sea otters and fur seals caused a sharp decline in the profitability of the fur trade, which was replaced by fishing, shipbuilding, and lumbering. Realizing that American traders and Britain's Hudson Bay Company already had interests in Alaska, Russia began to lose enthusiasm for its distant and increasingly unproductive colony. In 1859, Tsar Alexander II authorized his agent, Baron Edward de Stoeckl, to negotiate the sale of Alaska to the United States.

Initially, Congress was reluctant to consider the purchase, especially during the 1861–65 Civil War. In 1866, California fur companies expressed interest in the Russian-American Company but it was not until 1867 that Secretary of State William H Seward championed the cause of purchasing Russian interests in North America. President Andrew Johnson and the US Congress agreed to buy Alaska for the paltry sum of $7.2 million or – as is frequently noted – about 2 cents an acre. At Sitka on October 18, 1867, ownership was officially transferred and the US flag was raised. Despite the low price, the American public generally thought Alaska was a waste of money, and dubbed the new acquisition "Seward's Folly," "Seward's Icebox," "Walrussia," and "Uncle Sam's Attic."

Hand-colored woodcut depicting Sitka in 1869

1799 Tsar Paul I grants trade monopoly to Russian-American Company; Baranov sets up Russian fort and political capital at Sitka

1867 political cartoon on the purchase of Alaska

1848 New England whalers begin commercial whaling in Alaskan waters

1867 US Secretary of State William H Seward purchases Alaska for $7.2 million

1800	1820	1840	1860

1791 George Vancouver of Britain and Alejandro Malaspina of Spain explore Southeast Alaska

1840 Russian Orthodox diocese established for Alaska

1859 Russian attaché Edward de Stoeckl is granted authority to negotiate the sale of Alaska to the US

1861 American Civil War begins

The Gold Rush

In the decade after the US purchase of Alaska, there was very little interest in the new acquisition, but this changed in 1880 when gold was found at the site of present-day Juneau. Little had come of earlier strikes on the Kenai Peninsula and in the Stikine Valley, but the Juneau find sparked off a fresh wave of interest. With the discovery of gold in the Klondike and in the beach sands of Nome in the late 1890s, a frenzied Gold Rush began. By the time it ended around 1905, interest in Alaska had waned again, but a small number of adventurous homesteaders continued to venture north in search of opportunity.

Key

☐ Gold Rush Territory 1867–1905

--- Key routes to gold mining areas

Transport and communication routes were set up as a result of the Klondike Gold Rush. Telegraph lines were laid and the White Pass and Yukon Route Railroad was built in 1898 to link Skagway with the Klondike, opening up the Interior to the outside world.

Gold pans were used to separate river gravel and alluvial gold.

Streams carried the gravel that contained gold.

Steamships were used by people who had the means to sail up the Yukon River to the goldfields. Others took the All-American Route from Valdez across Valdez Glacier and up the Copper River system to the Yukon River.

"Grubstakes" were carried by all prospectors on the Chilkoot Trail, who hauled load after load of supplies over the steep pass. Fearing that unprepared miners would face starvation, Canadian officials required each man to carry a year's worth of supplies and food.

Women travelers such as Edith Van Buren *(left)* and Mary Hitchcock ushered in a new phase of Klondike history – while prospectors struggled to reach the goldfields, they sailed up the Yukon into Dawson as tourists in 1898.

Capturing the popular imagination, the Gold Rush was well represented in prose, poetry, and movies. Charlie Chaplin's *The Gold Rush* (1925), with the Tramp as a gold prospector in the Klondike, portrayed the harsh conditions faced by the prospectors.

Tents served as home to prospectors in the northern wilderness, and tent cities sprang up around major discoveries.

Gold Rush literature includes the works of Robert Service *(see pp200–201)*. Known as the "Bard of the Yukon," Service immortalized this era with his poetry, which includes "The Spell of the Yukon," "The Cremation of Sam McGee," and "The Call of the Wild," which are popular even today.

Gold Panning

In the river valleys of Interior Alaska and the Klondike, prospectors staked claims and set up operations to extract placer gold, particles of gold found in alluvial or glacial deposits concentrated in wilderness streams. Early prospectors used little more than shovels and gold pans, while others set up simple water-powered dredges.

Gold Rush mining tools were usually basic, and included sluice boxes, gold pans, pickaxes, and shovels. Modern placer miners use gasoline dredges to process the gravel.

After the Gold Rush, most prospectors returned home penniless, having squandered their riches on frontier vices. By the 1920s, seams began to play out, and although the World War II ban on gold mining was lifted in 1946, postwar inflation made mining unprofitable. Operations such as Independence Mine *(see pp90–91)* began closing down, leaving derelict mines and dredges strewn across Alaska.

Timber structures under construction on Main Street in Anchorage in 1915

The Gold Rush

After the purchase of Alaska, few Americans had any interest in the state. However, the discovery of gold near Juneau in 1880 and subsequently in the Canadian Klondike focused outside attention on Alaska and led to a Gold Rush that lasted for nearly two decades. By the time the Gold Rush era ended around 1905, most Americans had lost interest in Alaska, but a small, steady stream of hardy men continued to head north in search of land to homestead. In 1900, the capital was moved from Sitka to Juneau, and by 1906, Alaska had a non-voting member in Congress; it gained official Territorial status barely six years after that.

Developing the New Territory

In the years leading up to World War II, an increasing population and interest in timber resources and seafood transformed the

Workers marching back to camp during the construction of the Alaska Highway, 1942

new territory from a useless outpost to a viable part of the USA. In the 1920s, Alaskan Natives, along with other Native Americans, were granted voting rights and then US citizenship. The Alaska Railroad between Seward and Fairbanks was completed in 1923, rejuvenating the city of Anchorage, which had sprung up in 1914 as a railway construction camp and service center for miners from the Kenai Peninsula.

During the Great Depression of the mid-1930s, President Franklin D Roosevelt's New Deal established the Matanuska Valley Colony at Palmer. Some 200 farming families, mostly from the Midwest states of Minnesota and Wisconsin, were resettled here to try their hand at farming and raising dairy cattle. Although the project enjoyed only limited success, the area remains Alaska's most productive farming region.

1884 US Congress passes Organic Act, providing education to all residents of Alaska	**1891** First oil claims staked in Cook Inlet	Gold panning in Nome	**1900** Alaska's capital moved from Sitka to Juneau	**1914** Tent city of Anchorage founded as a construction camp for the Alaska Railroad
1880	**1890**		**1900**	**1910**
1872 Gold discovered around Sitka	**1880** Joe Juneau and Richard Harris unearth gold near present-day Juneau	**1896** Gold discovered in the Klondike in Canada	**1902** Gold found near Fairbanks	**1912** Novarupta erupts; Alaska becomes a US Territory

The War Years

When Japan attacked Pearl Harbor on December 7, 1941, the American government realized the vulnerability of Alaska's position in the North Pacific, with Anchorage as close to Tokyo as it is to Washington, DC. Fears of invasion were well-founded and the Japanese launched an air attack on the Aleutians on June 3, 1942. Four days later, they captured Attu Island, taking the locals

US troops carrying a wounded soldier on Attu Island in 1943

prisoner. The US government was quick to retaliate. Hundreds of other islanders were evacuated to Southeast Alaska, troops and about 70 US Navy ships were dispatched to the Aleutians, and military bases were established at Akutan, Amchitka, and Adak. The islands were successfully recaptured by August 1943.

During this period, a large portion of the state's current highway system was developed. The greatest project was the 1,440-mile (2,304-km) Alaska Highway, which connected Alaska to the rest of the US by road *(see pp290–91)*. This phenomenal feat involved punching a route through trackless territory, felling trees, and bridging wild rivers. Despite incredible hardships, the project was completed in eight months and 12 days, and the road was opened on October 25, 1942.

Statehood

In 1942, Anchorage had a population of just 7,724, but the development brought about by the war caused that number to

increase to 43,314 by 1945. Several other towns grew almost as dramatically. At this point, it was clear that Alaska had matured and was on the road to eventual statehood. In 1955, Alaskans elected delegates to a constitutional convention, which would draft a constitution for the new state. The resulting document was adopted the following year, and in 1958 President Dwight D Eisenhower signed the Statehood Bill that made Alaska the 49th state of the US on January 3, 1959.

Mile 0 marker of the Alaska Highway in the town of Dawson Creek, Canada

1923 Completion of the Alaska Railroad

Alaska State flag and US flag

1942 Japanese invade the Aleutian Islands; Alaska Highway completed

1955 Alaskans elect delegates to a constitutional convention

1956 Voters adopt the new Alaskan constitution

1920   1930   1940   1950   1960

1924 Congress extends citizenship to Native Americans

1935 Matanuska Valley Project brings families from the US Midwest to farm in Alaska

1943 US forces finally repel the Japanese from the Aleutians

1959 Alaska becomes a state on January 3

1922 Native voting rights established

Anchorage's 4th Avenue, a day after the massive 1964 Good Friday earthquake

The Oil Boom

In 1957, oil was discovered in Cook Inlet and by the mid-1960s, platform installations were producing 200,000 barrels of oil per day. However, a major setback occurred on March 27, 1964, when one of the 20th century's strongest earthquakes – 9.2 on the Richter scale – rocked Southcentral Alaska, causing widespread destruction. Due to the low population density, loss of life was minimal and property damage was limited to $500 million. Despite this tragedy, Alaska continued to grow. In 1968, the Atlantic-Richfield Company (ARCO) drilled an exploratory well at Prudhoe Bay on the Arctic coast and discovered an estimated 9.6 billion barrels of recoverable oil reserves on state-controlled land. Alaska sold oil leases worth $900 million, and six years later, the Alyeska Corporation began construction of the Trans-Alaska Pipeline and the black gold rush was on. Thousands of workers flooded into Alaska for well-paying pipeline jobs and 39 months and $8 billion later, the oil began to flow. The resulting oil revenues were used to establish the Alaska Permanent Fund in 1982, which now serves as a state savings account and pays an annual dividend to every resident of Alaska.

ANCSA and ANILCA

In 1971, Congress passed the then controversial Alaska Native Claims Settlement Act (ANCSA), which attempted to compensate Alaska Natives for the loss of

Endicott Oil Production Island at Prudhoe Bay on Alaska's North Slope

1968 The first oil is pumped at Prudhoe Bay

1971 ANCSA (Alaska Native Claims Settlement Act) passed

1980 ANILCA (Alaska National Interest Lands Conservation Act) passed

1985 Alaska purchases Alaska Railroad from federal government

| 1965 | 1970 | 1975 | 1980 | 1985 | 1990 |

1964 Good Friday earthquake seriously damages Anchorage, Valdez, Seward, and Kodiak

1969 North Slope oil leases sold for $900 million

1976 Willow selected as the new capital site

1977 Trans-Alaska Pipeline completed

1989 *Exxon Valdez* hits Bligh Reef and spills oil into Prince William Sound

Workers cleaning oil-covered rocks after the *Exxon Valdez* spill

their lands. The Act transferred 68,750 sq miles (178,000 sq km) of land to 12 newly established and potentially profit-making Native Corporations, which roughly coincided with tribal and sub-tribal boundaries. Alaska Natives were made shareholders in their respective corporations and were given substantial control over the assets. This arrangement effectively avoided the Reservation system used in the Lower 48 and nullified any claims to Native sovereignty.

In 1980, President Jimmy Carter signed the Alaska National Interest Lands Conservation Act (ANILCA), which set aside 162,500 sq miles (420,870 sq km) as protected wilderness. As a result, a host of national parks were created, including Wrangell-St. Elias, Kenai Fjords, Gates of the Arctic, and Katmai. Unfortunately, interpretation of other facets of ANILCA have since created rifts between urban residents and rural Alaska Natives, who do not consider their homeland to be "wilderness." Many of them feel that

they should have priority access to the land for subsistence purposes. City and town dwellers, however, who are constitutionally entitled to the same access to fish, water, and wildlife, also want to be permitted to exercise their rights. After more than three decades, the dispute continues.

The 1989 *Exxon Valdez* oil spill *(see p121)* just off the coast of Valdez cost the company billions of dollars and damaged both the delicate ecology of Prince William Sound and the public opinion of Alaska's oil industry. However, fossil fuels continue to finance state government and fuel the enormous US market for petroleum products. Debates about opening the remote Arctic National Wildlife Refuge to oil drilling and developing a natural gas pipeline are continuing, although a diversifying economy has lessened Alaska's reliance on primary natural resources in favor of tourism and service industries.

Aialik Bay in Kenai Fjords National Park, which was created in 1980 under ANILCA

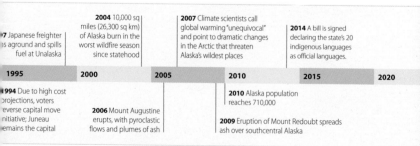

2004 10,000 sq miles (26,300 sq km) of Alaska burn in the worst wildfire season since statehood

2007 Climate scientists call global warming "unequivocal" and point to dramatic changes in the Arctic that threaten Alaska's wildest places

2014 A bill is signed declaring the state's 20 indigenous languages as official languages.

...7 Japanese freighter ...s aground and spills fuel at Unalaska

1995 | 2000 | 2005 | 2010 | 2015 | 2020

1994 Due to high cost projections, voters reverse capital move initiative; Juneau remains the capital

2006 Mount Augustine erupts, with pyroclastic flows and plumes of ash

2010 Alaska population reaches 710,000

2009 Eruption of Mount Redoubt spreads ash over southcentral Alaska

ALASKA AREA BY AREA

Alaska at a Glance

Thanks to its plate tectonics and glaciation, Alaska has a magnificent array of landforms. In the Southeast, forested hills and ice-covered peaks rise above deep, winding fjords. Farther north, rugged mountains and rivers fringe the highways. Beyond the main routes, Alaska offers a wealth of variations on the wilderness theme, including temperate rainforests, Arctic tundra, volcanic islands, and boreal forests. Wildlife is plentiful and adventure activities abound, ranging from Nordic skiing to whitewater rafting. Anchorage, Fairbanks, and Juneau provide urban counterpoints to Alaska's wild expanses, offering excellent museums, restaurants, hotels, and shopping opportunities.

Barrow *(see pp226–7)*, well above the Arctic Circle, is the northernmost settlement in the US.

• Barrow

ARCTIC AND WESTERN ALASKA
(See pp218–35)

• Kotzebue

Denali National Park *(see pp166–9)* is Alaska's top visitor attraction. Its name comes from Mount McKinley, known to the Native peoples as Denali, which is an Athabaskan word meaning "The Great One." The park is home to moose, Dall sheep, caribou, and grizzlies.

• Nome

SOUTHWEST ALASKA
(see pp202–17)

Bethel •

THE KE PENINS
(See pp96

The Aleutians *(see pp212–15)* are a long chain of stormy volcanic islands.

Kodia

Unalaska •   *Islands*

Aleutian

Katmai National Park *(see pp210–11)* takes in a vast wilderness of icy lakes, volcanic landscapes, and a wild sea coast. The McNeil and Brooks Rivers have bountiful salmon runs that attract brown bears.

◀ Glacial blue pools seen from a flightseeing trip over forested wetland south of Anchorage

Kenai Fjords National Park *(see pp106–7)*, near Seward, draws kayakers and day cruisers with its rugged coastlines, high peaks, icefields, and glaciers. The seas here, rich in crustaceans, fish, and plankton, host a wide variety of marine mammals.

Kennicott *(see pp188–9)* in Wrangell-St. Elias National Park, was the processing site for the area's prolific copper mines. The remaining ghost town is now the park's most popular destination.

0 km 300
0 miles 300

EASTERN
INTERIOR
ALASKA
(See pp180–201)

WESTERN
INTERIOR
ALASKA
(See pp156–79)

ANCHORAGE
(See pp66–95)

PRINCE
WILLIAM SOUND
(See pp114–23)

Juneau

SOUTHEAST
ALASKA
(See pp124–55)

Ketchikan

Columbia Glacier *(see p119)*, west of Valdez, spills down from the Chugach Mountains to calve icebergs into Prince William Sound, whose waters are a favorite of kayakers and anglers.

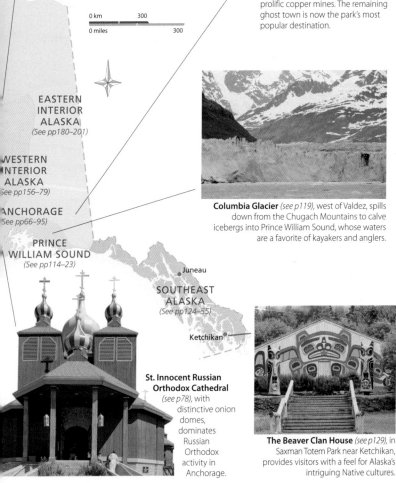

St. Innocent Russian Orthodox Cathedral *(see p78)*, with distinctive onion domes, dominates Russian Orthodox activity in Anchorage.

The Beaver Clan House *(see p129)*, in Saxman Totem Park near Ketchikan, provides visitors with a feel for Alaska's intriguing Native cultures.

ANCHORAGE

Spread across an alluvial plain between the lofty Chugach Range and the waters of Cook Inlet, Anchorage is Alaska's largest city. In less than a century since its founding in 1914, this former tent city has grown into the economic, commercial, and transport hub of the state. With excellent museums, theaters, parks, and shops, Anchorage is not only the perfect urban foil for Alaska's wilderness, but an ideal jumping-off point for adventures farther afield.

The original tent city on the shores of Ship Creek was a service camp for the Alaska Railroad. An early sale of lots led to the growth of downtown Anchorage on the nearby bluffs, while the banks of Ship Creek developed into the town's port, shipping, and industrial district.

The massive Good Friday earthquake of 1964 destroyed parts of Anchorage, but construction of the Trans-Alaska Pipeline in the 1970s completely changed the profile of the city. A large share of oil revenue came to Anchorage, leading to an explosion of growth. The downtown area was revitalized with new sports arenas, civic centers, and performing arts venues, and outlying suburbs were integrated into the urban area. Today, the municipality of Anchorage, with a population of over 300,000 people, includes not only the city proper, but also the Elmendorf Air Force Base and Fort Richardson Military Reservation, several villages along Turnagain Arm, and a string of suburbs, including Eagle River and Eklutna, along Knik Arm. It also takes in the vast swathe of Chugach State Park, which brings the "real Alaska" right to the city's back door. To the north, the growing Matanuska-Susitna (Mat-Su) Borough provides space and a more outdoorsy lifestyle than is possible in Anchorage proper.

All year round, travelers will find numerous good hotels and excellent restaurants. In the summer, however, downtown Anchorage comes into its own, bustling with visitors from across the world who stop off to see the sights and prepare for adventures in the more remote parts of the state.

Native Alaskans performing traditional dances at the Alaska Native Heritage Center

◀ *Crystal Lattice*, a contemporary sculpture by Robert Pfitzenmeier, Anchorage Museum

Exploring Anchorage

The historic downtown area and the older neighborhoods of Smuggler's Cove and Turnagain form the core of Anchorage. The main sights of interest – including the Alaska Public Lands Information Center, Anchorage Museum, and Town Square – are centered around this core, within walking distance of one another. Avenues in this central area run east-west and are numbered. Streets run north-south and are lettered from A Street westward and named alphabetically for Alaskan towns from Barrow Street eastward.

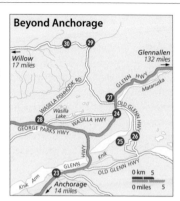

Beyond Anchorage

Sights at a Glance

Areas of Natural Beauty
- ⓫ Ship Creek Salmon Viewing Platform
- ⓬ Tony Knowles Coastal Trail
- ⓮ Lake Hood and Lake Spenard
- ⓲ Hilltop Ski Area
- ㉖ Bodenburg Butte
- ㉚ Hatcher Pass

Parks and Theme Parks
- ❼ Resolution Park
- ⓱ H2Oasis
- ⓲ Alaska Zoo
- ⓴ Chugach State Park pp82–3
- ㉑ Alaska Botanical Garden
- ㉓ Eklutna Historical Park
- ㉕ Reindeer Farm
- ㉗ Musk Ox Farm
- ㉙ Independence Mine State Historical Park pp90–91

Museums and Theaters
- ❶ Anchorage Museum pp72–3
- ❷ Alaska State Trooper Museum
- ❻ 4th Avenue Theater
- ❾ Alaska Native Heritage Center pp76–7
- ⓭ Alaska Aviation Heritage Museum

Buildings, Neighborhoods, and Towns
- ❸ Anchorage Market & Festival
- ❹ Log Cabin Visitor Information Center
- ❺ Alaska Public Lands Information Center
- ❽ Oscar Anderson House
- ❿ St. Innocent Russian Orthodox Cathedral
- ⓯ Spenard
- ⓰ Alaska Wild Berry Products
- ㉔ Palmer
- ㉘ Wasilla

Tour
- ㉒ Turnagain Arm Tour pp84–5

Signpost reflecting the city's self-proclaimed status as an air crossroads

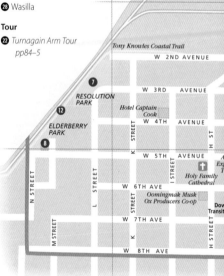

Getting Around

The main sights, concentrated in downtown Anchorage, are best explored on foot. While People Mover buses connect the Dimond Center, Downtown, and Muldoon Transit Centers with most parts of town, the most convenient way to explore farther afield is by car. The Seward Highway is the main north-south corridor, while the main east-west route is the Glenn Highway. Anchorage International Airport, 4 miles (6 km) southwest of the city center, handles domestic and international flights and is served by taxis and buses. Alaska Railroad operates a year-round service between Anchorage and Fairbanks and summer trains to Seward and Whittier.

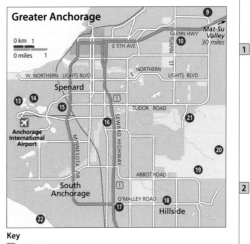

Greater Anchorage

0 km 1
0 miles 1

Key

Area of the main map

Key

Place of interest

0 meters 200
0 yards 200

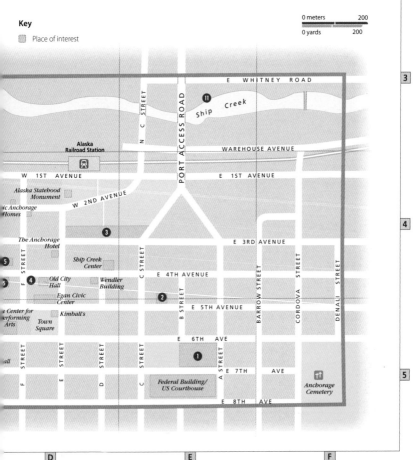

Street-by-Street: Downtown Anchorage

Although Anchorage began as a tented construction camp on the shores of Ship Creek, the 1915 sale of lots shifted its center to the site of present-day downtown Anchorage. After almost a century of growth and development, along with restoration work after the massive 1964 earthquake, downtown Anchorage today features a mix of historic buildings and modern high-rises interspersed with small private homes. Containing an open-air weekend market, a variety of shops, and most of the city's main sights, as well as a lovely town square and pleasant ornamentation including public artwork and flower baskets hanging from lampposts, this compact area is a joy to explore on foot.

Anchorage's busy 4th Avenue filled with visitors and locals

❸ **The Anchorage Market and Festival** Alaskan arts and crafts, snacks, and fresh produce are on sale here.

❺ **Alaska Public Lands Information Center** The Center has details on Alaska's millions of acres of wild places, including Denali and 14 other national parks.

❻ **4th Avenue Theater**
The Art Deco-style 4th Avenue Theater, which was built in 1947, survived the Good Friday earthquake of 1964.

❹ **Log Cabin Visitor Information Center** This picturesque downtown log building has an oft-photographed sign showing the distance to other cities around the globe.

★ **Town Square**
With over 9,000 plants, this is a popular lunch and concert spot. In the winter, it boasts an ice rink and hosts the New Year's fireworks display.

The Wyland Whale Mural
Created freehand by Robert Wyland in 1994, the mural depicting a family of whales is painted on a wall east of the Town Square.

Locator Map
See Street Map pp68–9, D4, D5 & E5

❷ Alaska State Trooper Museum
Founded in 1991, one of the most prominent exhibits in the museum is a sparkling, fully restored 1952 Hudson Hornet patrol car.

Key

— Suggested route

0 meters 100
0 yards 100

❶ ★ Anchorage Museum
One of the state's premier museums, this houses excellent collections of historical artifacts, as well as traditional Native and modern Alaskan art.

Balto's Statue
This champion sled dog's bronze statue stands outside the turreted Wendler Building.

Baseball in Alaska

Each summer, top baseball players from major American colleges come to Alaska to play on six semi-pro teams. Two teams, the Anchorage Bucs and the Anchorage Glacier Pilots, play at Muchay Stadium at E. 16th and Cordova. This is a great chance to watch the players of tomorrow –

many Bucs and Glacier Pilots have gone on to play in the majors, including Reggie Jackson, Dave Winfield, Mark McGuire, Randy Johnson, Kurt Suzuki, J D Drew, Rick Aguilera, and Jered Weaver. Other Alaska Baseball League teams are in Fairbanks, Palmer, and Kenai.

● Anchorage Museum

Covering 170,000 square feet, including 2 acres (1 ha) of landscaped public space, Alaska's largest museum reopened in 2009 following a $106-million expansion. The museum houses exhibits on Alaskan history, science, and Native culture, along with some of the state's finest art. The Imaginarium Discovery Center is a highlight, as are the planetarium and artifacts from Alaskan Native cultures. Additionally, the museum hosts approximately 20 visiting exhibits annually from around the world.

The slick, modern facade of the Anchorage Museum

The Smithsonian Arctic Studies Center houses a remarkable collection of Native artifacts on loan from the Smithsonian.

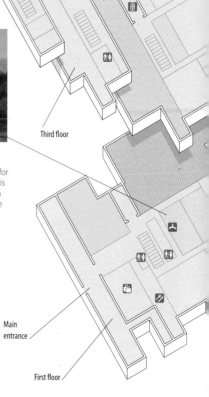

Fourth floor

Third floor

Main entrance

First floor

★ Mount McKinley by Sydney Laurence
Considered one of Alaska's most popular painters, Sydney Laurence (1865–1940) is perhaps best known for his series of paintings of Mount McKinley, including this iconic depiction of the mountain in enigmatic Alaskan light. Several of Laurence's atmospheric landscapes are on display at the museum.

Gallery Guide

The Imaginarium Discovery Center covers much of the first floor, which also houses the Alaska Resource Center (open for public research) and the Art of the North gallery, which features a broad scope of Alaskan and Circumpolar North art through the ages. The second-level galleries exhibit native and contemporary art, and explore 10,000 years of Alaskan history. Changing exhibits are displayed on level three, which also gives access to the fourth floor gallery from where there are views of the Chugach Mountains.

Key

- The Alaska History Gallery
- Imaginarium Discovery Center
- Special exhibits
- Art of the North
- Arctic Studies Center
- Conoco Phillips Gallery
- Alaska Resource Center
- Planetarium
- Non-exhibition space

Vintage Hudson Hornet patrol car, Alaska State Trooper Museum

Second floor

Prospector's Cabin
A diorama in the Alaska Gallery shows a log cabin with a prospector weighing gold using a small balance scale.

Yup'ik Ceremonial Mask
This traditional Yup'ik mask, made of wood, feathers, and pigment, was created in the Kuskokwim Delta circa 1900. Masks represented characters and experiences in performances and stories.

★ **Imaginarium Discovery Center**
This kid-friendly science space has many hands-on attractions, such as a floor that responds to human movement.

❷ Alaska State Trooper Museum

245 W 5th Ave. Map E4. Tel 279-5050. 🚌 to Downtown Transit Center. Open 10am–4pm Mon–Fri, noon–4pm Sat. ♿ 📷
W alaskatroopermuseum.com

Founded with a handful of officers in 1941 as the Alaska State Highway Patrol, Alaska's law enforcement agency also served as the Territorial Police and the State Police before being named the Alaska State Troopers in 1967. The museum was established in 1991.

In the early days, the Troopers protected half a million square miles (1,295,000 sq km) of territory using the fairly basic technology of the time. One display exhibits a typical 1940s law enforcement office, where sealskin boots, snowshoes, a clunky period radio, typewriter, and telephone illustrate the wide range of duties a trooper was expected to fulfill.

The most popular exhibit is the shiny 1952 Hudson Hornet patrol car, one of the fastest vehicles of its era, now lovingly restored. Other displays showcase memorabilia from the days of the US Marshals, including a poster offering a $1,000 reward for Alaska's first serial killer, Edward Krause, who killed ten people between 1912 and 1915. Another intriguing device is the Harger Drunkometer, a confounding forerunner of the modern breathalyzer.

The picturesque Log Cabin Visitor Information Center

❸ Anchorage Market & Festival

3rd Ave at E St. **Map** D4. **Tel** 272-5634. 🚍 to Downtown Transit Center. **Open** mid-May–mid-Sep: 10am–6pm Sat & Sun. ♿

A favorite of both locals and tourists, this weekend market attracts hundreds of people on summer weekends to a large downtown parking lot across from the Hilton Hotel. The event combines a farmers' market, craft booths, food, and entertainment. You'll find more than 300 vendors selling made-in-Alaska pottery, nature photography, clothing, home-made jams and birch syrup, Alaskan keepsakes, nesting dolls, colorful flowers, and an array of fresh Mat-Su Valley produce. There are plenty of fast food stalls too, selling a range of tasty snacks from pizza slices and Kachemak Bay oysters to sweet funnel cakes. The market is open rain or shine.

❹ Log Cabin Visitor Information Center

546 W 4th Ave. **Map** D4. **Tel** 257-2363. 🚍 to Downtown Transit Center. **Open** Jun–Aug: 8am–7pm daily (to 6pm first and last 2 weeks of season); May & Sep: 8am–6pm daily; Oct–Apr: 9am–4pm daily. ♿ 🌐 anchorage.net

Operated by the Anchorage Convention and Visitors Bureau, this helpful center is in the heart of downtown Anchorage. The flower-bedecked, sod-roofed log cabin is a favorite spot for photos, and outside there are equally picturesque signposts showing the distance in miles to many international cities. The main visitor center fills a second building. Here you'll find visitor brochures, free guides to nearby parks, and other publications, plus helpful staff to answer travel questions.

❺ Alaska Public Lands Information Center

605 W 4th Ave. **Map** D4. **Tel** 644-3661, (866) 869-6887. 🚍 to Downtown Transit Center. **Open** last Mon May (Memorial Day)–first Mon Sep (Labor Day: 9am–5pm daily; remainder of Sep: 9am–5pm Mon–Fri; Oct–Memorial Day: 10am–5pm Mon–Fri. 🌐 alaskacenters.gov

The Federal government manages more than 60 percent of Alaska lands, including

Classic neon sign of Anchorage's 4th Avenue Theater

15 national parks, the nation's 2 largest national forests, 16 national wildlife refuges, and millions of acres of other public lands. This information center, which is housed within the old Federal Building, has displays on Alaska's wildlife and natural areas, a plethora of books and other publications, and an auditorium for nature videos and talks.

If you're looking for advice on anything from buses into Denali or bush flights into the Arctic National Wildlife Refuge, this is a great place to ask experienced staff. Daily historical walks are also offered. It is located across the street from the Log Cabin Visitor Information Center. There are also branches in Fairbanks, Tok, and Ketchikan.

❻ 4th Avenue Theater

630 W 4th Ave. **Map** D4. 🚍 to Downtown Transit Center. **Closed** to the public.

Designed in 1941 in classic Art Deco style by B Marcus Priteca, the old 4th Avenue Theater, also known as the Lathrop Building, is the quintessential Anchorage landmark. Construction began in 1941 at the cost of one million US dollars, and the building opened to the public with the film *The Al Jolson Story*. With 960 seats spread over its main floor and the balcony, the 4th Avenue Theater served as the city's only movie house for over four decades. Remarkably, the theater survived the enormously destructive 1964 Good Friday earthquake (*see p29*), which leveled other buildings along 4th Avenue. A restoration project in the mid-1980s revived its opulent Italian marble and walnut wood interiors, which are adorned with impressive bronze relief murals depicting scenes from Alaskan history. Though currently closed, there are plans to redevelop the building; however, the theater's historic significance means that this has met with opposition.

Urban Wildlife in Anchorage

Urban moose climbing up the front steps of an Anchorage house

While Anchorage may not be representative of the Alaskan wilderness, it is home to an array of wild denizens. Along with a host of birds and squirrels, moose are resident across the city. All year round, lone bulls and mothers with calves may be seen raiding gardens, snarling at traffic, and causing serious accidents that often do more damage to the car than to the moose. In addition, both brown and black bears inhabit city parks and have been known to harass joggers and cyclists on city trails, while red foxes may be observed prowling the sidewalks.

The Captain Cook Monument, a life-size bronze statue in Resolution Park

❼ Resolution Park

320 L St. **Map** B4. 🚌 to Downtown Transit Center. **Open** 24 hrs daily. ♿

Named after Captain Cook's flagship, Resolution Park offers visitors one of the best views in Anchorage, taking in Cook Inlet and both Mount Susitna (a magnificent low mountain to the northwest, also known as The Sleeping Lady) and spectacular Mount McKinley on a clear day. The active volcanoes south of Mount McKinley, Mount Spur and Redoubt, are also visible.

The centerpiece of this small park is the **Captain Cook Monument**, commemorating the 200th anniversary of James Cook's exploration of Alaska. An 18th-century British naval officer and explorer with a natural talent for physics and mathematics, Cook led several expeditions around the world. In 1776, on his third voyage in HMS *Resolution*, he sailed north along the continent's west coast in search of the Northwest Passage (a navigable link between the Atlantic and Pacific Oceans), and passed the present-day site of Anchorage, giving his name to Cook Inlet. Derek Freeborn's life-sized bronze statue, based on the one in Whitby, UK, from where Cook first set sail, was donated to Anchorage during the US Bicentennial celebrations in 1976.

Just one block east, in front of the Carr-Gottstein Building, is Josef Princiotta's fabulous 1973 bronze sculpture, **The Last Blue Whale**. Adding a wonderful sense of perspective is a small beleaguered boat on the ripples of water near the tail of the gigantic whale.

❽ Oscar Anderson House

420 M St. **Map** B4. **Tel** 274-2336. 🚌 to Downtown Transit Center. **Open** Jun–Aug: noon–4pm Tue–Sun. 🐾 📷 ♿

This historic home was built in 1915 by Oscar Anderson, a Swede who is said to have been the 18th resident of the original tent city of Anchorage. While still living on the beach after his arrival in town, Anderson established the Ship Creek Meat Company and the Evan Jones Fuel Company. Due to a shortage of building materials, his house, the first permanent wood-frame structure in town, had only one and a half stories and measured just 800 sq ft (72 sq m). Anderson lived here until his death in 1974, and two years later, it was deeded to the City of Anchorage by his widow.

The building has since been meticulously restored to reflect the period in which it was built, and is listed on the National Register of Historic Places. Various exhibits reveal the history of the city, and many of Anderson's original belongings are on display, including a working 1909 player piano. A Swedish Christmas open house is held here in traditional style each December. Next to the house, **Elderberry Park** offers great views of Knik Arm and the chance to spot beluga whales.

Oscar Anderson House, Anchorage's oldest wood-frame building

❾ Alaska Native Heritage Center

Situated in a lovely wooded corner of Anchorage, the Alaska Native Heritage Center uses exhibits, workshops, and outdoor displays to preserve and perpetuate Native Alaskan culture. One of Anchorage's most popular attractions, this educational and cultural institution gives visitors the opportunity to experience a range of diverse Native traditions at a single site. Among the center's highlights are five Native "villages," which are based on broad tribal groupings that draw upon cultural similarities or geographic proximity. Native Alaskans throughout the site interpret aspects of their cultures.

Raven the Creator, by John Hoover, at the Welcome House

Southeast Alaska Natives Village Site
Revealing the cultures of the Tsimshian, Eyak, Tlingit, and Haida peoples of Southeast Alaska, this site consists of a simple, undecorated clan house and a carving shed where Native artists work on totem poles.

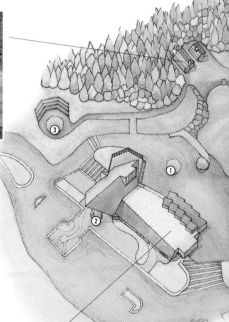

KEY

① **Village Circle**

② **Raven the Creator**

③ **Talking Circle**

④ **The Aleut (Unangax̂) and Alutiiq (Sugpiaq) Village Site** occupies a *ciqlluaq* (also called a *barabara* or *ulax*), a traditional semi-subterranean sod-covered home.

⑤ **The Inupiat and St. Lawrence Yup'ik Village Site** is housed in a *qargi*, a community house usually made from sod blocks laid over whalebone frames.

⑥ **The Yup'ik and Cup'ik Village Site** features a circular *qasgiq*, or men's house. Here, visitors can watch Native Alaskans in traditional clothing interpret the Yup'ik way of life.

⑦ **Lake Tiulana** forms a natural centerpiece for the village tour.

★ **Welcome House**
The first stop for visitors, the Welcome House contains the Hall of Cultures, with craft displays and historical exhibits, and the Gathering Place, where Native dancers, storytellers, and drummers perform.

Exploring the Center

The center sprawls across 26 acres (10 ha) of land not far from down-town Anchorage. A trail winds around a large central lake, leading past five Native villages and a Village Circle and Talking Circle where Native games are often demonstrated. The center also presents workshops, films, storytelling, and numerous other cultural programs. To fully explore the site will take at least half a day.

VISITORS' CHECKLIST

Practical Information
Muldoon Rd North, exit from
Glenn Hwy. **Map** F1.
Tel 330-8000, (800) 315-6608.
Open May–mid-Sep: 9am–5pm
daily; open for special events in
winter (late Sep–early May).
discounted rates for seniors
and children up to 16, free for
kids under 6.
W alaskanative.net

Transport
Free shuttle from Anchorage
Museum and from some hotels.

★ **Athabaskan Village Site**
This site consists of a large earth-floored log cabin that served as a traditional Athabaskan home. Here, Athabaskan docents explain the use of the home's various rooms and demonstrate traditional tools and implements.

The Welcome House

Beyond the information desk and gift shop in the entrance area is the circular Gathering Place, an arena for traditional performances. Beyond the Crossroads foyer are the theater and the Hall of Cultures, with exhibits and stands where Native artisans create and sell their work. There is also a large research library.

The unique Welcome House entrance ushers visitors into the center

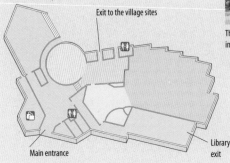

Exit to the village sites

Main entrance

Library exit

Key
- Crossroads
- Theater
- Hall of Cultures
- Library
- Gathering Place
- Non-exhibition space

Traditional domes and crosses of St. Innocent Russian Orthodox Cathedral

❿ St. Innocent Russian Orthodox Cathedral

401 Turpin St. **Map** F1. **Tel** 333-9723.
🚌 8. **Open** only for services. ♿ ✉
✝ 6pm Sat, 9am Sun, 6pm Thu.
🆆 sicanc.org

The heart of Russian Orthodox activity in the Anchorage area, this beautiful cathedral was named in honor of the erudite 18th-century bishop Ioan Veniaminov. Arriving in Unalaska in the early 1820s, he built churches and schools, developed a written version of the Aleut language, and produced an Aleut Bible, for which he was canonized in 1977 as St. Innocent. Due largely to the efforts of such missionaries, Alaska is today the leading diocese of the Russian Orthodox Church in the Western Hemisphere.

The most striking features of St. Innocent are its 12 blue onion domes. As with most Orthodox places of worship, the cathedral is full of beautifully colored icons, paintings, and religious artifacts. Although the cathedral is usually closed to the public, its opulent interior

can be seen during services, on feast days, or during other significant events of the Russian Orthodox calendar.

⓫ Ship Creek Salmon Viewing Platform

North side of Ship Creek footbridge, off Whitney Ave. **Map** E3. **Open** 24 hrs. Derby tickets: available at the cabin next to Comfort Inn on the south bank of Ship Creek.

Flowing between downtown and the Port of Anchorage, Ship Creek is a mecca for urban fishermen. Each year, the nearby salmon hatchery releases up

to 250,000 king salmon smolt, which swim downstream into Cook Inlet, spending seven years at sea before returning to spawn. To the north of the bridge across Ship Creek, a viewing platform gives visitors the opportunity to observe the salmon crowding their way upstream and jumping at the weir.

In the summer, anglers in hip-waders descend to the riverbanks in hopes of reeling in one of the 5,000 fish that are caught here each year. To fish here requires an Alaska fishing license, which is available in local shops. Fishing derbies may yield up to $10,000 for lucky anglers who catch specially tagged fish.

⓬ Tony Knowles Coastal Trail

Western end of 2nd Ave. **Map** B4.
🚌 7A. ♿

The most popular biking and jogging trail in Anchorage, the Tony Knowles Coastal Trail passes the attractive Elderberry Park on the downtown waterfront and follows the coastline south to Kincaid Park. One of the highlights along the 11 mile (17 km) trail is Westchester Lagoon, where walkers can observe waterfowl or cross over to the gravel beaches of Knik Arm. On clear days, there are great views across Cook Inlet to the volcano, Mount Spurr. Midway along the route, Earthquake Park has exhibits on the devastating 1964 Good Friday earthquake, which created the

Cyclists pedaling down Anchorage's scenic Tony Knowles Coastal Trail

1928 Stearman on display, Alaska Aviation Heritage Museum

dramatic bluff visible here. At the southern end of the trail, the 2 sq miles (5.7 sq km) Kincaid Park, a forested glacial moraine area, offers excellent summer hiking and a network of Nordic ski trails in the winter. The park also has the city's largest population of moose.

⑬ Alaska Aviation Heritage Museum

4721 Aircraft Dr. **Map** E1. **Tel** 248-5325. 🚌 7A. **Open** mid-May–mid-Sep: 9am–5pm daily; mid-Sep–mid-May: 9am–5pm Wed–Sun. 🅿️ ♿ 📷 🆆 alaskaairmuseum.org

Located on the shores of Lake Hood, the Alaska Aviation Heritage Museum is a must-see for anyone interested in the lives and achievements of traditional bush pilots and their planes. There is detailed coverage of the state's World War II history, including the Japanese invasion, along with collections of artifacts, photographs, aviators' clothing, and newspaper accounts of highlights in Alaskan aviation.

The museum also preserves an extensive collection of historic aircraft, including a 1928 Stearman bush plane that was among the first to land on Mount McKinley in 1932, one of only two remaining 1928 Hamilton Metalplanes, Merle "Mudhole" Smith's 1929 Cordova Airways TravelAir, and a 1929 Loening seaplane first flown to Alaska Territory in 1946 by former governor Jay Hammond. A 100-seat theater is available for viewing a library of film footage about Alaska's early pilots.

⑭ Lake Hood and Lake Spenard

Lakeshore Drive. **Map** E1. 🚌 7A. **Open** 24 hrs. ♿

Keeping Anchorage in touch with the Alaska that exists beyond its urban boundaries, this is the largest and busiest floatplane base in the US. It handles up to 800 takeoffs and landings per day and anyone chartering a bush flight into a remote area will probably depart from here. The best viewpoint to watch the flights is behind the Department of Transportation building. A lakeside park features a roped-off swimming area.

Anchorage's Lake Hood and Lake Spenard floatplane base

⑮ Spenard

Map E1. 🚌 7.

Anchorage's funky Spenard district was once a separate town, connected to downtown by the winding Spenard Road. Visitors to the neighborhood may come across a scattering of less-than-reputable businesses, throwbacks to Spenard's grittier days.

Despite its past and its somewhat unsavory reputation, Spenard is rapidly becoming a fashionable neighborhood. The derelict buildings and trailer parks are giving way to houses, health food eateries, second-hand shops, motels, and atmospheric bars and clubs. The corner of Spenard and Northern Lights has a REI store (see p93), along with a Kaladi Brothers coffee shop and one of Alaska's finest bookstores, Title Wave Books.

Floatplane taking off from the Lake Hood and Lake Spenard complex

Bush Flying in Alaska

Visitors who wish to fly into a remote lodge or enjoy a wilderness fishing trip are likely to employ an Alaskan bush pilot. These legendary aviators fly across untracked country, land on lakes and gravel bars, and defy natural conditions that most conventional pilots prefer to avoid. About 1 in 50 Alaskans has a pilot's license, and the state supports over 290 charter companies. Careful preparations are essential as drop-offs and pickups are prescheduled and can be disrupted by bad weather or unforeseen circumstances.

Village buildings at Anchorage's popular Alaska Wild Berry Products

⑯ Alaska Wild Berry Products

5225 Juneau St. **Map** F2. **Tel** 562-8858.
🚌 60. **Open** Jan– May: 10am–8pm
Mon–Sat, noon–6pm Sun; Jun–Aug:
10am–9pm daily; Sep–Oct:10am–
8pm Mon–Thu, 10am–9pm Fri & Sat,
11am–8pm Sun; Nov–Dec: 10am–9pm
Mon–Sat, 11am–8pm Sun. **Closed**
Thanksgiving, Christmas, and New
Year's Day. 🚗 ♿ 🎫 📷
🅦 alaskawildberryproducts.com

Located on the banks of the
scenic Campbell Creek, Alaska
Wild Berry Products is a popular
tourist attraction. It boasts the
world's largest chocolate
waterfall, a 20 ft (6 m) cascade
of melted chocolate, which
conjures up images of Roald
Dahl's *Charlie and the Chocolate
Factory*. Through observation
windows, visitors can watch as
the company's jams and sweets
are made.

A stroll around the Wild Berry
Park and Village leads to a trail
and reindeer enclosures. The
attached Sourdough Mining
Company serves traditional
Alaskan fare and holds gold
panning demonstrations.
Visitors staying downtown can
call for a free pickup. There's
another outlet in Wasilla *(see p89)*.

⑰ H2Oasis

1520 O'Malley Rd. **Map** F2. **Tel** 522-
4420. 🚌 2. **Open** mid-May–mid-Sep:
10am–9pm daily; mid-Sep–mid-May:
3–8pm Fri, 10am–8pm Sat, 11am–
7pm Sun. 🚗 ♿ 🖥 Riverwalk:
Open 7–10am Mon, Wed, & Fri.
🅦 h2oasiswaterpark.com

Alaska's only indoor water park,
H2Oasis has activities for all ages.
The Lazy River encircling the

park offers tubing opportunities
as well as a **Riverwalk**, a fitness
walk in slow running water,
three times a week. A Wave Pool
provides body surfing at a
balmy 27° C (80° F) – even in
winter. The Pirate
Ship features
slides for chil-
dren. Visitors can
barrel down a
500-ft (150-m)
water coaster on
an inflatable raft, or body-slide
down the tamer enclosed water
tube. Adult swimmers can later
relax in a whirlpool spa.

⑱ Alaska Zoo

4731 O'Malley Rd. **Map** F2. **Tel** 346-
2133. 🚌 shuttle from downtown.
Open Mar, Apr, Oct: 10am–5pm daily;
May & Sep: 9am–6pm daily; Jun–Aug:
9am–9pm daily; Nov–Feb: 10am–4pm
daily. 🚗 ♿ 🖥 📷 🅦 alaskazoo.org

In 1966, the Crown Zellerbach
Pulp Company staged a contest,
offering either $3,000 or a baby

elephant as the grand prize. To
the company's surprise, the
Anchorage grocer who won
chose the baby elephant.
Eventually, Annabelle the Asian
elephant was donated to local
horse rancher Mrs. Seawell, who
decided that the community
needed a public zoo. The Alaska
Children's Zoo opened in 1969,
developing slowly into what is
today the sprawling Alaska Zoo.

Although Annabelle is no
longer alive, visitors can see a
host of Alaskan and exotic
animals. There are enclosures
for moose, reindeer, and Dall
sheep. Waterfowl ponds provide
a habitat for tundra and trumpeter swans. There are snow

Sign at Alaska Zoo, south
of Anchorage

leopards and
Siberian tigers, as
well as a brown
bear, polar
bears, Bactrian
camels, and even
a yak. Children
will enjoy the petting zoo.

⑲ Hilltop Ski Area

Upper Abbot Rd. **Map** F2. **Tel** 346-
2167. **Open** winter: 3–8pm Mon–Thu,
3–9pm Fri, 9am–9pm Sat, 9am–5pm
Sun. 🚗 ♿ disabled adaptive skiing
programs available. 🖥 🎫 📷
🅦 hilltopskiarea.org

New skiers and those without
the time or money to head for
the larger Alyeska Resort in
Girdwood will appreciate the
30-acre (12-ha) Hilltop Ski Area,
Anchorage proper's only ski

Families enjoying the tropical environs of H2Oasis

Cemetery of the Eklutna Historical Park with its brightly painted "spirit house" graves

resort. Here, the longest run (2,090 ft/637 m) offers a gradient that drops a gentle 295 ft (90 m). There are numerous other runs of varying difficulty. Access to the ski slopes is provided by a rope tow and a chairlift. In the adjacent Hillside Park, Nordic skiers will find 22 miles (32 km) of groomed cross-country trails.

⓴ Chugach State Park

See pp82–3.

㉑ Alaska Botanical Garden

4601 Campbell Airstrip Rd. **Map** F2. **Tel** 770-3692. 🚌 1, 75. **Open** daylight hours daily, year-round. 🅿️ 🍴 Jun–Aug: 1pm daily. 🅰️ limited access. 📷 🌐 alaskabg.org

Amid the beautiful birch and spruce forests of Far North Bicentennial Park nestles the 110-acre (44-ha) Alaska Botanical Garden. Opened in 1993, the area features a formal herb garden, two perennial gardens, an alpine rock garden, and a wildflower path dotted with erratic boulders left behind by glaciers. Boreal flora is showcased with more than 1,100 perennials and 150 native species of hardy flowering plants, shrubs, and other northern vegetation *(see p161)*. The 1-mile (2-km) long interpretive Lowenfels Family

Nature Trail follows the north fork of Campbell Creek, which is home to a summer run of king salmon. The trail offers views of the Chugach Range and reveals the geological history of the Anchorage Bowl. In the summer, the area is ideal for photography and bird-watching, and during the winter, the various trails serve as Nordic ski routes. As moose and bears inhabit the area, dogs are not allowed.

Blue poppies, Alaska Botanical Garden

㉒ Turnagain Arm Tour

See pp84–5.

㉓ Eklutna Historical Park

Mile 26, Glenn Hwy. **Map** B2. **Tel** 688-6026. 🚌 Anchorage–Mat-Su. **Open** mid-May–mid-Sep: 10am–5pm Mon–Sat. 📷 🅰️ 📅 9–10:30am Sun. 📷 🌐 eklutnahistoricalpark.org

Forming the centerpiece of the tiny village of Eklutna, the Eklutna Historical Park was established to preserve and portray the heritage of the Athabaskan people. Founded in 1650, it is the oldest continually inhabited village in the Anchorage area. With the coming of Russian missionaries in the early 19th century, most of the locals converted to Russian

Orthodoxy, as evidenced by the onion-domed St. Nicholas church. The adjacent cemetery has over 100 graves covered with colorful "spirit houses," decorated according to individual family traditions. Early 20th-century implements used here and Athabaskan beadwork and snowshoes can be seen at the Heritage House museum.

A 3-mile (5-km) return walk, over the Glenn Highway and through birch forests, leads to scenic **Thunderbird Falls**. During the winter, this 200-ft-(60-m-) high cascade becomes a spectacular icefall.

Hiking in the lush landscape below Thunderbird Falls near Eklutna

⑳ Chugach State Park

Encompassing almost 770 sq miles (2,000 sq km), Chugach State Park is America's third largest state park, and one of the most accessible from an urban area. This fabulously scenic glaciated region, situated right in Anchorage's backyard, includes icefields, glaciers, high peaks, forests, and mountain lakes, all within hiking distance of the city. While no roads cross the park, there are several hiking trails through spectacular scenery, as well as plenty of opportunities to view wildlife, including moose, black and brown bears, Dall sheep, mountain goats, marmots, and a host of smaller animals. Birdlife is profuse, especially along the park's many rivers, and close-up views of salmon are available from a platform near the Eagle River Nature Center.

Hikers passing through meadows on Crow Pass Crossing

Symphony Lake
Cold, clear Symphony Lake, along the South Fork of the Eagle River, lies in a deep valley between the glaciated peaks of the Harmony Mountains.

Key

═══ Highway

═══ Minor road

▬ ▬ Trail

━━━ Alaska Railroad

▬ ▬ Park boundary

△ Peak

★ Flattop Mountain
Alaska's most climbed mountain, the 3,510 ft (1,070 m) Flattop makes a popular outing for visitors who can manage the steep 1,310 ft (393 m), two-hour-long ascent.

Exploring the Park

From the Eagle River Nature Center, the easy half-mile (1 km) Rodak Nature Trail and 3 mile (5 km) Albert Loop Trail lead to grand views of the Eagle River Valley. A popular day hike is the 6 mile (10 km) return hike to Echo Bend on the Old Iditarod Trail, which connects Eagle River with Girdwood.

For hotels and restaurants see pp242–5 and pp250–55

★ Eklutna Lake
The glacial blue waters of Eklutna Lake sparkle in the sun. The camp-ground at the lake offers pleasant picnic and camping spots, while the lakeshore trail provides access to challenging alpine hikes up Twin Peaks and Bold Ridge.

VISITORS' CHECKLIST

Practical Information
Eastern part of the Municipality of Anchorage. **Map** F2. ℹ Potter Section House, Mile 115, Seward Hwy. 🏕 🏔 🌐 **dnr.alaska.gov/parks/units/chugach**
Eagle River Nature Center: Mile 12, Eagle River Road. **Tel** 694-2108. **Open** May–Sep: 10am–5pm daily; Oct–Apr: 10am–5pm Fri–Sun. **Closed** Mondays in May and Sep. 🅿 only for trailhead parking. 🌐 **ernc.org**

Transport
Taxi from Anchorage, Eagle River, and Eklutna; by trail from Peter's Creek and Girdwood.

The Mitre
Hikers on the trail to Eklutna Glacier are treated to close-up views of this spectacular 6,600-ft (2,000-m) high peak. The mountain is best viewed along the East Fork of the Eklutna River.

Hikers on the Crow Pass Crossing can book the Forest Service public use cabin at the toe of Raven Glacier.

★ Eagle River Nature Center
The center has maps, books, and exhibits on the landscape and wildlife of the park. Viewing decks and spotting scopes offer visitors great views of the river valley and the surrounding peaks.

For keys to symbols *see back flap*

❷ Turnagain Arm Tour

The curious name of the 50-mile (80-km) long fjord known as Turnagain Arm was bestowed by explorer Captain James Cook in 1778. He was forced to "turn again" after discovering that it was impossible to navigate a sea route between Cook Inlet and the fabled Northwest Passage. Today, a drive along the Arm's shore makes a rewarding day trip from Anchorage. A lovely stretch of the 120-mile (200-km) Seward Highway, which connects Anchorage and Seward (see pp102–3), follows the fjord's north shore through Chugach State Park, offering spectacular views of the Kenai Mountains and Chugach National Forest.

Driving along the scenic Seward Highway next to Turnagain Arm

① **Anchorage Coastal Wildlife Refuge**
Just south of Anchorage at Mile 117, a series of boardwalks provide views across Potter Marsh, frequented in the summer by nesting ducks, geese, swans, and other waterfowl.

Key

▬▬ Tour
▬▬ Main road
▭▭ Minor road
▬ ▬ Trail
▬ Alaska Railroad
⠿ Road-rail tunnel
△ Peak

② **Beluga Point**
At Beluga Point (Mile 110) visitors can observe Turnagain Arm empty and refill twice daily in a wall of water known as the bore tide, which ranges from 2 to 6 ft (60 cm–2 m), occasionally topping a dramatic 8 ft (2.5 m).

Anchorage
Cook Inlet
Bird
Hope
Chugach
Turnaga[in]
Sunrise
National
Resurrection Creek

Beluga Whales

The distinctive whale known as the beluga (*Delphinapterus leucas*) is one of several beaked whales that inhabit the Arctic, North Atlantic, and North Pacific Oceans. The name beluga, meaning "the white one," was given by Russian explorers, who probably first observed them in the Bering Sea. These mammals are 13 to 15 ft (4 to 4.5 m) in length and weigh about 2,500 to 3,500 lbs (1,100 to 1,600 kg). In the summer, pods migrate into Turnagain Arm to feed and may be observed from the shore, although the Cook Inlet population has been declining dramatically in recent years, alarming scientists.

Beluga whale breaking the surface

③ Girdwood and Alyeska Resort
The village of Girdwood, 40 miles (65 km) from Anchorage, revolves around Alyeska, Alaska's most popular ski resort. Summer visitors can ride the gondola to the top of Mount Alyeska for sweeping views over the fjord and surrounding mountains.

④ Crow Creek Trail
From the end of Crow Creek Road, a 4-mile (6-km) trail climbs past Gold Rush relics to Crow Pass, which has fine views of Raven Glacier.

Tips for Drivers

Starting point: 12 miles (19 km) S of downtown Anchorage.
Length: 40 miles (64 km).
Stopping-off points: Bird Ridge Café and Bakery at Mile 100 is a good place to stop for a quick bite. The McHugh Creek Wayside at Mile 112 offers pleasant picnic spots. Potter Section House at Mile 115 houses the Chugach State Park Headquarters.
Campgrounds: Bird Creek at Mile 101 offers good, basic sites.

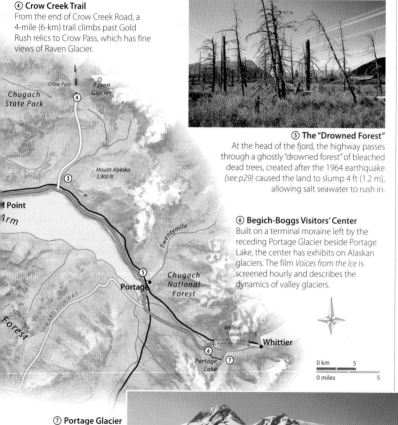

⑤ The "Drowned Forest"
At the head of the fjord, the highway passes through a ghostly "drowned forest" of bleached dead trees, created after the 1964 earthquake (*see p29*) caused the land to slump 4 ft (1.2 m), allowing salt seawater to rush in.

⑥ Begich-Boggs Visitors' Center
Built on a terminal moraine left by the receding Portage Glacier beside Portage Lake, the center has exhibits on Alaskan glaciers. The film *Voices from the Ice* is screened hourly and describes the dynamics of valley glaciers.

⑦ Portage Glacier
One of Alaska's most visited glaciers, Portage Glacier extends into Portage Lake and is best viewed on cruises from the visitors' center. A level 2-mile (3-km) loop track leads to the foot of nearby Byron Glacier.

Alaska Railroad train travelling along Turnagain Arm between Anchorage and Seward ▶

Hay bales on a Mat-Su Valley farm near Palmer

㉔ Palmer

42 miles (70 km) NE of Anchorage.
Map C1. 🚹 6,000. 🚌 from
Anchorage. 🚹 723 S Valley Way,
745-2880. 🚌 Fri. 🎪 Alaska State Fair
(Aug–Sep), Colony Christmas (Dec).
🌐 palmerchamber.org

Best known as a farming
community, the compact town
of Palmer nestles below the
peaks of the Talkeetna Range in
the narrow valley of the glacial
Matanuska River. Founded as a
social experiment in 1935 as
part of President Franklin D
Roosevelt's New Deal, it was
settled by 200 Midwestern
families (see p58). Each family
in the newly established
Matanuska Colony was given
40 acres (16 ha) of land for
vegetable farming, growing
hay, and raising dairy cattle.

Today, while farming is still
important, Palmer's outskirts
are rapidly turning into bedroom suburbs for Anchorage,
due mainly to the city's
dwindling land and high costs.
The surrounding Matanuska
and Susitna Valleys, popularly
abbreviated to Mat-
Su, are now among
the fastest-growing
regions of Alaska.

Well worth visiting
is the **Colony House
Museum**, which
reflects one of the five
basic farmhouse styles
available to the Colony
farmers. Inside, their story
is told with old newspaper
articles, period furnishings,
and artifacts.

For 12 days in August and
September, Palmer hosts the
Alaska State Fair (see p48),
the state's biggest annual
event, drawing nearly half of
Alaska's population. The fair
features the valley's famous
giant vegetables, as well as
other agricultural displays,
crafts, livestock, food and
retail booths, live music, a
rodeo, Native dancing and
blanket tossing, and a range
of competitions.

🏛 Colony House Museum
316 E Elmwood Ave, Palmer.
Tel 745-1935. **Open** Jun–Aug:
10am–4pm Tue–Sat. 🐾

㉕ Reindeer Farm

5561 S. Bodenburg Loop Rd.
Palmer, AK 99645. **Map** C2.
Tel 745-4000. **Open** May–mid-Sep:
10am–6pm daily. 🐾 🅿 ♿
🌐 reindeerfarm.com

Located in one of the original
Colony farmhouses on the flat
farmlands off the
Old Glenn Highway,
the Reindeer Farm
lets visitors see
reindeer close-up.
Children are invited
to hand-feed and pet
the animals, and meet
an elk, a moose, and
a black-tailed deer.
Those inclined to
outdoor activities can join
a horseback trail ride.

Reindeer at the farm
near Palmer

㉖ Bodenburg Butte

Adjacent to the Reindeer Farm at Mile
11.5, Old Glenn Hwy. **Map** C2.

Rising out of the farmlands on
the Knik River flats south of
Palmer, the 900 ft- (270m-) high
Bodenburg Butte is one of the
Matanuska Valley's most
prominent landmarks. It was
created when Knik Glacier rode
over a small knob of resistant
bedrock, leaving a glacier-
scraped dome known as a roche
moutonnée. Once used for
military training, it is now a
popular picnic and hiking spot
with a windy summit from where
parasailers can launch out over
the flats. The steep trail leading
to the summit starts opposite
Reindeer Farm and soon passes
from the stands of birch at the
base into open grassy ridges and
rocky bluffs near the top. The
two-hour-long round trek is
worth it for the views from the
summit, which take in the Palmer
area and Knik Glacier.

Green Giants

Alaskans are rightfully proud of the produce grown in the
Matanuska Valley. The growing season may be short, but thanks
to the long summer days, vegetables continue to grow around
the clock, resulting in enormous carrots, turnips, zucchini, and
other produce. At the annual Alaska State
Fair, awards are given for the largest vegetable of each variety. The record-winning
rutabaga (swede) was 75 lb (34 kg), while
the largest pumpkin weighed in at a whop-
ping 942 lb (428 kg). The most popular
annual competition is for the cabbage –
the world-record holder, grown in Wasilla
in 2009, tipped the scales at 127 lb (38 kg),
winning the $2,000 grand prize. Local
farmers and gardeners are still trying to
break that record.

Gargantuan cabbage from
the Mat-Su

Abandoned snow-covered Mat-Su Valley barn near Bodenburg Butte

❷ Musk Ox Farm

8 miles (13 km) N of Palmer at 12850 E Archie Rd, Mile 50, Glenn Hwy. **Map** C1. **Tel** 745-4151. **Open** May–Sep: 10am–6pm daily; Oct–Apr: by appt. 🚌 📷 🏠 **w** muskoxfarm.org

The Musk Ox Farm is home to the only domestic herd of musk oxen in the world. Hunted to extinction in Alaska in the 19th century, they were reintroduced from Greenland in the 1930s. Musk oxen now inhabit Nunivak Island, the Seward Peninsula, and the North Slope of Alaska.

Anthropologist John Teal started the farm in Fairbanks in 1964. Now located in Palmer, the farm gathers *qiviut*, the fine underwool of the musk ox, and distributes it to Native women. They spin and knit the *qiviut* into soft, warm garments using patterns and motifs unique to their villages. The farm is open to the public and runs short tours.

❷ Wasilla

45 miles (72 km) N of Anchorage. **Map** B1. 🚠 5,500. 🚉 🚌 from Anchorage. ℹ Mat-Su Convention and Visitors Bureau, Tel 746-5000. **w** cityofwasilla.com

Home to former governor Sarah Palin, Wasilla is a long strip of unfocused development along the Parks Highway. The town was founded in 1917 and began to grow when the Parks Highway was completed in the 1970s, eventually becoming the commercial center of the Mat-Su Borough. Although not the prettiest Alaskan town, Wasilla does have several worthwhile attractions. Most of these sights are clustered north of the railroad station, off the highway at the Old Wasilla Townsite Park. The park includes historic homes, the original Wasilla School, an old barn and blacksmith shop, a reconstructed bathhouse, and

the Dorothy Page Museum, named for the woman who founded the Iditarod Trail Sled Dog Race *(see p43)* with musher Joe Redington.

The **Museum of Alaska Transportation and Industry**, formerly the Air Progress Museum of Anchorage, was renamed and shifted to Palmer after a fire. When it outgrew that site in 1992, it moved to its present home west of Wasilla. In addition to a large gallery and exhibit hall, the museum has an outdoor collection that includes *umiaqs* (skin boats), railway memorabilia, and vintage steam engines, aircraft, and vehicles.

Situated on the Iditarod Trail, the **Knik Museum and Musher's Hall of Fame** is located in an old roadhouse. Visitors can see objects from the now-defunct town of Knik, as well as Iditarod exhibits such as race trophies, charcoal drawings of past winners, and a presentation on famous Alaskan mushers.

🏛 **Museum of Alaska Transport and Industry**
5 miles (8 km) W of Wasilla at 3800 W. Museum Drive. **Tel** 376-1211. **Open** May–Sep: 10am–5pm daily. 🚌 **w** museumofalaska.org

🏛 **Knik Museum and Musher's Hall of Fame**
Mile 13.9, Knik Rd. **Tel** 376-2005. **Open** Jun–Aug: noon–6pm daily. 🚌

Bull musk oxen facing off on a snowy plain

㉙ Independence Mine State Historical Park

Most people associate gold mining in Alaska with the placer gold (see p57) diggings in the Klondike. However, starting in 1906, a gold-bearing quartz lode was being tapped in the Talkeetna Mountains. Two mines were established in the scenic mountain valley of the Little Susitna River, the Alaska Free Gold Mine on Skyscraper Mountain and the Independence Mine on Granite Mountain. In 1938, the two were merged into the Alaska-Pacific Consolidated Mining Company. Although the mines were producing large amounts of gold, the activity was deemed non-essential during World War II, and after the war, government restrictions on private ownership of gold spelled the end of the mine. The site was designated a State Historical Park in the late 1970s.

Mine buildings scattered across Fishhook Valley

★ Bunk Houses
Three of the larger buildings at Independence Mine served as bunk houses. One was built in 1939 and functioned as a supply warehouse, engineering office, and school. A small, well-appointed building nearby had self-contained housing units for top mine officials.

Key

① **The New Bunk House** was built in 1940 to accommodate 50 people. It also contained rooms used for classes and for screening films.

② **The Manager's House** was constructed in 1939 to house the mine manager's family and guests. Today, the distinctive building serves as the park's Visitor Center and administrative headquarters.

③ **The New Mess Hall**, constructed in 1941, had a well-equipped kitchen, bakery, butchery, scullery, and a dining hall that seated 160 people.

④ **The Administrative Building** was used as an office, storeroom, and bunk house during an attempt to reopen the mine in 1946.

⑤ **Mechanical and repair shops** housed plumbing, carpentry, and electrical operations.

⑥ **The Assay Office** now houses the site museum.

⑦ **An ore conveyor** brought ore into the mill where it was sorted and crushed to extract the gold.

⑧ **The Hard Rock Trail** leads to a park overlook near the Water Tunnel Portal.

Exploring the Mine

To fully explore the park's historic buildings and ruins will take two to three hours. The Main Trail is an easy, level route that begins at the Manager's House and loops past the Mess Hall, Administrative Building, and Bunk Houses, with a short detour to the Museum (Assay Office). The more challenging 20-minute Hard Rock Trail climbs the tundra-covered hillside to an overlook near the Water Tunnel Portal and Mine Shops. Guided tours of the mine last between 60 and 90 minutes.

Hatcher Pass Road winding through the
Independence Mine area

⓿ Hatcher Pass

21 miles (34 km) N of Palmer at Mile
19 of the Hatcher Pass Road. **Map** B1.
Taxi from Anchorage, Willow, &
Palmer. The pass may be closed from
September to May; check in advance.

Beyond Independence Mine,
the Hatcher Pass Road climbs
up onto the "tail" of the
Talkeetna Range that reaches
westward toward Willow and
makes a wonderful driving or
biking route. The road is paved
only as far as the Independence
Mine turn-off and Hatcher Pass
Lodge at Mile 17. Shortly after,
at Mile 19, it crosses 3,886-ft
(1,166-m) Hatcher Pass, one of
Alaska's highest road passes,
before twisting for another
31 miles (50 km) to Willow.

Just beyond the pass, the
road passes through the
Summit Lake State Recreation
Site. The lake itself is a small
alpine tarn in a glacial cirque,
or steep-walled basin, and is
accessed by a trail around its
perimeter and along the bluff
overlooking it. The inspiring
views take in the Susitna Valley,
Willow Creek, and the Alaska
Range in the distance.

In the summer, Hatcher Pass
is an excellent paragliding
venue, and a number of hiking
trails, including the popular
Gold Mint Trail, take off into
the peaks and valleys. In the
winter, the attraction is the
network of Nordic skiing and
snowmachining trails that
lead into the wilds of the
Talkeetna Mountains.

★ Mill Complex
The 1937 mill complex, uphill from the mine
offices, includes a welding shed, ore sorting
plant, machine shop, and blacksmith. An aerial
tramway carried supplies up the hill and
returned laden with ore.

Plan of Site

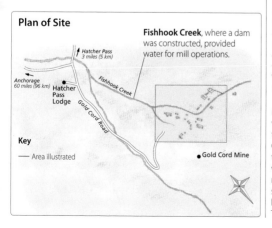

Fishhook Creek, where a dam
was constructed, provided
water for mill operations.

Hatcher Pass
3 miles (5 km)

Anchorage
60 miles (96 km)

Hatcher
Pass
Lodge

Fishhook Creek

Gold Cord Road

Gold Cord Mine

Key
— Area illustrated

SHOPPING IN ANCHORAGE

Anchorage is arguably the best place in Alaska to pick up gifts and souvenirs that are unique to the state. Throughout downtown, numerous small shops sell inexpensive gifts and mementos, while a range of higher-quality shops and art galleries offer Alaskan art and photography, furs, local foods, Native arts and crafts, and antiques. Mainstream shopping ranges from warehouse-like box stores, such as Fred Meyer outlets, to large shopping malls and the more upmarket Nordstrom store. Due to its position as a jumping-off point for adventure activities, the city is also an excellent place to pick up outdoor supplies, and several local outlets sell camping, hiking, cycling, boating, hunting, and fishing gear to help prepare for outdoor adventures.

Soapstone carvings on display at Anchorage's Weekend Market

Markets and Fairs

Every Saturday and Sunday, between mid-May and mid-September, the **Anchorage Market and Festival** (see p74) fills the parking lot downtown at 3rd Avenue and E Street, selling Alaskan crafts, souvenirs, freshly cooked food, and clothing. From June to August, at the Northway Mall grounds in East Anchorage, the **Wednesday Market** sells similar items from 11am to 5pm. The **Center Market** inside the Sears Mall offers gourmet and farm foods every Wednesday and Saturday year-round. The ultimate informal shopping experience is undoubtedly the annual **Alaska State Fair** (see p48) in Palmer.

Alaskan Arts and Antiques

One of the best ways to find unusual Alaskan photography, art, and original creations is to attend the First Friday openings of art galleries. The **Iditarod**

Trail Store sells official Last Great Race patches, dog booties, posters, and other memorabilia. A legacy of the Gold Rush, Alaskan gold makes excellent jewelry, souvenirs, and investment items. The **Alaska Mint** sells Alaskan gold and silver coins and medallions. The gift shop at the **Anchorage Museum** has a fine selection of works by Alaskan artists, including traditional pieces. In the summer, local artists have their wares on display in the atrium. In addition, fine art galleries are dotted throughout downtown Anchorage.

Native Arts and Crafts

Alaska's most unique product is clothing made of *qiviut*, the fine underwool of the musk ox, sold at the **Oomingmak Musk Ox Producers' Co-operative**. *Ulus*, rounded knives used by Native women, are also popular. Most gift shops sell them but the **Ulu Factory** has the largest selection of authentic knives. Other gifts include baskets made of grass, bark, and baleen (also called whalebone), beaded purses and belts, and fine scrimshaw art on ivory and bone. The **Alaska Native Medical Center Craft Shop** sells high quality Native objects from all over Alaska. At the **Alaska Native Heritage Center** (see pp76–7), visitors can watch artists at work and purchase gifts from the on-site shop. **One People** is a cooperative shop selling authentic Native arts and crafts.

While shopping for Native art, especially soapstone carvings, it is best to be careful, as items mass-produced abroad are occasionally sold as Native art. The state-run Silver Hand program guarantees that products tagged with the Silver Hand label were made by Native Alaskans using Alaskan materials. However, the program is not universal, and plenty of legitimate crafts do not carry the label.

Pottery and wood-crafted ducks for sale in an Anchorage shop

Alaskan Foods

10th and M Seafoods sells smoked fish and freshly caught salmon, and will also smoke, freeze, and package visitors' own catch of fish or game for the trip home. **Alaska Sausage and Seafood** will turn hunters' moose, caribou, or deer into sausage products, and sells smoked salmon and reindeer sausage. **Alaska Wild Berry Products** *(see p80)* is the best place for Alaskan berries made into jam and sweets. Exotic seafood is available at the three **New Sagaya's Markets**, the city's prominent Oriental groceries.

Department Stores

The main shopping malls in Anchorage are occupied by department stores of varying price and quality. The most down-to-earth choice is the **Dimond Center**, which features Gap and Old Navy for clothing and Best Buy for electronics.

The midtown **Sears Mall** has a large Sears Department Store, which sells clothing and appliances, while the downtown **5th Avenue Mall** is best known for its Nordstrom store. There are also a large number of box stores, massive outlets that sell just about everything at discounted prices. The most pleasant of these are the **Fred Meyer** stores, which also have a grocer, bakery, and deli. The cheapest places are the membership warehouses **Costco** and **Sam's Club**. **Wal-Mart** stores sell a variety of functional items at low prices.

Sporting Goods

Due to its outdoor orientation, Anchorage is an excellent place to stock up on gear before heading out into the wilderness on a camping, hiking, backpacking, fishing, hunting, whitewater rafting, or kayaking trip. One of the most popular stores in town is **REI** (Recreational Equipment Incorporated), a membership retailer that mainly stocks equipment, clothing, and lightweight gear for non-motorized sports. **Alaska Mountaineering and Hiking**, a similar outlet nearby, sells gear from a range of manufacturers and is aimed primarily at rock climbers and mountaineers. For keen hunters, anglers, and campers, there is no better outfitter than the mind-boggling **Sportsman's Warehouse**, which offers everything from camouflage clothing, winter gear, footwear, and salmon smokers to hunting hides, rifles, pontoon boats, and skinning knives.

Visitors who are in town in the cold season and want to try out some winter sports can drop by **Play It Again Sports** and pick up warm clothing, as well as used and new skiing, skating, snowshoeing, and hockey equipment at discounted prices.

DIRECTORY

Markets and Fairs

Anchorage Market and Festival
3rd Ave & E St. **Map** D4.
Tel 272-5634.
W anchoragemarkets.com

The Center Market
The Mall at Sears, 600 N. Lights Blvd. **Map** E1. W the centermarket.com

Wednesday Market
Northway Mall. **Map** F1.
Tel 272-5634. W anchor agemarkets.com

Arts, Crafts, and Antiques

Alaska Mint
429 W 4th Ave. **Map** D4.
Tel 278-8414.
W alaskamint.com

Alaska Native Medical Center Craft Shop
4315 Diplomacy Dr.
Map F1. **Tel** 729-1122.
W anthc.org

Iditarod Trail Store
5th Avenue Mall, 320 W

5th Ave. **Map** E5. **Tel** 276-2350. W iditarod.com

One People
425 D St. **Map** D4.
Tel 274-4063.

Oomingmak Musk Ox Producers' Co-operative
604 H St. **Map** C5. **Tel** 272-9225. W qiviut.com

Ulu Factory
211 W Ship Creek Ave.
Map E3. **Tel** 276-3119.
W theulufactory.com

Alaskan Foods

10th and M Seafoods
1020 M St. **Map** E1. **Tel** 272-3474, 800-770-2722.
W 10thandmseafoods. com

Alaska Sausage and Seafood
2914 Arctic Blvd. **Map** E1.
Tel 562-3636.
W alaskasausage.com

New Sagaya's Markets
3700 Old Seward Hwy.
Map F1. **Tel** 561-5173.

900 W 13th Ave.
Map E1. **Tel** 561-5173.
2525 Blueberry Road.
Map E1. **Tel** 563-0220.
W newsagaya.com

Department Stores

5th Avenue Mall
320 W 5th Ave.
Map E5.

Costco
330 W Dimond Blvd.
Map E2. **Tel** 344-6436.
4125 Debarr Road.
Map F2. **Tel** 269-9510.
W costco.com

Dimond Center
Dimond Blvd & Old Seward. **Map** F2.
Tel 344-2581.
W dimondcenter.com

Fred Meyer
7701 Debarr Rd.
Map F1. **Tel** 269-1700.
W fredmeyer.com

Sam's Club
8801 Old Seward Hwy.
Map F2. **Tel** 522-2333.
W samsclub.com

Sears Mall
Benson & Seward Hwy.
Map E1. **Tel** 264-6695.
W mallatsears.com

Wal-Mart
8900 Old Seward Hwy.
Map F2. **Tel** 344-5300.
W walmart.com

Sporting Goods

Alaska Mountaineering and Hiking
2633 Spenard Rd.
Map E1. **Tel** 272-1811.
W alaska mountaineering.com

Play It Again Sports
2636 Spenard Rd. **Map** E1. **Tel** 278-7529. W play itagainsports.com

REI
1200 W Northern Lights Blvd. **Map** E1.
Tel 272-4565. W rei.com

Sportsman's Warehouse
8681 Old Seward Hwy.
Map F2. **Tel** 644-1400.
W sportsmans warehouse.com

ENTERTAINMENT IN ANCHORAGE

While Anchorage may be better known as a launch pad to the wilderness, it nonetheless offers a range of entertainment that is more vibrant than any other Alaskan city. The seemingly endless daylight hours of summer are ideal for outdoor activities, while in autumn and winter, indoor pursuits such as concerts, theater, opera, and ballet are available. The Alaska Center for the Performing Arts, in downtown Anchorage, is renowned for its cultural events, while the Sullivan Arena hosts rock concerts and sporting events. The city also has numerous cinemas, bars, and nightclubs, many of which offer live entertainment and excellent locally produced brews.

Information and Tickets

Published every Thursday, the *Anchorage Press* is the best source of information on art exhibitions, concerts, festivals, and sports. This free weekly paper is distributed to businesses across the city. The **Anchorage Convention and Visitors' Bureau** also keeps abreast of upcoming events. Tickets for most programs can be easily bought at the Alaska Center for the Performing Arts or obtained directly from the various venues. Alternatively, **Ticketmaster** outlets can be found at Fred Meyer stores around the city.

Theater and Concerts

Major theater and musical productions are staged at the Atwood Concert Hall, the Discovery Theater, and the Sydney Laurence Theater, all located in the **Alaska Center for the Performing Arts**. The

The log cabin theme at Chilkoot Charlie's in Anchorage

Traditional dance performance at the Alaska Native Heritage Center

Anchorage Opera, the **Alaska Dance Theatre**, the **Anchorage Symphony Orchestra**, and the **Anchorage Concert Association** perform at the center. The **Sullivan Arena** hosts pop and rock concerts, while plays and small classical music shows are held at the Wendy Williamson Auditorium, the Arts Theater, and the Arts Recital Hall at the **University of Alaska Anchorage**.

Cinema

While there are no art film venues in Anchorage, a number of multiplex cinemas such as **Dimond Center 9 Cinemas** and **Century 16 Cinemas** screen popular first-run films. Showing inexpensive second-run movies, the **Bear Tooth Theatre Pub** also offers some excellent microbrewery beer and good food in a bar-and-restaurant environment. For extensive film reviews, there is the *Anchorage Press*, while cinema listings are outlined in the city's main newspaper, the *Anchorage Daily News*.

Cultural Presentations

The large open theater at the **Alaska Native Heritage Center** *(see pp76–7)* plays host to a range of Native arts, theater, dance, and sports demonstrations. The **Anchorage Museum** *(see pp72–3)* often features visiting art exhibitions. On the first Friday of every month, galleries across Anchorage hold art openings, usually attended by showcased artists. During the winter, the downtown **Dena'ina Civic and Convention Center** hosts a variety of cultural events as well.

Clubs and Bars

Anchorage enjoys a vibrant nightlife, with a good variety of clubbing and drinking venues on offer. For rock, pop, and sheer mayhem, the hotspot is **Chilkoot Charlie's**, popularly nicknamed "Koot's." Downtown, head to **Humpy's Great Alaskan Alehouse** *(see p250)* for live music, a packed dance floor, microbrews on draught, and tasty pub grub. **Cyrano's Off**

Anchorage Glacier Pilots playing the Bucs at Mulcahy Stadium

Center Playhouse often showcases live jazz evenings. For fans of the amber fluid, the **Glacier Brewhouse**, the **Moose's Tooth** pub-cum-pizzeria (sister joint to the Bear Tooth Theatre Pub) and the **Snow Goose** (see p250 for all three venues) can between them serve up a limitless selection of microbrewery beers.

Sports

Although Anchorage has no major league baseball or NHL hockey team, it takes pride in sport. During the summer, the Alaska Minor Baseball League's **Anchorage Glacier Pilots** and **Anchorage Bucs** play in town. The **University of Alaska Anchorage (UAA) Seawolves**

basketball team hosts the **Great Alaska Shootout** in late November, and the **Alaska Aces** hockey team play at the Sullivan Arena in winter. The **World Championship Sled Dog Races** are held in February, while the **Iditarod Trail Sled Dog Race** is flagged off in early March.

Children

With an array of children's activities on offer, Anchorage promises to be a fun experience for the family. The Children's Gallery at the **Anchorage Museum** (see pp72–3) caters specifically to youngsters with its extraordinary **Imaginarium Discovery Center**, home to a host of fun activities. The **Alaska Zoo** (see p80) offers a wonderful day out for kids.

DIRECTORY

Information and Tickets

Anchorage Convention and Visitors' Bureau
546 W 4th Ave. **Map** D4. **Tel** 274-3531.
W anchorage.net

Anchorage Press
540 E 5th Ave. **Map** E5/F5. **Tel** 561-7737.
W anchoragepress.com

Ticketmaster
W ticketmaster.com

Theater and concerts

Alaska Center for the Performing Arts
621 W 6th Ave. **Map** D5. **Tel** 263-2900.
W myalaskacenter.com

Alaska Dance Theatre
550 E 33rd Ave. **Map** F1. **Tel** 277-9591.
W alaskadancetheatre.org

Anchorage Concert Association
430 W 7th Ave, No. 200. **Map** D5. **Tel** 272-1471.
W anchorageconcerts.org

Anchorage Opera
1507 Spar Ave. **Map** E4. **Tel** 279-2557.
W anchorageopera.org

Anchorage Symphony Orchestra
400 D St No. 230. **Map** D4. **Tel** 274-8668.
W anchoragesymphony.org

Sullivan Arena
1600 Gambell St. **Map** F1. **Tel** 279-0618 (Box Office).
W sullivanarena.com

University of Alaska Anchorage
Department of Theatre and Dance, 3211 Providence Dr. **Map** F1. **Tel** 786-4849 (Box Office).
W theatre.uaa.alaska.edu

Cinema

Bear Tooth Theatre Pub
1230 W 27th Ave. **Map** E1. **Tel** 276-4200.
W beartooththeatre.net

Century 16 Cinemas
301 E 36th Ave. **Map** F1. **Tel** 770-2602.

Dimond Center 9 Cinemas
800 E Dimond Blvd. **Map** F2. **Tel** 344-0008.

Cultural Presentations

Dena'ina Civic and Convention Center
600 W 7th Ave. **Map** D5. **Tel** 263-2850.
W anchorageconventioncenters.com

Clubs and Bars

Chilkoot Charlie's
2435 Spenard Road. **Map** E1. **Tel** 272-1010.
W koots.com

Cyrano's Off Center Playhouse
413 D St. **Map** D4. **Tel** 274-2599. W cyranos.org

Sports

Alaska Aces
724 E 15th Ave, Suite C. **Map** E1. **Tel** 258-2237.
W alaskaaces.com

Anchorage Bucs
Tel 561-2827.
W anchoragebucs.com

Anchorage Glacier Pilots
207 E Northern Lights Blvd No. 105. **Map** E1. **Tel** 274-3627.
W glacierpilots.com

Great Alaska Shootout
3211 Providence Dr. **Map** F1. **Tel** 786-1250.
W goseawolves.com

Iditarod Trail Sled Dog Race
2100 S.Knik-Goosebay Road, Wasilla. **Map** B1. **Tel** 376-5155.
W iditarod.com

University of Alaska Anchorage (UAA) Seawolves
3211 Providence Dr. **Map** F1. **Tel** 786-1250.
W goseawolves.com

World Championship Sled Dog Races
400 D St No. 110. **Map** D4. **Tel** 274-1177.
W furrondy.net

THE KENAI PENINSULA

Frequently referred to as Alaska's Playground for the range of outdoor activities it offers, the Kenai Peninsula is a microcosm of the state. Its eastern half has forested slopes and icefields, and a coast cut by deep fjords and dramatic valleys that usher glacier ice into the sea. The west is gentler, with muskeg bog, rolling, lake-studded lowlands full of wildlife, and seas that brim with marine life.

Situated on the western edge of the Gulf of Alaska, the peninsula derives its name from the Kenaitze people of the Dena'ina Athabaskans, who moved here from the interior regions of Alaska. With the coming of the Russians in the late 18th century and the establishment of the towns of Ninilchik and Kenai, Native culture began to gradually fade away and the peninsula became one of the main centers of Russian influence in Alaska.

After the US purchased Alaska in 1867, the area remained a backwater until the discovery of gold near Hope in the 1890s. Since then, Seward has gained importance as a center for transportation and shipping, Homer thrives on its fisheries, and the production of oil and natural gas in Cook Inlet drives the economy around Kenai and Soldotna. The entire peninsula has also benefitted from tourism. Its proximity to Anchorage and its diverse landscape has helped make the region one of the most populated, best connected, and most visited in the state. With its relatively dense road network, the Alaska Railroad, the Marine Highway, and the cruise ship port at Seward, the peninsula is an easily accessible destination for most independent travelers and those on package tours.

The area offers stunning drives that wind through the spruce forests of the Kenai Range. Kenai Fjords National Park and many state parks offer campsites, beaches, and miles of hiking trails. In the summer, outdoors enthusiasts bound for activity-packed weekends crowd onto the scenic Seward Highway, while anglers gravitate toward the Kenai River, or opt for deep-sea fishing in Kachemak Bay. For those interested in soaking up Russian ambience and history, the towns of Ninilchik, Nikolaevsk, and Seldovia make good stopping-off points.

Rolling fields and verdant mountains of the Kenai Peninsula

◄ Fresh catch of halibut and other fish displayed on the dock at Seward

Exploring the Kenai Peninsula

The varied landscape of the Kenai Peninsula takes in everything from fjords and glaciers to forests and muskeg. Kenai Fjords National Park contains the Harding Icefield, one of the largest in the US. The peninsula also features three very distinctive urban areas – practical Seward, the bustling, commercial Kenai-Soldotna region, and free-spirited Homer. These towns boast some excellent attractions, including Seward's Alaska SeaLife Center and Homer's Oceans and Islands Visitors' Center, as well as good places to stock up on supplies for outdoor activities. For the adventurous, the Kenai River is ideal for rafting and fishing, while the Resurrection Pass Trail is Alaska's most popular multi-day hiking route.

Resurrection Creek along Resurrection Pass Trail, near Hope

Sights at a Glance

Towns and Cities

1 Hope
2 Moose Pass
3 Cooper Landing
6 *Seward pp102–5*
8 Sterling
9 Soldotna
10 Kenai
13 Clam Gulch
14 Ninilchik
15 Anchor Point
16 Nikolaevsk
17 *Homer pp112–3*

National and State Parks

7 *Kenai Fjords National Park pp106–7*
11 Captain Cook State Recreation Area
12 Kenai National Wildlife Refuge

Area of Natural Beauty

4 Kenai River

Tour

5 *Resurrection Pass Trail p101*

Getting Around

It is easiest to explore the region with an organized tour or by car. The Seward Highway links the Kenai Peninsula to Anchorage, while the Sterling Highway runs along the peninsula's west coast. In the summer, daily Homer Stage Lines buses connect the main sights and Park Connection buses run directly to Denali National Park. Also in the summer, there is a daily Alaska Railroad service from Seward, and the Marine Highway ferry *Tustumena* calls at Homer and Seldovia. Homer and Kenai are served by year-round scheduled flights from Anchorage.

For hotels and restaurants see pp242–5 and pp250–55

Anchorage

SEWARD HIGHWAY

Chickaloon Bay

Barabara Lake

Chickaloon

1 HOPE

RESURRECTION PASS TRAIL

5

3 COOPER LANDING

2 MOOSE PASS

Cooper Lake

Kenai Lake

SEWARD HIGHWAY

Skilak Lake

Skilak Glacier

Exit Glacier

9

12

Harding Icefield

SEWARD 6

Caines Head State Recreation Area

Tustumena Glacier

Bear Glacier

7

Malik Bay

Resurrection Bay

RDS NATIONAL PARK

Harris Bay

SKA MARINE HIGHWAY

Transfiguration of Our Lord Russian Orthodox Church, Ninilchik

Key

- ▬ Highway
- ▭ Minor road
- - - Alaska Marine Highway
- ─ Alaska Railroad

Charter vessels and fishing boats at the Small Boat Harbor on the Homer Spit

For keys to symbols *see back flap*

Seaview Café and Bar on the main street of Hope

❶ Hope

88 miles (141 km) S of Anchorage.
Transport map B3. 🚌 190. ✈
🏃 Wagon Trail Run (3rd weekend
in Jul). 🌐 hopealaska.info

The historic gold-mining town
of Hope nestles in a deep valley
next to the south shore of
Turnagain Arm *(see pp84–5)*.
Named after Percy Hope, a
17-year-old prospector, Hope's
heyday was in the late 1890s,
when it was a rollicking Gold
Rush town. By the end of the
decade, however, many of the
town's inhabitants had pulled
up stakes and headed for the
Klondike goldfields.

Today, despite its proximity
to Anchorage and the Seward
Highway, Hope remains a quiet
place. Most visitors stroll around
town and visit the 1902 log
social hall and the old 1896
general store, now home to
the Seaview Café and Bar.
Recreational opportunities here
include camping at Porcupine
Campground, rafting on Six-
Mile Creek, and hiking the Gull
Rock Trail. More energetic hikers
can try the **Resurrection Pass
Trail**, which passes both historic
and modern-day gold diggings.

❷ Moose Pass

98 miles (158 km) S of Anchorage.
Transport map B3. 🚌 220.
🚌 Anchorage–Seward. **Tel** 288-3101
(Trail Lake Lodge). 🏃 Moose Pass
Solstice Festival (weekend nearest
June 21). 🌐 moosepassalaska.com

Moose Pass village began life
in 1912 as a construction camp
on the Alaska Railroad. The area
was named in 1903, after, it is
said, a moose blocked the

passage of a mail-carrying dog
team. To the west of the Seward
Highway stands a landmark
waterwheel, constructed in
1976 by the Estes Brothers who
still run a grocery located in the
adjacent 1928 building. Moose
Pass sits on the south side of
Trail Lake, and a local air taxi
provides flightseeing trips.

North of Moose Pass, a
salmon hatchery next to North
Trail Lake is the starting point
of the **Johnson Pass Trail**.
Following the lakeshore, the
trail climbs over its namesake
before descending to Granite
Creek at Mile 62.9 of the
Seward Highway.

❸ Cooper Landing

98 miles (158 km) S of Anchorage.
Transport map B3. 🚌 290.
🚌 Anchorage–Homer. **Tel** 595-8888.
ℹ Mile 48, Sterling Hwy.
🌐 cooperlandingchamber.com

Named after Joseph Cooper,
who was the first to discover
gold in the area in 1894,

Cooper Landing was one of
the few places in Alaska that
continued producing gold into
the 20th century. The town
sprawls along the Sterling
Highway in a string of eateries,
lodges, gift shops, and fishing
fitters. At the **K'Beq Kenaitze
Footprints Heritage Site**,
Dena'ina Natives share their
traditions through interpretive
walks featuring archeological
sites. Local artists make and sell
Dena'ina arts and crafts.

❹ Kenai River

Transport map A3. 🚌 Anchorage–
Homer. 🎣

Originating between high peaks
above the glacier-blue Kenai
Lake, the Kenai River rushes
westward from Cooper Landing,
where whitewater rafting,
kayaking, and canoeing are on
offer. The Kenai then passes the
mouth of the Russian River
before flowing out of the
mountains and onto the flats
around Skilak Lake.

Among the world's most
productive salmon streams,
the lower Kenai is the original
combat fishing river, with fierce
competition among anglers for
fishing space. People flock to
the river on summer weekends,
temporarily making the Sterling
Highway one of Alaska's busiest
roads. Continuing west from its
Skilak Lake outlet, the river flows
past innumerable public
campsites and private cabins
to its mouth at Kenai.

The Kenai River flowing swiftly past Cooper Landing

❺ Resurrection Pass Trail

The 38 mile (61 km) Resurrection Pass Trail on the Kenai Peninsula is Alaska's most popular multi-day hiking route. Beginning at the Kenai River along the Sterling Highway, it climbs through spruce forest and past Juneau Creek Falls into the subalpine zone. The trail crosses the 2,600 ft (780 m) Resurrection Pass before descending along Resurrection Creek to the trailhead near the gold mining village of Hope. An alternative is to hike the 10 mile (16 km) Devil's Pass Trail from Mile 39.5 on the Seward Highway, and then take the Resurrection Pass Trail to either Hope or the Sterling Highway.

Tips for Walkers

Starting point: Kenai River at the Sterling Highway. Due to the net altitude loss, it is best to hike the trail from south to north.
Length: the 38 mile (61 km) trail can take between two and six days to cover.
Accommodation: there are several forest service public use cabins along the trail. It is essential to pre-book (see p241).

⑤ Abandoned Gold Diggings
The northern end of the trail passes through a gold mining area, where prospectors have been mining and leaving behind detritus since the Gold Rush days.

⑥ Footbridge
A wooden footbridge spans Resurrection Creek near the northern end of the trail.

③ Resurrection Pass Summit
For 5 miles (8 km) the trail passes through a treeless alpine zone. Its highest point is the 2,500-ft (780-m) Resurrection Pass.

② Hoary Marmot Area
The distinctive whistles of hoary marmots accompany hikers through the alpine area of the hike.

① Juneau Creek Falls
The roaring Juneau Creek Falls are one of the most dramatic sights along the trail.

Turnagain Arm

Hope

HOPE HWY

Sunrise

Resurrection Creek

Palmer Creek

Caribou Creek

Pass Creek

Fox Creek

East Creek

DEVIL'S PASS TRAIL

Swan Lake

Juneau Lake

Trout Lake

Juneau Creek

Soldotna

STERLING HWY

Cooper Landing

Kenai

Kenai Lake

Moose Pass

④ Camping along Resurrection Creek
Campers will find lovely wild campsites near the northern end of the Resurrection Pass Trail.

Key

− − Trail
═ Highway
═ Minor road

0 km   5
0 miles   5

❻ Seward

Considered to have one of Alaska's most scenic locations, Seward is also known for its saltwater salmon fishing, its rollicking Independence Day celebrations, and its access to Kenai Fjords National Park (see pp106–7). Although the Russians set up a shipyard here in 1793, the town was founded in 1903 by John Ballaine, who decided that its deepwater port would be an ideal location for a railhead. The railway came to fruition in 1923 and Seward thrived, but the 1964 earthquake destroyed most of the town. However, Seward was rebuilt, and to mark its revitalisation, its newspaper was named the *Phoenix Log*.

Ship's anchor on display at Seward's waterfront

🏛 Benny Benson Memorial
♿

Located next to the lagoon just to the west of the Seward Highway stands a memorial honoring Benny Benson and his contribution to Alaska. Carved on Alaska stone by artist Damon Capurro, the memorial is engraved with the words of the Alaska flag song by Marie Drake and Elinor Dusenbury.

In 1926, George Parks, the governor of Alaska, asked schoolchildren to submit ideas for a state flag with essays explaining their design. Of the 142 entries submitted, the judges' unanimous choice was that of Benny Benson, a 13-year-old Alutiiq boy who lived at Seward's Jesse Lee Orphanage. Benson's essay explained that the flag's blue field represented the Alaska sky as well as the forget-me-not, the state flower. The North Star stood for the future State of Alaska, the most northerly in the Union, while the Great Bear constellation symbolized strength. Alaska's flag is now generally regarded as the most beautiful of all the US state flags (see p59).

🐟 Seward Waterfront
♿ ✏ 🖥 📷

Situated a short distance away from the small boat harbor and downtown Seward, the waterfront lies within easy reach of the port, rail depot, and airport. For most of the year, row upon row of yachts, pleasure craft, and fishing boats peacefully bob in the waters beneath the snow-covered peaks across the bay.

In the summer, however, the waterfront transforms into a bustling tourist complex. Here, the town's thousands of visitors and cruise ship passengers can organize tours and fishing trips, join Kenai Fjords cruises, plan outdoor activities, and shop for gifts in a growing number of souvenir shops. At the southern end, the shops give way to an often packed tent and RV campground that stretches along the shore for almost 2 miles (3 km).

🏛 Kenai Fjords National Park Information Center
1212 4th Ave. **Tel** 422-0500. **Open** late May–early Sep: 8:30am–7pm daily; May & Sep: 9am–5pm daily. ♿ 📷
Ⓦ nps.gov/kefj

The handsome building that houses the Kenai Fjords National Park Information Center sits on the Seward waterfront. It features several exhibits detailing aspects of the glaciation that created the park's spectacular landscapes, as well as the wildlife and prolific birdlife that inhabits it (see pp106–7). A free video runs intermittently, outlining natural history and park landscapes, including remote sites that few visitors are able to reach.

🏛 Seward Community Library and Museum
6th & Adams. **Tel** 224-3902. **Open** mid-May–mid-Sep: 10am–5pm; winter: noon–1pm Tue–Fri, noon–4pm Sat. ☀ summer only. ♿ 📷

Located on the first floor of the town's library, the Seward Museum offers a glimpse of the

Kenai Fjords National Park Information Center on the Seward Waterfront

Visitors exploring the magnificent Exit Glacier

🧊 Exit Glacier
8 miles (13 km) W of Seward on Exit
Glacier/Herman Leirer Rd. ℹ️ 422-
0500. 🅿️ 🚻 ♿ limited. ⛺ 🏕️
🌐 nps.gov/kefj

The impressive Exit Glacier,
2,500 ft (762 m) high and
3 miles (5 km) long, is the only
part of Kenai Fjords National
Park that is accessible by road.
Pouring down from Harding
Icefield, it is the most readily
accessible walk-up glacier in
Alaska. From the seasonal
visitors' center at the end of
the road, a short wheelchair-
accessible trail leads to a hiking
route across the rocky terminal
moraines to the glacier face. The
energetic can hike the steep
4-mile (6-km) Harding Icefield
Trail up the western flank of
Exit Glacier to the vast Harding
Icefield. Camping is not permitted on the trail, but there is
a public use cabin and free
campground nearby.

history of the Resurrection Bay
area, from pre-Russian contact
to the 1964 Good Friday earthquake. As well as the permanent
exhibition, rotating temporary
displays focus on interesting
aspects of social history, such
as a collection of items from the
Brown & Hawkins store, in business here from 1904 to 2013.

🐟 Alaska SeaLife Center
See pp104–5.

🏞️ Caines Head State Recreation Area
🚤 water taxi from Seward. 🚤 ⛺
🏕️ 🌐 alaskastateparks.org
During World War II, the US
Army built Fort McGilvray on
the rocky headland known as
Caines Head, as well as a
dock at North Beach and
a garrison at South Beach.
The area still has ammunition
storage bunkers and gun
emplacements used to guard
the port and Resurrection
Bay when Alaska's Aleutian
Islands were attacked by
Japanese forces.

The shale-covered beaches
are ideal for anglers, and sea
kayakers will enjoy paddling
here. Hiking is also possible,
but the 3-mile (5-km) walk
from Tonsina Point is possible
only at low tide, so hikers on
the return trip will probably
need to camp overnight. Note
that the remains of the South
Beach garrison are unstable.

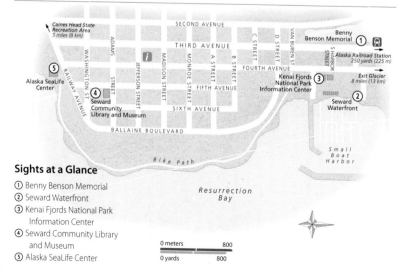

Sights at a Glance
① Benny Benson Memorial
② Seward Waterfront
③ Kenai Fjords National Park Information Center
④ Seward Community Library and Museum
⑤ Alaska SeaLife Center

0 meters 800
0 yards 800

Seward: Alaska SeaLife Center

On the lovely Resurrection Bay waterfront in Seward, the Alaska SeaLife Center integrates museum exhibits, aquarium displays, and hands-on experiences to provide an educational introduction to the maritime world of Alaska's southern coasts. Initially conceived as a coldwater marine research and rehabilitation facility to study and protect sealife and provide public education – especially in the aftermath of the 1989 *Exxon Valdez* oil spill *(see p121)* – the center was opened in May 1998 and has since grown into one of Alaska's best-loved attractions. Highlights include several innovative tours and a series of spectacular tanks with underwater viewing windows that allow visitors to look at a variety of creatures in naturalistic habitats.

Facade of the extensive Alaska SeaLife Center in Seward

The Resurrection Bay Overlook provides an opportunity to view harbor seals, sea otters, whales, and birds in their natural habitat.

The Harbor Seal Habitat resembles a rocky coastline where seals can be seen in great numbers.

★ **Windows to the Sea**
Visitors enjoy close-up views of fish, harbor seals, octopuses, and several affable Steller sea lions.

★ **Denizens of the Deep**
Among several hands-on Encounter Tours is the Octopus Encounter, where participants meet a giant Pacific octopus, and there is also the chance to join a harbor seal training session.

Gallery Guide

Windows to the Sea on the first floor provides underwater views of Alaskan sealife. The second floor has a host of exhibits, including the Discovery Pool and the Seabird Habitat, showcasing various aspects of the marine world.

Entrance

★ **Discovery Touch Pool**
The pool offers a hands-on experience of Alaska's underwater world. Children can enjoy touching such creatures as sea cucumbers, starfish, anemones, and sea urchins, as well as underwater plant life.

The Research Deck Overlook provides a view of the animals involved in rehabilitation or research projects.

Discovery Classroom

★ **Seabird Habitat**
A large aviary on the second floor encloses cliffs housing a selection of the bird species that inhabit the islets in the Gulf of Alaska. Diving seabirds are visible in the tank in the Windows to the Sea exhibit below.

Second floor

Steller Sea Lion Habitat

The research and rehabilitation facilities are designed to combine scientific study, wildlife rehabilitation, and public education.

First floor

Key

- Windows to the Sea
- Aquariums
- Rocky Coast Gallery
- Salmon Stream
- The Resurrection Bay Overlook
- Research Facilities
- A Closer Look
- Non-exhibition space

Bering Sea Gallery
This gallery contains a series of images and illustrative displays about Alaska's marine ecosystem. Attractive cutouts and interactive kiosks explain various facets of the state's sealife and address rehabilitation concerns.

Kenai Fjords National Park

Covering 950 sq miles (2,460 sq km), Kenai Fjords National Park takes in some of Alaska's finest and most accessible coastal scenery, glacial landscapes, and diverse marine wildlife. The crown of the park is the Harding Icefield. This vast expanse of ice, interrupted only by an occasional *nunatak* (*see p31*), feeds the glaciers that flow down from the heights to form the park's deep valleys and fjords. The seas, rich in fish, crustaceans, shellfish, and plankton, also provide a habitat for a range of readily observed birds and marine mammals, including sea otters, Dall porpoises, Steller sea lions, and several whale species.

Cook Inlet
Soldotna
Seward
Area of map illustrated
Gulf of Alaska

Locator Map
Kenai Fjords National Park

Calving Glaciers
Tidewater glaciers such as Holgate Glacier regularly calve icebergs into the fjords in the park. Kayakers must watch out for large waves generated by falling house-sized chunks.

0 km   5
0 miles   5

Key
Highway
Minor road
Park boundary

Harding Icefield

Peders Gla

Northwestern Glacier
Holgate Glacier

Harris Penins

Northwestern Fjord

McCarty Glacier

Harris Bay

McCarty Fjord

Gra Isla

Whale-Watching
Summer visitors often spot sounding or breaching whales in these waters, which serve as summer feeding grounds for humpbacks and migratory routes each spring and fall for gray whales. Minke whales and pods of porpoises are also seen in the summer.

Gulf of Alaska

★ Harding Icefield
The 70-mile- (113-km-) long and 30-mile- (48-km-) wide Harding Icefield stretches across the Kenai Mountains and creates all of Kenai Fjord's glaciers. Hikers can access it via a steep trail from Exit Glacier. The icefield also draws experienced backcountry skiers keen to explore its farthest reaches.

VISITORS' CHECKLIST

Practical Information
Seward. **Transport map** A4.
🚌 to Seward. 🛈 1212 4th Ave, Seward; 422-0500. 🛈 Information Center; Exit Glacier Nature Center and trail. 🏕 🏕 Permits required for backcountry camping are free and unlimited; available at the Information Center. Exit Glacier Nature Center: Mile 9, Exit Glacier Rd. 🌐 **nps.gov/kefj**

Transport
🚌 to Seward, then shuttle van to Exit Glacier. 🚢 day cruises to the fjords.

[Map showing Exit Glacier, Seward, Resurrection Bay, Bear Glacier, Aialik Glacier, Aialik Peninsula, Fox Island, Rugged Island, Aialik Bay, Chiswell Islands]

The Kenai Fjords National Park Information Center *(see p102)* in Seward issues backcountry permits and provides information.

★ Fjord Cruises in Aialik Bay
This 20-mile- (32-km-) long fjord is the most popular destination for day cruises. Visitors are usually guaranteed a dynamic show as huge chunks of ice calve off the towering face of Aialik Glacier.

Exploring the Park
Kenai Fjords' only road ends at the Exit Glacier parking lot, where an easy half-mile (1-km) trail leads to good views of the glacier face. A challenging 6-mile (10-km) return trail goes up to Harding Icefield. To see the park's wildlife and calving glaciers, visitors can join a half- or full-day fjords cruise with Seward-based operators (see p267). Several local companies also offer guided multi-day kayak trips into the park.

★ Steller Sea Lion Rookery
On the lonely, rocky outcrops of the Chiswell Islands, passengers on day cruises can approach one of Alaska's most prominent Steller sea lion rookeries. The islands also have impressive bird cliffs with nesting puffins and kittiwakes.

For keys to symbols *see back flap*

❽ Sterling

134 miles (215 km) SW of Anchorage. **Transport map** A3. 🏔 5,000. 🚌 Anchorage–Homer.

The name of the game in the 5 mile (8 km) strip known as Sterling is fish. Nearly all the businesses along the Sterling Highway cater to the anglers who flock to the town when the salmon are running. This community is also home to numerous private recreational cabins on the banks of the Kenai river.

Anyone who has ever wanted to try their hand at landing a monster salmon will find plenty of equipment and advice in Sterling, as well as along the highway between here, Soldotna, Kenai, and Homer. The area's most worthwhile site is **Skilak Lake**, which features lovely wild lakeside campsites and hiking trails. In the winter, the area's many frozen lakes, including Seven Lakes and Hidden Lake, make a pretty sight, but in the summer, the congestion around this area can be frustrating.

❾ Soldotna

148 miles (238 km) SW of Anchorage. **Transport map** A3. 🏔 4,000. ✈ 🚌 Anchorage–Homer. 🛈 44790 Sterling Hwy; 262-9814. 🛒 Farmer's Market, 10am–2pm Saturdays in summer. 🌐 **soldotnachamber.com**

As the primary commercial and service center of the Kenai Peninsula, Soldotna features

Log cabin at the Soldotna Historical Society Museum

fast-food franchises, stores, and visitor accommodation options. Founded in the 1940s as a retail hub at the junction of the Sterling and Kenai Spur Highways, it was incorporated only in 1967. While the area experienced steady growth, unbridled sprawl, and congestion in the late 20th century, much of the surrounding land remains protected under federal management.

Five sites around town – the Soldotna Visitors' Center, Rotary Park, Soldotna Creek Park, and the Centennial and Swiftwater Campgrounds – have set up "Fishwalks" along the Kenai River. These boardwalks, designed to protect the fragile riverbank, allow public access to the river for fishing and salmon-viewing.

On Centennial Park Road, the **Soldotna Historical Society Museum** features a collection of homesteaders' cabins from the 1940s. It also has a Territorial log school, Native artifacts, and a collection of stuffed wildlife.

Holy Assumption of the Virgin Mary Russian Orthodox Church, Kenai

❿ Kenai

11 miles (18 km) NW of Soldotna. **Transport map** A3. 🏔 7,000. ✈ 🚌 Anchorage–Homer. 🛈 11471 Kenai Spur Hwy; 283-1991. 🎉 Kenai River Festival (2nd weekend in Jun). 🌐 **visitkenai.com**

The Kenai Peninsula's largest city, Kenai also ranks as one of Alaska's best-preserved historic communities. In 1791, Russian fur traders came in contact with the region's Dena'ina Athabaskan people and established St. Nicholas Redoubt, the second permanent Russian settlement in Alaska. In 1869, two years after the purchase of Alaska, the US Army built Fort Kenay to provide a military presence in the Cook Inlet region. Extensive oil exploration began in the 1950s, and the Tesoro Alaska refinery at Nikiski is now a major economic player.

Visitors can stroll around the historic Old Town near the beach, which has the 1881 Parish Rectory House, the 1906

St. Nicholas Chapel, a replica of Fort Kenay, and the onion-domed **Holy Assumption of the Virgin Mary Russian Orthodox Church**. Founded in 1846, the church's present building was constructed between 1894 and 1895. The interior is decorated with Russian artifacts, some from the early 19th century.

In spring, the salt marsh at **Kenai Flats State Recreation Site**, across the Warren Ames Bridge over the Kenai River, attracts large flocks of Siberian snow geese. With interpretive panels, picnic tables, a board-walk, and viewing scope, it will delight birders. A little farther west, on Cannery Road, a salmon cannery compound dating from 1922 has been converted into Kenai Landing, an atmospheric complex consisting of shops, a restaurant, bar, theater, and museum.

The old salmon cannery complex at Kenai Landing, Kenai

⓫ Captain Cook State Recreation Area

25 miles (40 km) N of Kenai at Mile 36, Kenai Spur Hwy. **Transport map** A3. 262-5581. dnr.alaska.gov/parks/units/captcook.htm

Located on the shores of Cook Inlet, the Captain Cook State Recreation Area is named after British explorer Captain James Cook, who explored the area in 1778. One of Alaska's quieter parks, its forests, lakes, streams, and beaches offer picnic sites, hiking routes, and camping at the large Discovery Campground, as well as swimming, canoeing, and fishing in Stormy Lake. Wildlife, including moose, bears, loons, and sandhill cranes, can be spotted in the park. The beach is popular with agate hunters, but visitors should avoid the dangerous mudflats just offshore.

Along the dead-end road to the recreation area, visitors can pick up supplies and look around the oil town of **Nikiski**, 9 miles (14 km) to the south. Formerly known as North Kenai, this town began as a homesteading area in the 1940s and grew with the discovery of oil in Cook Inlet. At the end of Nikiski Beach Road, fine views open up across Nikishka Bay and the Cook Inlet oil drilling platforms, and beyond to the active volcano Mount Spurr. The large domed Nikiski pool, funded by the oil companies, boasts a hot tub and a winding 136 ft (41 m) water slide that is very popular with residents and visitors.

⓬ Kenai National Wildlife Refuge

Transport map A4. Anchorage–Homer. Ski Hill Rd, 43655 Kalifornsky Beach Rd, Soldotna; 262-7021. kenai.fws.gov

The Alaska National Interest Lands Conservation Act of 1980 (see p61) changed the name of the Kenai National Moose Range to the Kenai National Wildlife Refuge, and expanded it to its current area of almost 3,125 sq miles (8,094 sq km). The refuge covers high peaks, glaciers, muskeg, and lake-studded bog. This landscape provides habitat for a range of wildlife, from mountain goats, Dall sheep, and bears to moose, caribou, and wolves. The refuge is also home to lynx, coyotes, and waterfowl such as trumpeter swans and migratory birds.

Kenai National Wildlife Refuge sign

Access to the refuge's wild southern part can be challenging, but the northern areas feature several public campgrounds, 200 miles (322 km) of hiking trails, and two world-class canoe routes. The 80 mile (128 km) **Swanson River Canoe Route** links over 40 lakes with the Swanson River, ending in the Captain Cook State Recreation Area. The 60 mile (96 km) **Swan Lakes Loop** is a system of 32 lakes, accessible from the Swanson River and Swan Lake Roads. Equipment can be hired and tours organized in nearby towns.

Lakes and forests at the Kenai National Wildlife Refuge

⓭ Clam Gulch

23 miles (37 km) S of Soldotna.
Transport map A3. 🚍 180.
🚌 Anchorage–Homer.

As its name might suggest, the highlight at Clam Gulch is clamming. The village itself is small, consisting of a few houses and some services, but beneath the sands of the beautiful Cook Inlet coast lie some of the world's most productive razor clam beds. At low tide, this is the best place in Alaska to dig for these delicious treats.

Diggers will need rubber boots, a clam shovel, bucket, and an Alaska fishing license (see p45). The daily limit per person is 60 clams. The clams are usually about 6 inches (15 cm) beneath the surface. A small dimple in the sand indicates the presence of a clam, but it is best to dig to the side to avoid breaking its shell. Clams will attempt to flee by burrowing into the sand, so diggers may well have to give chase. It is best to carry the clams in a bucket of saltwater, adding a bit of corn meal to let them clean themselves before they are cooked.

⓮ Ninilchik

40 miles (65 km) S of Soldotna.
Transport map A4. 🚍 880.
🚌 Anchorage–Homer. 📞 567-3571. 🎵 Salmonstock Music Festival, first weekend Aug.
🌐 ninilchikchamber.com

This traditional Russian-era Native village, whose name means "peaceful riverside place," is centered around the 1901 **Transfiguration of Our Lord Church**. The photogenic onion-domed church sits beside a rambling Russian Orthodox cemetery and offers fine views across the inlet. While the church is open for Sunday services, it is closed to the public on other days.

The Ninilchik River, a short walk to the north of the Visitors' Center, and Deep Creek, to the south, are world-class salmon fishing streams. Deep-sea charters provide access to offshore halibut and salmon. When the king salmon are running upstream (usually the first two weeks of June), the Deep Creek State Recreation Area Campground and the Ninilchik River Campground fill up and spill over into surrounding private sites and RV parks. Anglers will probably enjoy the scene, while others may prefer quieter areas.

Anchor Point sign highlighting its location on the highway system

⓯ Anchor Point

61 miles (98 km) S of Soldotna.
Transport map A4. 🚍 1,900.
🚌 Anchorage–Homer. ℹ️ Sterling Hwy, opposite Anchor River Inn; 235-2600. 🌐 anchorpointchamber.org

Named after an anchor that the British explorer Captain James Cook lost on his voyage up Cook Inlet, the Anchor Point community was established by homesteaders in 1949. The major attraction at this westernmost point on the contiguous US Highway system is the Anchor River, with its abundant supply of king and silver salmon, and rainbow, Dolly Varden, and steelhead trout. The seas around the area are rich in saltwater salmon and halibut.

Anglers usually stay at the Anchor River State Recreation Area at Anchor Point. Those who prefer a quieter campsite can opt for the beautiful (and angler-free) Stariski State Recreation Area north of Anchor Point. The park is perched on a bluff with views across Cook Inlet to the volcanoes beyond.

⓰ Nikolaevsk

64 miles (103 km) S of Soldotna.
Transport map A4. 🚍 320.

Settled in 1960, Nikolaevsk village is home to the Old Believers, a sect of Russian Orthodoxy that broke away from the mother church and settled in Siberia after the 17th-century religious reforms (see pp36–7). Those who wound up in Alaska established Nikolaevsk and several surrounding villages.

Visitors arriving along the 9-mile (14-km) drive from Anchor Point might feel as if they have passed through a time warp. With distinctive architecture and demeanor, the villagers' lifestyle has only been lightly touched by the 21st century. One exception is an enterprising local woman who runs the Samovar Café and a gallery of costumes and artwork.

There is a lovely Russian Orthodox Church which is worth a look, but its interior is closed to the public.

The traditional Transfiguration of Our Lord Church, Ninilchik

The Bears of Alaska

Most visitors to Alaska want to see bears, and nearly everyone does. One often hears, "When you're in Alaska, you're never far from a bear," and while that does not hold true for the Aleutian Islands, the rest of the state is prime bear habitat. Alaska is home to three species of bears – black, brown, and polar. Alaskan brown bears are further divided into two kinds, the smaller grizzlies of the Interior and the enormous brown bears of Southwest Alaska. They are not a true subspecies, however, and the size variations are due only to differences in their diet. Active in summer, many bears become dormant in winter, retreating to dens and living on fat reserves. Cubs are often born during dormancy. Bears can be aggressive, particularly when protecting cubs or competing with each other during the breeding season.

Brown bears, numbering about 40,000 in Alaska, are resident from the Southeast to the Arctic. The smaller grizzlies eat more vegetation, whereas Kodiaks (see p207), which can measure up to 12 ft (4 m) tall when standing on their hind legs, eat a high-protein fish diet.

Black bears, which measure an average of 5 ft (1.5 m) in length, are the smallest Alaskan bears. These predominantly vegetarian bears are found everywhere in Alaska except the Arctic tundra and the Aleutian Islands.

Bear Safety

- Store food in a bear-proof container, and cook away from tents. Never eat or keep snacks in your tent.

> YOU ARE IN BEAR TERRITORY
> Do Not Leave Food Unattended
> Unattended items subject to
> Impound and $50 Fine
> 11 AAC 12.230J

Bear safety sign

- In a bear encounter, do not run, as that may elicit a chase response.
- In a defensive attack, curl up in a ball with knees tucked into the stomach, arms wrapped around the face, and hands laced behind the back of the neck.
- In an aggressive attack, fight back with as much strength as possible. Poke at the bear's eyes and nose, punch it in the face, and try to hit it with a hiking pole or stick.
- Polar bears are the only species that stalk humans, and in an aggressive attack, a firearm will provide the only reasonable protection.

Polar bears, which inhabit the Arctic Ocean coastline, subsist mainly on marine mammals. Swimming across open water, they spend most of their lives roaming the ice floes in search of seals, but come ashore in the fall to breed (see p227).

Bear	Identification	Best Times to See	Best Places to See
Black (Ursus americanus)	Black or cinnamon coat; pointed muzzle	Spring, summer, and fall	Anan Creek Wildlife Observatory
Brown (Ursus arctos)	Dark brown to blond coat; prominent shoulder hump	Summer to fall	Denali National Park and Katmai National Park
Polar (Ursus maritimus)	Creamy coat; longer neck than other bears	Spring and fall	Barrow and Kaktovik

Ramp to the small boat harbor on Homer Spit

⑰ Homer

84 miles (135 km) S of Soldotna.
Transport map A4. 🚋 5,000. ✈
🚌 🚌 ℹ 201 Sterling Highway,
235-7740. 🎏 Kachemak Bay
Shorebird Festival (2nd weekend
in May). 🖥 **homeralaska.org**

Founded in 1895 and named
for Homer Pennock, a New
York con man who spent a few
months in the area, Homer
sells itself as the "end of the
road." It is a refuge for visitors,
artists, and anglers, as well as
some modern-day Pennocks.
In 1886, Homer got its first
post office, and in the late
1890s, a coal-shipping
settlement occupied the tip
of Homer Spit that runs into
Kachemak Bay. However, the
village was abandoned in 1902
when the coal seams became
unviable. The handful of
residents who remained in
town turned to farming and
fishing. From 1910 onwards,
Homer expanded from a
fishing village into a pleasant
small town.

Homer continues to attract
outsiders, causing rapid development of its bluffs and foot-
hills. For visitors, the town
means bird-watching, halibut
fishing, shopping for local
arts, and visits to the nearby
Kachemak Bay State Park.
Homer also boasts the world-
class Alaska Islands and Oceans
Visitors' Center and several
interesting museums.

🏛 Pratt Museum
3779 Bartlett St. **Tel** 235-8635.
Open mid-May–mid-Sep:
10am–6pm daily; mid-Sep–mid-May:
noon–5pm Tue–Sun. 🔲 🔲 🔲
botanical garden only. 🔲
🖥 **prattmuseum.org**

Homer's natural history
museum covers the geology,
flora, fauna, and oceanography
of the peninsula, as well as
homesteader and Native
cultures. The Kachemak Bay
exhibit uses photographs,
videos, and interactive computer
programs to provide a sense of
the place. Detailed coverage
of the 1964 earthquake and the
1989 *Exxon Valdez* oil spill *(see
p121)* is displayed downstairs.
Trails through the botanical
gardens outside the main
building lead past 150 identified
species of local plants. The
Harrington Cabin displays
artifacts from Homer's 1940s
homesteading era.

Engaging exhibits inside Homer's
Pratt Museum

🏛 Bunnell Street Arts Center
106 W Bunnell Ave. **Tel** 235-2662.
🔲 🔲 🔲 🖥 **bunnellarts.org**

Drawn by its scenic location,
several artists made Homer
their home, and as a result,
sundry street fairs, workshops,
and galleries sprang up.
One of the most renowned
is the Bunnell Street Arts
Center, which was founded
by an artists' group in 1989.
Housed in the 1937 Old
Inlet Trading Post building,
which was once a commercial
hub for homesteaders, the
gallery now showcases
contemporary fine art.

🏛 Alaska Islands and Ocean Visitors' Center
95 Sterling Hwy. **Tel** 235-6961.
Open late May–early Sep: 9am–5pm
daily; winter: noon–5pm Tue–Sat. 🔲
🔲 🖥 **islandsandocean.org**

This highly worthwhile stop is
probably the finest center of its
kind in Alaska. A wealth of
original exhibits, including a
replica of a Bering Sea seabird
rookery and a recording of
conservationist and researcher
Olaus Murie dictating his
journal, detail the natural
history of the Alaska Maritime
National Wildlife Refuge and
the Kachemak Bay Research
Reserve. Visitors can also hike
along a boardwalk to Beluga
Slough's tidal marshes or watch
an award-winning film on the
Aleutian Islands.

Carl E. Wynn Nature Center

E Skyline Dr. **Tel** 235-5266.
Open mid-Jun–early Sep: 10am–6pm
daily. 🚐 📷 🚻 limited. 📷
🅦 akcoastalstudies.org

This center is set amid spruce forests and meadows on the bluffs overlooking Homer. Formerly the homestead of naturalist Carl E Wynn, it was donated to the Center for Alaskan Coastal Studies in 1990. Visitors can enjoy bird-watching, stroll amid wildflowers, or explore the variety of vegetation from upland coastal forests to boreal forests. The center also offers guided walks highlighting local wildlife and shrubs.

Wildflowers at the Carl E. Wynn Nature Center outside Homer

Homer Spit

Thought to be a remnant of an ancient glacial moraine, Homer Spit has been spared from the ravages of the sea by reclamation and rock walls. This is Homer's main tourist district, taking in the small boat harbor, the ferry terminal, a hotel, myriad eateries, and a host of fishing charter companies. The **Salty Dawg Saloon**, with its distinctive lighthouse tower, is listed as a maritime landmark. Around 1900, it served as the headquarters for the Cook Inlet Coal Fields Company. Today, this atmospheric drinking den is unmissable.

The Spit is also a camping venue with communities of RVs and tents strung along the northern shore.

Rocky Island off Kachemak Bay State Park

Seldovia

20 nautical miles (32 km) S of Homer.
🚶 260. ✈ charter floatplane from Homer. 🚢 from Homer. 🎊 July 4 parade and canoe jousting.
🅦 seldoviachamber.org

Seldovia was inhabited by Dena'ina people as early as the 16th century. Russians settled here around 1800, naming the place Zaliv Seldevoe (Herring Bay). In the early 20th century, the area's flourishing herring trade increased the town's population to about 2,000, but the boom was shortlived.

Today, Seldovia is a small fishing village with an active Native association. Visitors can stroll along the waterfront boardwalk, explore the Village Tribe Museum and Visitors' Center, and visit the 1891 St. Nicholas Russian Orthodox Church, which crowns a hill overlooking the harbor.

Salty Dawg Saloon lighthouse, Homer Spit

Kachemak Bay State Park

8 nautical miles (12 km) across the bay from Homer. **Tel** 262-5581.
🚢 from Homer. 🏔 🏕
🅦 alaskastateparks.org

Alaska's first state park and one of the largest coastal state parks in the US, the Kachemak Bay State Park and the adjoining Kachemak Bay State Wilderness Park take in 625 sq miles (1,619 sq km) of islands, forests, glaciers, beaches, and rocky coastlines. This critical habitat area supports several species of marine life, including whales and sea otters, land mammals such as coyotes and black bears, and birds that include eagles and puffins. About 80 miles (130 km) of hiking trails lace the waterfront area of the park, across the bay from Homer. Trails from primitive beach campsites lead to ridges and remote coastlines.

Halibut Cove

12 miles (19 km) SE of Homer.
🚶 75. 🚢 from Homer.
🅦 halibutcove.com

Halibut Cove happily receives short-term visitors, but is keen to avoid the unbridled growth of Homer. This scenic little cove makes an excellent launch point for hikes into the adjacent Kachemak Bay State Park. There is also a restaurant and several lodges, as well as a number of artists' galleries. The most renowned of these is the Cove Gallery of the late Diana Tillion, who used octopus ink for her works. A local charter boat company provides twice-daily summertime tours from Homer to Halibut Cove.

PRINCE WILLIAM SOUND

The northernmost extent of the Gulf of Alaska, Prince William Sound is a large bay studded with forested islands. Lying to the east of the Kenai Range and south of the heavily glaciated Chugach Range, the massive sound is roughly twice the size of Massachusetts, with convoluted coasts lined with large tidewater glaciers and sheltered waters that harbor a rich variety of wildlife.

Home to the Eyak, Dena'ina, and other Native peoples, the Prince William Sound area was first explored in 1778 by the British captain James Cook and by the Spanish explorer Don Salvador Fidalgo in 1790, both of whom were searching for the elusive Northwest Passage. The first serious scientific study of the area was conducted in June 1899 by the Harriman Expedition, which included eminent scientists and artists. Much of their vast collection of specimens, illustrations, and photographs is now at the Smithsonian Institution in Washington, DC.

In the early decades of the 20th century, the area's economy received a boost when the town of Cordova became the railhead for the Copper River and Northwestern Railway. In the 1970s, Valdez, by virtue of being the northernmost ice-free port in North America, was chosen as the site of the marine terminal for the Trans-Alaska Pipeline. Since then, oil tankers have shared the shipping lanes with Marine Highway ferries, fishing boats, kayakers, and, more recently, cruise ships calling into the port of Whittier.

Despite the environmental damage suffered in the 1989 *Exxon Valdez* oil spill, most of the sound has come back, at least on the surface, although herring fisheries have never recovered. Marine life is recovering and wildlife watching cruises can be very rewarding. Bird-watchers will enjoy the kittiwake colonies near Whittier and the migratory birds of the Copper River Delta. Kayaking among the ice floes in the bay is another popular activity, as is hiking on the glaciers.

Fisherman's Memorial overlooking Cordova's boat harbor

◀ Meltwater cascading down forested slopes near Whittier, Prince William Sound

Exploring Prince William Sound

Alaska's greatest concentration of tidewater glaciers form the highlight of Prince William Sound. Three main towns, prosperous Valdez, cozy Cordova, and tiny Whittier, flank the sound. They serve as bases for popular cruises that visit Blackstone Bay, College Fjord, and the massive Columbia Glacier, and offer opportunities to view seals, whales, and sea otters. East of Cordova, the arresting beauty of the Copper River Road makes for a wonderful drive through the bird-watching area of Alaganik Slough and the Copper River Delta to the Childs Glacier and famed Million Dollar Bridge.

Sign for Childs Glacier next to Million Dollar Bridge, Cordova

Private yachts and boats crowding Whittier's Small Boat Harbor

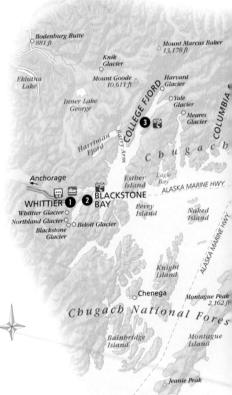

Sights at a Glance

Towns and Cities

① Whittier
⑤ Valdez
⑥ Cordova

Areas of Natural Beauty

② Blackstone Bay
③ College Fjord
④ Columbia Glacier
⑦ Copper River Highway

Getting Around

Scheduled flights operate between Anchorage, Valdez, and Cordova. In the summer, Alaska Marine Highway ferries do daily runs between Whittier, Valdez, and Cordova. Private vehicles can get to Valdez on the Richardson Highway. A toll tunnel from the Seward Highway provides access to Whittier. While there's no outside road access to Cordova, it's worth taking a vehicle on the ferry in order to drive the Copper River Highway. Perhaps the best way to see the sound, however, is on an organized cruise from Whittier or Valdez.

For hotels and restaurants see pp242–5 and pp250–55

Marshland at Alaganik Slough near Cordova, Prince William Sound

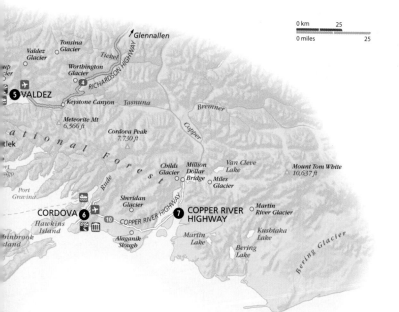

0 km   25
0 miles   25

Glennallen

Tonsina Glacier
Valdez Glacier
Tiekel
Wortbington Glacier
RICHARDSON HIGHWAY
5 VALDEZ
Keystone Canyon
Tasnuna
Bremner
Meteorite Mt 6,566 ft
Copper
Cordova Peak 7,730 ft
National Forest
Childs Glacier
Million Dollar Bridge
Van Cleve Lake
Mount Tom White 10,637 ft
Miles Glacier
Sheridan Glacier
Hinchinbrook Island
COPPER RIVER HIGHWAY
7 COPPER RIVER HIGHWAY
Martin River Glacier
CORDOVA 6
Ride
10
Hawkins Island
Alaganik Slough
Martin Lake
Kushtaka Lake
Bering Lake
Bering Glacier
Port Gravina

Key

━━ Highway

┈┈ Minor road

─── Alaska Railroad

┄┄ Alaska Marine Highway

△ Peak

Ice floes in the bay near Columbia Glacier, Prince William Sound

For keys to symbols *see back flap*

Pleasure boats docked at Whittier, at the western edge of Prince William Sound

❶ Whittier

59 miles (95 km) SE of Anchorage.
Transport map E4. ✈ 220.
🚂 from Anchorage via Portage.
⛴ from Valdez and Cordova.
Ⓦ **whittieralaska.gov**
Anton Anderson Memorial Tunnel:
Open 15 mins hourly in each
direction. Ⓦ **tunnel.alaska.gov**

Whittier's name came from
the adjacent Whittier Glacier,
named after the American
poet John Greenleaf Whittier.
Founded in 1943, when the US
Army used this ice-free port to
build an Alaska base, the town
was made accessible by the
3-mile (5-km) Anton Anderson
road-rail toll tunnel, which
connects Turnagain Arm with
Passage Canal, an arm of Prince
William Sound.

Despite its spectacular
setting, surrounded as it is by
glaciers and thundering waterfalls, Whittier is probably one
of Alaska's oddest towns. The
army, not especially concerned
with aesthetics, housed their
personnel in Soviet-style high-
rise apartment buildings. After

the army left in 1960, the few
hundred residents who stayed
behind continued to live in
two towers, one of which, the
14-story Begich Towers, has
now been converted into con-
dominiums. The town's other
occupied building is the less
obtrusive Whittier Manor. Most
residents are accustomed to
unflattering remarks about
these buildings, and even
seem proud of the undeniably
quirky architecture.

One of Whittier's main
attractions is a large colony
of black-legged kittiwakes in
the cliffs across Passage Arm,
which can be viewed on sea
kayaking trips. Lovers of the
outdoors will also enjoy the
26 Glacier Cruise run by
Phillips Cruises and Tours. The
cruise boats travel deep into
Barry Arm and College Fjord,
offering visitors close-up views
of wildlife and glaciers.

Phillips Cruises and Tours
Cliffside Marina. **Tel** 276-8023, (800)
544-0529. Cruises depart May–Sep
12:30pm daily. Ⓦ **26glaciers.com**

❷ Blackstone Bay

Transport map E4. ⛴ from Whittier.

One of Alaska's most dramatic
sights, the 18-mile- (29-km-)
long Blackstone Bay lies at the
foot of three calving tidewater
glaciers – Blackstone, Beloit,
and Northland. These choke
the upper portion of this
spectacular fjord with growler
ice, bergy bits, and small
icebergs (see pp30–31).

From the campground at
the southern end of Willard
Island, campers have a front-
row view of nature's intriguing
displays, as well as a minor
lesson in physics. As chunks
calve off the glaciers, three
types of waves appear. First,
light waves make the calving
visible to observers. Several
seconds later, a sound wave
arrives, carrying the thunder-
like crack of the breaking ice.
Finally, after a minute or so,
the waves created by the big
splash roll onto the shore.

Most visitors to Blackstone
Bay arrive on day cruises from
Whittier, but it is also popular
as a venue for ocean kayaking
(see 266–7). Kayakers typically
take two days to reach Willard
Island in the middle of the
fjord. Although it can be an
enjoyable experience to paddle
around between the bergs,
visitors should be careful not
to approach the glacier faces
or be caught on an incoming
tide. Pieces of ice, pushed
by the forceful current, can
crush a kayak.

Sea kayakers gliding past Blackstone Glacier, Blackstone Bay

For hotels and restaurants see pp242–5 and pp250–55

❸ College Fjord

Transport map E4. 🚢 tour from Whittier. 📷

The College Fjord arm of Prince William Sound and the neighboring Harriman Fjord include an impressive concentration of easily accessible tidewater glaciers, as well as myriad valley glaciers and hanging glaciers *(see pp30–31)*.

In 1899, New York railroad magnate Edward Harriman launched a scientific expedition along the Alaskan coast, including College Fjord, where he named the glaciers after the Ivy League colleges attended by the scientists on board his ship, the *George W. Elder*. As one travels into the fjord, the glaciers on the left are named for women's colleges and those on the right for men's schools. Chunks as large as a house often calve from the massive 300-ft- (90-m-) high glacier faces.

❹ Columbia Glacier

Transport map E3. 🚢 tour boats from Valdez. 📷

During the 1980s, 40-mile- (64-km-) long, 2,000-ft- (600-m-) thick Columbia Glacier was a highlight on the Alaska Marine Highway route between Whittier and Valdez. Ferries would typically stop amid the

Black-legged kittiwakes perching on a small ice floe

Kittiwakes

The towering cliffs across Passage Arm from Whittier are home to a colony of thousands of black-legged kittiwakes *(Rissa tridactyla)*. During the summer nesting season they can be seen wheeling around the precarious cliff faces where they nest, breed, and hatch their chicks. With a relatively rapid wingbeat, kittiwakes are highly maneuverable and able to land on narrow cliff ledges even in strong winds. In the winter, these pelagic gulls spend most of their time on the open ocean, feeding on small fish and plankton.

groups or rafts of sea otters and icebergs laden with harbor seals, and blast their horns with the hope that the vibrations would cause the glacier to calve.

However, in the early 1980s, Columbia Glacier began to surge at a pace as great as 115 ft (35 m) per day, calving icebergs into Prince William Sound much faster than snow compression on the ice field could replace it. It is thought that the melting ice created a cushion of water beneath the main ice sheet, allowing the glacier to progress without being impeded by the friction of ice against rock. As a result of the calving, however, the glacier has receded about 9 miles (15 km) since 1982 and can no longer be readily accessed by ferry. It calved so much ice that it choked the waters between its 3-mile- (5-km) wide face and its terminal moraine with large icebergs that froze together. Currently, this active glacier is most readily accessed on day cruises (check out www. stephenscruises.com) and private tour boats from Valdez.

Cruisers aboard a tour boat approaching Columbia Glacier, Prince William Sound

Display of a trapper's cabin, Valdez Museum

❺ Valdez

304 miles (487 km) E of Anchorage.
Transport map E4. 🛩 4,000. ✈
🚌 irregular service from Fairbanks.
🚢 from Whittier, Cordova.
ℹ️ 200 Chenega St, 835-4636.
🅦 valdezalaska.org

The most important town of
the Prince William Sound region,
Valdez was named after the bay
Port Valdez, which in turn, was
named by Spanish explorer Don
Salvador Fidalgo after Spanish
naval officer Antonio Valdes y
Basan in 1790. The town was
founded in 1897 about 4 miles
(6 km) east of its current
location as a jumping-off point
for prospectors heading to the
Klondike goldfields.

With the discovery of copper
in the Wrangell Mountains,
Cordova became the terminus
of the Copper River and
Northwestern Railway (see p187)
and Valdez slid into decline. In
the early 20th century, however,

Valdez became the terminus
for a wagon road to connect
the nearby Fort Liscum with
Fort Egbert on the Yukon River.
After the 1964 earthquake
utterly destroyed Old Valdez,
the town was rebuilt at its
present location.

As the northernmost ice-free
port in North America, it was
chosen to be the terminus of the
Trans-Alaska Pipeline (see p186),
which brought prosperity to the
town during its construction.

Modern Valdez enjoys a lovely
setting between
the mountains and
the sea. Day trips
and organized
cruises to north-
eastern Prince
William Sound pro-
vide good wildlife
viewing, including
sightings of whales,
seals, sea otters,
and birds around
Columbia Glacier.

Pipeline Workers'
Monument

🏛 Valdez Museum

217 Egan Dr. **Tel** 835-2764.
Open summer (Memorial Day to
Labor Day): 9am–5pm daily; winter:
noon–5pm Tue–Sun. 📷 ♿ 📸
Remembering Old Valdez: 436
S Hazelet Dr. **Tel** 835-5407. **Open**
summer only, 9am–5pm daily. 📷
♿ 🅦 valdezmuseum.org

This excellent museum, which
takes at least two hours to
explore fully, reveals the history
of Valdez and Prince William
Sound, as well as the Alaskan oil
industry. The museum's most
well-known display is probably
the 1886 hand-pumped Ahrens
steam fire engine, lovingly

Ahrens steam fire engine occupying pride
of place in Valdez Museum

polished and tended. A replica of
the Pipeline Workers' Monument,
dedicated to the men who built
the pipeline, is among the
displays. There are photographs
depicting the 1964 earthquake
and Valdez's rebirth as an oil
town, as well as Native artifacts
and mockups of an old miner's
cabin, a period photography
studio, and a historic 1880s bar.
The Exxon Valdez spill gets rather
minimal coverage.

The **Remembering Old
Valdez** exhibit, housed in an old
warehouse nearby, contains a
1:20 scale model of Old Valdez
as it appeared before the 1964
earthquake. It also has historic
vehicles and a high-tech exhibit
on earthquakes. A visit to the
actual site of Old Valdez, east of
town, gives a vivid idea of the
devastation that occurred there.

🏛 Whitney Museum

303 Lowe St. **Tel** 834-1690. **Open**
May–mid-Sep: 9am–7pm daily. ♿
♿ 🅦 mjwhitneymuseum.org

For more than half a century,
philanthropists Maxine and Jesse
Whitney traveled around the
villages of Alaska, buying art and
other items directly from
artists and craftsmen. In
the 1980s, they donated
their collection to the
Prince William Sound
Community College.
This museum is thought
to have the world's
largest private
collection of Native
Alaskan art, artifacts,
and stuffed wildlife.
It houses some of
the finest examples of
Inuit scrimshaw, as well
as a ship and an aircraft carved
entirely of ivory. One room is
filled with nothing but baskets,
another is dedicated to historic
Gold Rush exhibits, and yet
another to fascinating rocks
and minerals.

There is also an extensive
collection of Native dolls,
garments, weapons, masks, and
household implements. In
addition, the museum contains
larger exhibits such as an old
Inuit kayak with whale baleen
stays, a lovely Russian prayer rug,
and a sofa made of moose horn.

Hiking the challenging trail up to the face of Worthington Glacier

🦋 Keystone Canyon

Mile 12.8–Mile 15.9 on the
Richardson Highway.

This canyon was named
after the Keystone State
(Pennsylvania) by Captain
William Ralph Abercrombie,
following a failed 1884 expe-
dition to sail up the Copper
River to the Yukon. Keystone
Canyon contains both the
Richardson Highway, one of
Alaska's most scenic highways
and buried stretches of the
Alaska Pipeline.

East of Valdez, at Mile 13, two
great waterfalls spill down the
slopes into the slate-gray Lowe
River. A paved turnout provides
access to **Horsetail Falls**, north
of the highway. A bit farther
along, the lovely **Bridal Veil
Falls** tumble down into a deep,
rainbow-flanked pool. Farther

east, the highway climbs out
of the canyon into an alpine
landscape beneath the ice-
sculpted spires of the eastern
reaches of the Chugach Range.

🦋 Worthington Glacier

Mile 28.7 on the Richardson Highway .
📷 🔺 🅦 **alaskageographic.org**

The Worthington Glacier,
protected in the Worthington
Glacier State Recreation Site,
flows steeply down the icy peak
of the 6,130-ft- (1,840-m-) high
Girls Mountain in a series of

fingers that extend to within
430 yards (400 m) of the road.
Visitors can admire the scene
from below or follow the
challenging Ridge Trail up the
glacier's lateral moraine and right
to its face. There is an information desk and a small shop,
which also provides shelter.

The Blueberry Lake State
Recreation Site, 4 miles
(7 km) south of the glacier,
makes a great stop. North of
the campground is **Thompson
Pass**, Alaska's snowiest spot.

Spectacular cascade of Horsetail Falls,
Keystone Canyon

Exxon Valdez Oil Spill

On March 23, 1989, the tanker
Exxon Valdez, under the command
of Captain Joseph Hazelwood,
was forced to change course to
avoid an iceberg near the mouth
of Columbia Bay. The ship struck
Bligh Reef and started leaking oil.
As much as 11 million gallons (42
million liters) of oil spilled into the
sound. Clean-up crews were slow
to respond, and although disper-
sants were eventually applied, the
weather was too calm for them to
be effective. Even a week later,
only a few skimmer vessels had
been deployed. The oil contamin-
ated 1,500 miles (2,400 km) of

Cleaning an oil-covered bird after the
oil spill

coastline, killing fish, whales, seals, sea otters, and birds. Nearly 10,000
workers were employed to count dead wildlife and clean up the
sound and surrounding areas, often wiping the black sludge off rocks
by hand. The effort cost Exxon $1.25 billion. In 1991, the State of
Alaska and the federal government reached an out-of-court
settlement, requiring Exxon to pay $1 billion in restitution. In 1994, a
class-action suit awarded $5.2 billion in damages but Exxon appealed
and a much smaller settlement of $507m was granted in 2009.

❻ Cordova

50 miles (80 km) SE of Valdez.
Transport map E4. 🚟 2,200. ✈
🚢 Valdez, Whittier. ℹ 404 1st St,
424-7260. 🎭 Iceworm Festival (1st
weekend in Feb), Copper River Delta
Shorebird Festival (1st week of May),
Copper River Wild Salmon Festival
(late July). 🌐 **cityofcordova.net**

Smaller than nearby Valdez, rainy
little Cordova offers a slice of the
independent, self-suffcient
character of "old Alaska" that has
faded in more accessible places
along the road system. There is a
quiet charm in wandering its
steets or strolling past the fish
canneries. This scenic town is
linked to the outside world only
by plane or the ferries of the
Marine Highway.

Initially a Gold Rush town,
Cordova became the Copper
River and Northwestern Railway
railhead, linking the copper
mines at Kennicott *(see pp188–9)*
with the coast.

Snow-capped mountains overlooking the boat harbor, Cordova

Fisherman's Memorial

The railroad
functioned
until the mines
closed down in
1938. Although
Cordova was
badly damaged
by the 1964
earthquake, it
bounced back
as a fishing
town and is
known for its
Copper River reds,
prized salmon that are shipped
fresh to restaurants both inside
and outside Alaska.

🏛 Cordova Historical Museum

622 1st St. **Tel** 424-6665. **Open** late
May–early Sep: 10am–5pm Tue–Sat.
📷 ♿ 🎁 🌐 **cordovamuseum.org**
This small museum, housed in
the Centennial Building, features
several interesting exhibits. In
addition to works by Alaskan
artists, including painter Sydney
Laurence (who spent some time
in Cordova around 1900), the
museum houses an old skin-
covered canoe and a collection
of antique photographs. One
exhibit explains the effects of
the 1964 earthquake and
another showcases Cordova's

Iceworm Festival *(see p49)*, held
in February to relieve the stress
of wintertime cabin fever. There
is a thoughtful display on the
Copper River and Northwestern
Railway, along with examples of
copper jewelry and implements.
A video showcases high points
in the town's history.

🏛 Prince William Sound Science Center

Seafood Lane, Cordova Harbor.
Tel 424-5800. **Open** 8:30am–5:30pm
Mon–Fri. ♿ 🌐 **pwssc.org**
Founded immediately after the
1989 oil spill, this scientific base
at Cordova harbor's entrance is
home to teams of research
scientists studying the Prince
William Sound ecosystem.
The center offers a fine view
from the deck over-
looking the water.
The researchers
here can answer
questions and
provide insights
into the long-
term effects of the
Exxon Valdez oil
spill on the sound
and its ecology.
The center also
offers numerous
educational programs. These
include holding field trips and
science projects for families and

Logo, Prince William Sound
Science Center

adults, informative scientific
seminars in isolated communities around Prince William
Sound, and summer camps for
local schoolchildren.

🏛 Ilanka Cultural Center

110 Nicholoff Way. **Tel** 424-7903.
Open summer: 10am–5pm Mon–Fri;
winter: 10am–5pm Tue–Fri. 📷
donations accepted. ♿ 📷
🌐 **nveyak.com/ilanka-cultural-
center**
Situated opposite the
Fisherman's Memorial on
Nicholoff Way, the Ilanka
Cultural Center was founded to
preserve the culture of the Eyak
tribe, and in fact the last Native
speaker of the Eyak language
died in 2008. The Eyak people's
stories are told in an interesting
collection of artifacts
and photographs.
Other exhibits
include a complete
orca skeleton and a
contemporary
subsistence totem
pole. The work of
carver Mike Webber,
the pole is intended
to reflect the foods,
clothing, and dance
regalia of the tribe.
The center also provides studio
space for Eyak artisans to
produce their work.

❼ Copper River Highway

Transport map E4. 🏔 Childs Glacier.
Forest Service: 612 2nd St, Cordova;
424-7661. **W** fs.usda.gov/chugach

Million Dollar Bridge across the Copper River near Cordova

There is little to prepare visitors for the arresting beauty of the 48-mile (77-km) drive along the Copper River Highway between Cordova and the end of the road at the **Million Dollar Bridge**. Along the way, a number of short hiking trails and roadside views, as well as abundant wildlife and a few obligatory sights, will easily fill up a full day.

The gravel road, which is always open for visitors, and usually free of snow by late April, follows the roadbed of the historic Copper River and Northwestern Railway. At Mile 4, a marker provides information on its construction and history. At Mile 5.7, the road passes the Forest Service's **Eyak River Trail**, a 2-mile (3-km) hike, which includes a long boardwalk over muskeg. The variety of birdlife found here makes it a favorite walking trail of birders.

About 7 miles (11 km) north along a side road from Mile 13.7, a short walk leads onto the terminal moraine of **Sheridan Glacier**, with fine views of its blue ice. The steep 3-mile (5-km) Sheridan Ridge Trail climbs to a good view. After another 4 miles (6 km) along the highway, a rugged side route leads south to **Alaganik Slough**, which has a picnic site and a 990-ft (300-m) elevated boardwalk over a wetland. Vast watery views are on offer, replete with colorful wildflowers such as irises. Every summer, thousands of waterfowl, including 7 percent of the world's trumpeter swans, descend on this spot to nest, and countless shorebirds screech overhead.

Beginning around Mile 25 for 10 miles (16 km), the view from the road takes in more water than land as the route crosses the **Copper River Delta** over a series of bridges and causeways.

Once across the river, the road passes through birch and cottonwood forests to its end at the Million Dollar Bridge. This impressive structure, a part of the Copper River and Northwestern Railway, actually cost a million dollars to build in 1910. It had to be constructed in the winter to avoid the summer advance of the adjacent **Childs**

Wild iris at Alaganik Slough

and **Miles Glaciers**. The northernmost span collapsed in the 1964 earthquake and it took nearly 40 years of makeshift repairs to reopen it to traffic. The road, however, ends barely a mile or so farther on. Views from the bridge take in both Childs Glacier and the expansive Miles Glaciers, which has receded over a mile (2 km) since the bridge was built.

There is a small five-site campground at Childs Glacier, offering excellent views of the glacier face across the roiling gray Copper River. Campers here are treated to an all-night symphony of thunder-like booms and cracks as the glacier calves. Signs dotted around the area warn visitors that about once a year, the calving of large chunks into the water generates waves of up to 40 ft (12 m) that have been known to wash across the campground.

Childs Glacier near Million Dollar Bridge along the Copper River Highway

SOUTHEAST ALASKA

Nature prevails throughout the Panhandle, a narrow 400-mile (640-km) strip of islands and coastline that reaches southeastward from the Alaskan mainland. The spectacular scenery of Southeast Alaska, from the threaded passageways of the Alexander Archipelago to the rugged Coast Mountains, combines with its easy accessibility to make it one of Alaska's most visited regions.

For the Tlingit, Haida, and Tsimshian peoples who have inhabited this area for thousands of years, Southeast Alaska has provided not only beauty, but also bounty – seas full of fish, wildlife to hunt, and a wealth of enormous trees to provide wood for homes and boats. When the first Russians arrived, the Native peoples fought to defend their homeland, but were ultimately forced to accept the inevitable political, economic, and lifestyle changes that were introduced by the newcomers.

Fortunately, many of the traditional ways of the Native peoples have been preserved, not only in museums, but in villages with significant indigenous populations. Several towns, especially Wrangell and Sitka, have grown around Russian forts, while the discovery of gold was the impetus for the creation of Juneau and Skagway. In 1900, the discovery of gold near Juneau along with its strategic location along the Klondike route led to its becoming the capital of Alaska, taking over from Sitka. Other towns, such as Ketchikan and Petersburg, grew around fisheries, canneries, and timber mills.

Today, Southeast Alaska is the favored venue for most Alaska cruises (see pp38–9), and the region sees large numbers of visitors each summer. With local economies increasingly dependent upon tourism, ports such as Ketchikan, Skagway, and Sitka cater to cruise ship passengers with a variety of day tours and shopping opportunities. A limited number of ships are also permitted to enter Glacier Bay National Park, a UNESCO World Heritage Site, with its renowned whale-watching and glacier viewing opportunities.

Tour boat passengers admiring a glacier in Glacier Bay National Park and Preserve

◀ St. Michael's Russian Orthodox Cathedral in Sitka

Exploring Southeast Alaska

The Southeast, often the first part of the state seen by visitors traveling north, is archetypal Alaska. The main towns – bustling Ketchikan, beautiful Sitka, friendly little Wrangell, and Juneau, the capital – enjoy spectacular settings along narrow ocean channels next to rainforested slopes and glaciated peaks. The Tongass National Forest covers almost the entire region, including lush Prince of Wales Island and Misty Fiords National Monument. Anan Creek Wildlife Observatory and Admiralty Island National Monument offer excellent bear viewing, while Glacier Bay National Park and Juneau Icefield provide awe-inspiring vistas.

Totem pole topped by a bald eagle at Saxman Totem Park near Ketchikan

Creek Street above Ketchikan Creek, Ketchikan

Getting Around

The best way to get around Southeast Alaska is by plane, both on the scheduled flights that connect Skagway, Juneau, Sitka, Wrangell, Petersburg, and Ketchikan, and the floatplanes that fly to remote homesteads and lodges. The Alaska Marine Highway is a lifeline, with ferries connecting most towns. Other companies provide access to Prince of Wales Island and Glacier Bay National Park. Although Haines, Skagway, and Hyder are linked to the Canadian highway system, the lack of continuous roads within the region means that cars are not very helpful in getting around, except along the limited highways around individual towns.

For hotels and restaurants see pp242–5 and pp250–55

Sights at a Glance

Towns, Cities, and Islands

- ❶ Ketchikan
- ❷ Metlakatla
- ❹ Hyder
- ❺ Prince of Wales Island
- ❻ Wrangell
- ❽ Petersburg
- ❿ Sitka
- ⓫ Tenakee Springs
- ⓭ *Juneau pp142–5*
- ⓯ Haines
- ⓰ Skagway
- ⓴ Yakutat

National and State Parks

- ❸ Misty Fiords National Monument
- ❼ Anan Creek Wildlife Observatory
- ⓬ Admiralty Island National Monument
- ⓮ *Glacier Bay National Park and Preserve pp146–7*

Areas of Natural Beauty

- ❾ Mitkof Highway
- ⓳ Tatshenshini-Alsek Rivers

Tours

- ⓱ *Gold Rush Routes pp152–3*
- ⓲ *Haines Cut-Off Tour p154*

Malaspina Glacier

Yakutat Bay

20 YAKUTAT

TATSHENSHINI ALSEK RIVERS

Gulf of Alas

The cloud-obscured eastern cliffs of Glacier Bay National Park

Key

══ Highway

═══ Minor road

– – – Alaska Marine Highway

▬▬ International border

△ Peak

0 km _____ 50
0 miles _____ 50

HAINES **18** CUT-OFF TOUR

GOLD RUSH **17** ROUTES

16 SKAGWAY

15 HAINES

GLACIER BAY NATIONAL PARK AND PRESERVE

14 Gustavus

Juneau Icefield

Saint Therese Shrine

Mendenhall Glacier

13 JUNEAU
Douglas

Spencer

Elfin Cove

Hoonah

12

Chichagof Island

Admiralty Island

Pelican

11 TENAKEE SPRINGS

Angoon

Kruzof Is

10 SITKA

Baranof Island

Chatham Strait

Frederick Sound

Kake

Kupreanof Island

8 PETERSBURG

Tongass National Forest

9 MITKOF HWY

WRANGELL **6**

Coast Mountains

Mt Willibert 6,759 ft

Point Baker

Port Alexander

Cape Ommaney

Christian Sound

Wrangell Island

7 ANAN CREEK WILDLIFE OBSERVATORY

Coffman Cove

Cleveland Peninsula

Meyers Chuck

Coronation Is

Klawock

Craig

Hollis

Revillagigedo Island

5

4 HYDER

Misty Fjords National Monument

1 KETCHIKAN

Saxman

Noyes Is

Baker Is

Hydaburg

Kasaan

2 METLAKATLA

3

Prince of Wales Island

Alexander Archipelago

Dall Is

For additional map symbols see back flap

Cruise ship anchored at Ketchikan, a popular stop on cruise routes

● Ketchikan

235 miles (378 km) S of Juneau.
Transport map F5. 🛪 8,000. ✈
🚢 Bellingham–Skagway. ℹ 131
Front St, 225-6166, (800) 770-3300. 🎨
Blueberry Arts Festival (1st weekend
in Aug). 🌐 **visit-ketchikan.com**

Situated on the southwestern
end of Revillagigedo Island,
Ketchikan likes to call itself
Alaska's First City, because it is
the first Alaskan city that visitors
see when arriving on a cruise
ship or ferry.

Originally a Tlingit fish camp
called Kitschk-Hin (meaning
"thundering eagle wings
creek"), the town's growth
started in 1885 when Irishman
Mike Martin staked a claim near
Ketchikan Creek and set up a
fish cannery. By the 1930s, the
town's dozen canneries had
earned it the title Salmon
Capital of the World. Its other
big economic resource, the
Ketchikan Pulp Company's
paper mill at Ward Cove,
operated for over 40 years until
it shut down in 1997.

Despite that major loss,
Ketchikan bounced back. Today,
Alaska's fourth largest city
thrives as a major stop for cruise
ships and as a regional service
center. Built on pilings, the city
center lies along the waterfront,
while older neighborhoods
climb the slopes of nearby hills
accessible by steep streets and
wooden staircases.

🏛 Great Alaskan Lumberjack Show

Spruce Mill Way. **Tel** 225-9050.
🚌 Ketchikan city bus. **Open** May–
Sep: four shows daily when cruise
ships are in port. 🎨 🐕 🏠
🌐 **lumberjacksports.com**

Held in an amphitheater on
the site of the old Ketchikan
Spruce Mill, this lively show
displays hand-sawing, tree-
climbing, and log-rolling. It
is all done in a spirit of fun,
and the actors and lumberjack
competitors are so engaging
that much of the audience
seems happy to participate.
The original 1898 mill was
the world's largest spruce
mill and provided work for
lumberjacks who prepared
timber to be used during the
Gold Rush, for building aircraft
during World War II, and for
local canneries. The mill finally
closed in 1993.

🏛 Southeast Alaska Discovery Center

50 Main St. **Tel** 228-6220. 🚌
Ketchikan city bus. **Open** May–Sep:
8am–5pm Mon–Sat, 8am–4pm
Sun; Oct–Apr: 12:30–7pm Fri. 🎨
🐕 🏠 🌐 **alaskacenters.gov/ketchikan.cfm**

Both a museum and a visitors'
center for the 26,000-sq mile
(68,000-sq km) Tongass National
Forest, the lush temperate
rainforest which covers the
region, the Southeast Alaska
Discovery Center is a mine of
information. Totem poles from
the region's three main Native
cultures, Tlingit, Haida, and
Tsimshian are displayed, and the
historical, cultural, natural, and
economic story of Southeast
Alaska is told through exhibits.
Other displays feature traditional
Tlingit salmon-drying, forest
ecosystems, and local fishing
techniques such as purse sein-
ing, gillnetting, and trawling.

Silver salmon sculptures at the Southeast
Alaska Discovery Center

🚪 Creek Street

🚌 Ketchikan city bus. 🎨 🖥
🏠 **Dolly's House Open** May–Sep:
8am–5pm daily when cruise ships
are in port. 🎨

A pedestrian boardwalk built on
pilings over Ketchikan Creek,
Creek Street was the town's red-
light district for half a century.

Dolly's House built on the pilings of Creek Street

For hotels and restaurants see pp242–5 and pp250–55

In the early 1900s, well-heeled newcomers to the north side of town decided to clean up the neighborhood by banishing the "working girls" to the south side. Creek Street was soon notorious for its bars and bordellos, and it was here that Frenchie, Black Mary, and Dolly Arthur plied their trade.

Most of their houses have been turned into shops and eateries, but **Dolly's House** is now a museum. Visitors learn interesting facts about those bawdy days, such as how Creek Street's construction lent itself to surreptitious trap-door deliveries of alcohol after it was banned by the 1917 Bone Dry Law.

The street is a perfect spot to watch spawning salmon swim upstream. Visitors can also take the funicular from the end of the street up to the Cape Fox Lodge or follow the Married Man's Trail, once used by men hoping for a clandestine Creek Street encounter.

Totems along a forest walkway, Totem Bight State Historical Park

🏛 Saxman Totem Park

2 miles (4 km) S of Ketchikan at Mile 2.5, S Tongass Hwy. **Tel** 225-4846. 🚌 Ketchikan city bus. **Open** daily in summer. 🛒 ♿ 📷
🌐 capefoxtours.com

Founded in 1894, the Native village of Saxman today has the finest display of totem poles in Southeast Alaska. The village was settled by Tlingit from the villages of Tongass and Cape Fox at the southern tip of Alaska, who were persuaded to move here by Presbyterian missionaries. Begun in the late 1930s as a Civilian Conservation Corps (CCC) project, Saxman Totem Park has grown into a popular attraction. In addition to the renovated poles brought from surrounding villages, there is the colorful Beaver Clan House and the Frog Wall, which features dozens of frog faces. A large carving shed houses the workshops of Alaska's best totem carvers.

🏛 Totem Bight State Historical Park

10 miles (16 km) N of Ketchikan. ℹ 9883 North Tongass Hwy, 247-8574. 🚌 Ketchikan city bus. ♿ 📷
🌐 dnr.alaska.gov/parks/units/totembgh.htm

As Europeans established permanent settlements in Southeast Alaska, many Natives joined them, and their traditional villages fell into ruins. In 1938, the CCC launched a project to restore old totem poles that lay rotting in abandoned villages. Native carvers were hired to re-create the damaged poles, which were placed in a forested site near the Tongass Narrows, and by 1942, 15 poles and a clan house had been completed. In 1970, Totem Bight was designated a State Historical Park. Today, a walkway between the totems leads to the water and a replica clan house that once would have held 30 to 50 people.

Detail of a totem pole at Saxman Totem Park near Ketchikan

Totem Poles

Alaska's Tlingit, Haida, and Tsimshian peoples carve at least six types of totem poles to support buildings, tell stories, and honor people or special events. Never meant to be objects of veneration, poles were cultural symbols, carved of western red cedar with designs that included stylized clan totems, such as Raven, Beaver, Frog, Bear, Wolf, and Killer Whale, and painted in symbolic colors. Due to the iron tools gained by trade with Europeans, the mid-19th century saw an especially prolific carving period. This ended with the arrival of missionaries in the late 19th century, who discouraged pole raisings and potlatches, the gifting feasts that accompanied them. Pole carving was revived in the 1930s by the CCC, which launched a project to restore old poles and commission locals to carve new ones. Today, master carvers still create poles and pass on the craft to apprentices.

Metlakatla's boat harbor on Annette Island

❷ Metlakatla

18 miles (29 km) SW of Ketchikan.
Transport map F5. 🚉 1,400.
✈ Ketchikan. ⛴ from Ketchikan.
ℹ 886-8687. 🌐 **metlakatla.com**

Located on Annette Island southwest of Ketchikan, Metlakatla was founded in 1887 by Scottish clergyman Father Duncan. After falling out with the church in Old Metlakatla, Canada, he fled to Annette Island with over 800 of his Tsimshian followers (see p27). In 1891, the US Congress gave them possession of the island. Because the Tsimshian rejected ANCSA in the early 1970s (see p60), they retained their sovereignty, and Annette Island is now Alaska's only Indian reservation, with an economy dependent on fishing and the timber industry.

Sign, Annette Island Reserve

Metlakatla's main appeal lies in its quiet, small-town atmosphere. The **Duncan**

Cottage Museum contains Father Duncan's educational and medical materials, musical instruments, and a phonograph built by Thomas Edison himself. The **Le Sha'as Tsimshian** clan house is worth a visit to watch dance performances and totem carvers at work. There's also a pleasant, short hike up Yellow Hill for great Inside Passage views.

❸ Misty Fiords National Monument

22 miles (35 km) E of Ketchikan.
Transport map F5. ✈ charter floatplane from Ketchikan.
🌐 **fs.usda.gov/tongass**

Misty Fiords is a hidden gem, not only because it is little-known outside the Southeast, but also because it's often hidden in rain behind a bank of clouds. Characterized by wild fjords, alpine lakes, roaring water-falls, rainforests, snowy peaks, and soaring 3,000-ft (915-m) granite cliffs, the site was first

identified in the 1793 journals of Captain George Vancouver, one of Captain Cook's lieutenants. The profuse wildlife includes bears, deer, mountain goats, bald eagles, and whales.

Many travelers opt for boat and floatplane tours, such as the boat-in, fly-out tour organized by **Allen Marine Tours**.

Allen Marine Tours
519 W 4th Ave, Anchorage.
Tel 225-8100, (877) 686-8100.
🌐 **allenmarinetours.com**

❹ Hyder

2 miles (4 km) W of Stewart (Canada), 75 miles (120 km) E of Ketchikan.
Transport map F5. 🚉 90.
✈ Stewart. ⛴ Stewart–Terrace.
ℹ 5th Ave, Stewart, (250) 636-9224.
🎪 International Stewart and Hyder Rodeo (2nd week in Jun), International Days (1st weekend in Jul).

Isolated from the rest of Alaska by a roadless range of moun-tains, Hyder sits on the US border at the end of Canada Route 37A. Despite the fact that it works on Canadian time, has a Canadian phone code, and sends its children to Canadian schools, it enjoys a very Alaskan atmosphere.

For visitors, the town is an attraction in itself, with its his-toric buildings and more bars per capita than any town in Alaska. The scenic but rough 25-mile- (40-km-) long **Granduc Road** heads north from Hyder, following the Salmon River past old gold mines to a grand view of Salmon Glacier. The area also has a large number of brown bears, and salmon crowd the streams in summer.

New Eddystone Rock rising from Behm Canal in the atmospheric Misty Fiords National Monument

For hotels and restaurants see pp242–5 and pp250–55

Alaska's Temperate Rainforests

Characterized by lush, rain-soaked mosses, lichens, shrubs, and ferns sheltering beneath enormous coniferous trees, the forests of Southeast Alaska make up the northern extent of the world's largest temperate rainforest. Much cooler than their tropical counterparts, temperate rainforests have climatic conditions that are marked by average summer temperatures of less than 16° C (61° F), a cool dormant season, and at least 55 inches (140 cm) of precipitation per year. At the southern end of the Panhandle, the rainfall can exceed 200 inches (508 cm) per year, but moving north, it decreases to around 60 inches (150 cm) near Juneau. The most prominent trees in Alaska's rainforest are the Sitka spruce and western hemlock, followed by mountain hemlock, yellow cedar, and western red cedar. Rarer conifers include mountain juniper, subalpine and silver fir, and Pacific yew.

Rainforest trees typically live from 200 to 1,000 years. When they fall, they decompose into a rich organic material that nourishes vegetation.

Ferns prefer moist conditions with low levels of light and thrive under the temperate rainforest cover.

Flora and Fauna

Alaska's temperate rainforest includes a canopy composed of tall coniferous trees, while smaller shade-loving trees and shrubs make up the understory. On the damp, shady forest floor grow ferns and large-leafed plants. Fauna species include river otters, pine martens, and boreal toads.

Devil's Club, a spiny plant, dominates the floor of the rainforest where little sunlight filters through.

Sitka black-tailed deer, endemic to the region, feed on the native hemlock, berries, and lichens.

Porcupines, second in size to beavers among Alaskan rodents, are nocturnal animals.

The Tongass National Forest, the world's largest temperate rainforest, covers the Southeast Alaskan mainland and over 1,000 islands, and includes Wrangell Narrows, a narrow waterway between Mitkof and Kupreanof Islands.

Epiphytic mosses and lichens draw nutrients and moisture directly from the air, using the host trees just for support.

❺ Prince of Wales Island

Named for the son of King George III by Captain George Vancouver in 1793, Prince of Wales Island lies mostly within the Tongass National Forest. The third largest island in the US after Hawaii and Kodiak, it is home to both the Haida and Tlingit peoples, as well as a number of outsiders attracted by its beauty and solitude. It is laced with 1,400 miles (2,240 km) of old logging roads, half of which are passable by cars. One of the most interesting activities here is simply to drive through the forests and muskeg of the interior. Access to the island is either by ferry from Ketchikan or Wrangell, or by floatplane.

Densely forested islets off Prince of Wales Island

Craig

90 miles (145 km) W of Ketchikan. 🚶 1,200. ✈ charter floatplane. ⛴ to Hollis. ℹ 300 A, Easy St, 755-2626. 🌐 **princeofwalescoc.org**

The largest town on the island, Craig is also its only community without a Native majority. It was named for Craig Millar who, with the help of local Haida, set up the first saltery on Fish Egg Island in 1907, followed by a sawmill and a salmon cannery. Due to poor salmon runs, fishing declined in the 1950s, but in 1972, the large Head Sawmill, north of Craig, boosted the town's faltering economy. Today, Craig is the island's service center, with a bank, hotel, gas station, and several restaurants.

Klawock

5 miles (8 km) N of Craig. 🚶 750. ✈ ⛴ to Hollis. ℹ Mile 23.4, Hollis–Craig Hwy, 755-2626.

Named for the first Tlingit settler, Kloo-wah, the village of Klawock was originally a summer fishing camp. A trading post and saltery were set up here in 1868, and a decade later, it became the site of Alaska's first salmon cannery. Today, the town boasts a hatchery on the shores of Klawock Lake, a sawmill, a log-sorting yard, and a dock for loading timber. In keeping with the timber theme, electricity is provided by a wood-fired generator.

Klawock Totem Park, next to the town library, has about 20 restored poles from Tuxekan, a Tlingit winter village to the north. Across the Hollis-Craig highway from the Chamber of Commerce is the Gaan Ax Adi Clan House, with a carving shed where visitors may sometimes see new totems being carved. The airport, the only one on the island, has an unattended 6,000-ft (1,800-m) paved runway with pilot-controlled lighting, remarkable given its location.

Key

═══ Minor road

0 km   30

0 miles   30

Tlingit totem poles in the village of Klawock

Students paddling a traditional Haida canoe that they have carved

Hydaburg

45 miles (72 km) SE of Craig. 🚶 380. ✈ charter floatplane.

As rural Alaskan towns go, the little Haida village of Hydaburg is as picturesque as it gets. Although the town was not founded until 1912, when the three villages of Sukkwan, Howkan and Klinkwan combined, Haida peoples have occupied the area since the 18th century, when they migrated from British Columbia. Today, the town has the largest Haida population in Alaska.

Hydaburg's totem park is well worth a visit. Its collection of restored totems, with their unique emphasis on pastel colors, stands apart from others in the region.

Thorne Bay

39 miles (63 km) NE of Craig. 🚶 480. ✈ floatplane from Ketchikan. 🏕

Nestled between rolling hills and the sea, Thorne Bay was named in honor of Frank Manley Thorn, superintendent of the US Coast and Geodetic Survey in the 1880s. During its heyday in the mid-20th century, Thorne Bay was North America's largest logging camp, but the mill closed in the 1990s and the economy now depends on fishing.

A popular visitor attraction here is the **Honker River Canoe Route**, which begins at Coffman Cove Road and winds through a chain of lakes down to Thorne Bay. The area also has several campsites, forest service cabins, hiking trails, and picnic areas.

Kasaan

49 miles E of Craig. 🚶 55. ✈ charter floatplane.

Deriving its name from the Tlingit word for "pretty town," Kasaan does indeed have a lovely setting between forested mountains and the sea. It was founded in 1892 when mining and fishing jobs attracted the Haida here from the now-abandoned Old Kasaan. Today, most Kasaan residents depend on their harvests of deer, fish, shrimp, and crab.

In the 1930s, the Haida Chief Sonihat built the Whale clan house, and the various totems around the village were transferred to the same site, forming the **Kasaan Totem Park**. A 15-minute trail through beachside woods leads to the park, where the decaying poles and clan house, almost swallowed by the undergrowth and unspoilt by commercial trappings, lend an authentic air to the picturesque scene.

El Capitan Cave

Mile 50, N Prince of Wales Rd. **Tel** 828-3304. ✈ **Open** mid-May–early Sep: Mon–Sat. 🅿 🎫 mandatory, at 9am, noon, & 3pm: book 2 days in advance.

Sited northwest of Whale Pass, El Capitan Cave is the largest and longest of the limestone caves dotted around the karst region of northern Prince of Wales Island. In these caves, paleontologists have uncovered human remains dating back about 9,500 years, the oldest found in the region. A 12,300-year-old brown bear skeleton was discovered in El Capitan Cave, while a more remote cave yielded a 45,000-year-old bear skeleton.

Over 2 miles (3 km) of passageways in El Capitan Cave have been surveyed. Guided tours using helmets and headlamps are offered. Reservations must be made two days in advance, but rare walk-ins are allowed. Young children under 7 years are not allowed in the cave. The tour begins with a steep climb up 367 steps, and a fair degree of physical fitness is required.

Forestry in Southeast Alaska

Since the late 19th century, forestry and forest products have been an economic factor in the Tongass National Forest, and from the 1940s to 1990s, they were the mainstay of Alaska's economy. The prime western hemlock and Sitka spruce of Southeast Alaska were exported, while lower quality timber was reduced to pulp for the paper industry. In the 1990s, economic and environmental pressures combined with decreasing harvest limits caused the closure of the Sitka and Ketchikan mills. Today the industry plays only a minor role in Alaska's economy.

Worker adjusting truckload of logs for delivery

For hotels and restaurants see pp242–5 and pp250–55

Wrangell's harbor against the backdrop of the Coast Mountains

❻ Wrangell

80 miles (128 km) N of Ketchikan.
Transport map F5. 🚄 2,400. ✈
from Ketchikan. 🚢 from Ketchikan,
Petersburg, or Juneau. ℹ Nolan
Center, 296 Campbell Drive, 874-
2829/800-367-9745. 🔺 🖼 Stikine
River Birding Festival (early May).
Ⓦ wrangell.com

Founded as Redoubt St. Dionysius
in 1833 by the Russians, the
original fort on this site was
intended to protect Russian fur
trading interests from the British
and Spanish. The local Tlingit,
under Chief Shakes V, recognized the economic benefits of
cooperation with the Russians
and joined them at the redoubt
in 1834. In the same year, combined Tlingit and Russian forces
managed to repel the British
forces led by Peter Skeen Odgen,
who had attempted to establish
a fur trading post. In 1868,
following Alaska's transfer to the
US, the Americans established a
military fort that they named
after the head of the Russian-
American Company, Baron
Ferdinand von Wrangel.

Today, Wrangell is a friendly
little town, attracting a few
adventurous visitors and a
handful of small cruise ships in
the summer. The real draw is the
Stikine River, just outside town,
as well as Anan Creek and
outlying parts of Wrangell
Island, both popular for wildlife
viewing. From the town, forest

roads lead to free campgrounds,
the best of which are at Nemo
Point, 14 miles (22 km) south,
offering wonderful high altitude
views over Zimovia Strait.

🏛 Wrangell Museum
Nolan Center, 296
Campbell Drive. **Tel** 874-
3770. **Open** May–Sep:
10am–5pm Mon–Sat;
Oct–Apr: noon–5pm Fri &
Sat. ♿ 🅿 🏠

Housed in the same
building as the town's
visitor information
office and convention
center, the Wrangell
Museum contains a
wonderful collection of
artifacts. The large entryway
features the original
17th-century houseposts of the
Frog Clan from the Tlingit Tribal

Tlingit housepost,
Wrangell Museum

House on Chief Shakes Island.
Electronic lighting on the
ceiling of the lobby simulates
the undulations of the aurora
borealis. Museum displays
begin with the natural history
of the region and proceed
chronologically
through exhibits on
Native culture, the fur
trade, military history,
the Stikine Gold Rush,
fishing, and forestry.
The museum is also a
repository for thou-
sands of historic
images and numerous
audio and video
records, which are
available for viewing.

🏠 Chief Shakes Island
Shakes St.
Accessible by a wooden walkway
across an arm of the harbor, Chief
Shakes Island is a park and a
repository for Tlingit totems
dating from 1840 to 1940.
Opened in 1940 and restored in
2013, the large replica **Tlingit
Tribal House**, a National Historic
Site, was named Ck! Udatc Hit
("House of Many Faces") in
reference to the human visages
in its design. Inside are replica
houseposts of the Frog Clan, and
dotted around the park are
several distinctive totems. The
peaceful park overlooks the
picturesque harbor, and on
sunny days, its green lawns
provide a perfect place to relax.

Totem pole and Tlingit Tribal House on
Chief Shakes Island

◀ The beautiful town of Sitka, on the west coast of Baranof Island

🗿 Petroglyph Beach State Historic Site

Half a mile (1 km) N of Wrangell at Grave St. **Open** 24 hrs. 🚻 limited.

Archeologists believe that an ancient culture already occupied the Wrangell area before the modern-day Tlingit arrived. Evidence suggests that these early groups were here around 10,000 years ago, at the end of the last Ice Age, and that they established subsequent settlements 5,000 and 3,000 years ago. It is thought that these early people made some of the 40 petroglyphs that adorn the rocks of the beach. However, the artwork reveals little information about their culture, except that the simplest spiral and sun designs match petroglyphs found as far away as South America. The petroglyphs of wolves, bears, and orcas found on the same beach were probably carved by the Tlingit. Most of the petroglyphs, carved on boulders scattered along several hundred feet of beach, have been eroded over time by the sea. A visitors' platform provides access to the beach, where the state has reproduced the most interesting petroglyphs to allow visitors to make rubbings of the carvings without damaging the originals.

Petroglyph of a fish on a boulder

🐟 Stikine River

🚤 tour boats. 🛶 ⛰ 🏔

The glacier-fed Stikine River is the biggest draw for visitors to Wrangell. Originating in the mountains of British Columbia, the 360-mile (576-km) river flows through 30 miles (48 km) of the Stikine-LeConte Wilderness on the Alaskan mainland to its mouth across the narrows near Wrangell.

Several companies organize jetboat tours, which head upstream through spectacular mountain scenery and past waterfalls and the iceberg choked face of Shakes Glacier. There is a delightful lunch spot here, overlooking the glacier. There are also good

Kayaking in the blue waters of the Stikine River

opportunities to see harbor seals, black bears, spawning salmon, and the world's largest summer concentration of bald eagles. A popular destination is **Chief Shakes Hot Springs**, where open-air hot tubs offer soaking in a wild setting.

⛳ Muskeg Meadows Golf Course

Mile 0.5, Ishiyama Dr. **Tel** 874-4653. or phone for pickup from town. **Open** Apr–Nov: 9am–6pm. 🏌 💻 🌐 **wrangellalaskagolf.com**

The non-profit Wrangell Golf Club was established in 1993 to carve a nine-hole, par 36 course from the muskeg bog for which it was named. From 1995 to 1998, volunteers laid wood pulp to create the fairways, planted grass, and installed the greens, resulting in a beautiful course set amid spruce and cedar rainforest. This is the world's only golf course with a rule that states that if a raven steals a golf ball, it can be replaced without penalty, provided the golfer has a witness.

❼ Anan Creek Wildlife Observatory

31 miles (50 km) S of Wrangell. **Transport map** F5. **Tel** 874-2323. ✈ by floatplane. 🚤 tour boat. **Open** year-round. 🏕 ⛰ book in advance. Permits: required Jul 5–Aug 25, book at 🌐 **fs.usda.gov/tongass**

Located on the Cleveland Peninsula, Anan Creek is the site of one of Alaska's greatest pink salmon runs. The fish are slowed by a waterfall half a mile (1 km) inland, which attracts large numbers of hungry brown and black bears. Adjacent to the falls, a wildlife observatory, which is actually a large viewing platform, allows visitors close-up views of the feeding bears. During the salmon run, sea otters, harbor seals, and bald eagles can also be spotted along the shore near the mouth of Anan Creek.

While wildlife is usually visible all summer, permits are needed to visit the observatory in July and August. Only 60 permits are issued for each day. Four permits are also available for those staying at the nearby Anan Bay public use cabin – the only accommodation available in the area. However, local tour operators pre-book permits and make them available to visitors on their tours.

Black bear feeding with cub at the rapidly flowing Anan Creek

Houses built on pilings above Hammer Slough in Petersburg

❽ Petersburg

32 miles (51 km) N of Ketchikan.
Transport map F5. 🚗 3,000. ✈
from Ketchikan, Wrangell & Juneau.
🚢 from Ketchikan, Sitka, Wrangell, &
Juneau. 🛈 1st & Fram St, 772-4636.
🎭 Little Norway Festival (weekend
nearest May 17). 🌐 **petersburg.org**

Named for Norwegian settler
Peter Buschmann, Petersburg
nestles on sheltered Mitkof
Island beside a calm sea.
Buschmann, who arrived to
homestead in the area in 1890,
initiated the development of
the town. By 1900, realizing that
glacier ice could be used to
preserve fish, he set up the Icy
Strait Packing Company
cannery. By the 1920s, jobs
created by the town's businesses had attracted over 600
people. Petersburg now has
crab, shrimp, salmon, and
herring fisheries, as well as
Alaska's largest halibut fleet.
Petersburg enjoys spectacular

mountain views that include
the precipitous Devil's Thumb,
towering at 9,077 ft (2,767 m)
and straddling the Canadian
border about 40 miles (64 km)
away. The major attractions for
visitors are the beautiful
hinterlands of Mitkof Island and
neighboring Kupreanof Island,
which offer superb hiking,
camping, fishing, boating,
and kayaking.

🚏 Sing Lee Alley

Built on pilings above
Hammer Slough, this
picturesque board-
walk is one of
Petersburg's oldest
historic streets. At
No. 23, the distinctive
Sons of Norway Hall,
built by Norwegian
immigrants in 1912,
has graceful decorative scroll
paintings called *rosemaling* on
its facade. The adjacent Bojer
Wikan Fishermen's Memorial

Park features a statue of Bojer
Wikan, a local fisherman lost at
sea. The replica Viking ship
Valhalla, used in the Little
Norway Festival, is kept here.
The street also has a pleasant
café and bookshop.

Bojer Wikan statue,
Sing Lee Alley

🏛 Clausen Memorial Museum

203 Fram St. **Tel** 772-3598.
Open May–early Sep:
10am–5pm Mon–Sat. **Closed**
public holidays. 🅿 📷
🌐 **clausen museum.net**

The compact Clausen
Memorial Museum
showcases the history
and culture of the
Petersburg and
Kupreanof Island area.
Besides a replica of a
1970s-era fish packer's
office, it features a fish
trap, a collection of old nautical
and fishing gear, and a Tlingit
dugout canoe. The most
popular exhibit, however,
representing every angler's
dream, is the 125-lb (56-kg)
stuffed king salmon.

❾ Mitkof Highway

Transport map F5. 🛈 12 N Nordic
Dr, 772-3871. 🏔 🌐 **fs.fed.us/r10/
tongass/districts/petersburg**

The scenic Mitkof Highway
follows the coastline from
Petersburg to the southern end
of Mitkof Island. At Mile 14.5, a
lovely boardwalk trail crosses

Sons of Norway Hall with the Viking ship *Valhalla*, Sing Lee Alley

the muskeg to access some picnic spots and the salmon run at **Blind River Rapids**. Wintering trumpeter swans can be seen from mid-October to December at the Swan Observatory at Mile 16. Not far ahead, at Mile 18, the Crystal Lake Hatchery and Blind Slough Recreation Area offer scenic picnic sites.

The beautiful **Man Made Hole** at Mile 20 was once a quarry that has filled with water to form a lake. A gentle trail winds around its perimeter on boardwalks and gravel. At Mile 22, the pretty Ohmer Creek Campground offers visitors free camping at the island's only public campsite.

❿ Sitka

See pp140–41.

Brightly painted houses at Tenakee Springs flanking the calm inlet

⓫ Tenakee Springs

48 miles (78 km) N of Sitka. **Transport map** E5. 🚠 130. 🚢 Sitka–Juneau. 🛈 736-2207. Bathhouse: at ferry dock. **Open** men: 2–6pm & 10pm–9am daily; women: 9am–2pm & 6–10pm daily. 🅦 tenakeespringsak.com

Situated on the eastern shores of Chichagof Island, the village of Tenakee Springs takes its name from the Tlingit Tinaghu, meaning "Copper Shield Bay," after three prized copper shields that were lost in a storm in Tenakee Inlet.

Historically, the town's main attraction was the 42° C (108° F) hot spring, which made the area bearable in all seasons. In 1895, a **Bathhouse** was built to enclose the spring, and 1899

Mud flats and forests on Admiralty Island

saw the launch of Snyder's Mercantile, which is still run as a general store.

Modern Tenakee Springs is a community of retirees, residents, and weekend visitors from Juneau, stretching along a single picturesque street. Vehicles are not allowed and most people walk in town.

⓬ Admiralty Island National Monument

43 miles (70 km) NE of Sitka. **Transport map** F5. 🛩 charter float-plane from Juneau. 🚢 Sitka–Angoon; tour boat Juneau–Pack Creek. 🛈 586-8800. 🏞 🛶 ⛺ ⚠ Permits required to visit Pack Creek Jun–mid-Sep.

Called Kootznoowoo (meaning "Fortress of Bears") by the Tlingit people, Admiralty Island National Monument sprawls across 1,492 sq miles (3,865 sq km). Lying within the Tongass National Forest,

almost 98 percent of this lush rainforest is a designated wilderness area. The main site of interest for wildlife enthusiasts is **Pack Creek** in the Stan Price State Wildlife Sanctuary at the island's northeast corner. This area is home to the world's densest population of brown bears. Sitka black-tailed deer can be seen along the shore, and Mitchell, Hood, Chaik, and Whitewater Bays contain porpoises, seals, and sea lions. Summer access to the tidal estuary and bear-viewing tower is by permit only; permits can be booked online at www.recreation.gov.

The sole settlement on the island is **Angoon**, a small Native village accessible via the Marine Highway. Kayakers and canoeists will enjoy the **Cross-Island Canoe Route**, which connects Angoon with Mole Harbor, on the island's eastern shore, by a series of lakes, streams, and portages.

Little Norway

Peter Buschmann's success in Petersburg inspired many of his countrymen to follow him to Alaska in search of fjords, fishing, and opportunity. Nicknamed Little Norway, the town reflects its Norwegian heritage in the decorative details on buildings and the souvenirs on offer. On the weekend nearest Norwegian Independence Day on May 17, the town celebrates the Little Norway Festival *(see p46)* with a Norwegian feast and *bunad* (traditional dress) fashion show. The *Valhalla* leads a parade of revelers clad in Norwegian flags and Viking attire. Even if it rains – and it usually does – a good time is had by all.

⑩ Sitka

One of Alaska's most beautiful towns, Sitka sits beside an island-studded sea on the west coast of Baranof Island. The lure of hunting sea otters for their pelts led the Russians to set up Redoubt St. Michael in the year 1799. After local Tlingit destroyed the fort in 1804, the Russians established the fortified town of Novo Archangelsk. By 1808, this was the capital of Russian America and was flourishing economically and culturally. When the US bought Alaska in 1867, the town's name was changed to Sitka, a contraction of Shee Atiká, the Tlingit name for the settlement. Today, Sitka's economy is based on tourism and a large fishing and cold-storage industry.

Tlingit totem poles on display at the Sheldon Jackson Museum

Detail of ceremonial Native canoe, Sitka Historical Museum

🏛 Sitka Historical Museum

330 Harbor Dr. **Tel** 747-6455, 747-5516 (performance information). **Open** mid-May–late Sep: 9am–5pm Mon–Fri, 10am–4pm Sat–Sun; late Sep–mid-May: 10am–4pm Tue–Sat. 🚫 donations accepted. ♿ 📷 ⓦ sitkahistory.org

Housed in the Harrigan Centennial Hall, this museum outlines Sitka's history from the Russian era to the present, including exhibits on mining, forestry, and World War II. In addition to a model of Sitka at the time of its transfer to the United States, the museum's highlights include Tlingit art, tools, and spruce baskets. There are also trade beads, Russian weapons, historic photographs, and a unique "tea brick." These bricks of compacted Cantonese tea were acquired by the Russians from the Chinese in exchange for the sea otter pelts that formed the basis of Russian Alaska's economy.

Outside, a large Haida ceremonial canoe is on display beneath a canopy. In the summer, the New Archangel Dancers perform in traditional Russian costume for tourists.

🏛 St. Michael's Russian Orthodox Cathedral

240 Lincoln St. **Tel** 747-8120. **Open** May–Sep: 9am–4pm Mon–Fri, or when cruise ships are in port; winter: by appt. 🚫 ♿ limited. 🏛 6pm Sat, 9:30am Sun. ⓦ oca.org/parishes/oca-ak-sitsmk

This onion-domed cathedral is the quintessential Sitka landmark. The cornerstone was laid by Bishop Veniaminov *(see p78)* in 1844, and construction was completed in 1848. The present church is a replica of the original, which burned down in a fire in 1966. Although locals managed to rescue the paintings, icons, chandelier, and the partially melted bronze bells, the large library of works in Russian, Tlingit, and Aleut languages was lost. One surviving artifact, the Madonna of Sitka, has been credited with miraculous healing. The reconstruction, in fire-resistant materials, took from 1967 to 1972, and the new cathedral was consecrated in 1976. Visitors can attend services.

Dome and spire of St. Michael's Russian Orthodox Cathedral

🏛 Sheldon Jackson Museum

104 College Dr. **Tel** 747-8981. **Open** mid-May–mid-Sep: 9am–5pm daily; mid-Sep–mid-May: 10am–4pm Tue–Sat. 🚫 ♿ 📷 ⓦ museums.state.ak.us

From 1888 to 1898, the Presbyterian Reverend Sheldon Jackson traveled around Alaska

representing the US educational system. In the course of his travels, he collected the indigenous artifacts that are displayed here, including hunting tools, masks, kayaks, and reindeer sleighs. Each summer, Native artisans come to the museum to demonstrate their crafts. The museum shop offers a variety of Native hand-crafted goods and artwork.

❑ Alaska Raptor Center

1000 Raptor Way. **Tel** 747-8662. 🚌
Community Ride. **Open** late May–
early Sep: 8am–4pm daily. 🗓 🅿 ♿
🏠 🌐 **alaskaraptor.org**

One of the state's best raptor
hospital and rehabilitation
centers, the non-profit Alaska
Raptor Center treats injured
ravens and raptors such as
eagles, falcons, owls, and
hawks, and tries to re-adapt
them to life in the wild. Seriously
wounded birds become Raptors-
in-Residence and are used in
educational programs for visitors.

❑ Russian Bishop's House

Lincoln & Monastery Sts. **Tel** 747-
0110/07. 🚌 Community Ride. **Open**
May–Sep: 8:30am–5pm daily; winter:
by appt. 🗓 🅿 ♿ 🌐 **nps.gov/sitk**

The oldest building in Sitka, this
1843 structure is one of the few
surviving examples of secular
Russian architecture. The original
building was made from spruce
by Finnish woodworkers, who
introduced Baltic-style
opulence to Russian

Bald eagle in the compound of the Alaska
Raptor Center

America. Despite the building's
flamboyance, its first occupant,
Bishop Veniaminov, lived a
simple monastic life.

Over the years, the building
has served as an orphanage,
seminary, and school. The last
Russian bishop moved out in
1969 and the building was
purchased in 1972 by the US
National Park Service for restoration. On the main floor is a
model of Novo Archangelsk as it
looked in 1845 and a collection
of icons and relics. To see the
library, chapel, and Bishop's
quarters, it is necessary to join
a guided tour.

Russian cemetery, where
hundreds of graves recall 18th-
and 19th-century Russian Sitka.

❑ Sitka National Historical Park

103 Monastery St. ℹ 747-0110.
Closed public hols. 🅿 ♿ 🏠
🌐 **nps.gov/sitk**

Alaska's oldest federal park
was established in 1910 to
commemorate the 1804 Battle
of Sitka. In 1802, Tlingit warriors
of the Kiks.ádi tribe attacked
the Russian redoubt, killing
most of the Russian and Aleut
personnel. Seeking revenge, the
Russians returned with four
ships and beseiged the Tlingit
fort. After much bloodshed,
Russians entered the fort to find
that it had been abandoned by
the Tlingit. Today, the site is part
of the park. From the visitors'
center and museum, trails lead
through rainforest past nearly a
dozen Northwest Coast totem
poles. To the east is the site of
the Tlingit fort and the actual
battleground, while to the
north, across the creek, trails
lead to the Russian Memorial.

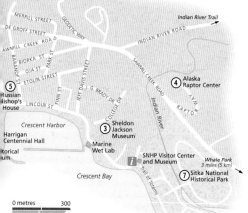

Prince of Wales Island totem pole, Sitka
National Historical Park

Sights at a Glance

① Sitka Historical Museum
② St. Michael's Russian Orthodox
  Cathedral
③ Sheldon Jackson Museum
④ Alaska Raptor Center
⑤ Russian Bishop's House
⑥ Blockhouse and Russian
  Cemetery
⑦ Sitka National Historical Park

❑ Blockhouse and Russian Cemetery

Kogwantan & Marine Sts. Blockhouse:
Open late May–early Sep: noon–4pm
Sun. Cemetery: **Open** 24 hrs.

North of St. Michael's sits a
reconstruction of an octagonal
two-story blockhouse used by the
Russians to shield their redoubt
from the Tlingit. Just behind the
Blockhouse lies the overgrown

⓭ Juneau

Often described as a little San Francisco due to its hilly setting, Alaska's capital is located between Mount Juneau and Mount Roberts along Gastineau Channel. Joe Juneau and Dick Harris' 1880 discovery of gold in Gold Creek and Juneau's strategic location on the route to the Klondike goldfields established its importance and led to it taking over the role of Alaska's capital from Sitka in 1900. In the mid-1970s, Alaskans voted to move the state capital to Willow, but due to projected costs, they reversed the decision in 1982.

Gold Rush-era mining display at the Alaska State Museum

Pleasure craft and fishing boats anchored in Juneau

🏛 Alaska State Capitol Building

4th & Main. 🚌 3 & 4. **Open** summer: 8:30am–5pm Mon–Fri, 9:30am–4pm Sat & Sun; winter: 8am–4:30pm Mon–Fri. 🅿

Designed to serve as the seat of Territorial Government, this gracious marble Art Deco building was completed in 1931. It now houses the Alaska State Legislature and the offices of the Governor and Lieutenant Governor. A state map made from a slice of the Alaska Pipeline is on display near the staircase, and decorative details throughout showcase aspects of Alaska's culture and economy. Free tours are available daily in summer. The Legislature is in session January to March.

🏛 Alaska State Museum

395 Whittier St. **Tel** 465-2901. 🚌 3 & 4. **Open** for new opening hours following closure for renovations, telephone or see website. 🅿 ♿ 🏠
🌐 **museums.state.ak.us**

The Alaska State Museum has an impressive collection reflecting many facets of Alaskan history, ranging from prehistoric times to modern days. On the ramp to the second floor is a mock rainforest, complete with recorded birdsong and a replica bald eagle nest. Displayed along the walls of the ramp are a range of Native artifacts, including dolls, masks, baskets, and models of traditional canoes. There is also a collection of Native ivory "billikens" upstairs. These chubby elf-like figurines have now become mainstays of the Alaskan tourist trade. Russian America is represented by a collection of icons and samovars, while numerous mining tools bring the Gold Rush to life. Other highlights include a mineral collection, the pen used by

President Dwight Eisenhower to sign the bill that gave Alaska its statehood, and a children's area with hands-on activities.

[Map of Juneau showing: Cope Park, Goldbelt Avenue, Calhoun Avenue, Capitol Avenue, Dixon Street, Indian St, Distin St, Village Street, Whittier Street, Willoughby Avenue, Egan Drive. Labeled sights: Wickersham State Historical Site ③, Governor's House, Alaska State Capitol Building, City Museum, State Office Building, Alaska State Museum ②, Centennial Hall. Airport 8 miles (13 km), Ferry Terminal 13 miles (21 km).]

0 meters	200
0 yards	200

Sights at a Glance

① Alaska State Capitol Building
② Alaska State Museum
③ Wickersham State Historical Site
④ Red Dog Saloon
⑤ Mount Roberts Tramway

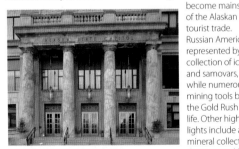

Facade of the Alaska State Capitol Building

🏛 Wickersham State Historical Site

213 7th St. **Tel** 586-9001. **Open** mid-May–mid-Sep: 10am–4pm Tue–Sat; winter: by appt. 🏛 donations accepted. W **alaskastateparks.org**

The historic Wickersham house, built in 1898, was once the home of Judge James Wickersham, who served as the voice of the law in over half of Territorial Alaska. As a

Last Chance Mining Museum 1 mile (2 km)

delegate to the US Congress, the judge introduced an Alaska Statehood Bill in 1916, planting the seeds of an idea that would come to fruition in the 1950s. After his death in 1939, his niece Ruth Allman opened the house to the public. In 1984, the house and its relics were purchased by the state and turned into a museum.

🍺 Red Dog Saloon

278 S Franklin St. **Tel** 463-3658. 🚌 3 & 4. **Open** May–Sep: 9am–10pm daily. 🅰🚻🖥📷 W **reddogsaloon.com**

During Juneau's mining heyday in the late 19th century, the Saloon offered alcohol, entertainment, and dancing to travelers and local miners. The Harris family bought the place in 1973 and turned it into a bar. Popular with cruise passengers and other visitors, it offers meals and drinks in a retro setting that includes a collection of interesting memorabilia, plus live music.

🚡 Mount Roberts Tramway

490 S Franklin St. **Tel** 463-3412. 🚌 3 & 4. **Open** May–Sep: 8am–9pm daily. 🅰🚻🖥 W **goldbelttours.com**

The tramway up the slopes of Mount Roberts offers panoramic views along Gastineau Channel and across to Douglas Island. At the summit, the Mountain House has a gift shop, restaurant,

and the Chilkat Theater, which screens a film on Tlingit culture. The short Alpine Loop trail winds through meadow and forest, past several Tlingit carvings, with a short side trip to Father Brown's Cross. The energetic can forgo the tramway and hike up the mountain from the end of Sixth Street.

Mount Roberts Tramway cable car moving past forested slopes

🏛 Last Chance Mining Museum

1001 Basin Rd. **Tel** 586-5338. **Open** mid-May–late Sep: 9:30am–12:30pm, 3:30–5:30pm daily. 🏛

The only remnants of the Juneau goldfields are the historic buildings and relics of the Last Chance Mining Museum. It is located in the mine's old service center, which once housed dormitories, assay offices, and machine repair shops. The museum displays what was once the world's largest air compressor, mining tools, and a three-dimensional representation of the mine tunnels that wind through the adjacent mountain.

View of downtown Juneau from the upper Mount Roberts Tramway station

Exploring Beyond Juneau

Downtown Juneau lies between the Coast Range and Gastineau Channel, so most of the city's residential areas are found on the coast of precipitous Douglas Island, as well as in the scenic side valleys and along the coastal, forest-studded Glacier Highway to the northwest. The city bus system extends only as far as the Mendenhall Valley loop, but with a rental car, it is possible to explore the spectacular hinterlands. More adventurous visitors can join helicopter tours of the Juneau Icefield.

Sights at a Glance

① Macauley Salmon Hatchery
② Alaska Brewing Company
③ Glacier Gardens
④ Juneau Icefield
⑤ Mendenhall Glacier
⑥ Shrine of St. Therese de Lisieux

Key

▢ Juneau
▬ Highway
═ Minor road

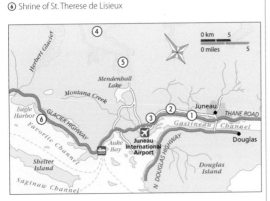

🏛 Macauley Salmon Hatchery

2697 Channel Dr, 3 miles (5 km) N of downtown Juneau. **Tel** 463-4810. 🚌 3 & 4. **Open** May–Sep: 10am–6pm Mon–Fri, 10am–5pm Sat & Sun. 🅿 🅲 🅶 ♿ **W** dipac.net

A working hatchery that provides fry to stock streams in many areas of Southeast Alaska, the Macauley Salmon Hatchery is an interesting place to visit. Inside, over 100 species of local sealife are on view in a number of large saltwater aquariums. Outside the building, walkways lead past several tanks where fry of various ages are fed and reared until they are ready for release into the surrounding waterways. Small salmon are also released into nearby Twin Lakes for recreational anglers. Between June and October, a 450-ft (135-m) fish ladder provides easy access for pink and chum salmon returning to the hatchery to spawn and produce their fry. Visitors can purchase a range of salmon products in the hatchery shop.

🏛 Alaska Brewing Company

5429 Shaune Dr. **Tel** 780-5866. 🚌 3 & 4. **Open** May–Sep: 11am–7pm daily; Oct–Apr: 11am–5:30pm Tue–Sat. 🅲 ♿ 🅶 **W** alaskanbeer.com

Home-brewers Geoff and Marcy Larsen started the Alaskan Brewing Company in 1986 when they uncovered an ingredient list for a popular beer brewed during the 19th-century Gold Rush. This recipe became the base for their winning formula for Alaskan Amber. The popularity of their beers grew, and today their company is the state's only fully-fledged brewery. In 1987, they produced 1,600 barrels of Amber and currently, the company annually distributes about 125,000 barrels of award-winning amber, pale ale, stout, and smoked porter throughout the western states.

A free hour-long tour explains the brewing process and includes displays of brewing equipment. Beer samples are available, and it is also possible to buy discounted cases of beer.

🅒 Glacier Gardens

7600 Glacier Hwy. **Tel** 790-3377. 🚌 3 & 4. **Open** May–Sep: 9am–6pm daily. 🅿 🅲 🅶 ♿ **W** glaciergardens.com

Nearly surrounded by the Tongass National Forest, the 52-acre (21-ha) Glacier Gardens is a pleasant blend of groomed gardens and natural rainforest, including a series of artificial streams and ponds flanked by lovely plantings. A collection of upended tree stumps, salvaged from a devastating 1984 mudslide, form planters for colorful hanging gardens of petunias, begonias, and fuschias.

From the greenhouse, a succession of rainforest trails leads to boardwalks and a platform offering dramatic views of Gastineau Channel. For those who do not want to climb the steep hillside, the admission price includes transport by an electric golf cart through the woods, as well as a running commentary on the rainforest environment.

Unusual tree-stump planters, Glacier Gardens

Mendenhall Glacier on the shores of Mendenhall Lake near Juneau

🏔 Juneau Icefield

🚁 accessible by flightseeing or helicopter tour only. 🎫

Juneau Icefield sprawls across 1,500 sq miles (3,885 sq km) of the Coast Range, with its highest peak, the 8,584-ft (2,616-m) Devil's Paw, straddling the US-Canada border.

The icefield feeds about 40 large and 100 small glaciers. Of all Juneau Icefield's glaciers, only Taku Glacier continues to advance and calve into Taku Inlet.

The most readily accessible portion of the icefield is the retreating Mendenhall Glacier. A hike to the rest of the vast white wilderness of the icefield can be quite challenging, and most visitors opt for helicopter or flightseeing tours, some of which additionally offer adventurous summer dog sled rides across the ice. Also available are ice climbing classes, with instruction and gear provided.

🏔 Mendenhall Glacier

Glacier Spur Hwy. **Tel** 789-0097.
🚌 3 & 4. ℹ 789-6640. **Open** May–mid-Sep: 8am–7:30pm daily; Oct–Mar: 10am–4pm Fri–Sun. **Closed** Apr 🅿 summer only; free in winter. 🎫 ♿
🏛 ⛰ 🌐 www.fs.usda.gov/main/tongass/home

Spilling into the Mendenhall Valley from the Juneau Icefield, the large Mendenhall Glacier was first called Auke Glacier after the nearby Tlingit village, Aak'w Kwaan. In 1892, it was renamed in honor of physicist Thomas Mendenhall, who surveyed the international border between Canada and Southeast Alaska.

There are several trails access the glacier. The East Glacier Loop follows the glacial trimline, while the West Glacier Trail goes up to the glacier's west face. The Moraine Ecology Trail has information panels explaining the regeneration of vegetation on deglaciated areas. The Photo Point Trail is lined with benches and interpretive panels, and provides the best vantage points to capture panoramic shots of the glacier.

At **Mendenhall Lake**, which is often choked with icebergs calved from the glacier, the huge curving glass wall of the visitor center offers fabulous views of the glacier across the lake. An exhibit hall has information on glaciers, and a theater shows films on icefield geology. A salmon-viewing platform and a fish-cam provide views of spawning salmon moving up Steep Creek.

⛪ Shrine of St. Therese of Lisieux

Mile 23, Glacier Hwy. **Tel** 780-6112.
Open Apr–Sep: 8:30am–10pm; Oct–Mar: 8:30am–8pm. ♿ limited.
⛪ late May–early Sep: 1:30pm Sun. 🎫 🅿
🌐 shrineofsainttherese.org

This peaceful Catholic pilgrimage site lies on Shrine Island at the end of a 400-ft (120-m) pedestrian causeway from the mainland. The serene chapel, built of beach stone, occupies a lovely forested spot with views across the sea to the distant peaks of the Chilkat Range. It is dedicated to the 19th-century French saint Therese de Lisieux, who was chosen by the first Bishop of Alaska, Joseph Raphael Crimont, as the patron saint of the state. The shrine also contains the 14 Stations of the Cross, a prayer labyrinth, and the Marian Gardens.

The Shrine of St. Therese on a forested islet west of Juneau

For hotels and restaurants see pp242–5 and pp250–55

⑭ Glacier Bay National Park

The 5,000-sq mile (13,000-sq km) area surrounding Glacier Bay was designated a National Park in 1980 and declared a UNESCO World Heritage Site in 1992. Historically, the park has served as an open-air laboratory for studies on the recolonization of formerly glaciated lands by plants and wildlife. For visitors, Glacier Bay is best known for its tidewater glaciers and deep fjords, and is also a popular destination for wildlife enthusiasts. Its forests and alpine areas are home to bears and mountain goats, while in the summer, its waters are alive with migrating humpback whales. Although most visitors take an organized cruise, kayaking is also an enjoyable option.

Locator Map

▦ Glacier Bay National Park

★ **Margerie Glacier**
Of the seven tidewater glaciers that calve icebergs into the bay, Margerie Glacier is the most visited. It was once a tributary of the Grand Pacific Glacier, which has retreated 70 miles (112 km) in the past 200 years.

★ **Fairweather Range**
The forbidding Fairweather Range, which culminates at the 15,300-ft- (4,590-m-) high Mount Fairweather, was the source of the ice that created the park's deeply indented fjords. The range continues to feed the glaciers on the western peninsula of the park.

For hotels and restaurants see pp242–5 and pp250–55

Whale-watching at Glacier Bay
Black and white killer whales (orcas) and humpback whales can frequently be spotted, along with sea otters, sea lions, and harbor porpoises. Boats are not allowed within 500 yards (450 m) of the whales, so bring binoculars.

VISITORS' CHECKLIST

Practical Information
75 miles (105 km) NW of Juneau.
Transport map E4. *i* NPS
Visitor Center, Glacier Bay Lodge,
Bartlett Cove, 697-2230. 🚻 🚻
Bartlett Cove only. 🚻 🚻 🚻 🚻
Permits for private boats & back-country camping available at
Bartlett Cove. Boat or floatplane drop-off required for backcountry access. **W** **nps.gov/glba.**

Transport
🚉 🚢 from Juneau.
🚌 Gustavus–Bartlett Cove shuttle bus.

Key

===== Minor road

▬▬ Park boundary

△ Peak

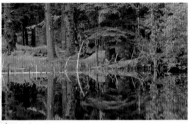

★ Bartlett Cove
Several easy hikes are available around Bartlett Cove, the only developed area within the park. It has a visitor center, park headquarters, a lodge, and a campground.

Exploring the Park

While short, easy hikes loop through the forests around Bartlett Cove, the best views of Glacier Bay are from the water, and most visitors see the park either on cruises or organized boat tours that typically go up to the face of Margerie and Grand Pacific Glaciers. Smaller boats provide drop-off services for people wishing to explore on their own.

Gustavus
The village of Gustavus, outside the southeast corner of the park, prospered in the 1920s as an agricultural homestead area. It offers lodging and visitor services, and operators run tours and rent kayaks for private trips.

For keys to symbols *see back flap*

Former officers' quarters at Fort Seward, Haines

⓰ Haines

75 miles (120 km) NW of Juneau.
Transport map E4. ⛰ 2,500. ✈ to
Juneau & Skagway. ⛴ ℹ 122 2nd
Ave, 766-2234. 🎪 Great Alaska Craft
Beer & Home Brew Festival (4th week
of May), Southeast Alaska State Fair
(last weekend of Jul), Alaska Bald Eagle
Festival (2nd week of Nov).
ⓦ haines.ak.us

Founded in 1881 by Presbyterian
missionaries, Haines sits on a site
known to indigenous peoples as
Dei-Shu, or "end of the trail."
Early residents were quick to
take advantage of the plentiful
fish in adjacent Lynn Canal, the
country's deepest and longest
fjord. By 1900, commercial fishing
and canning had grown into
major enterprises. The building of
Fort Seward brought further
economic benefits. In 1939, a
sawmill was developed to support a nascent timber industry.

Haines boasts a mild climate
and spectacular setting and
over the years has attracted
many artists and entrepreneurs.
In addition to several galleries
and a renowned microbrewery,
it has a winery that makes
unusual wines from fireweed,
birch sap, and onions.
There are excellent
hiking trails around
town, including the
Mount Ripinsky and
Mount Riley Trails and
the easy 2-mile (4-km)
Battery Point Trail.

🏚 Fort Seward
Open 24 hrs. 🏊 🚶
Named for William
H Seward, President
Andrew Johnson's Secretary
of State who instigated the
purchase of Alaska, Fort Seward
was built in 1903. Complete
with barracks, officers' quarters,

carpentry shops, and smithies,
the fort was the state's first
permanent army post and the
mainstay of Haines' economy.
Locally refered to as Chilkoot
Barracks to avoid confusion with
the town of Seward (*see pp102–3*),
the fort was used as a training
base during the two World Wars.
Decommissioned in 1947, it was
bought by five World War II
veterans who set up a series of
small businesses. Today, it
houses art galleries, restaurants,
a replica Tlingit clan house, and
a center for Native arts.

🏛 Sheldon Museum
11 Main St. **Tel** 766-2366. **Open** mid-
May–Sep: 10am–5pm Mon–Fri,
1–4pm Sat & Sun. 🅿 📷
ⓦ sheldonmuseum.org

Established in 1924, this
museum grew around a private
collection of artifacts
from the early days of
European settlement
in the upper Chilkat
Inlet area. The original
collection has been
augmented by relics
from the Gold Rush era
and the fishing and
timber industries, as well
as by Chilkat blankets,
basketry, and a single-log
dugout canoe. The area's
Russian history is reflected in
colorfully painted Russian trunks.
There are also shipping artifacts,
including an old lens from Lynn
Canal's Eldred Rock Lighthouse.

Indigenous copper
shield

Eldred Rock Lighthouse sitting in the middle of spectacular Lynn Canal

Model woodcarver at the Hammer Museum

🏛 Hammer Museum

108 Main St. **Tel** 766-2374. **Open** May–Sep: 10am–5pm Mon–Fri; all other times: by appt. **Closed** public holidays.
🛇 📷 🌐 **hammermuseum.org**

The Hammer Museum is Alaska's contribution to the world's most unique museums. Over 1,500 hammers of varying sizes are on display, all painstakingly collected by owner Dave Pahl. They served a variety of purposes, from blacksmithing and mining to cracking nuts and stunning cattle. Highlights include Colonial-era and Industrial Revolution hammers, and an 800-year-old Tlingit slave-killing hammer found on a Southeast Alaska beach, all put into historical context. There are also some model woodcarvers salvaged from the Smithsonian Institution in Washington, DC. Visitors are invited to identify hammers whose purpose is not yet known.

🏔 Mount Ripinsky

Rising above Haines, the 3,610-ft (1,083-m) Mount Ripinsky affords the best view over the town and its stunning hinterlands, extending as far as Skagway and almost to Juneau. North of the town center, from the trailhead at Young Road, a trail winds up the peak. Climbing gently for about 3 miles (5 km), it then ascends steeply through alpine meadows to the summit. Hikers should carry bear spray and plenty of water, and allow at least seven hours for the strenuous round trip. Overnight camping is also possible beyond the North Summit. The less energetic can opt for an easier hike up 1,760-ft (528-m) Mount Riley, which is accessed by a trail from Mud Bay Road near Fort Seward, or along a spur trail from the Battery Point Trail that starts at the end of Beach Road, south of the town center.

⚡ Chilkat Bald Eagle Preserve

Mile 9.4 to Mile 25, Haines Cut-Off. ♿ limited. American Bald Eagle Foundation Center: 113 Haines Rd at 2nd Ave. **Tel** 766-3094. **Open** late May–Aug: 9am–5pm Mon–Fri, noon–4pm Sat & Sun. 🛇 ♿ 📷
🌐 **baldeagles.org**

In the summer, Haines hosts a modest number of bald eagles that can be seen at the waterfront or along streams. In October and November, however, cottonwood trees along the Chilkat and Klehini River valleys in the 75-sq-mile (195-sq-km) Chilkat Bald Eagle Preserve fill with up to 3,500 eagles, who arrive to feed on Alaska's last salmon run after most other waterways have frozen solid. Within the preserve, several pull-offs along the Haines Cut-Off afford excellent viewing of this phenomenon, known as the Gathering of the Eagles, which has inspired Haines' annual Alaska Bald Eagle Festival.

Summer visitors who will miss this November event can stop by the **American Bald Eagle Foundation Center** in town, only 20 miles (32 km) away, dedicated to the protection and preservation of bald eagles. Using a diorama of the Chilkat Preserve, this non-profit center gives visitors a better understanding of how the eagles live in a delicate balance with their environment. The center also has a screening room where visitors can watch videos of the Gathering of the Eagles.

Bald Eagles

The national bird of the US, the bald eagle *(Haliaeetus leucocephalus)* is the only eagle unique to North America. In this case, the word "bald" means not hairless, but white, a reference to its distinctive head color. In 1963, the bald eagle population in the Lower 48 states included just 417 breeding pairs, but by 2004 stringent conservation measures had raised that number to about 10,000 pairs. Currently, North America is home to 100,000 bald eagles – about half of which live in Alaska – leading the US Fish and Wildlife Service to suggest that they can be removed from the official threatened species list. While the Bald Eagle Protection Act makes it illegal to transport, trade, or possess any part of an eagle without a permit, indigenous peoples are allowed to use eagle feathers in their traditional dresses and ceremonies.

Bald eagle taking flight from a tree

⑯ Skagway

After pioneers George Washington Carmack, Skookum Jim Mason, and Dawson Charlie discovered gold in the Klondike in the late 1890s, steamboat captain William Moore founded Skagway as a gateway to the goldfields. Over 30,000 hopeful prospectors passed through in the first year, seeking supplies and entertainment and helping the town to boom. The 1900 completion of the White Pass and Yukon Route Railroad (WP&YR) made the trip easier, but the Gold Rush was already subsiding. Skagway was revived in the 1940s as an Alaska Highway construction staging camp, and today, the town's economy is driven mainly by tourism.

Locator Map

— Area illustrated

★ **Arctic Brotherhood Hall**
The front of this building, housing the Skagway Visitor Information Center, is decorated with thousands of pieces of driftwood.

★ **Red Onion Saloon**
The 1898 Red Onion still retains the bar from the days when it served as a saloon and brothel. It offers the Brothel Tour, conducted by appropriately clad young ladies.

White Pass and Yukon Route Railroad Depot
In the summer, trains set off from here daily, offering journeys through stunning scenery (see pp152–3).

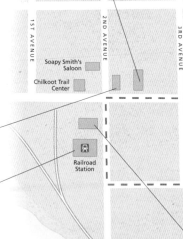

Klondike Gold Rush NHP Visitors' Center
Now the Klondike Gold Rush National Historical Park Visitors' Center, the original WP&YR depot, built using packing crates and salvaged lumber, was hurriedly constructed in 1898 to handle the flood of prospectors.

Key

— Suggested route

Corrington Museum
Built in 1975, the Corrington Building houses an ivory gift shop and displays Native basketry, a mammoth tusk, and a collection of walrus ivory scrimshaw.

Eagle's Hall, built in 1898, hosts the Days of '98 show, re-creating the Frank Reid-Soapy Smith shootout.

Nome Saloon, a Gold Rush drinking hall, now houses a jewelry shop.

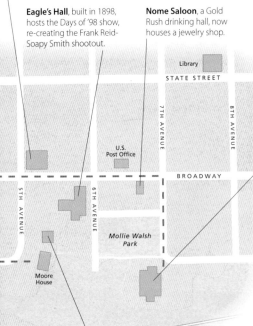

★ Skagway Museum
The 1899 faux-Gothic McCabe College first functioned as a private school, then the Federal Courthouse, jail, and Town Hall. It now houses the town museum, with displays on the Gold Rush, local Tlingit culture, and the infamous Soapy Smith.

Moore Cabin
Built in 1888 by Captain Moore, the town's founder, this is Skagway's oldest building. Its walls are papered with newspapers from the late 1800s.

Soapy Smith

Born Jefferson Randolph Smith in Georgia in 1860, Soapy earned his nickname after a swindle involving soap. In 1896, he arrived in Skagway, opened a saloon, and set himself up as an underworld boss and local philanthropist. His most notorious scams included a phony freight company and a fake telegraph office that would "wire" money across non-existent wires. In 1898, this uncrowned "king" of Skagway was killed after a shootout with city surveyor Frank Reid.

Historic image of Soapy Smith at the bar of his saloon

⓱ Gold Rush Routes

Along the old Gold Rush trail from Skagway, three separate routes link the port with the interior. The most famous is the Chilkoot Trail, starting at the site of Dyea and crossing Chilkoot Pass to Bennett Lake in Canada's British Columbia. Hikers can return by the narrow-gauge 1898 White Pass and Yukon Route Railroad, which runs from Skagway past vertical cliffs, over old bridges, and through tunnels from sea level to the 2,865-ft (860-m) high White Pass in just 20 miles (32 km). The third route, the picturesque Klondike Highway, is a good driving route that passes spectacular scenery on the opposite side of the Skagway River from the railway and continues to the Yukon Territory.

Rafting on the Chilkoot River at Dyea near Skagway

③ Chilkoot Pass
After struggling up the 3,525-ft (1,058-m) Chilkoot Pass on the US-Canada border, hikers can look forward to a downhill run all the way to Bennett Lake. During the Gold Rush, stampeders crossing the border had to stop here to pay customs duties to the Royal Canadian Mounted Police.

② Canyon City
In 1898, Canyon City had 1,500 residents and 24 businesses, but the town had disappeared within two years. All that is left today is the remains of a boiler once owned by a transportation company.

④ Lindeman
Now a campsite, Lindeman was a bustling lakeside tent town of 4,000 during the Gold Rush. While stampeders and their gear were carried by a steamer and barges across the lake in the summer, they had to walk across the frozen lake in the winter.

Mount Hoffman
6,080 ft

Irene Glacier

Mount Yeatman
5,670 ft

Mount Carmack
6,229 ft

Goa
Lake

0 km   2
0 miles   2

Skagway

① Dyea
Although it rivaled Skagway as Alaska's largest town during the Gold Rush *(see pp56–7)*, nothing remains of Dyea but a few harbor pilings, a cemetery, and the wooden frontage of a land office. Thousands of prospectors, also called stampeders, set off from Dyea for the Klondike. Today, it is the trailhead for the Chilkoot Trail.

⑤ Bennett Lake, British Columbia

In the winter of 1897, a town of over 20,000 people sprang up at Bennett Lake, as stampeders waited for the ice to break up. In May 1898, in the week after the thaw, about 7,000 boats set off for the goldfields. For modern hikers, the lake is the end of the Chilkoot Trail.

Key

═ Klondike Highway

━ ━ Chilkoot Trail

── White Pass and Yukon Route Railroad

▬ ▬ International border

△ Peak

⑥ Fraser, near Bernard Lake

Beside beautiful Bernard Lake in an alpine valley, Fraser is a stop on the modern White Pass and Yukon Route Railroad. It also serves as Canada's Customs and Immigration post for travelers on both the railway and the Klondike Highway.

⑧ Denver

At Denver, the railway line crosses the east fork of the Skagway River. Here, the US Forest Service rents out a public use cabin sited in a historic railway caboose.

⑦ White Pass

About 7 miles (11 km) from Fraser, the railway crosses White Pass where, during the Gold Rush, Canadian police checked the grubstakes (see p56) of stampeders on the White Pass Route. The modern trains, made up of 1890s rolling stock, are pulled by either steam or diesel locomotives.

⓲ Haines Cut-Off Tour

The scenic 146-mile (234-km) Haines Cut-Off, or Haines Highway, links Haines with the Alaska Highway. From Haines, the route follows the Chilkat and Klehini Rivers northward. Near the Canadian border, the road climbs steeply, gaining 3,000 ft (900 m) over 18 miles (29 km). For the next 50 miles (80 km), the road passes through the high alpine country of northern British Columbia before dropping into lake-studded forests to join the Alaska Highway at Haines Junction.

Tips for Drivers

Starting point: Haines.
Length: 146 miles (234 km).
Stopping-off points: there is excellent whitewater rafting at Tatshenshini-Alsek Park at Dalton Post off the Haines Cut-Off. An overlook at Mile 78 offers photo opportunities. Dezadeash Lake at Mile 114 has primitive campsites.

Key

══ Alaska Highway
══ Tour
══ Major road
▪▪ International border
▬▬ Provincial border
△ Peak

⑦ **Haines Junction**
This service center appeared in 1942 with the construction of the Alaska Highway, and is a staging point for trips into Kluane National Park.

⑥ **Kathleen Lake**
This spectacular glacier-fed lake and campground in Canada's Kluane National Park is well worth a stop. On summer evenings, park rangers often conduct naturalist programs.

⑤ **Klukshu Village**
Visitors to this indigenous village can admire the traditional fish traps, shop for Native crafts, and stop by the small museum.

④ **Million Dollar Falls**
Boardwalk trails and viewing platforms at the Million Dollar Falls campground provide great views of the tumbling Takhanne River.

③ **Chilkat Pass**
The 40-mile (64-km) alpine portion of the route reaches its highest point at 3,510-ft (1,070-m) Chilkat Pass. Much of this stretch may be impassable in the winter.

② **Three Guardsmen Lake and Peaks**
The imposing Three Guardsmen Lake and Peaks lie in the alpine portion of the route.

① **Mosquito Lake**
The small Mosquito Lake State Recreation Site includes a basic campground with fantastic views of high peaks across Mosquito Lake.

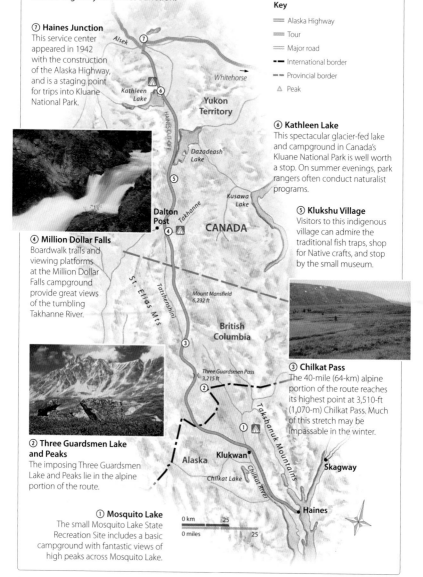

For keys to symbols *see back flap*

⑲ Tatshenshini-Alsek Rivers

Transport map E4.
Permits: mandatory, contact the Visitor Reception Center, Haines Junction, YT.
W env.gov.bc.ca/bcparks/explore/parkpgs/tatshens

The Tatshenshini River and its tributary, the Alsek, which are considered two of the world's best whitewater rafting and kayaking rivers, rise in the St. Elias Range of British Columbia and the Yukon Territory, respectively. From there, they flow 160 miles (256 km) through canyons and rapids and past numerous glaciers to the coast at the northern end of Glacier Bay National Park (see pp146–7). Once a vital Tlingit trade route, the Tatshenshini supports productive salmon runs, and visitors to Klukshu can see how the First Nations once caught salmon with fish traps and dried them for use in the winter.

The usual put-in site for the glacial Alsek is near Haines Junction, while Tatshenshini rafters put in at Dalton Post, near the Yukon Territory-British Columbia border. Most rafters run the rivers with commercial operators and experienced guides. For private trips on the Alsek, rafters need a wilderness permit from Canada's Kluane National Park. Rafters on both rivers must also obtain a permit for Glacier Bay National Park, citing a pre-specified take-out time from Dry Bay at the

Floating houses in Yakutat's harbor with Mount Augusta in the distance

mouth of the Alsek, which will require a bush flight to Haines or Yakutat.

Rafters on the Alsek should be aware that the 10-mile (16-km) stretch through Turnback Canyon in British Columbia presents serious whitewater, and must be bypassed using a pre-organized helicopter portage. A highlight is the paddle past the icebergs of Alsek Glacier. There are no services along the way, so river runners need to be fully self-sufficient.

⑳ Yakutat

225 miles (362 km) NW of Juneau.
Transport map E4. 660.
i Yakutat Chamber of Commerce 784-3933. Fairweather Days (early Aug). **W** yakutatalaska.com

Located on the Gulf of Alaska at the southern edge of Wrangell-St. Elias National Park (see pp192–3), Yakutat is just 70 miles

(110 km) from the 18,008-ft (5,490-m) Mount St. Elias, the second highest peak in the US.

The Russians were among the first outsiders in Yakutat, whose name means "where the canoes rest" in the Tlingit language. In 1805, the Russian-American Company built a fur trading post here, but it was destroyed by the Tlingit, who had been denied access to their traditional hunting and fishing lands. In 1886, minor gold deposits were discovered in the beach sands, but the area's economy took off only in 1903, when a cannery, sawmill, and railroad were established. Yakutat also served as a garrison and airstrip during World War II.

Due to its remote location, modern Yakutat sees few casual visitors. However, it has been discovered by fly-fishermen, who come for steelhead, and surfers who head to **Cannon Beach**, a popular place to surf the waves. The town also enjoys good views of a host of peaks and glaciers, including the galloping **Hubbard Glacier** (see p31) and the vast **Malaspina Glacier**, which is one of the largest in North America. Yakutat is a good base for exploring the southeast corner of Wrangell-St. Elias National Park, while the Russell Fjord Wilderness, which includes Harlequin Lake and Yakutat Glacier, is a 26-mile (42-km) drive away.

Rafters passing through a calm section of the Tatshenshini River

WESTERN INTERIOR ALASKA

The landscape of the sparsely populated Western Interior is covered with boreal forest, muskeg, taiga, and lakes. Dominated by a continental climate that creates the state's greatest climatic extremes, the region enjoys long summer days with almost round-the-clock sunlight and dramatic storms, and long, cold winter nights illuminated by the undulating colors of the aurora borealis.

This territory was first settled by Native Athabaskan peoples who, despite its exceedingly harsh environment, found it a region rich in wildlife and capable of providing meat for food, and skins for clothing and shelter during the bitterly cold winters. While much of the land is deemed unproductive by modern definitions, the first Europeans in the area, like the Athabaskans before them, managed to eke out a living in these bleak and difficult conditions. These pioneers, including early 20th-century prospectors near Fairbanks, built up a semblance of civilization in what was then considered the country's last frontier.

By the 1920s, engineers were using dredges to exploit deep seams of gold after placer gold *(see p57)* started to play out. World War II boosted the region's fluctuating fortunes and population, when huge military bases were set up to counter the Japanese threat *(see p59)*. There was another growth spurt in the 1970s when Fairbanks was chosen as the logistical headquarters of the Trans-Alaska Pipeline.

Across the heart of the region stretches the massive Alaska Range, crowned by Mount McKinley. Located within the popular Denali National Park, the peak is now the area's main draw. Denali and various state parks provide excellent hiking and wildlife viewing. Winter activities range from Nordic skiing to soaking in hot springs and viewing the aurora. Attractive towns, including Fairbanks, Alaska's second-largest city, historic gold dredges, and whitewater rafting all combine to draw steadily increasing numbers of visitors.

Brilliant aurora borealis undulating across the sky

◀ A Riverboat Discovery cruise on the Chena River near Fairbanks

Exploring Western Interior Alaska

Dominating the landscape of the Western Interior is Mount McKinley, North America's highest mountain. Popular Denali National Park, home of the massive peak, is on the itinerary of nearly every visitor to the state. Beyond Denali, summer visitors also enjoy Denali State Park, the rustic little town of Talkeetna, and the excellent museums of Fairbanks. The region also contains such little-known gems as Nancy Lake State Recreation Area to the south and Chena Hot Springs to the north. The uncrowded and mostly untarred Elliott, Steese, and Denali highways, which lead into the heart of the northern wilderness, make not-to-be-missed drives.

Rafting the Nenana on the border of Denali National Park

Key

═══ Highway

┄┄┄ Minor road

──── Alaska Railroad

△ Peak

Map labels:

Prudhoe Bay

Stev
Villa

DALTON HIGHWAY

Mount Tozi
5,500 ft

Rampart

Liveng

Yukon

ELLIOT HIGHWAY

Tanana

Minto

Chate

Manley
Hot Springs

Tanana

Tolovana
Hot Springs

NENANA

Anderson

Nenana

Kantishna

HEAL

DENALI

DEN.
(MCKINLE
VILLA

NATIONAL

Toklat

Kantishna

Wonder
Lake

CANTW

PARK

Mount McKinley
(Denali) 20,320 ft

Mount Foraker
17,344 ft

DENALI STATE PARK

Petersville

TALKEETNA

Trapper Creek

Yentna

Mc
Cre

Skwentna

WILLOW

NANCY LAKE STATE
RECREATION AREA

BI
LA

Sights at a Glance

Towns and Cities

① Big Lake
② Houston
④ Willow
⑤ Talkeetna
⑦ Cantwell
⑩ Denali (McKinley) Village
⑫ Healy
⑬ Nenana
⑭ Ester
⑮ Fairbanks

National and State Parks

③ Nancy Lake State Recreation Area
⑥ Denali State Park
⑨ *Denali National Park pp166–9*

Area of Natural Beauty

⑪ Nenana River

Tours

⑧ *Denali Highway Tour p165*
⑯ *Steese Highway Tour p179*

For keys to symbols *see back flap*

Moose dredging for pond weed, Denali National Park

Getting Around

The Western Interior has evolved around one thin lifeline, the Parks Highway, which connects the northern part of the Mat-Su to Fairbanks. Daily summer bus and train services link Anchorage, Denali National Park, and Fairbanks. Daily flights operate between Anchorage and Fairbanks; the Interior's largest city is also the most convenient airport for scheduled and chartered flights to bush communities in Arctic and Western Alaska. Radiating out from Fairbanks, the Chena Hot Springs Road, the Steese Highway, and the Elliott Highway link the city with outlying areas that are best accessed with an organized tour or by car.

A floatplane flying across Mount McKinley and the Alaska Range

For hotels and restaurants see pp242–5 and pp250–55

Cottages lining the shoreline along Big Lake

❶ Big Lake

60 miles (96 km) N of Anchorage.
Transport map E3. 🏕 3,300. 🛈 892-
6109. 🎣 Big Lake Ice Fishing Derby
(Mar). 🅦 biglakechamber.org

Dubbed Alaska's "Year Round
Playground", Big Lake lives up to
the moniker. In the summer, the
lake echoes with the roars of
motorboats, floatplanes, jet skis,
and fireworks, while in the
winter, it buzzes as snow-
machiners take to the trails.

While the community itself is
small, most of the surrounding
lakes are lined with the vacation
cabins of city dwellers trying to
get away to the outdoors.
However, in contrast to Big
Lake's constant hum of activity,
many of these lakes, including
the Papoose Twins, Big Beaver
Lake, and Horseshoe Lake, are
quieter. Nearly all have public
boat launches that offer access
to quiet sailing, kayaking, and
canoeing, as well as the chance
to view otters, muskrats, and
nesting waterfowl.

Devastating forest fires in
1996 burned much of the area,
but it now provides a first-hand
look at the regeneration of the
boreal forest.

❷ Houston

60 miles (96 km) N of Anchorage.
Transport map E3. 🏕 1,900. 🚌
Anchorage–Fairbanks.

Stretched out along the Parks
Highway, this small service
center is the only place in the
Matanuska-Susitna Valley where
fireworks can be purchased

legally. They are banned in
some parts of the state,
including Anchorage and much
of the Mat-Su, due to the
possibility of setting wildfires.
Fireworks stands are permitted
in only one area near the
southern end of the town, and
it is worth visiting for their
advertising alone. The most
imaginative is Gorilla Fireworks,
featuring enormous inflatable
gorillas and a range of
psychedelic vehicles.

❸ Nancy Lake State Recreation Area

Nancy Lake Parkway, Mile 67.3 Parks
Hwy. **Transport map** E3. 🛈 Nancy
Lake Ranger Station, 495-6273. 🚣 🏕
🏕 🅦 alaskastateparks.org

The Susitna Valley landscape is
dominated by the winding
ridges and small hills – eskers
and drumlins – left behind by
retreating glaciers. Here, the
low-lying bogs, forested slopes,
and lakes of Nancy Lake State

Recreation Area provide a
serene environment for
canoeing, fishing, and wildlife
watching. The highlight is the
two-day **Lynx Lake Loop**
canoe trail, which winds
through 14 lakes and ponds.
Canoes can be rented at South
Rolly Lake in the summer. Many
lakes in this area have beaver
lodges and dams, and every
lake has at least one pair of
loons, whose haunting calls
punctuate summer evenings.
During the winter, the park's
trails and canoe route become
excellent Nordic ski trails and
snowmachine routes.

❹ Willow

70 miles (113 km) N of Anchorage.
Transport map E3. 🏕 2,100. 🚌
Anchorage–Fairbanks.
🅦 willowchamber.org

Founded in 1897 after the
discovery of gold in the
Talkeetna Mountains, Willow
flourished until the 1940s, when
mining stopped and the town
lapsed into obscurity. It gained
national visibility in 1976, when
voters selected it as their new
state capital. Investment poured
in, land prices skyrocketed, and
myriad plans surfaced for the
new "capital in the wilderness."
The hype evaporated after a
1982 referendum in which
Alaskans declined to fund the
predicted costs of the move
from Juneau. The town now
serves as a Parks Highway snack
stop, and, more importantly, as
the restart location for the
Iditarod (see p49).

Small roadside museum on the Parks Highway at Willow

The Boreal Forest

Most of Interior Alaska is cloaked in the vast circumpolar boreal forest that also covers much of subarctic Canada, northwestern Russia, Scandinavia, and Siberia. In hilly or well-drained regions, the term "boreal forest" includes dry lands, such as the rolling country around Fairbanks, which are typically covered in white or black spruce and birch. This region also includes taiga, "little sticks" in Russian, which refers to the stick-like black spruce forest that dominates the typically boggy and low-lying muskeg that prevails in much of Alaska's Interior. These rich, lake-dotted lands produce a wealth of berries and are home to most of Alaska's lynx, bears, and forest-dwelling rodents such as beavers, porcupines, martens, and ermines.

Shrubs, mosses, and lichens form the ground cover beneath the trees.

Spruce, birch, and aspen are well-adapted to the typically thin topsoil.

Boreal Fauna

At different stages in its regrowth after a wildfire, the boreal forest supports a changing succession of wildlife. Northern hawk owls are among the first to inhabit the forest, followed by red foxes, martens, and spruce hens as the forest matures.

Black-capped chickadees, tiny song birds, do not migrate in the winter and are evident all year round.

Red squirrels spend summer cutting and storing green spruce cones. They nest in trees, using ground burrows mostly as caches.

Spruce hens, marked by mottled feathers, usually nest at the base of a spruce tree.

Northern hawk owls are atypical of most owls because they hunt during the day, preying on voles, mice, and occasionally small birds.

Martens, who feed mainly on voles, have non-retractable claws, used for climbing as well as holding prey.

Red foxes are recognized by their white-tipped tails and black "stockings." These omnivores are found across the Alaskan Interior in hilly, forested country.

❺ Talkeetna

114 miles (183 km) N of Anchorage.
Transport map E3. ⛰ 900.
✈ 🚃 Anchorage–Fairbanks. 🚌
Anchorage–Fairbanks. ℹ Parks Hwy
& Talkeetna Spur Rd, 733-2688. 🎿
Talkeetna Bluegrass Festival (1st
weekend in Aug), Bachelor Auction
and Wilderness Woman (1st weekend
in Dec). 🔲 talkeetnadenali.com

Possibly the only town to have
had a ginger cat – Stubbs – as
its honorary mayor for some
15 years, Talkeetna, meaning
"meeting of the rivers" in the
local Athabaskan language,
began in 1896 as a trading post
and grew into a riverboat port
supplying the 1910 Susitna
Valley Gold Rush. There was a
second wave of development
when the Alaska
Engineering
Commission set up
its headquarters
here during the
construction of
the Alaska Railroad.
Modern growth has
been fueled by its
favorable location near
Mount McKinley.
    Any illusions of
Talkeetna being the prototype
of a small, quiet, pioneer town
will be quickly dispelled by the
summer crowds. Although the
town was bypassed by the Parks

Climbers planning a trip at the Talkeetna Ranger Station

Highway when it was built in
the early 1970s, it still attracts a
lot of traveler traffic: busloads of
tourists admire its old-fashioned
air, young backpackers wonder
how to settle in permanently,
and prospective climbers hope
to scale Mount McKinley.
    Popular activities include
flightseeing trips over
the mountain and
touring the
junction of the
Susitna, Talkeetna,
and Chulitna rivers
with **Mahay's Riverboat
Service**. Mahay's also
runs Denali wilderness
tours and fishing tours
on the Talkeetna river.

**Road sign,
Talkeetna**

AIRCRAFT
CROSSING

Mahay's Riverboat Service
Main St, Talkeetna. **Tel** 733-2223.
🔲 mahaysriverboat.com

Talkeetna Ranger Station
22241 B St. **Tel** 733-2231. **Open** mid-
Apr–early Sep: 8am–5:30pm daily;
winter: 8am–4:30pm Mon–Fri. ♿
🔲 nps.gov/dena/planyourvisit/
mountaineering.html

Maintained by the National Park
Service, this ranger station
provides year-round information
for prospective climbers of
Mount McKinley and other peaks
of the Alaska Range. The staff also
mails out free information on
mountaineering regulations and
fees. Inside, there is a reference
library of books and maps on
mountaineering and Mount
McKinley. Rangers conduct free
orientation programs for
climbing expeditions, as well as
general interest programs at the
Talkeetna Historical Society
Museum and the Talkeetna
Alaskan Lodge.

🏛 Talkeetna Historical
Society Museum
Off 1st St. **Tel** 733-2487. **Open**
summer: 10am–6pm daily; winter:
11am–4pm Sat & Sun. 📷
🔲 talkeetnahistoricalsociety.org

Located next to the old
airstrip, the Talkeetna Historical
Society Museum consists of a
complex of seven buildings. The
main displays are housed in the
red 1937 **Schoolhouse**, which
had rooms for teachers on the
floor above. Used as a school
until 1971, it became the
museum headquarters three
years later. Today, it is packed
with pioneer artifacts, photographs, and articles on old
Talkeetna, including relics of
bush pilot Don Sheldon and
mountaineer Ray Genet.
    The museum also includes
the 1933 **Railroad Depot**,

Climbers and bush plane on Kahiltna Glacier

Mountaineers and Glacier Pilots

Mount McKinley, looming on the horizon, is Talkeetna's main draw. In
1947, Bradford and Barbara Washburn pioneered the West Buttress
Route, which is the standard route in use today. Starting with a flight
to the 7,200-ft (2,160-m) level of Kahiltna Glacier, it eliminates a long
walk on Muldrow Glacier from McKinley's northern slope. Talkeetna
legend Ray Genet became the first McKinley guide, and his friend
Don Sheldon ferried climbers to and from Kahiltna Glacier. Today,
dozens of Talkeetna pilots fly climbers, skiers, and sightseers to
McKinley's slopes.

complete with a historic ticket office, which replaced the original 1920s structure that burned to the ground. It was moved from the railway yard to its present location in 1990. The 1923 **Railroad Section House** was originally the home of the railway foreman and his family and crew. It now houses a mountaineering exhibit, including a 12-sq-ft (3.5-sq-m) scale model of Mount McKinley that is based on aerial photographs taken by renowned photographer, Bradford Washburn.

The town's oldest building, the 1916 **Ole Dahl Cabin**, the home of miner and barber Ole Dahl, was also salvaged by the museum, as were the 1924 **Harry Robb Cabin** and the 1920s **stables** operated by Belle McDonald.

🏛 Fairview Inn

101 Main St (corner of D St)
Tel 733-2423.

Built by Ben Nauman in 1923 as the overnight stop on the Alaska Railroad between Seward and Fairbanks, the Fairview Inn holds the laudable distinction of having possessed Talkeetna's first bathtub. Decorated with antlers, pelts, and local memorabilia, it was a community hall and drinking den for both locals and visitors. In 2003, it was decreed that

Fairview Inn sign, downtown Talkeetna

no building in downtown Talkeetna could be higher than the inn. After closing briefly, the Fairview reopened in 2006 and is now smoke-free. It is a great spot to meet locals and climbers, and to enjoy the occasional live band.

🏛 Nagley's Store

13650 North Main Street. **Tel** 733-3663. 📷 🇼 nagleysstore.com

Across the street from the Fairview Inn, Nagley's Store is one of Talkeetna's most charming buildings. Horace Nagley ran a shop at Susitna Station on the Big Su (the Susitna River), but dismantled it and reconstructed it on the Talkeetna riverfront between 1917 and 1921. In 1945, it was moved again on log rollers to its current site. Amazingly, it stayed open during the move. The store houses the town's only grocery and general store. Farther down

McKinley Climbers Memorial in Talkeetna's wooded cemetery

Main Street is the 1930s **Ole Dahl Cabin No. 2**, the home of miner Ole Dahl, the 1930s Norwegian-style **Helmer Ronning House**, and the 1917 **Frank Lee Cabin and Barn**, now housing the popular Talkeetna Roadhouse.

🏛 Talkeetna Cemetery

2nd & F Sts.

Talkeetna's quiet cemetery would be of little interest to visitors if it were not for the memorial commemorating climbers who have died on Mount McKinley over the years. It is a sobering reminder to those setting out that the mountain and its weather can be harsh opponents and are not to be taken lightly. Among the headstones is that of Talkeetna glacier pilot Don Sheldon, whose exploits are immortalized in the book, *Wager with the Wind*. He died in 1975 at the age of 56. Talkeetna's other hero, Ray Genet, is missing here as he was lost on Mount Everest in 1979 at the age of 48 and his body was never found.

Historic Nagley's Store in downtown Talkeetna

The enormous concrete Igloo at Mile 188.5 of the Parks Highway serving as a local landmark

❻ Denali State Park

135 miles (215 km) N of Anchorage. **Transport map** E3. 🚌 Anchorage–Fairbanks. 🛈 Alaska State Parks Office (Wasilla), 745-3975. ♿ limited. ⚠ 🌐 dnr.alaska.gov/parks/units/denali1.htm

The majority of travelers drive past Denali State Park en route to the better-known Denali National Park *(see pp166–9)*, effectively creating this park's quieter charm. Established in 1970, Denali State Park sprawls over 507 sq miles (1,313 sq km), which is about half the size of Rhode Island.

The park offers uncrowded campgrounds, fabulous hiking trails, and views that equal those of its more renowned neighbor. **Denali Viewpoint South**, at Mile 134.7 of the Parks Highway, which bisects the park, offers the best panorama of Mount McKinley along the road system. The park's **Kesugi Ridge Trail**, a challenging 13- to 35-mile-(21- to 56-km-) long hike, follows an alpine ridge east of the Parks Highway, with superb mountain and glacier views from beginning to end. It is accessed from Little Coal Creek Trailhead at Mile 163.9 of the Parks Highway, with exits back to the highway via the Troublesome Creek, Ermine Hill, or Cascade Trails.

The flora of the park is dominated by white spruce and paper birch, as well as moss campion and mountain avens.

The park's varied landscape, with valley glaciers and great alpine ridges, as well as meandering lowland streams and Arctic tundra, make it the favored habitat of a wide range of wildlife, including caribou, moose, bears, wolves, and lynx. Beavers and muskrats inhabit the park's wet areas, while both marmots and pikas (small rabbit-like mammals) can be seen on treeless hillsides and rocky outcrops.

A few sights along the Parks Highway beyond the Denali State Park boundary at Mile 168.6 also demand attention. These include the dramatic **Hurricane Gulch** at Mile 174 and the **Igloo** at Mile 188.5. Built in the 1970s, this enormous, now abandoned structure roughly marks the midway point between Anchorage and Fairbanks.

❼ Cantwell

210 miles (340 km) N of Anchorage. **Transport map** E3. 🚐 220. 🚌 Anchorage–Fairbanks.

This small village takes its name from the Cantwell River, the former name of the Nenana River. This scenic area was originally inhabited by itinerant Athabaskan hunters, but the first person to settle there was trapper Oley Nicklie in the early 20th century. As more people settled there, Cantwell was designated a federally recognized tribal community. Today, a quarter of its residents are of Native descent. Cantwell, with a food shop and a motel, is a convenient refueling stop. It is also the western terminus of the Denali Highway.

No-See-Ums

The biting midges known as no-see-ums are the smallest of the biting flies. Their peskiness quotient often surpasses that of mosquitoes, as they appear in thick swarms that are impossible to ignore. Alaska has 50 midge species, of which only a few actually bite. The variety found in the boreal forests of Interior Alaska, *Culicoides sanguisuga* (the Latin name appropriately means bloodsucker), raises large itchy welts, and can make life intolerable from late June through July. A DEET-based repellant will be effective, although some people swear by the widely available Avon Skin-So-Soft moisturizer, which acts as a repellant.

Tiny midges appear in swarms in the summer

❾ Denali Highway Tour

A trip across the fabulously scenic Denali Highway is an unforgettable experience. Built in 1957, it was the only link between Anchorage and Denali National Park until the completion of the Parks Highway in 1972. The Alaska Range runs along its length, offering spectacular views, and tundra and taiga forests on the route are home to moose, caribou, and grizzlies. Except for the first 21 miles (34 km) westward from Paxson and the last couple of miles, the route is gravel that ranges from smooth to rough and rutted.

Tips for Drivers

Starting point: Paxson.
Length: 134 miles (214 km).
Accommodation: Tangle River Inn, Mile 20 (Tangle Lakes).
🅦 tangleriverinn.com
Gracious House, Mile 82 (Susitna River). 🅦 alaskaone.com/gracious
Stopping-off points: waysides and parking areas along the route offer great photo opportunities.
Note: the highway is closed to traffic from October to mid-May.

Key
▭▭ Tour route
▭▭ Main road

0 km   100
0 miles   100

⑥ **Brushkana River**
The highway crosses the Brushkana River at Mile 104.3. The campsite near the bridge is ideal for fishing.

⑤ **Susitna River**
The 260-mile (416-km) Susitna River, popularly called the Big Su, has its headwaters in the Susitna Glacier in the Alaska Range. The river has Class III to Class V rapids between here and Talkeetna.

④ **Clearwater Creek Controlled Use Area**
Gold was mined in the Clearwater Creek area in the early 20th century. Today, there is good hunting and fishing available here.

③ **McLaren Summit**
At 4,086 ft (1,226 m), this is Alaska's second highest pass. The view north takes in several glaciers, including Susitna Glacier.

② **Tangle Lakes**
Tangle Lakes, the headwaters of the Delta River, are popular for kayaking and fishing. The surrounding 350-sq-mile (900-sq-km) area includes several ancient Native hunting sites.

① **Summit Lake**
Around Mile 4, several highway turnouts afford great views north to Summit Lake and Gakona Glacier.

❾ Denali National Park

Alaska's top attraction, the expansive Denali National Park, sprawls across 9,420 sq miles (24,395 sq km) and is larger than the entire state of New Hampshire. Its highlight is, of course, the 20,320-ft (6,195-m) Mount McKinley, which dominates the surrounding landscape and is North America's highest peak. The park is world-renowned for its wildlife viewing, and visitors can expect to see a wide variety of animals. In the summer, Denali's tundra regions explode with wildflowers, while in September, they blaze with autumnal yellows, reds, and oranges. Just one road penetrates the backcountry; after Mile 15 this single route is accessible only in summer by the park's shuttle buses, crossing open tundra, boggy lowlands, and mountain passes to wind up at beautiful Wonder Lake.

Alaska Railroad
The train is a convenient way to get to the park from Anchorage or Fairbanks.

★ **Wonder Lake**
Wonder Lake, near the end of the park's shuttle route, affords one of the finest views of Mount McKinley. Visitors will find excellent late-summer blueberry picking around the lake campground.

Kantishna

McKinley

Exploring the Park

With a full day, it is possible to take an early morning shuttle bus to Wonder Lake and still have an hour or two to explore on foot before catching the last bus back. As long as no wildlife is visible in the area, day hikers can get off the bus wherever they like and flag down a later bus back on a space-available basis. Some of the finest day hiking is found around the site of the Eielson Visitors' Center. Backcountry hiking and camping can be strenuous and requires a permit from the Backcountry Information Center.

Mount McKinley
20,320 ft

Mount Foraker
17,400 ft

Mount Hunt
14,573 ft

Alaska Range

Yentna Glacier

Lacuna Glacier

Kahiltna Glacier

Kahiltna Glacier

Mount McKinley
The snow-clad Mount McKinley is visible from many points on the Denali National Park Road. Athabaskans called the peak Denali, "The Great One," and most Alaskans continue to refer to Mount McKinley by its old name.

Polychrome Pass
The Park Road crosses four high passes between Riley Creek and Wonder Lake. The overlook on Polychrome Pass offers a fabulous view across a wildly multicolored landscape.

Whitewater Rafting
The Nenana River *(see p172)*, on the park's eastern boundary, offers exciting whitewater rafting.

Key

═══ Highway

═══ Minor road

━━━ Alaska Railroad

– – Park boundary

△ Peak

Wildlife Viewing at Denali

Wildlife viewing is one of Alaska's major attractions, and Denali National Park offers excellent opportunities to see Alaska's "Big Four" – grizzlies, moose, caribou, and Dall sheep *(see p33)*. A variety of other animals and birds are routinely sighted, including the well-known wolf packs of Denali.

Grizzly bear roaming the park

Moose dredging for pond weed

Caribou browsing on the tundra

For keys to symbols *see back flap*

Exploring Denali National Park

Most summer visitors to Alaska have Denali National Park on their itineraries, so a smooth visit requires pre-booking and advance planning. In the June to August peak season, it is not uncommon to have to wait several days for shuttle tickets or campsite bookings. For hikers, the park is divided into 43 backcountry units, each of which accommodates one group per night. Backcountry permits cannot be reserved, so access to high-demand units can require long waits. To get to the most appealing parts of the park, those without bookings should stop off at the Wilderness Access Center to organize their visit. Note that no private vehicles are allowed on the Denali National Park Road beyond Savage River.

Horseshoe Lake, a popular and easy hike from Park Headquarters

Denali National Park Headquarters Area

PO Box 9, Denali National Park. **Tel** 683-2294. ♿ ✏ 🚻 🏕

The Park Headquarters area, near the main entrance at the eastern end of the park, is a necessary stop for all visitors. Around the Denali Visitor Center, which has an information desk, there is a general store, a restaurant, a bookshop, a gas station, showers, and lockers. A mile (1.6 km) away, the Wilderness Access Center handles shuttle bus tickets and campsite reservations, while next door, the Backcountry Information Center issues free backcountry permits. Also worth a visit are the **Sled Dog Kennels**, accessible by free shuttle bus from the Denali Visitor Center. Since the 1920s, rangers have used dog sleds to patrol the park. The dogs are so popular that rangers now offer mushing demonstrations in the summer. The entrance area also has some smooth, well-managed trails. The Rock Creek and Mount Healy Overlook Trails both take half a day, while the Horseshoe Lake and Taiga Trails take an hour or two. As the park proper has no managed trails, hikers must be prepared for rough terrain and unbridged river crossings. They need to carry their camping gear and food, and must be adept at route-finding with a map and a compass or GPS.

Park shuttles go to all six of the park's campgrounds. All the sites have toilets; four have potable tap water. Reserve a place as far in advance as possible.

🚌 Denali National Park Road

Tel (866) 761-6629 (bus reservations). 🚌 late May–mid-Sep: 6am–3pm at half-hour intervals from Wilderness Access Center; reserve in advance. ✏ ♿ on some buses. 🌐 **reservedenali.com**

The Denali National Park Road leads 85 miles (136 km) into the heart of the park through a picturesque and wildlife-rich forest and tundra landscape. The area between the Park Headquarters and **Savage River**, 15 miles (24 km) west of the entrance, is moose habitat. In the spring, visitors should look out for cow moose with calves. Beyond the river, the road grows increasingly scenic as it climbs onto alpine tundra, with herds of Dall sheep often visible on Primrose Ridge to the north.

Winding past braided rivers and colorful peaks, the road continues above the treeline to **Sable Pass**. **Polychrome Pass** at Mile 45 is another highlight. The stunning, vividly colored rocks of Polychrome Mountain were formed by volcanic action about 50 million years ago. Wolves sometimes hunt migrating caribou in this area, and visitors

Park shuttle buses at the Stony Hill Overlook on the Denali National Park Road

might spot a lone wolf on the road in the summer. Shortly after the road's highest point at the 3,980-ft (1,213-m) **Highway Pass**, visitors get their first good view of Mount McKinley at the **Stony Hill Overlook**. The road continues west to the **Eielson Visitor Center**. West of here, the road passes the foot of **Muldrow Glacier** and follows the wildly braided McKinley River to Wonder Lake. The one-way trip from Park Headquarters to the lake takes about six hours.

In an effort to control traffic pollution, only park shuttle buses are allowed on the Park Road beyond Savage River. The only exceptions are RV drivers who have a minimum three-night stay booked at the Teklanika campground.

🏕 Wonder Lake

Mile 85, Denali National Park Road. 🚌 from Wilderness Access Center. ⚠

Lovely Wonder Lake, at an altitude of just 2,090 ft (627 m), enjoys an unobstructed view of Mount McKinley, which rises a dramatic 18,230 ft (5,569 m) above the level of the lake. By comparison, the 29,035-ft- (8,710-m-) high Mount Everest rises only about 10,000 ft (3,000 m) from its base. On rare clear days, visitors are treated to the remarkable sight of the mountain reflected in the still waters of Wonder Lake. The

The original log-built 1919 Kantishna Roadhouse

region around the lake, characterized by expanses of tundra and blueberry bushes, is favored grizzly habitat, and campers at the Wonder Lake Campground frequently see bears and caribou. In nearby ponds, beavers can often be seen cutting willows, and moose can be spotted dredging for pond weed. For most visitors, the lake is the end of the usual route through the park, although the road and shuttle bus services continue on to Kantishna.

Kantishna

93 miles (150 km) W of Denali (McKinley) Village. 🚐 *130*. ✈ air taxi from Denali (McKinley) Village. 🚌 from Wilderness Access Center.

Located 7 miles (11 km) beyond Wonder Lake, tiny Kantishna is one of many Alaskan settlements that started as mining camps. In 1905, the initial rush brought in at least 2,000 stampeders, who arrived to profit from the area's deposits of gold, silver, lead, zinc, and antimony. After ANILCA was passed in 1980 *(see p61)*, Denali National Park was expanded and Kantishna found itself surrounded by the park. In 1985, all mining, including that on private claims, was banned.

Today, Kantishna is little more than an airstrip and a collection of lodges. The 1906 recorder's and assayer's office and the original 1919 **Kantishna Roadhouse** can still be seen near the current roadhouse. Anglers who hold a state fishing license can also fish around Kantishna.

The Wolves of Denali

While most people come to Denali to see the "Big Four" – grizzly bears, moose, caribou, and Dall sheep – a very lucky few also have the chance to see timber wolves in the wild, or hear their haunting choruses. These canines number only 7,000 to 10,000 in Alaska, and only 100 or so individuals, in about a dozen packs, inhabit Denali National Park. Each pack, which includes an alpha male, a female, and their pups, requires between 200 and 800 sq miles (518 to 2,072 sq km). Adults usually weigh around 100 lb (45 kg), and have a brain twice as large as that of a domestic

Timber wolf wandering through the scrub, Denali National Park

dog. Currently, Alaska's wolf population is healthy, but some sport and subsistence hunters maintain that wolves kill too many moose and caribou, and the state government has instituted highly controversial predator control programs. Denali's wolves are safe from officially sanctioned hunts, but once a pack roams beyond the boundaries of the park, there are no guarantees. Wolf researchers in Denali employ aircraft, radio collaring, and genetic studies to track and study the packs.

McKinley River flowing through vibrant tundra against the backdrop of Mount McKinley ▶

Denali (McKinley) Village, the main service center for Denali National Park

❿ Denali (McKinley) Village

124 miles (200 km) S of Fairbanks. **Transport map** E3. 🚐 170. 🚌 Anchorage–Fairbanks. 🚌 Anchorage–Fairbanks, park shuttle buses.

This cluster of huge hotels, RV parks, lodges, restaurants, and outdoor activity operators is the main service center for the Denali National Park area *(see pp166–9)*. Normally referred to as either Denali Village or Denali Park, this place was formerly just a roadside stretch of development, but a growing number of hotels, shops, and tourist-driven businesses have earned it the moniker "Glitter Gulch." By any name, however, it would still be one of the busiest villages in the summer. Since the demolition of the Denali National Park Hotel, which provided well-heeled accommodations inside the park, visitors who want to appreciate Denali in comfort usually take hotel rooms

here. Visitors can also opt for less expensive options in Healy to the north, or Carlo Creek, 13 miles (21 km) south on the Parks Highway.

⓫ Nenana River

S of Nenana Bridge in Denali (McKinley) Village. **Transport map** E3.

Rising on Nenana Mountain in the Alaska Range, the 150-mile (240-km) long Nenana River tumbles down to join the Parks Highway at Mile 215. From this point on, the river and highway flow side by side. Spruce occasionally topple off the eroding banks, forming "sweepers," logs that float in the water and are a real navigation hazard for rafts and canoes.

Beyond Healy, the Nenana enters the flats north of the Alaska Range and flows more lethargically until it merges with the Tanana River at the village of Nenana. From the south side of the Nenana Bridge in Denali

Park, thrilling whitewater rafting through the steep-sided Nenana Canyon is provided by three main outfitters: **Nenana Raft Adventures**, the **Denali Outdoor Center**, and **Denali Raft Adventures**. Difficulty levels range from easy Class I rapids to more challenging Class IV white-water. In the price of a half-day trip are included raingear, boots, personal flotation devices, and transfers to and from hotels in the area.

Denali Outdoor Center
Mile 238.5, Parks Hwy. **Tel** 683-1925, (888) 303-1925.
🆆 denalioutdoorcenter.com

Denali Raft Adventures
Mile 238, Parks Hwy. **Tel** 683-2234, (888) 683-2234. 🆆 denaliraft.com

Nenana Raft Adventures
Mile 238, Parks Hwy. **Tel** (800) 789-7238. 🆆 raftdenali.com

⓬ Healy

113 miles (182 km) S of Fairbanks. **Transport map** E3. 🚐 1,000. 🚌 Anchorage–Fairbanks. 🚹 Mile 0.4, Healy Spur Rd; 683-4636.
🆆 denalichamber.com

North of Denali, the village of Healy has long been the service center for the Usibelli coal fields 3 miles (5 km) to the east. Discovered by Emil Usibelli in 1943, these fields contain the state's largest deposits of sub-bituminous coal. The mine now provides energy for Alaska's military bases, fuels Fairbanks' power plant, and exports coal. Healy is best known as an inexpensive place to stay and

Thrilling whitewater rafting on the Nenana River

For hotels and restaurants see pp242–5 and pp250–55

plan a visit to Denali National Park. It is also well-known for the rough winter route from here to Kantishna *(see p169)*. Known as the **Stampede Trail**, the route is accessible by snowmachine in winter, but river crossings make it practically impassable in the summer. About 4 miles (6 km) north of Healy, the trail passes an old Fairbanks city bus. It was here that 24-year-old Chris McCandless died of injury and starvation in 1992. He intended to live off the land, away from civilization, and to experience the raw Alaskan wilderness. His story is documented in Jon Krakauer's book *Into the Wild* and film of the same name.

⑬ Nenana

58 miles (93 km) S of Fairbanks.
Transport map E3. 🚌 400. 🚍
Anchorage–Fairbanks. ℹ A St & Parks
Hwy, 832-5446. 🎿 Nenana Ice Classic
(Feb–Apr). 🌐 **nenana.org**

The little service center of Nenana lies at the confluence of the Nenana and Tanana Rivers. At the turn of the 20th century, it was known as Tortella or Tortilli, apparently derivations of a long forgotten

Old river tug, the *Taku Chief*, outside the Nenana Visitor Center

Athabaskan word. The town began as a trading post for river travelers, and eventually came to be called Nenana, which means "a good campsite between the rivers." In the 1920s, it served as a railroad construction camp, and gained fame on July 15, 1923, when President Warren G Harding drove in the golden spike that completed the Alaska Railroad between Seward and Fairbanks.

The old railroad depot at the end of Main Street houses the **Alaska Railroad Museum**. A block away, the log-built **St. Mark's Mission Church** is worth a visit, as is the *Taku Chief*, a river tug that once pushed barges down the Tanana. Today, it stands outside the Nenana Visitor Center. The **Alfred Starr Cultural Center** has displays on Native culture, plus a small gift shop.

Nenana is the site of the **Nenana Ice Classic** competition.

Each year, people from all across the state place bets on when the ice will go out on the Tanana. Any surge in the river ice shifts a four-legged "tripod" on shore, which pulls a cord, which in turn trips the clock on the adjacent tower. All correct entries split half the take and the organizers get the other half.

Four-legged "tripod" for determining ice breakup

⑭ Ester

6 miles (10 km) W of Fairbanks.
Transport map E3. 🚌 2,400. 🚍
Anchorage–Fairbanks. 🌐 **fairbanks-alaska.com/ester-alaska.htm**

Northeast of Nenana on the Parks Highway is the old mining and Gold Rush town of Ester. In 1906, in its heyday, Ester had a population of 5,000. The Fairbanks Exploration Company built the Ester Gold Camp in the mid-1930s to service the area's dredging operations. The camp closed in the 1950s, but it was reopened as a tourist site in 1958. It closed in 2008. Regardless, the town retains a pleasant, small mining village feel and has grown as a rural residential area. Most residents are employed in Fairbanks or at the University of Alaska Fairbanks *(see p175)*, although there are some small local businesses: a saloon, a library, fire station, post office, arts and crafts studios, three active gold mines and a summer farmers' market.

Now closed, the Healy Clean Coal Plant generated energy using Usibelli coal

⑮ Fairbanks

Known as Alaska's Golden Heart, Fairbanks sprawls across the broad Tanana Valley. Italian immigrant Felix Pedro, who discovered gold near Chatanika, met miner E T Barnette, who was forced ashore here when his boat ran aground, and together, they founded Fairbanks in 1901. The two men convinced Dawson prospectors to come to Fairbanks, swelling its population to 18,000. Most boomers left when the seam played out in the 1920s, but the town's economy was bolstered by World War II and the construction of the Trans-Alaska Pipeline in the mid-1970s. Today, Alaska's second largest city enjoys a sense of stability that has outlasted both its rapid urbanization and its economic fluctuations.

Sandhill crane at Creamer's Field Migratory Waterfowl Refuge

The broad Chena River curving through the city of Fairbanks

University of Alaska Fairbanks
Museum of the North
1 mile (1.6 km)

④ Pioneer Park

Growden Memorial Park

Riverboat Discovery
1 mile (1.6 km)

🏛 Morris Thompson Cultural & Visitor Center

101 Dunkel St. **Tel** 459-3700. 🚌 Blue and Red Lines. **Open** mid-May–mid-Sep: 8am–9pm daily; mid-Sep–mid-May: 8am–5pm daily. ♿
W morristhompsoncenter.org

On the Chena River in the heart of Fairbanks, this lovely modern building has state-of-the-art exhibits portraying traditional cultures and the natural world. Watch artisans at work, or enjoy a film on Alaskan life. A block away, Golden Heart Plaza's fountain features Malcolm Alexander's sculpture, *The Unknown First Family*, depicting an Inuit family and dedicated to the spirit of all Alaskans.

🏛 Fairbanks Ice Museum

500 2nd Ave. **Tel** 451-8222. 🚌
Open May–Sep: 10am–8pm daily. 🎟
🌐 W icemuseum.com

Housed in the historic Lacey Street Theater, the Fairbanks Ice Museum displays beautifully carved ice sculptures at a chilly -7° C (20° F). The World Ice Art Championships in early March draws top ice sculptors from around the world, who turn massive 7,800-lb (3,500-kg) blocks of ice into works of art. Children can enjoy the ice slides and mazes.

❎ Creamer's Field Migratory Waterfowl Refuge

1300 College Rd. **Tel** 452-5162.
🚌 Red Line. **Open** 24 hrs. 🎟 Jun–Aug: 10am Mon–Thu, 7pm Wed. ♿ 🐦 Bird banding: May: 6:30am–noon daily; Jun–mid-Jul & mid-Aug–Sep: 6am–noon daily.
W creamersfield.org

The refuge was originally a dairy farm but was sold to the state in 1975, and as it had always attracted migratory birds, the Alaska Conservation Society expanded the acreage to turn it into Creamer's Field Migratory Waterfowl Refuge. Today, the site offers good opportunities to view harriers, falcons, and swans. Sandhill cranes can be seen performing their unique dance, consisting of a series of bowing and hopping movements, through much of the summer. Visitors can watch birds being banded at the Alaska Bird Observatory near the edge of the refuge.

⌂ Pioneer Park

2300 Airport Way. **Tel** 459-1087. 🚌
Blue & Red Lines. **Open** year-round.
♿ for some attractions. ♿ 📷 🅿
Museums: **Open** Mar & Apr: 1–5pm Fri–
Sun; early May: 1–5pm daily; mid-May–
mid-Sep: 11am–8pm daily; late Sep:
1–5pm daily. 🌐 **co.fairbanks.ak.us**

This historical theme park in the
heart of Fairbanks features gold
panning, a reconstructed Gold
Rush town, the railway car that
President Warren G Harding used
while visiting Nenana in 1923,
and the SS *Nenana*, a
sternwheeler which operated on
the Chena River from 1933 to
1956. The Alaska Native Museum
highlights Athabaskan culture,
while the Alaska Pioneer Museum
outlines the lives of early settlers.
Don't miss the **Pioneer Park Air**

Vintage mining equipment in
Pioneer Park

Museum, with its collection of
vintage aircraft and exhibits on
Alaska's aviation history.

⌂ University of Alaska Museum of the North

907 Yukon Dr, University of Alaska
Fairbanks. **Tel** 474-7505. 🚌 Blue,
Yellow, & Red Lines. **Open** mid-May–
mid-Sep: 9am–9pm daily; mid-Sep–
mid-May: 9am–5pm Mon–Sat. ♿ 🅿
📷 🌐 **uaf.edu/museum** Georgeson
Botanical Garden: 117 W Tanana Dr,
UAF. **Open** May–Sep: 8am–8pm daily.
♿ 📷 LARS: Yankovich Dr, UAF.
Tel 474-5724. ♿ 📷 May–Sep:
7 tours daily.

Packed with natural history,
cultural, and geographical
displays, the old wing of the
University of Alaska Museum of
the North is well worth a visit.
Exhibits include the famous
Blue Babe, a mummified Ice
Age bison, a large collection of
Inuit carvings, and Native
costumes. The architecturally
inspiring new wing is designed
to represent mountain ridges,
ice, the aurora, and the tail
flukes of a sounding whale.
Inside, the two-story glass
view of the Alaska Range
complements the Rose Berry
Gallery of Alaska Art, which
exhibits works by renowned

Alaskan artists. The university's
**Large Animal Research Station
(LARS)**, which studies musk
oxen and caribou, and the
Georgeson Botanical Garden
are open to visitors as well.

⌂ Riverboat Discovery

Discovery Dr. **Tel** 479-6673. 🚌 Yellow
Line. **Open** mid-May–mid-Sep:
8:45am & 2pm daily. ♿ ♿ 📷 🅿
🌐 **riverboatdiscovery.com**

Perhaps the town's most
popular attraction, Riverboat
Discovery offers three-hour-
long sternwheeler riverboat
cruises down the Chena River
on the *Discovery I*, *Discovery II*, or
Discovery III. En route, a bush
pilot displays field take-offs and
landings from a grass runway
on the bank. There are visits to
the kennels of the late Iditarod
champion Susan Butcher and to
a reconstructed Athabaskan
village, where guides explain
Native traditions. The cruise also
sails past the confluence of the
clear black waters of the Chena
River and the silty, glacial
Tanana River.

---

0 meters   700

0 yards   700

Sights at a Glance

① Morris Thompson Cultural &
   Visitor Centre

② Fairbanks Ice Museum

③ Creamer's Field Migratory
   Waterfowl Refuge

④ Pioneer Park

Riverboat Discovery sternwheeler cruising on the Chena River

The Aurora Borealis

The Fairbanks area is one of the best places in the world to see the aurora borealis, or northern lights. The effect is visible as faint green, light yellow, or rose curtains, pillars, pinwheels, wisps, and haloes of undulating, vibrating light. During the greatest auroral storms, it appears as bright yellow, crimson, or violet streaks of light across the sky. While summer visitors will miss out due to the 24-hour daylight, there is a good chance of catching the celestial show on clear nights between late September and early April. Indigenous peoples had various explanations for these dancing lights. One legend said that they were the spirits of their ancestors, while another held that they were past and future events playing out across the sky.

Auroral undulations are due to the eddies, fluctuations, and directional changes in the earth's magnetic field. During a single storm, the aurora can produce up to a trillion watts of electricity with a million-amp current. Some people claim that they can hear the aurora crackling and whirring, or feel its charged particles, although scientists doubt this.

The Northern Lights Phenomenon

The aurora is caused by the interaction of the Earth's magnetic field with charged particles from the sun. As the sun fuses hydrogen into helium, it emits particles of radiation – protons and electrons – that are shot into space. When this plasma stream of particles, known as the solar wind, blows past the earth, the earth's lines of magnetism draw them toward the points where these lines converge, at the north and south magnetic poles. As the particles arrive in the ionosphere, they collide with gas atoms, causing them to emit light. The type of gas determines the color of the aurora.

Rare crimson aurora borealis over spruce and birch trees, Fairbanks

Vivid green aurora borealis shining above Bear Lake on Eielson Air Force Base

Exploring Beyond Fairbanks

Moving away from Fairbanks into the Fairbanks North Star Borough, the population thins and the vistas open up. This landscape of seemingly endless forested hills, broad river flats, and distant views of snow-capped peaks is the essence of Interior Alaska. Typically blue summer skies oversee it all, and in the winter, the aurora borealis is clearer and brighter than in Fairbanks, where it is obscured by the city lights.

Sights at a Glance

① North Pole
② Chena River State Recreation Area
③ Chena Hot Springs
④ Gold Dredge No. 8
⑤ Elliott Highway

Key

▬ Main road
═ Minor road
– – Trail
— Alaska Railroad

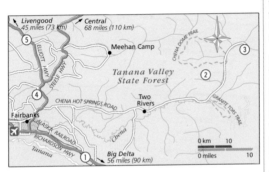

North Pole

15 miles (24 km) SE of Fairbanks. 🏔 2,100. 🚌 Fairbanks' Green Line. 🛈 125 Snowman Lane, 488-2281. 🅦 **northpolealaska.com** Santa Claus House: 101 St. Nicholas Dr. **Tel** 488-2200. 🅦 **santaclaushouse.com**

This town is nowhere near the North Pole, or even within the Arctic Circle, but here, the name is everything. Homesteaded in 1944, it was eventually sold to a developer who hoped to attract toy manufacturers by naming the new town North Pole. While manufacturers never materialized, the name inspired a Christmas spirit, as evidenced by such street names as Kris Kringle Drive, Mistletoe Lane, and Reindeer Alley. The **Santa Claus House**, next to the Richardson Highway, has a charming history and attracts youngsters with its enormous Christmas store, live reindeer, and the chance to speak with Santa. The community ushers in the Christmas season with a tree-lighting ceremony.

🏕 Chena River State Recreation Area

Mile 26, Chena Hot Spring Rd. **Tel** 269-8400. 🏔 🅦 **dnr.alaska.gov/parks/units/chena**

A wonderful park in Fairbanks' backyard, the Chena River State Recreation Area follows the clear Chena River as it winds between low, forested hills topped by rocky tors sprouting from alpine tundra. The river is ideal for Arctic grayling fishing as well as for easy kayaking.

The surrounding hills have hiking trails, from short walks to multi-day routes. One popular walk goes uphill through birch and spruce to Angel Rocks, large outcrops with superb views. The excellent two-day **Granite Tors Trail** leads up into the hills to a free shelter overlooking the Plain of Monuments, a wide expanse dotted with towering volcanic rocks. It loops back down through forest and over boardwalks across a berry-studded muskeg bog. The three-day 29-mile (46-km) **Chena Dome Trail** climbs above the timberline onto alpine tundra, with views across the wilderness. In the winter, there is plenty of scope for Nordic skiing and aurora viewing.

🏕 Chena Hot Springs

Chena Hot Springs Rd, 57 miles (91 km) E of Fairbanks. **Tel** 451-8104. 🚖 Chena Hot Springs. **Open** year-round. 🎣 🚲 🏇 🏊 🖥 📷 🏠 ⛺ 🏔 🅦 **chenahotsprings.com**

The most developed thermal spa in the state, Chena Hot Springs has functioned since 1905. It offers a complete resort experience with hot springs, pools (adults only), an indoor pool, spa therapies, and a range of other activities, such as canoeing and fishing.

Nordic skiing, sleigh rides, snowmachining, dog sledding, and, of course, aurora viewing make the spa more popular in the winter. An addition is the unique **Aurora Ice Museum**, which is open all year. It boasts an ice bar, elaborate ice carvings, and average room temperatures of -2° C (28° F).

Visitors enjoying a soak in a rock pool at Chena Hot Springs

For keys to map symbols see back flap

🎰 Gold Dredge No. 8

1755 Old Steese Hwy N. **Tel** 479-6673, (866) 479-6673. **Open** mid-May–mid-Sep: tours daily at 10:45am and 1:45pm (advance booking required).
🚗 ♿ 🖥 🌐 golddredgeno8.com

A brief taste of the Fairbanks Gold Rush of 1902 can be experienced at Gold Dredge No. 8, which gives visitors a two-hour long tour that faithfully explains gold-mining methods used in the early days. The tour begins with a ride on a replica of the Tanana Valley Railroad, with commentary and, if longtime conductor Earl is on board, old-time country songs along the way. First stop is by a section of the Trans-Alaska Pipeline, which carries approximately 15 per cent of the nation's oil production. (Top tip: stand under the pipe, raise your arms and have your photo taken "holding up" the structure.)

The train then moves on to Dredge No. 8 – a huge, mechanical gold pan which between 1928 and 1959 extracted over 7.5 million ounces (210,000 kg) of gold. Miners demonstrate the use of a sluice box and also give a brief history of mining in Alaska. Prospectors then demonstrate panning and washing gravel to extract the gold, and the guides encourage visitors to try it themselves using "pay dirt." Any gold found is weighed to determine its current value, and can then be kept by the lucky finder. Exit is, inevitably, through the gift shop, where your gold

Historic Manley Roadhouse in the village of Manley Hot Springs

pannings can be encased in a locket if you wish, while everyone enjoys complimentary coffee and cookies.

This attraction is run by the Binkleys, a fifth-generation Alaskan steamboating family who also operate the Riverboat Discovery trip on a picturesque sternwheeler *(see p175)*; the two tours can be combined in a day.

🏞 Elliott Highway

Starts 11 miles (18 km) NW of Fairbanks, off the Dalton Highway. **Tolovana Hot Springs** 100 miles (160 km) W of Fairbanks. **Tel** 455-6706. 🚗
🌐 tolovanahotsprings.com
Manley Hot Springs 152 miles (245 km) W of Fox. **Tel** 672-3171. 🚗

Connecting Fairbanks with **Manley Hot Springs**, the winding, undulating Elliott Highway is a 152-mile (245-km) wilderness route through some of Interior Alaska's finest scenery. The landscape it passes through is especially lovely in early September, with the fall colors of the birch and aspen forests.

At the tiny village of Livengood, the Dalton Highway *(see pp222–3)* turns north toward Prudhoe Bay while the Elliott Highway continues westward. At Mile 87, the road begins to climb to the trailhead for **Tolovana Hot Springs**, 11 miles (18 km) off the highway to the southeast. Pre-booking is essential for the springs. At Mile 98, the view opens up to take in the lake-studded Minto Flats, and a few miles later, a long side road turns south to the Athabaskan village of Minto.

The Elliott Highway ends at the pretty village of Manley Hot Springs, which boasts the Gold Rush-era Manley Roadhouse. The village's growth dates from 1902, when the site became a supply center for the nearby Tofty and Eureka Mining Districts. Today, the hot springs consist of three tubs in a spring-fed greenhouse filled with tropical plants.

Gold Dredge No. 8 moored along the Old Steese Highway

Dredging for Gold

After early prospectors had taken most of Alaska's easily available gold, large mining companies employed mechanical dredges, which resembled massive houseboats beset with machinery. To get at the gold-bearing quartz, water cannons blasted away soil and gravel permafrost layers. Upon reaching the bedrock, a dredge was brought in, usually to a streambed, to gouge out the rock using steel buckets on a conveyor belt. The rock was then sifted by screens of diminishing size until it reached a riffle board, where mercury was introduced to bind with the gold. Dredges crawled slowly upstream, creating dredge ponds in front of them and leaving artificial moraines behind.

Steel bucket used in gold dredging

⑯ Steese Highway Tour

From its start in Fox, the Steese Highway winds through the Alaskan Interior to Circle on the Yukon River (see pp198–9). Built in 1927, the highway follows an early mail route. After passing rolling hills and low-lying muskeg, it travels through several river valleys, which are choked with mining residue, and then crosses a scenic alpine stretch. After Twelvemile Summit, it starts descending into the flatlands around the Yukon River. While the first 44 miles (71 km) are tarred, the rest of the route is gravel of variable quality.

Tips for Drivers

Starting point: Fox, 11 miles (18 km) N of Fairbanks.
Length: 161 miles (259 km).
Accommodation: Chatanika Gold Camp Lodge at Mile 28.5 Steese Highway has rooms and a good restaurant. At Mile 39, the Upper Chatanika River State Recreation Site has wooded riverside campsites, as does Cripple Creek Campground at Mile 60.

Key

▬ Tour route
═ Minor road
– – Trail
△ Peak

0 km — 20
0 miles — 20

⑥ Circle
The highway ends at Circle, the largest town in the region until the rise of Dawson in the late 1890s. Early settlers chose its name believing that it lay astride the Arctic Circle – it is, in fact, about 55 miles (88 km) south of it.

⑤ Central
Unique exhibits at the town museum detail the history of Central, which was the heart of the Circle Mining District during the Gold Rush.

④ Birch Creek Access
River runners can launch at a facility at Mile 94, and put-in for a float to Mile 147.

③ Pinnell Mountain Trail
This 27-mile (43-km) trail follows an alpine ridge from Eagle Summit to Twelvemile Summit. Two free public shelters provide a roof for hikers along the route.

② Chatanika and Gold Dredge No. 3
Chatanika was built in 1925 to supply local dredging operations. Dredge No. 3, which closed in 1962, stands a short hike away from Chatanika Lodge.

① Fox
This former gold-mining camp is the site of such attractions as the Howling Dog Saloon. Also worth visiting is the nearby Gold Dredge No. 8.

Twelvemile House
Circle Hot Springs
Porcupine Dome 4,915 ft
Twelvemile Summit 2,982 ft
Birch Creek
Yukon
STEESE HIGHWAY
Chena Hot Springs
Little Chena
Chatanika
Chena
Fairbanks
Tanana

EASTERN INTERIOR ALASKA

The heart of the Klondike Gold Rush of 1898, the wild Eastern Interior reflects the popular image of Alaska for most outsiders. This "great, big, broad land 'way up yonder," so evocatively extolled in the poetry of Robert Service, is typified by hills laced with the gold-bearing streams that were the destinations of hopeful prospectors, and the icy peaks and glacial valleys that barred their way.

During the Gold Rush, towns sprang up in remote areas along the Yukon River and its tributaries. Dawson City, lying at the confluence of the Yukon and Klondike Rivers in Canada's Yukon Territory, became the commercial heart of the region. After most of the claims had been staked and the readily accessible gold had been extracted, many penniless prospectors opted to stay to homestead and pursue frontier lifestyles.

Shortly after the Gold Rush ended, copper was discovered at the turn of the century near Kennicott in the Wrangell Mountains, and the Copper River and Northwestern Railway was built from Cordova to export ore to the outside world. World War II necessitated the construction of the Alaska Highway in 1942, and the road not only opened up an access route through the Interior, but also boosted the economy of the region. In the 1970s, the area experienced a new boom – a black gold rush – as the Richardson Highway became the corridor for the Trans-Alaska Pipeline that connected the Prudhoe Bay oilfields with the Valdez terminal.

With the creation of Wrangell-St. Elias National Park in 1980, a thriving tourist industry took shape in the region. The park, a UNESCO World Heritage Site, is now on the itinerary of an increasing number of visitors. Visitors are also drawn by the numerous wildlife refuges and the mighty Yukon River, which flows across the northern part of the region, as well as by adventure activities, scenic drives, and historic towns.

The broad Yukon River winding across the Alaskan Interior near Circle

◀ Abandoned buildings at Kennicott within Wrangell-St. Elias National Park

Exploring Eastern Interior Alaska

Eastern Interior Alaska takes in not only vast swaths of landscape crossed by gold-bearing streams, but also the peaks of the Wrangell-St. Elias Mountains and the eastern Alaska Range. Cutting through Wrangell-St. Elias National Park is one of North America's most scenic drives, the Edgerton Highway/McCarthy Road, which leads to Kennicott, an abandoned mining town that is one of the state's most unusual attractions. Paxson is famous for hosting the Arctic Man, a demanding snowmachining challenge, while farther north lie the appealing communities of Eagle and Chicken. The mighty Yukon River offers canoeing and whitewater rafting.

Hiking across the ridges of Matanuska Glacier

Sights at a Glance

Towns and Cities

③ Glennallen
④ Copper Center
⑤ Paxson
⑥ Delta Junction
⑧ *Kennicott pp188–9*
⑪ Tok
⑬ Northway
⑮ Chicken
⑱ Eagle
⑳ Dawson City

National and State Parks

② Lake Louise State Recreation Area
⑨ *Wrangell-St. Elias National Park pp192–3*
⑫ Tok River State Recreation Site
⑭ Tetlin National Wildlife Refuge
⑯ Jack Wade Dredge No. 1
⑰ Yukon-Charley Rivers National Preserve

Areas of Natural Beauty

① Matanuska Glacier
⑦ Edgerton Highway/McCarthy Road
⑩ Tok Cut-Off
⑲ *The Yukon River pp198–9*

Birch Creek

Twenty Mile Vil

Fairbanks

West Point
5,870 ft

Salcha

Goodp

Fairbanks

Mount H
6,

Big Delta

⑥ DELTA JUNC

De
Lak

Black Rapid

*Isabel Pass
3,510 ft*

DENALI HIGHWAY

⑧

⑤ PAXSON

Paxson Lake

TOK CUT

Chistochina

Copper

Susitna Lake   Lake Louise   Gakona

LAKE LOUISE STATE RECREATION AREA ②

Gulkana

③ GLENNALLEN

Anchorage   Chickaloon   GLENN HIGHWAY   COPPER CENTER ④

Matanuska   *Tazlina Lake*

① MATANUSKA GLACIER

Tonsina

EDGERTON McCARTHY

W

Chugach   Chitina

④

Valdez

Mountains

0 km   50

0 miles   50

Key

━━━ Alaska Highway
━━━ Highway
═══ Minor road
━━━ International border
△ Peak

Fall colors in the forests around Dawson City, Canada

Swift-flowing creek in Wrangell-St. Elias National Park

Getting Around

In this region of great distances, a car or SUV will open up the spectacular country along the Alaska, Glenn, and Richardson Highways. There are relatively few public transport links. One bus line connects Whitehorse, in Canada, with Anchorage and Fairbanks via the Glenn and Alaska Highways, respectively. In the summer, there is a daily van service between Glennallen and McCarthy. Popular guided tours serve as de facto bus links between Fairbanks, Tok, Chicken, Dawson City, and Eagle. In the summer, a riverboat operates daily along the Yukon River between Eagle and Dawson City. Bush planes provide scheduled flights to most regional tours.

For keys to symbols see back flap

The wide face of the Matanuska Glacier visible from the Glenn Highway

❶ Matanuska Glacier

Mile 101 on the Glenn Highway. **Transport map** E3. **Tel** 745-2534, (888) 253-4480. **Open** May–mid-Oct. 🎿 📷 🖥 🏠 **W** micaguides.com

Drivers on the Glenn Highway cannot fail to notice the Matanuska Glacier, a broad, blue river of ice, descending 12,000 ft (3,600 m) to its 2-mile (3-km) wide face. It is thought that about 18,000 years ago, the glacier filled the entire Matanuska Valley and probably even flowed into Knik Arm near Palmer. Presently, it is advancing a foot (30 cm) a day.

Access to the glacier is via the privately owned Glacier Park, where hiking to the glacier face is permitted. Mica Guides leads ice treks and climbing classes on the ice. Drivers can stop at the free Matanuska Glacier State Recreation Site, which provides a lofty vantage point and interpretive panels. The Edge Nature Trail loops from here to another point with fine views.

❷ Lake Louise State Recreation Area

Mile 160 on the Glenn Highway. **Transport map** E3. ℹ️ 441-7575. **Open** May–Sep.

Not often visited by outsiders, the 26-sq-mile (67-sq-km) Lake Louise lies 19 miles (30 km) north of the Glenn Highway. It was named in 1889 by Major Edwin F Glenn of the US Geological Survey who reported its existence. Much of the lakeshore lies within the Lake Louise State Recreation Area, which offers camping, swimming, berry picking, boating, and fishing for trout and grayling in the summer, and snowmachining and ice fishing in the winter.

❸ Glennallen

Mile 187 on the Glenn Highway. **Transport map** E3. 🚍 480. 🚌 Anchorage–Whitehorse. ℹ️ junction of Glenn & Richardson Highways, 822-5555. **W** traveltoalaska.com

Deriving its name from two early explorers in the Copper River Valley, Major Edwin F Glenn and Lieutenant Henry T Allen, Glennallen is mainly a food and fuel service center at the junction of the Glenn and Richardson Highways, with a supermarket, restaurants, and a hotel. However, the town is beautifully situated. Approaching on the Glenn Highway from Palmer, the mountains Sanford, Drum, and Wrangell, which seem impossibly lofty, rise above the flats beyond the town. In the summer, the haze of humidity and wildfire smoke make them appear even more dreamlike.

❹ Copper Center

100 miles (161 km) N of Valdez. **Transport map** E3. 🚍 330. 🚌 from Fairbanks to Valdez.

Dotted with historic buildings, the small town of Copper Center makes a worthwhile side trip off the Richardson Highway. In operation since 1896, the Old Town Copper Center Inn and Restaurant offers rooms and meals. In an old bunkhouse next to it, the **Copper Center Museum** is filled with artifacts such as birch baskets, an enormous mouse trap, and a kerosene tin cradle. It also has information on the Copper River and Northwestern Railway *(see p187)*. The annex next door displays old tools and an antique snowmachine.

Abandoned cabins around the small town of Copper Center

A block away, in the Copper Center Inn, a scale replica of the railway winds around the beer garden, and a collection of historic railway photos decorates the walls. The town also boasts the region's first church, the 1942 log Chapel on the Hill; occasionally, the church screens historic videos about Copper Center.

Outside town, the beautiful **Wrangell-St. Elias National Park Visitors' Center** (see pp192–3) features a shop, information office, interpretive displays, and a nature trail.

🏛 Copper Center Museum

Copper Center Loop Road. **Open** Jun–Sep: 11am–5pm daily. 🖾 donations accepted.

Rivers winding by the Denali Highway near Paxson

❺ Paxson

176 miles (283 km) SE of Fairbanks. **Transport map** E3. 🚌 40. 🚍 from Fairbanks to Valdez. 🎿 Arctic Man Classic (early–mid-Apr). 🖥 arcticman.com

The eastern anchor of the Denali Highway, the tiny village of Paxson consists of little more than a roadhouse, a café, and a gas station. However, for five days in early April, attendance at the Arctic Man Classic contest (see box, above) makes it the fourth largest city in the state.

The area is dotted with vacation cabins along the shores of Paxson and Summit Lakes, and Paxson Lake has one of the best-maintained campgrounds in Alaska. The lake itself serves as a launching point for four-day

The Arctic Man

The Arctic Man Classic held annually at Paxson is unsurpassed for sheer craziness. The contest attracts as many as 15,000 spectators to this tiny hamlet. Each team consists of a snowmachine driver and a skier. After schussing down 1,700 ft (518 m) in less than 2 miles (3 km), the skier grabs a tow rope attached to the snowmachine. Pulled uphill at 80 miles (128 km) an hour, the skier lets go of the rope, slides over another mountain, and descends 1,200 ft (360 m) to the finish line.

Team participating in the Arctic Man Classic, Paxson

rafting and kayaking trips on the Gulkana River, with Class II to Class III rapids (see p266).

North of Paxson, the area around Summit Lake provides long views across open tundra and beyond to glaciers on the southern slopes of the mighty Alaska Range.

❻ Delta Junction

98 miles (158 km) SE of Fairbanks. **Transport map** E3. 🚌 1,000. 🚍 from Fairbanks to Valdez. ℹ️ Richardson Hwy, 895-5068. 🎿 Deltana Fair (last weekend in Jul). 🖥 deltachamber.org

In 1910, Delta Junction was little more than a roadhouse on the wagon road from Valdez to Fairbanks, but in the early 1920s, it grew as a construction camp for the Richardson Highway. After the Alaska Highway connected with the Richardson Highway here in the early 1940s, the town developed into a major service center. Several private

and governmental projects were set up here, including an Alaska Pipeline pump station and reindeer, yak, and elk farms. There were also bison farms, following the relocation of a herd from the Lower 48 states in the 1920s.

Delta Junction remains a small, rural outpost. The 1905 **Sullivan Roadhouse Museum** reveals pioneer life in Interior Alaska. Once located in the wilderness 14 miles (22 km) west of the modern town, it was moved here in 1996. Just outside town, the **Big Delta State Historical Park** includes the historic Rika's Roadhouse, with sweeping views along the Tanana River.

🏛 Sullivan Roadhouse Museum

Mile 267, Richardson Hwy. **Tel** 895-5068. **Open** 9am–6pm daily. 🖾 donations accepted.

🚍 Big Delta State Historical Park

Mile 275, Richardson Hwy. **Open** May–Sep: 8am–8pm daily. ♿ 🖾 📷

Log facade of Rika's Roadhouse in Big Delta State Historical Park

The Trans-Alaska Pipeline

When oil was discovered at Prudhoe Bay in 1968, no one knew how to transport it to market. It was eventually decided to lay an 800-mile (1,280-km) pipeline from the North Slope oil fields to the ice-free port of Valdez, where a pipeline terminal and shipping facility were to be built to handle the crude. Through the early 1970s, the Alyeska Pipeline Service Company worked on the pipeline design. Construction began on April 29, 1974, and was completed three years later at a cost of $8 billion. The first tanker, the *ARCO Juneau*, left Valdez filled with crude on August 1, 1977. Now run by a consortium, the pipeline transports 630,000 barrels of oil per day.

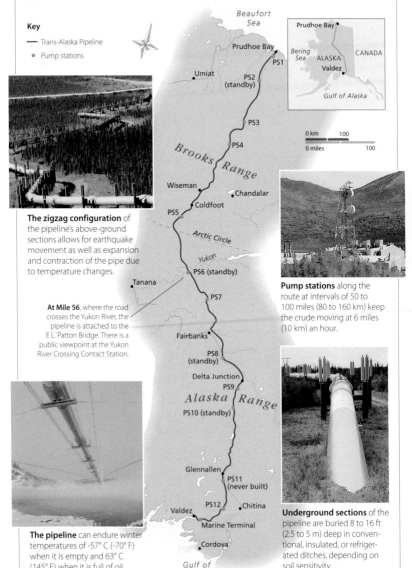

Key

— Trans-Alaska Pipeline

• Pump stations

The zigzag configuration of the pipeline's above-ground sections allows for earthquake movement as well as expansion and contraction of the pipe due to temperature changes.

At Mile 56, where the road crosses the Yukon River, the pipeline is attached to the E. L. Patton Bridge. There is a public viewpoint at the Yukon River Crossing Contact Station.

Pump stations along the route at intervals of 50 to 100 miles (80 to 160 km) keep the crude moving at 6 miles (10 km) an hour.

The pipeline can endure winter temperatures of -57° C (-70° F) when it is empty and 63° C (145° F) when it is full of oil.

Underground sections of the pipeline are buried 8 to 16 ft (2.5 to 5 m) deep in conventional, insulated, or refrigerated ditches, depending on soil sensitivity.

Camping at the Liberty Falls State Recreation Site

❼ Edgerton Highway/McCarthy Road

Off the Richardson Hwy at Mile 82.6. **Transport map** E3. 🚐 Backcountry Connection shuttle bus.

The Edgerton Highway/ McCarthy Road is among the most picturesque drives in North America. It begins calmly, gradually descending from the Richardson Highway into the Copper River Valley, with long views of the river's characteristic eroded bluffs. Entering Wrangell-St. Elias National Park *(see pp192–3)* at Chitina, the often rutted and dusty road follows the Copper River and Northwestern Railway (CR&NW) as it twists along above the Chitina River. Dramatically crossing the Kuskulana River, the road parallels the glaciated Wrangell Mountains to McCarthy, deep inside the park.

Chitina

66 miles (106 km) SE of Glennallen. 🚉 130. ✈ scheduled flights. 🚐 Glennallen–McCarthy. 🛈 Chitina Ranger Station, 823-2205.

Huddling in a narrow valley, Chitina was founded in 1908 as a halt on the CR&NW railway and a supply center for the copper mines at Kennicott. Of the few remaining original buildings, the former tinsmith's shop is the best restored and now houses an art gallery.

About 10 miles (16 miles) short of Chitina, the road passes camping and picnic spots at the **Liberty Falls State Recreation Site**. Entering a narrow canyon, it passes three lovely blackwater lakes before it reaches Chitina. Heading east from town, the road crosses the 1,378-ft- (413-m-) long Copper River Bridge, where subsistence fish wheels are visible. The river current turns the wheels, trapping salmon in the rotating baskets.

🚉 Kuskulana Bridge and Gilahina Trestle

🚐 Glennallen–McCarthy.
Perhaps the most dramatic reminders of the days when ore trains clattered along the CR&NW route are the two large railway trestles between Chitina and McCarthy. The incredible Kuskulana Bridge at Mile 17, built in 1910, is a three-span former trestle above the roiling Kuskulana River. At Mile 29, the road crosses the Gilahina River just downstream from the towering wooden Gilahina Trestle.

McCarthy

60 miles (96 km) W of Chitina. 🚉 30. 🚐 Glennallen–Kennicott River bridge, then on foot or by shuttle bus.

Homesteaded in 1906, McCarthy was a lively rest and supply town for workers at the Kennicott Mine in the early 20th century. During World War I, the rise in copper prices boosted McCarthy's economy. The town declined in 1938 when the mines and railway closed down, but its fortunes revived in the 1980s with the creation of Wrangell-St. Elias National Park.

Scenic little McCarthy retains much of its original flavor due to the well-preserved and restored buildings, some of which are still in use. The free **McCarthy-Kennicott Museum**, housed in the old Railway Depot, features historic photographs and artifacts from the two towns. Kennicott can be accessed by a shuttle bus or on foot along the Old Wagon Road out of McCarthy.

🏛 McCarthy-Kennicott Museum

Kennicott Road. **Open** late May– early Sep: 10am–5pm daily.

The narrow Kuskulana Bridge 283 ft (85 m) above the Kuskulana River

Copper River and Northwestern Railway

With the discovery of copper in the Wrangell Mountains in 1900, railway builder Michael J Heney began surveying the route and laying the track for the Copper River and Northwestern Railway from Cordova to the copper veins in the mountains. Given the difficult terrain, pessimists dubbed it the "Can't Run and Never Will." The Kennecott Corporation started a rival operation, but when a storm destroyed their railhead, they bought Heney's project and with an investment of $23 million, completed the railway in 1911.

❽ Kennicott

Overlooking the spectacular Kennicott Glacier, Kennicott is a fascinating historical attraction. In 1900, while exploring the mountain east of the glacier, prospectors Clarence Warner and "Tarantula Jack" Smith discovered some of the richest deposits of copper ever found. Mining engineer Stephen Birch convinced wealthy East Coast families to finance the completion of the Copper River and Northwestern Railway to transport ore to Cordova. Over the years, nearly $200 million in copper was mined, but declining copper deposits and the high cost of railway maintenance led to the closure of the mine in 1938.

Kennicott Glacier Lodge, housed in a replica of a historic mine building

Mine buildings against the Wrangell Mountains

KEY

① **Workers' cottages**, dotted around the site and perched on the hillsides are now used as private homes.

② **Electrical shop**

③ **Storage shed**

④ **The machine shop**, one of the most prominent buildings at Kennicott, held the metal-working and maintenance operations of the mine.

⑤ **The General Manager's Office**, Kennicott's oldest standing structure, had a large drafting room and was the heart of the mine's operations.

★ **Power House**
Power at Kennicott was generated by the large power plant which overlooks Kennicott Glacier. In this now partially restored building, four coal-fired steam boilers and two diesel generators provided enough steam and electricity for the entire mining operation.

★ Concentration/Crusher Mill
In Kennicott's heyday, low-grade ore was processed in the mill, which is the most striking building in the town. Remnants of the tramways that brought ore from the Bonanza and Jumbo Mines to the mill are still visible.

★ Ammonia Leaching Plant
Here, copper carbonates were extracted from treated ore that had passed through the crusher mill.

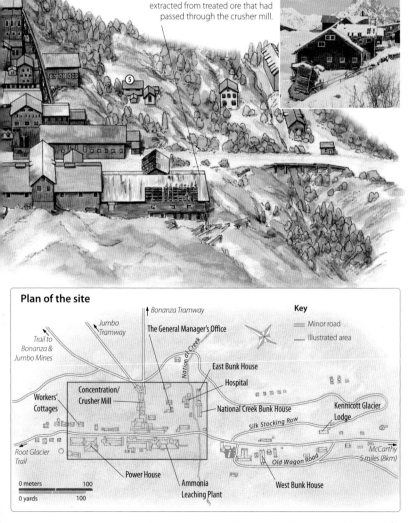

Plan of the site

Bonanza Tramway
Jumbo Tramway
Trail to Bonanza & Jumbo Mines
The General Manager's Office
Nation of Creek

Key
— Minor road
— Illustrated area

East Bunk House
Hospital
Workers' Cottages
Concentration/Crusher Mill
National Creek Bunk House
Kennicott Glacier Lodge
Silk Stocking Row
Root Glacier Trail
Power House
Ammonia Leaching Plant
Old Wagon Road
West Bunk House
McCarthy 5 miles (8km)

0 meters 100
0 yards 100

Spoil heaps surrounding the Kennicott mine buildings, against the Wrangell Mountains ▶

❾ Wrangell-St. Elias National Park

Wrangell-St. Elias National Park, the largest national park in the US – six times the size of Yellowstone – is a 20,000 sq mile (52,500 sq km) wilderness sprawling across the southeast corner of the Alaskan mainland. Dominated by the volcanic Wrangell Mountains and the glaciated St. Elias Range, the park has nine of the 16 highest mountains in the US. Designated a UNESCO World Heritage Site in 1992, the park contains remnants of historic mining sites and harbors a wealth of wildlife. Major activities include hiking, whitewater rafting, and taking flightseeing tours over the park's vast expanses.

Locator Map

■ Wrangell-St. Elias National Park

Mount Wrangell
This 14,160 ft (4,300 m) volcano, which last erupted in 1900, was known to the Ahtna Athabaskans as K'elt'aeni, "The One That Controls." Recent rumbles suggest it may be waking once again.

The Wrangell-St. Elias National Park Visitors' Center provides information and has a short nature trail leading to spectacular mountain views.

Copper River at Chitina
East of Chitina, the McCarthy Road (see p187) crosses the Copper River. The river crossing is surrounded by hills that are sometimes obscured by clouds of billowing dust.

★ Nabesna Road
Built in 1933 to access Nabesna Mine, this 42-mile (67-km) gravel road leads through muskeg and hills to the eponymous village. At Mile 36, a tough 5-mile (8-km) loop hike explores the area around the inactive Skookum Volcano.

Key

══ Highway
══ Minor road
▪▪ Trail
▪▪ Park boundary
△ Peak

★ Kennicott
In the early 20th century, Kennicott *(see pp188–9)* was the site of rich copper mines. In the summer, rangers conduct tours of the abandoned buildings.

Exploring the Park
Given the distances, flights are needed to get to the heart of the park. Only the Nabesna and McCarthy Roads (see p187) penetrate the park, which offers hikes of varying lengths and difficulty levels. Two short trails at Kennicott, the easy 3-mile (5-km) return hike to Root Glacier and the straightforward but strenuous 9-mile (14-km) return hike to Bonanza Mine, offer magnificent views. Longer routes are accessible off the McCarthy Road, including the challenging Dixie Pass Trail and the easier Nugget Creek Trail, both two- to four-day hikes.

★ McCarthy
The old mining town of McCarthy *(see p187)* was a supply and support center for the workers at Kennicott. It is now accessed via a short walk or shuttle ride from the Kennicott River footbridge.

For keys to symbols *see back flap*

Swans paddling in a lake, just off Tok Cut-Off

centuries, the modern town came up as a housing site for workers during the construction of the Alaska and Glenn Highways in the 1940s. Tok's economy was later enhanced by a fuel line from Haines to Fairbanks in 1954 and the opening of a Loran station, built in 1976 as an aid to long-range navigation.

Tok is now a service center with a range of accommodation, RV parks, eateries, and gas stations. It also has three information centers: the Tok Main Street Visitors Center, the Alaska Public Lands Information Center next door, and a Tetlin National Wildlife Refuge ranger station about 5 miles (8 km) southwest of town. The Fortymile Country, a gold mining region with historic and active claims, stretches north over undulating landscape along the Taylor Highway to the Yukon River.

⓾ Tok Cut-Off

Gakona Junct. to Tok. **Transport map** E3. 🚌 Anchorage–Whitehorse. ⛺

For drivers heading from Anchorage to the Alaska Highway, the scenic 125-mile (200-km) Tok Cut-Off links Glennallen with the village of Tok. The southern half of the route looks eastward on to broad vistas of Mount Drum, Mount Sanford, Mount Jarvis, and Mount Blackburn in the Wrangell Mountains. At Mile 60 is the junction with the Nabesna Road, which leads east, past the town of Slana and several hiking trailheads into the northern reaches of Wrangell-St. Elias National Park (see pp192–3).

The Native village of Mentasta Lake, the northernmost outpost of the Ahtna Athabaskans, lies in the heart of the Mentasta Mountains, which form the easternmost extent of the Alaska Range. About 16 miles (26 km) short of Tok, the Eagle Trail State Recreation Site includes a large campground and a steep 2-mile (3-km) trail to spectacular views over the surrounding hills and valleys.

⓫ Tok

206 miles (331 km) SE of Fairbanks. **Transport map** F3. 🚶 1,300. 🚌 from Fairbanks and Anchorage to Whitehorse. ℹ️ Tok Main St Visitors Center, Mile 1314, Alaska Hwy; 883-5775. 🌐 tokalaskainfo.com

Situated in the upper Tanana River Valley, at the junction of the Tok Cut-Off and the Alaska Highway, Tok is the first major Alaskan town west of the Canadian border. While there have been Athabaskan settlements in the region for

⓬ Tok River State Recreation Site

5 miles (8 km) E of Tok at Mile 1309, Alaska Hwy. **Transport map** F3. 🚌 Anchorage–Whitehorse. **Open** mid-May–mid-Sep: daily. 🎣 ⛺ 🌐 alaskastateparks.org

Located beside a sandy beach on the eastern bank of the Tok River, the Tok River State Recreation Site is a popular venue with both locals and highway travelers. Families spend sunny afternoons fishing

Arctic poppies produce a burst of color in the village of Tok

and picnicking at this lovely site, which also offers good boating opportunities. Although the area was burned in the Tok wildfire in 1990 and in the devastating fires of 2004, the campground itself was spared and remains a pleasantly green place to stop and take a break.

In addition to 43 campsites, 10 of which have room for RVs up to 60 ft (18 m) long, there is a picnic shelter with drinking water and facilities, a boat launch, a short nature loop, and interpretive sign boards that describe the human and natural history of this part of Interior Alaska. A campfire area is provided on the beach.

🔞 Northway

59 miles (95 km) E of Tok. **Transport map** F3. 🛬 70. 🛩 charter plane only. 🚌 Anchorage–Fairbanks.

This small village was named in 1942 to honor the local Athabaskan chief, Walter Northway, who passed away in 1993 at the age of 117. During the 1940s, the village served as an airstrip on the Northwest Staging Route, a chain of air bases and radio ranging stations that were built every 100 miles (160 km) from Edmonton, Alberta in Canada to Fairbanks, Alaska, to provide defense during World War II.

Visitors' Center at the Tetlin National Wildlife Refuge

Today, Northway remains the main US port of entry for private aviators arriving from the Lower 48 states. It is also the first US town for travelers arriving via the Alaska Highway. The modern settlement consists of three separate villages. Northway Junction lies right on the Alaska Highway, with a café, lodge, and gas station. The airstrip is on the Northway Road, 6 miles (10 km) south of the Alaska Highway, and another 2 miles (3 km) to the south is the Athabaskan Native village of Northway, where visitors can purchase basketry, Native moosehide and fur clothing, hats, gloves, and shoes decorated with fine beadwork.

Sandhill crane, a migratory visitor

Wildfire raging through forests in Interior Alaska

Wildfires in Alaska

In 2004, a record-breaking 10,156 sq miles (26,304 sq km) of Alaskan forest was destroyed by wildfires. Fires burning every 80 to 200 years are a necessary part of forest development, as they consume dead vegetation and recycle vital nutrients without destroying the soil's organic matter, so fires that do not threaten populated areas are allowed to burn. After the fire, vegetation returns in a well-defined succession. As the forest matures, leaf litter collects on the forest floor, until a lightning strike restarts the cycle.

🔞 Tetlin National Wildlife Refuge

E of Tok on the Alaska Highway. **Transport map** F3. 🚌 Anchorage–Whitehorse. 🛈 Mile 1229, Alaska Highway, 883-5312. 🅿 🦽 visitors' center only. 🏕 🏞 🌐 tetlin.fws.gov

Snow-capped peaks, glacial rivers, open tundra, lakes, and endless forests and muskeg flats mark the 1,140-sq mile (2,955-sq km) Tetlin National Wildlife Refuge. Along with the Kenai National Wildlife Refuge *(see p109)*, it is one of the two Alaskan refuges that are accessible by road. Situated under a bird migration corridor, the refuge attracts over 185 species of waterfowl, songbirds, and raptors. At least 115 of these, including the once threatened trumpeter swan, breed and nest in the refuge, and the annual migrations of sandhill cranes through the Tetlin corridor are spectacular events. In addition, some 25 hardy bird species remain in the refuge through the frigid winters of the Alaskan Interior.

The northern boundary of the refuge runs along the Alaska Highway, with seven interpretive turnouts and two free campsites. At Mile 1229 of the Alaska Highway, just west of the Canadian border, the visitors' center presents a wealth of natural history, wildlife, and cultural exhibits, as well as a spectacular view from its elevated deck.

Administrative office of the Yukon-Charley Rivers National Preserve in Eagle

⓯ Chicken

71 miles (114 km) N of Tok. **Transport map** F3. 🚗 7. 🚌 tour bus from Tok to Eagle. 🅿️

Chicken reputedly got its unusual name when early gold miners were unable to spell the chosen name, Ptarmigan, which is a bird that somewhat resembles a chicken. Today, the chicken theme is rather pronounced, with chicken T-shirts, stuffed chickens, a cutout of a chicken-pulled dog sled, and even a set of Chicken Poop outhouses.

Modern Chicken, south of the Taylor Highway, is divided into three main communities, Chicken Center, Beautiful Downtown Chicken, and Chicken Gold Camp. The Pedro Creek Dredge, which operated on Chicken Creek in the 1960s, lies on the grounds of Chicken Gold Camp and can be viewed on a guided tour. The historic town lies north of the highway. The Goldpanner in Chicken Center arranges guided tours, including panning opportunities and taking in the schoolhouse made famous in Anne Purdy's 1976 book, *Tisha*.

⓰ Jack Wade Dredge No. 1

Mile 86, Taylor Highway. **Transport map** F3. 🚌 tour bus from Tok to Eagle.

Gold mining in the Alaskan Interior began as early as 1881 with the discovery of gold on the North Fork of the Fortymile River. It proved to be one of the richest veins in Alaska, with its ore assaying $20,000 per ton (900 kg). The remnants of both historic and active mining claims are strewn along the graveled Taylor Highway between Chicken and Eagle.

One of the most prominent claims is the Jack Wade Dredge No. 1 at Mile 86. Such mining dredges (see p178) were used throughout Interior Alaska and in the Nome area from 1910 to the 1950s and even later. Dating from 1934, Jack Wade Dredge No. 1 is now in such an unsafe condition that it is possible to view it only from the exterior. Visitors should note that streams in this area are lined with active gold claims that are off limits to the public. Bureau of Land Management (BLM) sites along the Taylor Highway are also closed to recreational panning.

The derelict Jack Wade Dredge No. 1, off the Taylor Highway

⓱ Yukon-Charley Rivers National Preserve

12 miles (20 km) N of Eagle. **Transport map** F2. 🚢 Dawson–Eagle cruise. ℹ️ Chamberlain St, Eagle; 547-2233. 📷 ⓦ **nps.gov/yuch**

Administered by the US National Park Service, the Yukon-Charley Rivers National Preserve spreads over 3,906 sq miles (10,117 sq km), protecting 115 miles (185 km) of the Yukon River and the entire Charley River basin. This New Jersey-sized preserve, with only 30 year-round residents, is one of the wildest places in the US.

During the Klondike Gold Rush, the rivers in the area served as the main highways for prospectors trying to reach their claims along smaller gold-bearing streams. Today, most visitors to the preserve are kayakers and rafters, who use the rivers for recreational trips through this vast wilderness floodplain. Most people begin in Dawson City, in Canada's Yukon Territory, or in Eagle, and float down the Yukon to Eagle or Circle respectively. To raft the more challenging Charley River requires good whitewater skills and a chartered bush flight to the Finger-Charley or Golvins airstrips within the park, with a take-out at Circle. The preserve's visitor center in Eagle provides maps, and canoes can be hired in either Dawson City or Eagle.

⑱ Eagle

166 miles (267 km) NE of Tok.
Transport map F2. 🚍 90. 🚢
Dawson–Eagle cruise. 🛈 3rd &
Chamberlain, 547-2325.

The historical town of Eagle
sits beside the Yukon River
(see pp198–9) at the end of the
Taylor Highway. Started as
the Belle Isle Trading Post, just
12 miles (19 km) west of the
Canadian border, the town
was founded in 1897 by
unsuccessful Klondike Gold
Rush prospectors. They
named it Eagle after the birds
nesting on the bluff.

As the Gold
Rush boomed, the
founders staked 400
town lots and sold
them to settlers for a
$5 recording fee. By
1898, the settlement
had grown into the
military, judicial, and
commercial heart of

Welcome sign at
Eagle Village

the region. New settlers set
up gambling halls, saloons,
restaurants, and businesses.
Fort Egbert was established in
1899, and a year later, the
legendary Judge Wickersham
(see p143) chose Eagle as the
site of the Interior's first federal
courthouse. In 1905, Norwegian
explorer Roald Amundsen
mushed a dog team from the
Beaufort Sea to Eagle to
announce that his ship, the
Gjoa, had successfully negoti-
ated the Northwest Passage.
This apparent boom ended
when the Gold Rush waned, but

Cannon turned monument at the historic site of Fort Egbert

there is still much to explore in
Eagle today. A popular town tour
takes in the historical
sights, the stroll to the
BLM campground is
pleasant, and the
summit of Eagle
Bluff offers great
views. The 8–10 day
"float" down the Yukon
between Whitehorse
and Dawson is a
popular paddling
trip for canoe enthusiasts.

🏛 Fort Egbert

4th St Extension. **Open** late May–early
Sep: 9am–5pm daily. 🎫 Eagle
Historical Society, 547-2325.

Fort Egbert was established
by the US Army in 1899 and
five of its 46 original buildings
at the fort were restored by the
BLM between 1974 and 1979.
Open to the public as a
National Historic Landmark, the
buildings include the **Mule
Barn**, built in 1900 to house the
army's horses and mules. It
now holds tools used in early

mining, woodcutting, trapping,
agriculture, and transportation.
The distinctive **Waterwagon
Shed** was used in the winter to
prevent the fort's water supply
from freezing. Sliding doors
admitted the horse-drawn
wagons and sleds that
delivered water. The building
now houses transportation
exhibits and vintage vehicles.
The Scandinavian-style **Non-
Commissioned Officers
Quarters**, built in 1901, is now
set up as a military residence,
complete with period furnishings.
There is also an 1899 **Quarter-
master Storehouse** and a
1903 **Storehouse**, which now
features an interpretive display
on the restoration.

🏛 Eagle Historical Society Museum Tour

Wickersham Courthouse. **Tel** 547-
2325. **Open** late May–early Sep. 🎫
🕐 9am daily (duration 3 hrs). 🎫

Many of Eagle's finest historic
buildings are still in place, and in
the summer, the Historical
Society conducts a walking tour
of the prominent sights. Built by
Judge James Wickersham, the
1901 **Wickersham Courthouse**
still contains his original court-
room, and also houses a
museum of town history. The old
Customs House, part of Fort
Egbert, contains a period
residence. The tour also covers
the 1904 **Improved Order of
Redmen Lodge** (now the home
of the Historical Society), and the
town icon, the 1903 **Wellhouse**.
A massive flood in 2009
damaged many buildings along
the Yukon River. Fortunately,
most of Eagle's historic structures
escaped the flooding.

Log cabin gift shop decorated with moose and caribou antlers, Eagle

⑲ The Yukon River

Rising in the high peaks of northwestern British Columbia in Canada and flowing 2,300 miles (3,680 km) across the Yukon Territory and Alaska to the Bering Sea, the Yukon River provides a vital transport route for the people who live along it. Only four bridges cross the river – at Tagish, Whitehorse, and Carmacks in Canada, and at Mile 56 of Alaska's Dalton Highway. In the winter, the frozen river is a venue for a part of the Yukon Quest International Sled Dog Race, while in the summer, it offers adventure activities ranging from afternoon paddles and catamaran cruises to longer expeditions from the river's headwaters to the Bering Sea.

Locator Map
◼ Area illustrated

★ **Alaska Pipeline Crossing**
The E L Patton Bridge spans the river at Mile 56 of the Dalton Highway (*see pp222–3*), providing a crossing for both the highway and the Trans-Alaska Pipeline (*see p186*).

★ **Yukon-Charley Rivers National Preserve**
This vast swath of wilderness floodplain (*see p196*) offers a range of activities, including hiking, skiing, and rafting on the Yukon and the more challenging Charley River.

For keys to symbols *see back flap*

Key

▬▬ Alaska Highway
══ Highway
══ Minor road
▬ ▬ International border
▬ ▬ Park boundary
••• Trans-Alaska Pipeline

KEY

① **Circle**, a village on the Yukon River (*see p179*), offers beautiful wilderness views across braided river channels.

Eagle
Founded by unsuccessful Gold Rush prospectors, Eagle *(see p197)* is one of Alaska's most interesting towns with numerous old artifact-filled buildings, most of which survived the damaging floods that hit the town in 2009.

0 Km 100
0 miles 100

Dawson City, Canada
One of the main centers of the Klondike Gold Rush, Dawson City *(see pp200–201)* has preserved its architectural legacy and makes a lovely stop on a Yukon tour.

CANADA

Eagle

TOP OF THE WORLD HWY

Chicken

Dawson City

KLONDIKE HWY

tlin nction

Yukon

Carmacks

Whitehorse

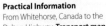

Whitehorse, Canada
Located in a valley, the town was at the head of the river's navigable waters during the Gold Rush. Today, Whitehorse is the capital of the Yukon Territory and a major stop on the Alaska Highway.

★ Canoe Trips
The Yukon offers exciting adventures for canoeists, kayakers, and rafters. The most popular routes are the 8–10 day float from Whitehorse to Dawson, the four-day float between Dawson and Eagle and the five-day trip from Eagle to Circle. Fly-in options and vehicle shuttles are available at Eagle, Dawson, and Circle.

For hotels and restaurants see pp242–5 and pp250–55

⑳ Dawson City

Over the international border in the Yukon Territory of Canada, Dawson City is a worthwhile side trip for visitors to Interior Alaska. Once an Athabaskan fishing camp at the confluence of the Yukon and Klondike Rivers, the area boomed in 1896 when gold was discovered in Rabbit Creek. In 1898, when the Yukon became a Canadian Territory, Dawson was designated its first capital. Along with government agencies, the thriving town was packed with saloons, brothels, and dance and gambling halls. Designated a Parks Canada National Historic Site in the 1960s, Dawson City is now a living museum. Although gold mining continues, the town's most reliable source of income is tourism.

The Yukon River curving past the Gold Rush town of Dawson City

🏛 Tr'ondëk Hwëch'in Dänojà Zho Cultural Center

Front St & York St. **Tel** (867) 993-6768. **Open** Jun–mid-Sep: 10am–6pm Mon–Sat. 🚌 🚗 2pm & 3pm daily. ♿ 📷 🌐 **trondekheritage.com/danoja-zho**

The center provides an insight into the cultural history and traditions of the Tr'ondëk Hwëch'in, the original inhabitants of the region. During the Klondike Gold Rush, many members of this Native group moved away to Mooseehide, about 4 miles (6 km) down the Yukon River. Some returned in the 1950s, eventually setting up the center in an effort to preserve their traditions.

The center's award-winning modern architecture reflects the traditional housing and fish drying racks that were so prominent in the indigenous way of life. Inside are displays of archeological artifacts, reproductions of traditional tools, historical photographs, and costumes. The center also hosts cultural events such as traditional dance performances.

🎭 Palace Grand Theatre

King St between 2nd & 3rd. **Tel** (867) 993-6217. **Open** late May–early Sep: 9am–5pm daily. 🚌 for tours and shows. 🚗 ♿ limited.

Built from the remnants of two wrecked sternwheelers in 1899 by the Wild West showman and notorious gunslinger "Arizona Charlie" Meadows, the Palace Grand Theatre was at Dawson's cultural heart during the Gold Rush. Everything from Wild West shows to opera was staged in its opulent auditorium. After gold was

Historic Palace Grand Theatre, built in 1899 and reconstructed in the 1960s

discovered in Nome (see pp233–5), Dawson began to decline, and in 1901, the theater was sold. Saved from destruction by the Klondike Visitors Association and reconstructed in the 1960s by the Canadian government, it is now open for tours.

🎰 Diamond Tooth Gertie's

4th Ave & Queen St. **Tel** (867) 993-5525. **Open** Jun–Aug: 7pm–2am Sun–Wed, 2pm–2am Fri & Sat. 🚗 📷 🌐 **dawsoncity.ca**

Constructed in 1910, the building was used for the town's most important social gatherings. In the 1970s, it was transformed into a casino and named after a popular dance hall queen. Diamond Tooth Gertie's is currently the only legalized gambling hall in the Yukon Territory. It is run by the non-profit Klondike Visitors' Association, who use the proceeds to promote tourism in Dawson City. Slot machines and all the major games are on offer for gaming enthusiasts. Nightly shows of garter-wearing, high-kicking dance hall girls attempt to re-create the bawdy atmosphere of the Gold Rush days.

🏚 Robert Service Cabin

8th Ave & Hanson St. **Tel** (867) 993-7210. **Open** May–Sep: 9am–5pm daily. 🚗 📷 1pm & 7pm daily.

One of Dawson City's most popular attractions is the humble two-room cabin once owned by "the Bard of the Yukon," Robert Service (1874–1958). Nestled amid willows and alders at the edge of town, the cabin is typical of the era. Built of logs and chinked with moss, it was originally heated with a wood stove and illuminated with coal oil lamps.

Although Service spent only three years in Dawson, between 1909 and 1912, he absorbed the essence of this wild region. His seminal works, "The Cremation of Sam McGee," "The Shooting of Dan McGrew," "The Call of the Wild," and "The Spell of the Yukon" have long defined the Gold Rush era and the magic of the North. Today, Service's poetry is brought to life through

VISITORS' CHECKLIST

Practical Information
328 miles (525 km) N of
Whitehorse. **Transport map** F3.
🚐 2,000. ℹ️ Front & King St,
(867) 667-4144.
🌐 dawsoncity.ca

Transport
✈️ from Whitehorse, Canada, &
Fairbanks. 🚌 from Whitehorse
(Husky Buslines). 🚌

Exterior of the original log cabin of Gold Rush poet Robert Service

the interpretations of engaging Park Service actors, who tell his story and recite his most popular works.

🏠 Jack London Cabin

8th Ave & Grant St. **Open** mid-May–mid-Sep: 11am–3pm daily. 🚌 🅿️ noon & 2:30pm. ♿ 📷

The renowned author Jack London (1876–1916) first came to the Yukon in search of gold, but instead found a wealth of material for the tales of adventure he spun about frontier life. The cabin he lived in was located on the North Fork of Henderson Creek, 72 miles (120 km) south of Dawson City. Local trappers rediscovered his cabin in 1936, and it was dismantled and shipped to Dawson in 1965 by Yukon author Dick North.

Two replicas were made from the original logs, one of which is on view in Oakland, London's California hometown. The other remains in Dawson and houses relics, photographs, documents, and newspaper articles from the Gold Rush days. Every summer, Dick North interprets the site for visitors.

Situated across the road from Jack London Cabin, the 1920s **Frank Berton Cabin** is worth a visit. The building now houses the Berton House Writer's Retreat Program.

🏠 The Goldfields

10 miles (16 km) SE of Dawson City on Bonanza Creek Rd. 🚌 only for tours. 📷 can be arranged with Husky Buslines; **Tel** (867) 993-3821.
🌐 huskybus.ca

Although numerous Gold Rush prospectors worked gravel for alluvial gold, the real environmental impact of mining came after 1910 with the introduction of dredges. For a close look at the effects of large-scale gold extraction, it is worth making a trip to Dredge No. 4. This enormous wooden-hulled dredge functioned from 1912 to 1966, when it was turned into a Parks Canada Historic Site. Down the road at Discovery Claim, a monument marks the spot where George Carmack found ore in 1896, launching the Gold Rush that changed the area forever. Nearby, Claim No. 6 is open to visitors for panning free of charge.

Sights at a Glance

1. Tr'ondëk Hwëch'in Dänojà Zho Cultural Center
2. Palace Grand Theater
3. Diamond Tooth Gertie's
4. Robert Service Cabin
5. Jack London Cabin

0 meters 200
0 yards 200

The Goldfields
10 miles (16 km)

For keys to symbols see back flap

SOUTHWEST ALASKA

The arc of volcanoes that form the Alaska Peninsula and Aleutian Islands stretches through the Southwest like a fiery necklace. Lying across the fault line where the North American and Pacific tectonic plates collide, flanked by the North Pacific and the Bering Sea, and almost continuously battered by the forces of the wind and sea, this is a land of great extremes.

The original inhabitants of the region were the Aleut islanders and the Alutiiq of the Alaska Peninsula. Over the millennia, they wrested a living from the stormy seas and managed to thrive despite the forbidding climate and volcanic activity.

The first outsiders to arrive were the Russians in the mid-1700s. As the first point of contact for the Russians in Alaska, the Southwest experienced tempestuous cultural clashes. The newcomers' quest for the valuable pelts of seals and sea otters led them to first employ the locals for their hunting expertise and to later forcibly exploit them for their labor.

Today, visitors to the region come for both the culture and the incredible wealth of natural beauty. The opulent churches that dominate nearly every town and village are a lasting legacy of the Russian era. Kodiak, the second-largest island in the US, was once the capital of Russian America and is the heart of the Alutiiq culture today.

While the national parks of the Alaska Peninsula are among the most remote in the US National Park System, they attract growing numbers of visitors with opportunities to hike through stark volcanic landscapes. Enthusiastic naturalists head to the remote Pribilof Islands, where cliffs are packed with thousands of nesting birds and basking seals. The ride down the stormy Aleutian chain on the ferry *Tustumena* makes an adventure-filled excursion.

The lovely Church of the Holy Ascension overlooking Illiuliuk Bay, Dutch Harbor/Unalaska

◀ Brown bears fishing for salmon at Brooks Falls, Katmai National Park

Exploring Southwest Alaska

Lying on the Pacific Ring of Fire and beset by stormy weather, this region is among the most difficult to access, but visitors who manage to get this far off the beaten track marvel at the region's history, abundant wildlife, and ethereal beauty. Aniakchak National Monument features the striking Surprise Lake, while Wood-Tikchik State Park's river systems are popular with boaters. Wildlife enthusiasts will enjoy Katmai National Park, which has the world's largest population of brown bears, and the Pribilofs, world-renowned for their bird and fur seal populations. Kodiak, part of a beautiful, rainy archipelago, has the area's largest town. It is also a busy fishing port, as are Dutch Harbor/Unalaska and Dillingham.

Hooper B

Hazen

Mekoryuk

Nunivak Island

Roberts Mountain
1,668 ft

PRIBILOF ISLANDS
St. Paul

St. George

*B e r i n g
S e a*

Horned puffins on St. Paul Island

0 kilometers   100

0 miles   100

Sights at a Glance

Towns and Cities

1 Kodiak

2 King Salmon

3 Dillingham

9 Sand Point

10 King Cove

11 Cold Bay and Izembek National Wildlife Refuge

12 Dutch Harbor/Unalaska

National and State Parks

4 Walrus Islands State Game Sanctuary

5 Wood-Tikchik State Park

6 Lake Clark National Park

7 *Katmai National Park pp210–11*

8 Aniakchak National Monument

Area of Natural Beauty

13 *Pribilof Islands pp216–17*

Key

::::: Minor road

– – Ferry route

△ Peak

Pogromni Volcano
6,547 ft △   False P.

Makushin Volcano
6,658 ft   Akutan   *Unimak Pass*   Unim
Isle

DUTCH HARBOR/ 12
UNALASKA

Fox Islands

Aleutian Islands

0 km   100

0 miles   100

Near Islands
Attu Island
Agattu Island   *Buldir Island*
Kiska Island

*P a c i f i c
O c e a n*

Rat Islands   *Semisopochnoi Island*   *Islands of Four Mountains*   *Umnak Is*   Dutch Harbor

Amchitka Island   *Great Sitkin Island*   *Atka Island*   *Seguam Island*   *Amukta Island*   *Fox Islands*
Adak Island   *Amlia Island*
Andreanof Islands

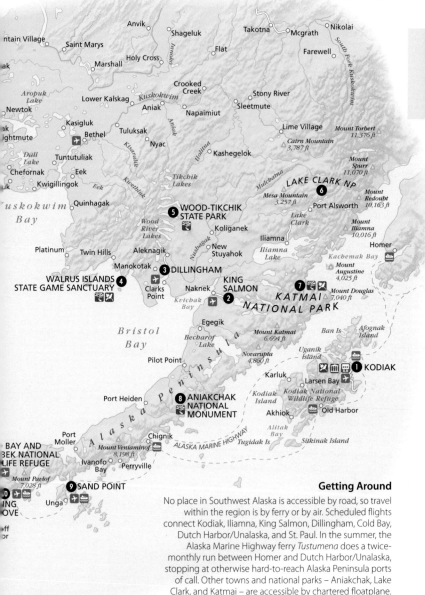

Getting Around

No place in Southwest Alaska is accessible by road, so travel within the region is by ferry or by air. Scheduled flights connect Kodiak, Iliamna, King Salmon, Dillingham, Cold Bay, Dutch Harbor/Unalaska, and St. Paul. In the summer, the Alaska Marine Highway ferry *Tustumena* does a twice-monthly run between Homer and Dutch Harbor/Unalaska, stopping at otherwise hard-to-reach Alaska Peninsula ports of call. Other towns and national parks – Aniakchak, Lake Clark, and Katmai – are accessible by chartered floatplane.

Russian Orthodox church overlooking Karluk Lagoon, Kodiak Island

For keys to symbols *see back flap*

Looking down on Kodiak town from Pillar Mountain

❶ Kodiak

150 miles (241 km) SW of Homer.
Transport map D4. ✈ 6,100. 🚢 🚌 from Homer. ℹ 100 Marine Way (Marine Hwy Terminal building), 486-4782. ⛳ Pillar Mountain Golf Classic (late Mar), Crab Festival (Memorial Day weekend), State Fair & Rodeo (1st weekend in Sep). 🖥 **kodiak.org**

Known as Alaska's Emerald Isle, Kodiak Island and its sur-roundings are famous for rain, bears, and fishing. Kodiak was settled by Alutiiq hunters and fishermen as many as 7,000 years ago. Its name, in fact, comes from the Alutiiq word Qiq'rtaq, which simply means "island" and was corrupted by the Russians to Kodiak. The first Russian explorer landed here in 1763, and a town was built by 1784. About a decade later, Alexander Baranov set up a trading post, designating it the capital of Russian America.

Kodiak suffered two major natural disasters in the last century: the 1912 explosion of Novarupta (see p211) and the 1964 earthquake (see p29). The island was once largely treeless, but spruce seeds and pollen blowing across from the mainland have taken hold of the northern end of the archi-pelago and the forests are slowly spreading southward.

🏛 Holy Resurrection Russian Orthodox Cathedral
Mission Road. **Tel** 486-3854. 🕐 late May–early Sep: 1–2pm daily. 🔔 6pm Sat, 9am Sun.

Following Russian colonists to Alaska in the 18th and 19th centuries, Orthodox priests converted large numbers of Natives, whose descendants still follow the faith. The present Holy Resurrection Russian Orthodox Cathedral is, in fact, the third on this site. A scale replica of the original 1794 church is kept at St. Herman's Theological Seminary next door. The second church, built in 1874, was destroyed by fire in 1943. The current building, with blue onion domes and gold-flecked windows, contains an original 1790s Russian icon, ornate candlestands, and the reliquary of the 18th-century Russian monk, St. Herman, canonized here in 1970. The neighboring chapel houses a collection of 17th-century manuscripts and a hand-carved chandelier. Each August, some 300 boats join a pilgrimage to nearby Spruce Island, the saint's retreat in his later years.

Holy Resurrection Russian Orthodox Cathedral

🏛 Baranov Museum
101 Marine Way. **Tel** 486-5920. **Open** summer: 10am–4pm Mon–Sat; winter: 10am–3pm Tue–Sat. 🖥 **baranovmuseum.org**

The Kodiak Historical Society's Baranov Museum occupies the white weatherboard Erskine House, built by Alexander Baranov in 1808 as a warehouse for otter pelts, and named after one of its later owners. Although minor changes have been made, this is the oldest existing building on the US West Coast. The museum features such oddities as an unusual three-seat baidarka (skin boat) and a Russian sealskin banknote. It also holds Alutiiq and Aleut artifacts such as woven grass baskets, seal gut bags, and bone carvings. The Russian era is reflected in a beautiful collection of brass samovars and icons, and the 1912 Novarupta eruption is chronicled in a photo-graphic display. The archives and extensive library are open to the public.

Samovar at the Baranov Museum

🏛 Alutiiq Museum
215 Mission Road. **Tel** 486-7004. **Open** 10am–4pm Tue–Fri, noon–4pm Sat. 🖥 **alutiiqmuseum.org**

With the arrival of the Russians in Alaska in the late 18th cen-tury, many aspects of Alutiiq culture on Kodiak and on the Alaska and Kenai Peninsulas were lost, but more than 1,000 archeological sites around the region reveal the original ways of the Alutiiq. This museum has put together an archive and collection of his-torical artifacts, includ-ing Alutiiq ornaments, a replica of an 1883 ground squirrel parka, and a fabulous awirnaq (spruce root hat), shared between this museum and the Anchorage Museum (see pp72–3) in alternating years. The renowned Alutiiq Dancers occasionally perform here.

Clouds hanging over the peaks of Afognak Island, north of Kodiak

Fort Abercrombie State Historical Park

Miller Point Road, 5 miles (8 km) E of Kodiak. **Tel** 486-6339. **Open** park: 24 hrs; visitors' center: 8:30am–noon, 1–5pm Mon–Fri. 🏔 🅦 **dnr.alaska. gov/parks/units/kodiak**

The lovely Fort Abercrombie State Historical Park lies on Miller Point along Rezanof Road. In June 1941, fearing a Japanese attack on Alaska, President Franklin D Roosevelt authorized the establishment of a 780-acre (312-ha) military post at Miller Point. After the attack on Pearl Harbor, coastal defense gun emplacements were installed on the site. Although the garrisons were removed some time ago, remnants of the searchlight bunkers, pillbox bunkers, ammunition dumps, and gun emplacements can still be seen around the lovely wooded site. The **Kodiak Military History Museum**, with a wealth of military artifacts, is housed in the Ready Ammunition Bunker on the Miller Point Headland.

The park, crisscrossed by numerous short hiking trails, is accessed on a forest road that leads past the picnic site at Lake Gertrude, where anglers can fish for stocked rainbow trout and grayling. Beyond is a campsite in lush, mossy spruce forest.

Kodiak Military History Museum

Tel 486-7015. **Open** Jun–Aug: 1–4pm Fri–Mon; May & Sep: 1–4pm Sat & Sun. 🏔 🅦 **kodiak.org/museums**

Kodiak National Wildlife Refuge

SW of Kodiak. ✈ chartered floatplane from Kodiak. 🚢 from Kodiak. 𝒊 402 Center St, 487-2626. 🏔 🏔 🅦 **kodiakwildliferefuge.org**

Established in 1941 to protect the Kodiak bear and sea mammals, the Kodiak National Wildlife Refuge covers most of the southwestern end of Kodiak Island, as well as Uganik and Ban Islands and much of the Red Peaks area on Afognak Island. This wild area sprawls over 3,405 sq miles (8,820 sq km) of rugged mountains, lakes, bogs, and meadows, and includes hundreds of miles of convoluted shoreline. It is

Alaskan wildflower

currently home to about 3,500 Kodiak brown bears, as well as 50 million wild salmon, representing all five Alaskan species. There are also 250 bird species and 1.5 million seabirds. The refuge has no roads or trails, so access is limited to float-plane, bush flights, or watercraft from Kodiak town. The most popular activity is taking a half- or one-day flightseeing trip to prime bear-viewing areas such as Frazer Lake and Karluk Lake. The refuge also offers backcountry camping, rafting, hunting, and fishing opportunities at the popular Karluk and Ayakulik Rivers.

Kodiak Bears

The Kodiak archipelago is home to around 3,500 Kodiak brown bears (*Ursos arctos middendorffi*), the world's largest land carnivores. While sows weigh 400 to 600 lbs (180 to 270 kg), the boars weigh from 800 to 1,500 lbs (360 to 675 kg) and can stand up to 12 ft (4 m) tall on their hind legs. The omnivorous

Solitary Kodiak bear on Kodiak Island

bears stay at sea level during spring, feeding on grasses, but as summer progresses, they move uphill to eat alpine shoots. In mid-July, they begin congregating around streams to partake in a feast of spawning salmon. Pregnant sows enter their winter dens, usually natural rock outcrops, in fall. They bear two to three cubs by late January, who emerge from the den when they are about four months old. Cubs typically stay with their mother for two to three years.

Boats docked at the bustling harbor in Dillingham

❷ King Salmon

285 miles (459 km) SW of Anchorage. **Transport map** D4. 370. Airport terminal, 246-4250.

The rugged little village of King Salmon occupies a lovely setting amid wide open spaces. The town overlooks the banks of the Naknek River, 15 miles (24 km) upstream from the fishing port of Naknek on Bristol Bay. Much of the current population of King Salmon is descended from people who were forced to relocate after the 1912 eruption of the Novarupta volcano, in what is now Katmai National Park *(see pp210–11)*.

As the gateway to Katmai National Park, King Salmon features an airstrip and lodging for those without reservations at Brooks Camp inside the national park. The Katmai National Park tourist office at the airport has natural history displays and videos on the park, as well as a gift shop selling maps and books.

❸ Dillingham

481 miles (774 km) SW of Anchorage. **Transport map** C4. 2,300. 348 D St, 842-5115. **dillinghamak.us**

Founded by Russian fur traders in 1822 as a fort called Alexandrovski Redoubt, Dillingham is the largest community in the Bristol Bay region, as a result of its commercial fishing industry.

In 1884, after the US took possession of Alaska, enormous runs of salmon in the Wood and Nushagak Rivers made Dillingham a logical fish processing and canning site. Today, up to 10,000 tons (9 million kg) of fish is processed every year from the Bristol Bay salmon fishery.

The chief attraction here is the **Sam Fox Museum**, which outlines the history of the Bristol Bay region, and features a gillnetter fishing boat with a sail, built around 1936. The town is a staging point for visits to Togiak National Wildlife Refuge, Walrus Islands State Game Sanctuary, and Wood-Tikchik State Park.

Sam Fox Museum
306 D St W. **Tel** 842-4831. **Open** 8am–5:30pm Mon–Fri.

❹ Walrus Islands State Game Sanctuary

100 miles (160 km) W of Dillingham. **Transport map** C4. Dillingham, then by charter boat. 267-2189. **Open** May–mid-Aug. Permits: 10 available for each 5-day period from Alaska Department of Fish and Game. **adfg.alaska.gov**

Located in the northwestern reaches of Bristol Bay, the Walrus Islands State Game Sanctuary is an archipelago of seven rocky islands. The most popular destination in the sanctuary is **Round Island**, where lounging walruses cover the beaches.

After the northern pack ice recedes in the spring, male walruses – as many as 14,000 a day – haul out onto the rocky, exposed beaches between feeding excursions at sea. In the summer, the surrounding seas abound with harbor seals, as well as gray, orca, and humpback whales. The beaches of Round Island and the neighboring islands also attract several hundred breeding Steller sea lions, and the cliffs above bustle with nearly 400,000 nesting sea birds. Red foxes roam the beaches to feed on seabird eggs and fallen chicks.

Access to Round Island is by permit only. Visitors need to be self-sufficient with gear that will accommodate a range of climatic conditions.

The Tusky Pinniped

Closely packed walruses lying on Round Island

The Pacific walrus *(Odobenus rosmarus divergens)*, a resident of the western Gulf of Alaska, Bristol Bay, the Bering Sea, and the Chukchi Sea, is a large, brown pinniped covered with coarse hair. Its most distinctive features are its shaggy "old man" moustache and its two ivory tusks, which are actually enlarged canine teeth. While breeding, males use the tusks to vanquish competitors for females. They also use the tusks to anchor themselves to the sea bottom while digging for mollusks. Male walruses can grow up to 12 ft (4 m) in length and weigh in at 3,700 lbs (1,480 kg). Only Alaska Natives are permitted to hunt walruses for food and for ivory, which they turn into their renowned scrimshaw carvings.

Red fox in Wood-Tikchik State Park

❺ Wood-Tikchik State Park

25 miles (40 km) N of Dillingham. **Transport map** C4. **Tel** 842-2641. ✈ Dillingham, then by floatplane or bus. ℹ Ranger Station, Dillingham. 🌐 **dnr.alaska.gov/parks/units/woodtik.htm**

America's largest state park, the 2,345-sq mile (6,070-sq km) Wood-Tikchik State Park is a vast landscape of two interconnected lake systems, that of the Wood River in the south and the Tikchik River in the north. The park is situated in a biological transition zone between coniferous forest and tundra, with willow and alder thickets as well as spruce and birch forests. Its eastern side consists of low, boggy wetlands studded with lakes and streams, while to the west rise the wild and untracked Wood River Mountains. The remoteness of the park makes it especially good wild-life habitat. Brown bears, caribou, and moose are abundant, as are porcupines, wolverines, marmots, beavers, land otters, and foxes. Throughout the park, well-appointed fly-in lodges serve as staging points for canoeing and fishing trips. Anglers will find all five Alaskan salmon species, especially sockeyes (reds), plus trout, Arctic char, Arctic grayling, and northern pike.

The most usual access for independent groups is to fly in to one of the lakes on the Wood River system, and then canoe downstream to Aleknagik on Lake Aleknagik, accessible via a gravel road. On the Tikchik system, most people fly into one of the lakes and then float downstream along the Nuyakuk and Nushagak Rivers, to be picked up at the airstrips at Ekwok or New Stuyahok.

Visitors who are considering an expedition but not planning to stay in one of the fly-in lodges should keep in mind that well-honed survival skills are essential for trips into the park's wilderness.

❻ Lake Clark National Park

200 miles (320 km) SW of Anchorage. **Transport map** D4. **Tel** 781-2218. ✈ Iliamna, then charter plane to Port Alsworth. 🛏 only in Port Alsworth. 🌐 **nps.gov/lacl**

When ANILCA was passed in 1980 *(see p61)*, the 6,250-sq mile (16,187-sq km) Lake Clark National Park came into being to protect the 50-mile- (80-km-) long Lake Clark and its surrounding ecosystems. These include the shores of Cook Inlet, which is prime bear territory, and the glaciated heights of the Chigmit Mountains and the Aleutian Range. The twin volcanoes, Mount Iliamna and Mount Redoubt, are also included. The park boasts an array of wildlife, most prominently brown bears and migrating herds of caribou. Activities include canoeing, kayaking, fishing, and hiking, but the only marked hiking trail leads from Port Alsworth to Tanalian Falls.

The park's headquarters are at the tiny village of Port Alsworth on Lake Clark's southern shore. While Port Alsworth has several small lodges, there are no shops or services anywhere in the park, so non-lodge visitors will need to carry camping and cooking gear. Access to remote parts of the park is by chartered bush flight only.

Fishing in Crescent Lake, surrounded by the Chigmit Mountains in Lake Clark National Park

❼ Katmai National Park

Katmai was proclaimed a National Monument in 1918 to preserve the unique geological features that were formed after the eruption of Novarupta in 1912. Designated a National Park when ANILCA was passed in 1980 *(see p61)*, it now encompasses 6,400 sq miles (17,000 sq km) of cold lakes, scenic valleys, volcanic landscapes, and wild seacoasts. Lakes and marshes serve as nesting sites for waterfowl, including swans, ducks, grebes, loons, and Arctic terns. Lake Brooks, which flows past Brooks Camp, and the McNeil River to the northeast draws large numbers of visitors to view bears feeding at the red salmon runs into Bristol Bay.

Fishing at Naknek Lake
Anglers flock to the park's rivers and lakes to fish for salmon, trout, and Arctic char.

★ Brooks Camp
This prime bear-viewing spot lies on the shores of Naknek Lake. It consists of a campground, ranger station, lodge, and elevated viewing platforms overlooking the Riffles and Brooks River Falls.

Exploring the Park

A rough 23-mile (37-km) road accesses the Valley of 10,000 Smokes. A steep trail descends into the valley, from where trails lead to Ukak Falls and the confluence of River Lethe and Windy River. A chartered bush plane is necessary to access remote areas of the park, while hiking to Mount Katmai or Novarupta is challenging and needs good backcountry skills. Camping is allowed throughout the park, but a permit is needed for backcountry camping.

Kukaklek

Alagnak

Nonvianuk Lake

Lake Coville

KING SALMON-NAKNEK RD

King Salmon ✈

Naknek Lake

Brooks Camp

Mount La Gorce △ 3,183 ft

Lake Brooks ✈

Iliuk Arm

Mount Kelez 3,250 ft

Three Forks •

Valley of

Windy R.

△ Mount Martin 6,050 ft

★ Valley of 10,000 Smokes
After the 1912 Novarupta eruption, thousands of fumaroles steamed from this bleak landscape of ash deposits, which is now slashed by deep river canyons.

0 km 10
0 miles 10

Brown bear with yearlings at McNeil River State Game Sanctuary

McNeil River State Game Sanctuary

The McNeil River State Game Sanctuary, at the northeast boundary of Katmai, provides the most reliable summer bear viewing. Often, a big group of brown bears congregates at the falls to feast on salmon, offering good opportunities for photographs. Access is by lottery permit only.

VISITORS' CHECKLIST

Practical Information
290 miles SW of Anchorage.
Transport map D4. **Tel** 246-3305, 365-2267. 🚌 🚍 daily guided bus tour from Brooks Lodge to Valley of 10,000 Smokes. 🏕 Permits required for Brooks Camp Campground: 🌐 recreation. gov; 🌐 nps.gov/katm
McNeil River State Game Sanctuary: N of Katmai National Park. **Tel** 267-2182.

Transport
✈ charter floatplane to Brooks Camp & Kulik Lodge.
✈ from Homer. 🌐 wildlife. alaska.gov/mcneil

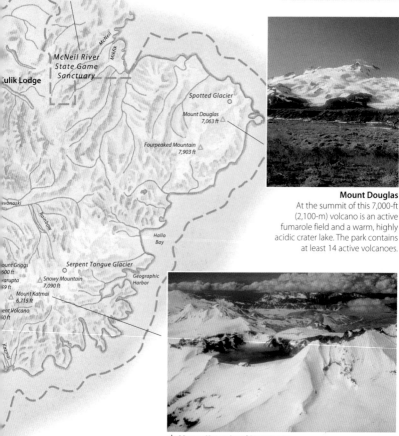

Mount Douglas
At the summit of this 7,000-ft (2,100-m) volcano is an active fumarole field and a warm, highly acidic crater lake. The park contains at least 14 active volcanoes.

★ **Mount Katmai and Novarupta**
In June 1912, severe earthquakes around Mount Katmai led to a cataclysmic eruption that covered the surrounding tundra with volcanic debris. It was initially thought that Mount Katmai had erupted, but Novarupta proved to be the source. As Novarupta's explosion emptied Mount Katmai's magma chamber, Katmai's summit collapsed, leaving a caldera with a crater lake.

Key

══ Minor road

── ─ Park boundary

△ Peak

For keys to symbols see back flap

Colorful iron springs at Surprise Lake in the Aniakchak Caldera

❽ Aniakchak National Monument

100 miles (160 km) SW of Kodiak.
Transport map D5. ✈ King Salmon, then chartered floatplane to Surprise Lake. ℹ King Salmon airport terminal, 246-3305. **W** nps.gov/ania

With the unofficial distinction of being the least visited unit in the US National Park System, Aniakchak National Monument is tucked away in a remote corner of the Alaska Peninsula. The park's most striking feature is the 2,000-ft (600-m) deep, 6-mile (10-km) wide **Aniakchak Caldera**, an ash-filled bowl formed 3,500 years ago when Aniakchak Volcano collapsed into its own empty magma chamber. Over the millennia, minor eruptions, including one in 1931, have added several small cinder cones and lava flows to the crater.

Located within the caldera, Surprise Lake is the remnant of a larger lake that once existed here. After a weakness developed in the caldera's southeastern wall, the lake drained. The resulting whitewater Aniakchak River created the canyon known as The Gates and flowed 27 miles (43 km) to the Gulf of Alaska. Fed by brilliant red iron springs, Surprise Lake provides floatplane access to the park and is the put-in point for whitewater rafting trips. The park has excellent hiking opportunities, but hikers and rafters need to be self-sufficient and prepared for long weather-related delays.

❾ Sand Point

440 miles (710 km) SW of Kodiak.
Transport map C5. ✈ 975. ✈ ⛴
W ci.sandpoint.ak.us

Situated on the northwest coast of Popof Island, the town of Sand Point was settled in the late 19th century by the Russians. Like nearby King Cove, it has Aleut and Scandinavian heritage, and these two groups still constitute the majority of its population. As with the rest of the region, the area's economy has always been based on the fishing industry. In 1898, a trading post and cod fishing station were set up by a San Francisco seafood company, and by the 1930s, fish processing had become the dominant activity. Today, Sand Point is home to one of the largest fishing fleets in the Aleutian region.

Visitors can view the large flocks of bald eagles that gather near the shore, ride the popular 14-mile (23-km) bike trail, and visit the 1933 Russian Orthodox Church, which is listed on the National Register of Historic Places.

To visit Sand Point, travelers will most likely take the Marine Highway ferry (see pp282–3) from Kodiak. The first stop on the journey is the tiny, beautifully situated village of **Chignik**, which is flanked by snow-capped peaks. Farther south is Perryville, founded by villagers from Katmai who migrated after their homes were destroyed in the 1912 eruption

Magnificent lagoon at the mouth of the Aniakchak River in Aniakchak National Monument

The active Shishaldin Volcano, best viewed from the Izembek National Wildlife Refuge

of Novarupta *(see pp210–11)*. The ferry arrives at Sand Point nine hours after leaving Chignik.

❿ King Cove

551 miles (887 km) SW of Kodiak.
Transport map C5. 🏔 750. ✈ 🚢
ℹ 497-2340. 🆆 **cityofkingcove.com**

Founded in 1911, King Cove developed around a salmon cannery belonging to the Pacific American Fisheries. The first settlers in the village were Scandinavian, Aleut, and Anglo fishermen who either hauled in the fish or worked in the processing plant. The plant operated until 1976, when it was damaged by fire and replaced by the Peter Pan Seafood Cannery.

Today, half the residents are of Native descent, while the rest are descended primarily from the early Scandinavian settlers. They continue to fish commercially or work for the cannery, which has grown into one of Alaska's most successful commercial operations. Locals also engage in subsistence fishing and hunting for geese, caribou, and ptarmigan.

Most visitors arrive on the Alaska Marine Highway's twice-monthly ferry between Homer and Dutch Harbor/Unalaska, which stops long enough for a visit to the Russian Orthodox Church. The church's bells and interior icons were brought here in the 1980s by residents who moved from the abandoned town of Belkofski, 12 miles (19 km) to the southeast.

Visitors should be wary of the unusually large numbers of bears that invade town, chasing dogs, tipping over trash cans, and trying to break into homes and buildings.

⓫ Cold Bay and Izembek National Wildlife Refuge

579 miles (930 km) SW of Kodiak.
Transport map C5. 🏔 100. ✈
🚢 Izembek National Wildlife Refuge: ℹ Izembek St, 532-2445.
🆆 **izembek.fws.gov**

The small town of Cold Bay, within view of the dramatic 9,370-ft (2,850-m) Shishaldin Volcano, officially came into existence in August 1941 as a covert US military base to ward off Japanese attacks. Its construction was classified and its military contractor, General William Buckner, assumed a civilian name and claimed to have built a salmon cannery.

Even after Fort Randall was constructed here in 1942, the Japanese failed to realize its military significance. In 1945, the US and Russia forged an alliance and made Fort Randall a training site for over 12,000 Russian troops. During the Vietnam War in the 1960s, Cold Bay sprang back to life as a freight hauling base and the headquarters of the famed Flying Tigers squadron. Cold Bay is today the air hub for the Aleutians.

The main attraction is the beautiful 650-sq mile (1,700-sq km) **Izembek National Wildlife Refuge**, partly accessible via gravel roads from Cold Bay. The refuge protects the habitat of brown bears, caribou, seals, sea lions, and whales. At the 150-sq mile (390-sq km) brackish Izembek Lagoon, 10 miles (16 km) from Cold Bay, vast beds of eelgrass provide food for migrating birds. These include 98 percent of the world's population of Pacific black brant, a small dark goose. Visitors can watch the wildlife from a viewing hide at the lagoon.

Caribou grazing in Izembek National Wildlife Refuge

⑫ Dutch Harbor/Unalaska

For thousands of years, Dutch Harbor and its sister town Unalaska have provided shelter from stormy seas. The Aleuts, or the Unangan, have lived here for centuries, fishing and hunting sea mammals from *iqax* (skin boats). The first outsiders to arrive were the Russians. Settling on Iliuliuk Bay, the site of Unalaska, in 1759, they conscripted the Aleuts to hunt fur seals and sea otters. After buying Alaska, the US also used the islands as a seal hunting base and, during World War II, as a military outpost. The king crab boom of the 1970s and the growth of the fishing industry have made this ice-free port the largest in the US in terms of the weight and value of the catch.

Fishermen repairing crab pots at Dutch Harbor

Sights at a Glance

① Church of the Holy Ascension
② Museum of the Aleutians
③ Aleutian World War II National Historical Park
④ Mount Ballyhoo

| 0 meters | | 500 |
| 0 yards | | 500 |

☩ Church of the Holy Ascension

Broadway Rd. **Tel** 581-3790. 📷 groups by appt. ✉ ☩ 6:30pm Sat & 9:30am Sun.

The focal point of Unalaska, the cruciform Church of the Holy Ascension stands on a small spit at the western end of the village. In 1808, it was the site of Alaska's first Russian Orthodox church, a basic structure that Bishop Veniaminov (*see p78*) reconstructed in a more opulent style in 1827. A third structure was built in 1858 by Aleut priest Innokenti Shaishnikov. The present building, dating from 1896, had suffered so much damage from Aleutian storms that by 1990 it needed repairs. The renovated church was rededicated in 1996, in time for its centenary.

Its interior is filled with a rich collection of icons from abandoned villages around Unalaska Islands, as well as an ornate candelabra, bronze bells, and paintings. The adjacent 1882 Bishop's House reflects a style characteristic of 1880s San Francisco.

Church of the Holy Ascension in Unalaska

🏛 Museum of the Aleutians

314 Salmon Way. **Tel** 581-5150. **Open** noon–6pm Tue–Sat. ♿ 🅿 📷 🆆 aleutians.org

Opened in 1999 on the site of an old World War II warehouse, the museum is one of the finest attractions in the area. The modern building, with lovely terrazzo tiles in the entryway, has an extensive collection that includes historic photographs, drawings, and relics from the Russian era, as well as objects salvaged from the World War II defense of the islands and a 1920s herring fishery.

Also on display are Aleut artifacts uncovered in several archeological digs around Unalaska, Amaknak, and other Aleutian Islands, including many of the 100,000 items recovered from the adjacent Margaret Bay village site. Once a flourishing fish camp, this village is thought to have thrived about 2,000 years ago. Volunteers and students are

Summer Bay Road winding across the tundra toward Ugadaga Pass

welcome to apply to participate in the ongoing museum-
sponsored digs around the
Aleutian Islands.

🏛️ Aleutian World War II National Historical Park

Dutch Harbor Airport. **Tel** 581-9944.
Open year-round; visitor center:
1–6pm Wed–Sat or by appt. 🅿️ ♿
🅦 nps.gov/aleu

Known as Unangax Tenganis,
which means "Our Islands" in
Aleut, the Aleutian World War II
National Historical Park was
designated by the US Congress
in 1996. It aims to showcase the
little-known war history of the
state, focusing on the culture
and role of the Aleuts and their
islands in the defense of the US.

The visitor center, at the
airport in Dutch Harbor, occupies the renovated Naval Air
Transport Service's Aerology
Building. Its displays include a
1940s-era radio room and
exhibits on the mass evacuation
of the Aleuts. The area's
remaining World War II structures and ruins convey the
grand scale of the war effort
mounted in the islands.

🏛️ Mount Ballyhoo

During World War II, Mount
Ballyhoo was the site of Fort
Schwatka, one of Dutch
Harbor's four coastal defense
posts. It was named for
Lt. Frederick Schwatka, who
was responsible for surveying
the Aleutians in the 1880s.

At this strategic location,
897 ft (269 m) above the
harbor, engineers built over 100
buildings designed to withstand
nature's fury. Today, the fort is a
part of the Aleutian World War II

National Historical Park. A stroll
across the site reveals concrete
bunkers, observation posts, and
gun emplacements from the
1940s. The site also offers views
across the sea and toward the
Makushin Volcano. While it is
possible to negotiate the steep,
twisting road with a hardy
vehicle, a pleasant day hike is
also an option.

🌾 Summer Bay

Heading east from Unalaska, a
gravel road along the scenic
coastline of Iliuliuk Bay turns
north to reach the beautiful
inlet known as Summer Bay.
Behind coastal sand dunes that
attract picnickers, the pristine
freshwater Summer Bay Lake
reflects the surrounding green

hills and magical Aleutian
light. At the head of the lake,
the road winds uphill across
the tundra to Ugadaga Pass.
From here, a relatively easy
hiking trail leads down to
Ugadaga Bay on the east
coast of Unalaska Island. In
fine weather, this makes an
excellent day hike.

Just northeast of Ugadaga
Bay at Ugadaga Head, it is
possible to see remnants of
another of the island's coastal
defense posts. The last mile
(2 km) or so is rough, so park
your vehicle and walk. Local
companies provide guided
birding and historical tours.

MV *Tustumena* sailing in Kachemak Bay

The Trusty Tusty

Built in 1964, the 296-ft- (89-m-) long ferry MV *Tustumena*, which is
affectionately known as the "Trusty Tusty," plies some of the roughest
waters on earth. Once a month from April to September, this sturdy
vessel – the oldest ship in the fleet of the Alaska Marine Highway
(see pp282–3) – does the difficult, stormy four-day run from Homer
to Dutch Harbor/Unalaska. This spectacular trip attracts adventurous
visitors hoping to see one of the most remote corners of the world.
Be forewarned though that the amenities are basic. Deck-class
passengers have access to a solarium where they can stake out
a warm spot to roll out their sleeping bags.

⑬ Pribilof Islands

In 1786, Gerassim Pribilof claimed the Pribilof Islands for Russia, and set up Russian trade interests based on the large fur seal colonies he found there. These five islands in the middle of the Bering Sea have been dubbed the "Northern Galapagos" due to their dense concentrations of breeding pinnipeds and nesting birds. While the larger islands of St. Paul and St. George have small Aleut communities, Otter Island, Walrus Island, and Sea Lion Rock are inhabited only by wildlife. Bird-watching groups dominate island tourism, but an increasing number of visitors also come to appreciate the local Aleut culture, the profusion of summer wildflowers across the volcanic landscapes, and the stark beauty of the islands.

St. Paul Island

St. Paul

Bering Sea

St. George

St. George Island

| 0 km | 10 |
| 0 miles | 10 |

Key

═══ Minor road

Village houses and the Russian Orthodox church, St. Paul Island

St. Paul Island

🏔 480. ✈ 🚤 ℹ Tanadgusix Corporation, PO Box 88, St. Paul; 546-3100. 📷 📅 📧 St. Peter and Paul Feast Day (Jul 12).
📧 **Permits** needed to camp on the island; see 🅦 **tanadgusix.com** St. Paul Island Tours: **Tel** 278-2312, (877) 424-5637. 🅦 **stpaultour.com**

St. Paul Island, with an area of only just over 40 sq miles (104 sq km), lies in the Bering Sea, 375 miles (600 km) west of the mainland. The island's only village, also called St. Paul, has the state's largest Aleut community, with 86 percent of the population consisting of indigenous people.

Life in the community revolves around the St. Peter and Paul Russian Orthodox Church, which is the only church on the island. For visitors, highlights include forays to the island's spectacular bird cliffs and northern fur seal rookeries, as well as the opportunity to hike through the wild interior to see reindeer

herds, volcanic formations, numerous small lakes, and a changing tableau of wildflowers. While it is possible to visit the island independently, tours are available only through St. Paul Island Tours, operated by the Native Tanadgusix Corporation.

St. George Island

🏔 100. ✈ 🚤 ℹ St. George Tanaq Corporation, St. George, 859-2255 or 4141 B St #301, Anchorage, 272-9886.
📷 📅 📧 **Permits** needed to camp on the island; issued by the St. George Tanaq Corporation.
🅦 **stgeorgetanaq.com**

Lying 47 miles (75 km) south of St. Paul, St. George Island is less visited, but is considered to be even more spectacular than its more easily accessed neighbor. Much wilder than St. Paul Island, it has six fur seal rookeries, harboring up to 250,000 animals, and the highest and most prolific bird cliffs in the Pribilofs.

About 90 percent of the islanders are Aleut or belong to other indigenous groups.

As with St. Paul Island, the beautiful Russian Orthodox church of St. George the Martyr dominates the local social scene and is one of the island's main attractions. Hiking around St. George or camping are other interesting options, but it is worth noting that there are few roads or trails, and in places, the going can be quite rough. Visits are organized by the St. George Tanaq Corporation, which is headquartered in Anchorage.

Towering cliffs with St. George village in the distance

Wildlife of the Pribilof Islands

The biodiversity of the Pribilof Islands is largely due to the Bering Sea, which is rich in fish, shellfish, seaweed, and plankton, as well as to the island's range of habitats, which include sand dunes, tundra, beaches, lagoons, and towering cliffs. Half of the world's population of northern fur seals breeds on St. Paul and St. George, while Steller sea lions breed on Walrus Island and harbor seals on Otter Island. In the summer, the spectacular cliffs that gird the islands hum with millions of nesting birds. Sea ice that once reached this far south from the Arctic brought a substantial population of Arctic foxes to the Pribilofs, while a reindeer herd that was introduced to St. Paul in the early 20th century still inhabits the interior of the island.

Bird cliffs are alive with thousands of nesting birds such as murres, a type of auk.

Horned puffins are awkward fliers, but can dive up to 20 ft (6 m) and swim underwater while retrieving the small fish that form their main diet.

The crested auklet sports a distinctive plume of dark feathers during the breeding season.

Birds

The towering cliffs of these tundra-covered, treeless islands annually attract over two million birds of at least 200 species, including Asian migrants that are blown off course by strong westerly winds.

Red-legged kittiwakes are similar in size and shape to black-legged kittiwakes *(see p119)*, but have red legs and darker wing undersides.

Animals

The abundance of wildlife attracts visitors to the Pribilofs, who come to view the world's largest colony of northern fur seals. Arctic foxes, reindeer, and harbor seals are easily spotted, while Steller sea lions are seen occasionally.

Arctic foxes den in grassy bluffs, foraging for sea bird eggs and chicks. They have both blue and white phases, when their coats change color, but the blue phase is most common in the Pribilofs.

Northern fur seals are "eared" seals, with a waxy coating in their ears and nostrils that prevents water from entering during dives. Their large bare flippers regulate body temperature by shedding heat while on land. Hunting them is now restricted to Alaska Natives, who take around 2,000 animals a year.

The reindeer herd on St. Paul Island, introduced in 1911, was originally of Russian stock. These domesticated caribou are shorter and stockier than their wild counterparts.

ARCTIC AND WESTERN ALASKA

Covering nearly two-thirds of Alaska, the vast coastal plain stretching from the Canadian border to Norton Sound is a quintessentially Arctic region. While this pristine wilderness is home to only a few thousand people, Arctic wildlife is abundant: great herds of caribou live on the tundra, musk oxen inhabit the North Slope, and millions of migrating birds flock to the region's lakes in summer.

Although the winters along the lonely coastline are not as harsh as those of the Alaskan Interior, the early Athabaskans chose to continue onward to the forested lands to the south, leaving the coast to the Inupiat and Yup'ik peoples that arrived later. Remarkably, these groups, known as First Nations, thrived in this barren region. They subsisted mainly on fish and sea mammals such as seals, sea lions, walrus, and whales, using their skins to make clothing and their fat to provide heat and light. While Native traditions are still followed to some extent, First Nation peoples now lead an increasingly modern way of life. They were the last Native people to be contacted by Europeans, mainly because their lands offered few natural resources. However, in the early 20th century, the Nome area experienced a surge of outside interest as prospectors stampeded in to mine the gold-bearing beach sands. Today, while the attractions of the region are undeniably spectacular, they are also universally difficult and expensive to access. This relative inaccessibility has resulted in swaths of untouched wilderness in parks such as the Arctic National Wildlife Refuge and Gates of the Arctic National Park. Several designated "Wild Rivers" offer rafting and fishing, and excellent bird-watching is available around Nome and Gambell. Adventure-seekers will enjoy driving the spectacular Dalton Highway to Deadhorse.

Caribou swimming across the Alatna River, Gates of the Arctic National Park

◀ Spectacular aurora borealis display reflected in icy water in the Arctic Brooks Range

Exploring Arctic and Western Alaska

Most visitors to the region want to experience its fierce, desolate beauty and venture north of the Arctic Circle. Of the three major towns, historical Nome has roads leading into spectacular country, Barrow is the largest Inupiat community in Alaska, and commercial Kotzebue is a gateway to four remote national parks. The rewarding Arctic National Wildlife Refuge is one of America's last true wildernesses and Prudhoe Bay displays the harsh conditions involved in Arctic oil extraction. Gambell and Nome are world-renowned bird-watching venues, and the Kobuk, Noatak, John, Kongukut, and Hulahula Rivers provide excellent kayaking, rafting, fishing, and access to wildlife viewing.

Kayaking on Walker Lake in the Brooks Range

Sights at a Glance

Towns and Cities
2 Prudhoe Bay
5 Barrow
6 Kotzebue
10 Nome
12 Gambell

Tour
1 *Dalton Highway Tour pp222–3*

National and State Parks
3 Arctic National Wildlife Refuge
4 Gates of the Arctic National Park
7 Kobuk Valley National Park
8 Noatak National Preserve
9 Cape Krusenstern National Monument
11 Bering Land Bridge National Preserve

Atigun River flowing along the Dalton Highway

Map labels

Wainwrig
Point Lay
Utukok
Kokolik
Kukpowruk
Wevok
B
Point Hope
Kukpuk
NOATAK NATIO
PRESERVE
8
Chukchi Sea
Kivalina
Noatak
Tututut Mounta 4,460 ft
Noatak
9
CAPE KRUSENSTERN
NATIONAL MONUMENT
KOBUK VAL
NATIONAL P
7
Kotzebue Sound
KOTZEBUE 6
Kiana
Am
Shishmaref
11
Goodhope Bay
Sel
BERING LAND BRIDGE
NATIONAL PRESERVE
Kiwalik
Selau Lake
Wales
Kougarok
Buckland
Port Clarence
Teller
Kuzitrin
Koyuk
Council
Koyuk
Bering Strait
NOME 10
Solomon
Elim
Norton Bay
Nu
GAMBELL
12
Savoonga
Shaktoolik
Kalta
St. Lawrence Island
Norton Sound
Unalakleet
Camp Kulowiye
Stebbins
Pastol Bay
Bering Sea
Kotlik
Grayling
Emmonak
Sheldon Point
Yukon
Amlıt *Nulato Hills*
Yukon

Key

===== Minor road
▪▪▪▪▪ International border
△ Peak
)(Pass

Native whalers launching an *umiaq* (skin boat) into the Arctic Ocean near Barrow

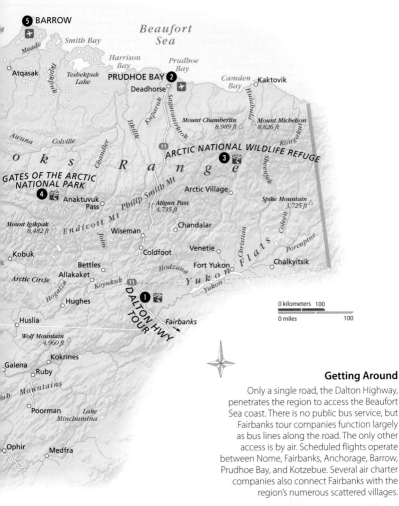

Getting Around

Only a single road, the Dalton Highway, penetrates the region to access the Beaufort Sea coast. There is no public bus service, but Fairbanks tour companies function largely as bus lines along the road. The only other access is by air. Scheduled flights operate between Nome, Fairbanks, Anchorage, Barrow, Prudhoe Bay, and Kotzebue. Several air charter companies also connect Fairbanks with the region's numerous scattered villages.

For keys to symbols *see back flap*

❶ Dalton Highway Tour

Originally built in the 1970s to supply equipment to the Prudhoe Bay oilfields and provide a service corridor for the Trans-Alaska Pipeline, the Dalton Highway is the only road in Alaska that crosses the Arctic Circle. Also known as the Haul Road, it was initially accessible only to supply trucks, but in the 1990s, the full route was opened to private drivers. While astoundingly scenic, much of the highway is a bone-jarring gravel route that should not be taken lightly. Services are available only in a handful of places, and drivers should travel with essentials such as food, water, a first aid kit, and spare tires.

⑥ Sukakpak Mountain
This dramatic 4,460 ft (1,360 m) peak was once a limestone deposit before heat and pressure metamorphosed it into marble.

⑤ Wiseman
The village of Wiseman was founded in 1907 as a camp to service the gold strike at nearby Nolan. Today, the site resembles an open-air museum, with equipment and several historic buildings still standing.

④ Arctic Interagency Visitors' Center, Coldfoot
An essential stop in Coldfoot, the center has exhibits and interpretive programs on the Arctic. Also worth a look is Coldfoot's temperature sign, which describes the day in 1989 when the temperature dropped to -63° C (-82° F), the coldest ever recorded in North America.

③ Arctic Circle Wayside
The highway crosses the Arctic Circle at Mile 115, where there is a wayside with a picnic area, a basic campsite, and interpretive signs.

Bettles
Middle Fork Koyukuk
Arctic Circle
Caribou Mountain 3,183 ft
Five-Mile Camp
Dall City
Big Lake
Minook Creek
Yukon
Manley Hot Springs
ELLIOTT HWY
DALTON HIGHWAY
Trans-Alaska Pipeline
Livengood
Fairbanks

① E. L. Patton Yukon Bridge
This 2,295-ft- (688-m-) long bridge carries both the Dalton Highway and the Alaska Pipeline. Built in 1975, this is the only US bridge across the Yukon (*see pp198–9*).

② Finger Mountain
Distant views from the Finger Mountain wayside take in the lovely tor-studded landscape and Caribou Mountain.

Tips for Drivers

Starting point: Livengood on the Elliot Highway, 73 miles (117 km) N of Fairbanks.
Length: 414 miles (662 km).
Accommodation: Coldfoot at Mile 175 has a hotel and café. There is a campground at Marion Creek, and Wiseman at Mile 188.6 has lodging and a general store. The Prudhoe Bay Hotel in Deadhorse serves meals.
Note: there are only four gas stations on the Dalton Highway – at Yukon Crossing, Five-Mile Camp, Coldfoot, and Deadhorse.

⑦ Atigun Pass

The highway crosses the Brooks Range at the 4,800-ft- (1,440-m-) high Atigun Pass, the highest point on Alaska's road system. Its steep grades should be driven with great caution.

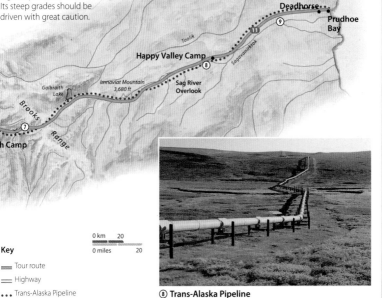

Kuparuk

Deadhorse

Prudhoe Bay

⑨

⑪

Toolik

Happy Valley Camp

⑧

Sagavanirktok

Galbraith Lake

Immaviat Mountain 3,680 ft

Sag River Overlook

Brooks Range

⑦

trich Camp

Key

—— Tour route

—— Highway

••• Trans-Alaska Pipeline

△ Peak

0 km   20
0 miles   20

⑧ Trans-Alaska Pipeline

Near the northern end of the highway, the gleaming pipeline winds across a vast tundra landscape along the western edge of the Arctic National Wildlife Refuge.

⑨ Franklin Bluffs

The iron-rich soil on the east bank of the Sagavanirktok River on the plains of the North Slope gives Franklin Bluffs their striking yellow, tan, and orange color.

Pipelines crisscrossing the oilfields at Prudhoe Bay on the North Slope

❷ Prudhoe Bay

487 miles (784 km) N of Fairbanks.
Transport map E1. ⛰ 2,100. ✈
from Anchorage. 🚌 tour bus from
Fair-banks. 🛈 Prudhoe Bay Hotel,
659-2449. 🅦 prudhoebayhotel.com

The North Slope oilfields, often
collectively called Prudhoe
Bay, make up the largest
oil-producing field in North
America. While geologic surveys
took place in the 1950s, the first
major discovery was made only
in 1968. The Alyeska Pipeline
Service Company was formed a
year later to construct a pipeline
(see p186) across the state to the
ice-free port of Valdez. Today,
the vast oilfields use the latest
technology to minimize their
impact on the delicate tundra.
Deadhorse, the oilfields'
service center, has a shop, a gas
station, a hotel, and restaurants.
Prudhoe Bay and the Arctic
Ocean coast, which lie beyond
a checkpoint, can only be
accessed on tours run by the
Prudhoe Bay Hotel.

❸ Arctic National Wildlife Refuge

200 miles (320 km) N of Fairbanks.
Transport map E1. ✈ air taxi to Fort
Yukon, Arctic Village, Deadhorse, or
Kaktovik, then bush plane. 🚌 tour
bus to Galbraith Lake, then hike. 🛈
101 12th Ave, Fairbanks; 456-0250,
(800) 362-4546. **Open** year-round.
🅦 http://arctic.fws.gov

The 30,000-sq mile (78,000-sq
km) Arctic National Wildlife
Refuge (ANWR, pronounced
AN-wahr) was established in
1960 to protect the region's
abundant wildlife, flocks of
migratory birds and its range
of ecosystems. However,
studies of the ANWR coastal
plain east of Prudhoe Bay have
determined that the northwestern corner of the refuge
holds vast amounts of natural
gas and oil. Political forces have
long tussled over ANWR, with
pro-development organizations
and many Republicans
lobbying to allow oil drilling,
while environmental groups
and most Democrats oppose
opening the wildlife refuge to
industrial development.
Scenically stunning, ANWR
is bisected by the Brooks
Range and crossed by the
Sheenjek, Kongukut, Hulahula,
and other "Wild Rivers" that are
popular for rafting trips. Wildlife
enthusiasts may have the
chance to spot all of Alaska's
bear species, as well
as musk oxen, bowhead
whales, and over 140 species
of birds. ANWR has no trails
or facilities, and visitors need
to be self-sufficient.

❹ Gates of the Arctic National Park

200 miles (320 km) NW of Fairbanks.
Transport map D1. ✈ to Anaktuvuk
Pass, Bettles, Coldfoot, or Kotzebue,
then bush plane. 🚌 tour bus to
Coldfoot, then bush plane. 🛈 Bettles
Visitors' Center, 692-5411. Also
Anaktuvuk Pass Ranger Station &
Arctic Interagency Visitors' Center
(Coldfoot). Note: no roads or facilities
in refuge. 🅦 nps.gov/gaar

The second-largest national
park in the US after Wrangell-
St. Elias (see pp192–3), Gates of
the Arctic National Park
encompasses 12,500 sq miles
(32,000 sq km). The park got
its name in the 1930s when
wilderness advocate Bob
Marshall described Frigid Crags
and the Boreal Mountains as the
"gates" to the Arctic Slope. The
heart of the park is the Brooks
Range, the northernmost extent
of the Rocky Mountains. The
abundant wildlife includes all
three bear species, caribou,
moose, and migratory birds, and
the vegetation away from the
bare, glaciated peaks ranges
from boreal forest of spruce,
birch, and aspen to alder
thickets, taiga, and muskeg.
Most visitors fly in for hiking or
rafting (see p266) on National
Wild and Scenic Rivers such as
the Kobuk, John, and Noatak.
Commercial trips are available,
but lone travelers usually take
an air taxi to Bettles, and then a
bush plane to a drop-off point.
Lodges at Bettles provide
accommodation and meals.

The mighty Brooks Range, Gates of the Arctic National Park

The Arctic Tundra

Lying north of the Brooks Range, Alaska's North Slope encompasses 88,000 sq miles (227,920 sq km) of largely flat, open Arctic tundra. Derived from the Finnish *tunturia*, meaning "treeless land," this circumpolar environment is characterized by low temperatures and thin topsoil that supports only ground-hugging vegetation such as reindeer mosses, sedges, lichens, liverworts, berries, dwarf birch, and miniature wildflowers. This thin surface is underlain by permanently frozen ground known as permafrost. Tundra areas typically have little precipitation, a growing season of less than 60 days, and average temperatures of 12° C (54° F) during the summer and around -34° C (-30° F) in the harsh winter.

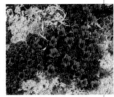

Vibrant miniature wildflowers carpet the tundra during the short flowering season in summer. Alaska has about 400 species of wildflowers.

Landscape
Underlying the thin tundra surface is permafrost. This permanently frozen ground cannot absorb surface water, resulting in numerous small shallow ponds and bogs.

Crater lakes are sometimes found in *pingos*, domed ice-cored mounds of earth. The expanding ice may cause the summit of the pingo to crack. This exposes the ice core and allows part of it to melt, forming the crater lake.

Wildlife
The tundra teems with wildlife, including Arctic hares, caribou, Arctic foxes, polar bears, and wolves, species that are well-adapted to the severe climatic conditions.

The Arctic ground squirrel digs burrows in the ground and hibernates through the long, cold winter.

Musk oxen live year-round on the open tundra, protected from the extreme cold by a soft insulating layer of hair known as *qiviut*. Musk oxen eat a wide variety of plants, including grasses, sedges, and woody plants.

Caribou have broad hooves that provide support in soft tundra and snow, function as paddles when the animal swims, and, in winter, help to scrape away snow to expose the limited grazing below. Unlike moose, both bulls and cows grow antlers.

❺ Barrow

The northernmost town in the US and seat of the vast North Slope Borough, Barrow sits on the tundra beside the Beaufort Sea. Its Inupiat name, Utqiagvik, means "the place to hunt snowy owls." Offshore ice huddles close to the shore almost all year round, retreating for just a few weeks in July and August. This isolated community experiences the midnight sun for 84 days in the summer; conversely, the sun does not rise at all for the same period in the winter. At 300 miles (480 km) north of the Arctic Circle, the people of this Inupiat outpost continue to live on subsistence fishing and hunting, as they have always done.

Whalers towing a whale out of the sea, Barrow

🏛 Ukkuqsi Archeological Site
Stevenson St.

Along the coast at the western end of town, a series of sod ruins and remnants of archeological digs sit on the bluffs overlooking a lonely stretch of beach. While contact between Europeans and indigenous peoples began around 1825, trade was not common until the 1870s. For that reason, the types of items unearthed – ivory points, weapons, tools, and artwork – are still familiar to the older residents of the town, who usually participate in the excavations. This grassy bluff makes a pleasant place to stroll and enjoy the views out over the Arctic Ocean.

🏛 Will Rogers and Wiley Post Monument
Akhovak & Momegana Sts. 🦽

This memorial honors the renowned pilot Wiley Post and his friend, Cherokee humorist Will Rogers. Post, famous for setting 1920s distance records in his Lockheed Vega, decided to survey an air route from California to Russia in 1935. Funded by interested airlines, he built a low-wing monoplane. In July 1935, Post and Rogers left Seattle for Alaska. Near Barrow they encountered bad weather and made an emergency landing. However, soon after they took off again, the engine failed and the plane plunged into a lagoon, killing both men. Visitors can hire ATVs or hike to the crash site 15 miles (24 km) to the south.

🏛 Inupiat Heritage Center
5421 North Star St. **Tel** 852-0422.
Open 8:30am–5pm Mon–Fri.
Closed public holidays. 🅿 📷 🦽
📷 🅦 nps.gov/inup

The town's main attraction, the Inupiat Heritage Center was set up in recognition of Inuit contribution to whaling. For hundreds of years, the Inuit hunted whales from their *umiaqs*, and in the 19th and 20th centuries, crewed on whaling ships and provided shelter for shipwrecked sailors.

In addition to the whaling connection, the center celebrates Inupiat culture, displaying diverse facets of local life, such as a whale baleen sled, spirit masks, and ivory implements. A large performance area hosts singing, drumming, and dance performances.

🏛 Whalebone Arch
Stevenson St.

This lonely spot on the coast of the Arctic Ocean is the historic site from where generations of Inuit whalers have set out across the icy seas in hopes of killing a whale to feed the community through the winter. An arch made from the massive jawbone of a

Prominent whalebone arch on the Arctic Ocean coast

For hotels and restaurants see pp242–5 and pp250–55

Polar Bears

Polar bear in Alaska's Arctic regions

Polar bears *(Ursus maritimus)* are marine mammals that wander across the Arctic ice in search of walruses and seals. Rivaling Kodiak bears as the world's largest four-footed carnivores, these bears keep warm due to their hollow tube-like hairs which seem white in the sunlight. Currently, about 3,000 to 5,000 polar bears live in Alaska, and one of the best places to see them is around Barrow's rubbish dump or on the nearby sea ice and gravel beaches. Sadly, global warming is starting to impact the bears as less ice makes it difficult for them to hunt.

VISITORS' CHECKLIST

Practical Information
580 miles (928 km) N of Fairbanks.
Transport map D1. 🛬 4,200. 🛥
Kivqiq Midwinter Festival (early Feb), Piuraagiaqta Spring Festival (Apr), Nalukataq (late Jun).
🌐 **cityofbarrow.org**

Transport
✈ 🛈 Momegana & Ahkovak St, 852-5211.

bowhead whale commemorates this indigenous tradition. Next to the arch is the former trading post (closed to the public) of the first European settler, Charles Dewitt Brower, who arrived in Barrow in 1884. Married twice to Inupiat women, he acted as postmaster, census taker, military recruiter, and unofficial surgeon. Brower's grave, marked by whalebones, is located beside the nearby lagoon.

🦴 Point Barrow
12 miles (19 km) N of Barrow. 🎫
North of Barrow, a coastal gravel road leads to the lonely cape, Point Barrow, which is the northernmost point of land in the US and divides the Chukchi Sea in the west from the Beaufort Sea in the east. At about 71 degrees N, it is roughly at the same latitude as North Cape in Norway, but without the warming waters of the Gulf Stream, it experiences considerably harsher climatic conditions. In the winter and spring, polar bears den in the area. Any sort of food will attract their attention so visitors should ensure they leave no waste on the beach.

Along the route to Point Barrow is the local Ilisagvik College, which works with the Barrow Arctic Science Consortium to research the Arctic environment.

Stress test being conducted on Arctic sea pack ice, Point Barrow

Sights at a Glance

① Ukkuqsi Archeological Site
② Will Rogers and Wiley Post Monument
③ Inupiat Heritage Center
④ Whalebone Arch

Point Barrow
12 miles (19 km) ➚

BOXER STREET
HERMAN STREET
OKAKOK STREET
KARLUK STREET
TAHAK STREET
LAURA MADISON ST
NORTH STAR STREET
C STREET
AVE C
AVE CAYE
B AVENUE

BROWERVILLE

Whalebone Arch ④

③ Inupiat Heritage Center

AHKOVAK STREET

Arctic Ocean

Tasigarook Lagoon

Isatqoaq Lagoon

HOPSON
AGVIK ST
AIVIK ST
NIGSAK ST
KONGEK ST
NACHIK ST
MOMEGANA STREET
NACHIK STREET
NANOK ST
STEVENSON STREET
KONGOSAK ST
EGASAK ST

TAKPUK STREET

OKPIK STREET

Ukkuqsi Archeological Site ①
APAYAUK ST
OGROOK STREET
Bus Station 🚌
② Will Rogers and Wiley Post Monument
✈ Airport Buildings
PISOKAK STREET

Freshwater Lake | *Will Rogers and Wiley Post Crash Site*
1 mile (2 km) | 15 miles (24 km)

0 meters 200
0 yards 200

❻ Kotzebue

550 miles (880 km) NW of Anchorage.
Transport map C2. ✈ 3,200. 🚌
ℹ 258A 3rd Ave, 442- 3401.
🅦 cityofkotzebue.com

The commercial, economic, and political center of the Northwest Arctic Borough, Kotzebue – with a 75 percent First Nation population – is a settlement located on the Chukchi Sea. A gateway to the Kobuk Valley National Park, the site, which has been occupied since at least the 15th century, lies 26 miles (43 km) north of the Arctic Circle on a 3-mile- (5-km-) long sandspit at the end of the Baldwin Peninsula. Kikiktagruk, its Inupiat name, simply means "the peninsula," and its modern name honors Otto von Kotzebue, a German who arrived in 1816.

The economy of modern Kotzebue depends largely on the Red Dog Mine, a lead and zinc mine 100 miles (160 km) north of town, which employs hundreds of workers and provides a good income for the Northwest Arctic Native Association (NANA). Kotzebue also has Alaska's only power grid that is supple-mented by electricity gener-ated by windmills.

Kotzebue is not a major tourist destination, however visitors to the area will get an idea of what life is like in this harsh place where the winters

An Inuit woman drying salmon near Kotzebue

are long and summers are brief and intense. Take a walk along the shore south of town to view local fish camps where fish, seal, and walrus meat are smoked and dried. In the heart of town, the cemetery is well worth a visit for its beautifully decorated graves, or head out on the dirt road east from Kotzebue to explore the rolling tundra stretching to the horizon. Be sure to pack head nets and mosquito repellent, as well as a good supply of water.

The National Park Service's **Northwest Arctic Heritage Center** has a wealth of exhibits on Kobuk Valley National Park, Cape Krusenstern National Monument, Noatak National Preserve, and Bering Land Bridge. These offer visitors a taste of some of the least-visited

units in the US National Park Service. (The parks themselves are very remote and require bush flights and total self-sufficiency for the duration of the trip.) The heritage center also provides an interesting introduction to Inupiat culture and houses a bookstore and gift shop. Educational programs are offered, along with occasional Native dance performances.

🏛 **Northwest Arctic Heritage Center**
Tel 442-3890, (800) 478-7252.
Open Jun–Sep: 8:30am–6:30pm Mon–Fri, 10:30am–6:30pm Sat. ♿ 📷
🅦 nps.gov/kova

❼ Kobuk Valley National Park

125 miles (200 km) E of Kotzebue.
Transport map D2. ✈ charter plane from Kotzebue. 🚤 charter boat from Ambler. ℹ 154 2nd Ave, Kotzebue; 442-3890, (800) 478-7252.
🅦 nps.gov/kova

Situated between the Baird and Waring Mountains, Kobuk Valley National Park is a sanctuary for the area's range of Arctic wildlife, including caribou, moose, and wolves.

The park's most unique sight is the Great Kobuk Sand Dunes which lie along Kavel Creek, a tributary of the Kobuk. Covering over 25 sq miles (65 sq km), the dunes, which rise as high as

Fall migration of caribou through Kobuk Valley National Park

DeLong Mountains rising from the tundra in Noatak National Preserve

250 ft (75 m), were created when glacier-ground rock was deposited and built up in an area where vegetation could not take hold.

The park is popular with river runners, who fly to Walker Lake and raft, canoe, or kayak 260 miles (416 km) down the Kobuk River over three weeks to the village of Kiana. Those who prefer a tamer adventure fly to Ambler, just east of the park entrance, and float the relatively mild 85-mile (136-km), six-day section to Kiana.

❽ Noatak National Preserve

200 miles (320 km) NE of Kotzebue.
Transport map C2. 🛩 charter bush plane from Kotzebue. 🛈 154 2nd Ave, Kotzebue; 442-3890, (800) 478-7252.
W nps.gov/noat

The wonderfully wild Noatak National Preserve, between the DeLong and Baird Mountain Ranges, encompasses some of the loneliest landscapes in the country and protects an array of plants and wildlife. The Noatak River, with its

headwaters in the Brooks Range inside Gates of the Arctic National Park *(see p224)*, is the preserve's main highway. River runners regard the wild 350-mile (550-km) descent of the Noatak as one of Alaska's best river trips. The trips, which can take up to three weeks, involve a bush flight into the Noatak headwaters from either Kotzebue or Bettles, with a pickup in Noatak village.

❾ Cape Krusenstern National Monument

50 miles (80 km) NW of Kotzebue.
Transport map C2. 🛩 charter bush plane from Kotzebue. 🛈 154 2nd Ave, Kotzebue; 442-3890, (800) 478-7252.
W nps.gov/cakr

The broad coastal plain of the haunting Cape Krusenstern National Monument is made up of 114 parallel limestone bluffs and ridges that create the Chukchi Sea coastline. In the autumn, this changing landscape of alternating lagoons and beaches attracts migrating waterfowl with its swarms of protein-rich insects. There is also rewarding bird-watching, hiking, and wildlife viewing.

However, the only facility here is a lonely summer ranger station at Anigaaq, near the beach ridges. There are no roads, trails, cabins, or campsites, and visits must be carefully planned.

The Blanket Toss

The blanket toss, in its most traditional form, is performed using a large walrus hide blanket held by a dozen or more people. The jumper stands in the middle of the blanket and while those holding the sides count to three, he or she makes increasingly higher jumps, as on a trampoline. Once a bit of altitude and momentum are gained, those holding the fringes provide a serious boost, and the jumper is propelled high into the air. Historically, the toss was used to allow lookouts to gain a bit of elevation over the largely flat coastline and determine whether whales, seals, walrus, or polar bears were visible on the ice or out at sea. Today, it is used mostly in celebration of a successful whaling season, hence the Inupiat name of Barrow's main festival, Nalukataq, which means "blanket toss." Blanket tosses are also staged for visitors in Barrow. Although they will not have a chance to be tossed in the air, they can participate as blanket holders.

Propelling a jumper skyward at a blanket toss, Kotzebue

Alaskan Wildflowers and Berries

Beginning in the spring and through the short northern summer, a series of wildflowers splash color across the Alaskan landscape. Plants of the same species may bloom as much as six weeks apart, depending on their location. Perhaps the finest show is in the Pribilof Islands, where the summer-long sequence of wildflower displays is renowned. From mid- to late summer, the edible berries emerge, many developing from the flowers of the early summer. In the late summer, after the salmon runs, this rich harvest provides sugar for the bears, to fatten them before they take to their winter dens.

Salmonberries can be either red or yellow in color.

Wild blueberries are popularly used in pies and desserts.

Lowbush cranberries are tart fruits that grow in both muskeg and tundra.

Berries

Wild strawberries grow in southern and central Alaska in late June, followed by the cloudberries and blueberries that carpet many parts of the state. Rose hips and lowbush cranberries ripen in late summer.

Labrador tea grows mainly in muskeg.

The aromatic leaves can be used as tea.

The chocolate lily, also called skunk lily due to its smell, is found in damp woodlands and open meadows.

Lupines, found in a range of elevations, bloom in June.

Wildflowers

During Alaska's short flowering season in the summer, the forests, bogs, and meadows are alive with the brilliant colors of blooming wildflowers. Tiny northern anemones and delicate pasqueflowers appear first, often just after the snow melts. At the height of summer, bright fireweed, lemon yellow Arctic poppies, skunk cabbage, and other flowers carpet the landscape.

The alpine forget-me-not, Alaska's state flower, blossoms between May and August.

Fireweed

Every summer, large swathes of the landscape turn purple as fireweed blooms. The young stems and leaves are rich in vitamins A and C, and Athabaskans have long eaten them either boiled or raw, and used raw cut stems to draw infection from boils. When the blooms go to seed and turn to cotton fluff, Alaskans say that the winter is only six weeks away.

Fireweed in full bloom

Villous cinquefoil, one of the first wildflowers to bloom, grows in cracks in boulders and cliff faces.

❿ Nome

650 miles (1,050 km) W of Fairbanks.
Transport map C2. 🚗 3,600. ℹ️ 301
Front St, 443-6624. 🎿 Iron Dog
Snowmobile Race (mid-Feb), Iditarod
Finish, Bering Sea Ice Classic Golf
Tournament (both after the Iditarod,
mid-Mar), Midnight Sun Festival (Jun
21). 🖥️ visitnomealaska.com

Nome's curious name probably
dates from the 1850s, when a
British officer scrawled "?Name"
across a naval chart. It is said that
a draughtsman later misread this
as "Nome." Attractively situated
on the shores of Norton
Sound, this mixed Inupiat and
Anglo community is the
commercial and transport
hub for northwest Alaska.

A former Gold Rush town,
Nome is today less busy than
it was in its heyday in the late
1890s, when Jafet Lindberg,
Erik Lindblom, and John
Brynteson discovered gold in
nearby Anvil Creek. In 1899, gold
was also found in the beach
sands (see pp56–7). Over 30,000
people staked claims, sparking a
boom that lasted until 1906,
when Nome quickly slipped
into obscurity.

However, gold fever has not
entirely faded in modern Nome.
The public beach, from the end
of the seawall to the roadhouse,
is open for recreational mining
and in the summer, a motley

Semipalmated sandpiper in the meadows
around Nome

colony of hopeful prospectors
camp here. Clad in wet suits,
they brave the freezing, ice-
choked waters of Norton Sound,
using diesel-powered dredges
to process the sands and collect
what remains of the gold.

Nome is also famous for its
superb bird-watching and as
the finish line of the Iditarod.
Visitors in January can see the
whimsical Nome National
Forest, created each year
when residents plant their
old Christmas trees in the sea
ice just outside town.

🎫 The Burled Arch

Front St. ♿ 🖥️ iditarod.com
Each March, the official finish
line, called the Red "Fox"
Olson Trail Monument and
better known as the Burled
Arch, becomes the ultimate

destination of all Iditarod
mushers (see pp42–3). The
original arch, with the inscrip-
tion "End of the Iditarod Dog
Race," was erected for the first
Iditarod in 1975. It succumbed
to dry rot after 26 years and was
replaced with a large burled
spruce log, which rests outside
the Town Hall in the summer.
During the race, a kerosene
lantern hangs from the arch
until the last competitor crosses
the finish line and retrieves it,
winning the Red Lantern Award.
This tradition recalls the early
days of transport in Alaska,
when mushers carrying goods
or mail would look for the
lanterns hanging outside
roadhouses along the route.

🏛️ Carrie M. McLain Museum

223 Front St. **Tel** 443-6630. **Closed** for
renovations: check website for
information on reopening dates.
🎫 donations accepted. ♿
🖥️ nomealaska.org/museum

Currently undergoing renovations, this city-owned museum
reveals Nome's colorful history
with original displays on its Gold
Rush days. Other exhibits focus
on modern Nome, as well as on
historic aviation, the arts and
culture of the Bering Strait Inuit,
the world-famous Iditarod, and
the original Nome Kennel Club
and its All Alaska Sweepstakes
sled dog race.

✝️ Old St. Joseph's Catholic Church

279 King Place, Anvil City Square.
Tel 443-7856.
Nome's oldest building, the
1901 St. Joseph's Catholic
Church, was built on the
waterfront as a counterpoint
to the rollicking Gold Rush
atmosphere of the time. On its
steeple, a cross lit by electric
lights served as a beacon to
guide mushers and miners into
town. Eventually, the building
fell into decay and a new one
was built. In 1996, the old church
was moved to its present site,
restored, and given a new
steeple. The church is now a
community hall. In front of it are
statues of Lindberg, Lindblom,
and Brynteson. The building is
only open for special events.

Dog team finishing the Iditarod in Nome

For hotels and restaurants see pp242–5 and pp250–55

Exploring Beyond Nome

Located on the Seward Peninsula, Nome may be remote, but it is the hub of an extensive wilderness road system. Most visitors rent a vehicle or join a tour to explore the area's wild hinterlands. The drive east along the coast to Council includes fine bird-watching and the remains of a failed railroad, while the Kougarok Road accesses remote hot springs. The Teller Road leads through spectacular scenery to the end-of-the-world village of Teller on the windswept coast of the Bering Sea.

Sights at a Glance

① Council Road
② Kougarok Road
③ Teller Road

Key

⋯⋯⋯ Minor road
– – Trail

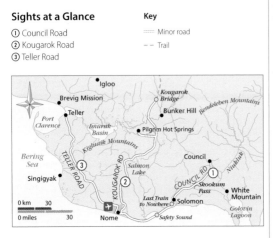

🏕 Council Road

72 miles (115 km) to Council.

The causeway-like Council Road follows the coastline east of Nome past campsites of wildcat prospectors, who mine the beach sands with gas-powered dredges. Passing superb bird-watching sites at the marshes of **Safety Sound**, it arrives at the photogenic **Last Train to Nowhere**, three locomotives and several decrepit railcars of the 1881 Council City and Solomon River Railroad that stand rusting on the tundra at Mile 33. The railway was envisioned as part of a link between Nome and the Lower 48, but the plans were abandoned in 1907 due to a lack of funds. At this point, the road turns inland, through the tiny village of **Solomon**, now virtually abandoned. After crossing scenic Skookum Pass, the road reaches its end at the Niukluk River. There is a ford into the Gold Rush village of **Council**, but the village is best accessed with the help of local boat owners.

🏕 Kougarok Road

89 miles (143 km) to Kougarok Bridge.
Pilgrim Hot Springs Turn-off at Mile 62. **Tel** 443-5252.

Also known as the Taylor Road, the wonderfully scenic Kougarok Road passes through the Kigluaik Mountains, paralleling the Wild Goose Pipeline, which was built in 1909 to transport water to Nome but never used. North of the mountains, a graveled spur road leads to an oasis of cottonwood trees at **Pilgrim Hot Springs**. The site has a simple wooden hot tank, which visitors can use after getting the owner's permission. Beyond the springs, the road passes through wetlands and tundra to its end at **Kougarok Bridge**. From here, a rough track leads to Taylor.

🏕 Teller Road

66 miles (110 km) to Teller.

Leaving Nome, this beautiful, lonely road follows clearwater streams, grasslands, and steep climbs on its way to **Teller**. Passing through the Kigluaik Mountains, it reaches rolling tundra, where there is a good chance of seeing wild musk oxen and domestic reindeer. Teller, at the westernmost tip of this westernmost road in North America, lies on a gray gravel spit at Port Clarence on the Bering Sea. It is known as the site where Norwegian explorer Roald Amundsen landed after his legendary 70-hour airship flight over the North Pole in 1926.

Rusting engines and railcars of the Last Train to Nowhere, on the tundra east of Nome

Granite tors at the Bering Land Bridge National Preserve

⓫ Bering Land Bridge National Preserve

100 miles (160 km) N of Nome.
Transport map C2. 🛪 charter bush plane from Nome. 🛈 Sitnasuak Building, 214 Front St, Nome; 443-2522. **Open** year-round. ⛺
🖥 nps.gov/bela

Designated a National Monument in 1978, Bering Land Bridge received National Preserve status when ANILCA was passed in 1980 *(see p61)*. Encompassing 4,200 sq miles (10,900 sq km), the preserve commemorates the 55-mile- (88-km-) long and 1,000-mile- (1,600-km-) wide land bridge that once connected North America and Asia *(see p53)*. It is believed that during the last major Ice Age, this bridge allowed the passage of both prehistoric wildlife and early human settlers from Asia into North America. Around 15,000 years ago, the melting of the ice caused a gradual rise in sea level, and the land bridge disappeared beneath the waves of the newly formed Bering Strait.

The broad Arctic landscape of the preserve includes wide expanses of tundra, as well as scenic granite tors that bear testament to the area's distant volcanic past. The six public use cabins scattered around the preserve, and the 20-bed bunkhouse and hot tub at the preserve's main attraction, **Serpentine Hot Springs**, may be used free of charge and require no reservations, although users may have to share the space with other parties. The preserve's visitor center in Nome has exhibits, maps, and videos showcasing its cultural and natural history.

Access into the preserve is almost exclusively by bush plane in the summer and snowmachine in the winter, although a few people do hike the 40 miles (64 km) to Serpentine Hot Springs from Kougarok Bridge.

⓬ Gambell

230 miles (370 km) E of Nome.
Transport map B3. ✈ 680. 🛪 from Nome. Permits: needed to access lagoons and other areas.

The small Yup'ik village of Gambell sits on beach gravel at the northwestern corner of St. Lawrence Island, which measures 70 miles (112 km) in length and includes the even more isolated village of **Savoonga**. Lying near the Siberian coast, the island is one of Alaska's most remote outposts.

When ANCSA was passed in 1971 *(see p60)*, Gambell and Savoonga decided not to participate, and thus gained title to about 1,780 sq miles (4,600 sq km) of land. The villagers are therefore able to charge an "outsider tax" from non-residents wishing to access the lagoons and areas around the village and farther afield.

Getting around the island requires an ATV, and visitors can usually get rides from the villagers for a small fee. Most visitors to the island come to view birds not seen elsewhere in North America, including several incidental Eurasian species such as Lapland longspurs. Summer visitors can also spot flocks of eider ducks, murres, kittiwakes, puffins, and auklets either nesting or heading north.

In addition to the birdlife, the island's main attractions include the unique boneyards south of the village and at the base of Sivaquaq Mountain, where waste from Native hunts – mainly whalebones – is tossed. Walrus ivory from the yards is now carved and sold to visitors.

The remote Yup'ik village of Gambell on St. Lawrence Island

TRAVELERS' NEEDS

WHERE TO STAY

The extensive range of accommodation offered in Alaska ranges from rustic campsites along remote hiking trails to business-class hotel rooms in Anchorage, Fairbanks, and Juneau. Those who prefer to experience local flavour have a choice of bed-and-breakfast accommodation ranging from simple lodges to well-appointed houses with home-grown vegetables and gourmet cuisine. Budget travelers will find a selection of low-priced hostels accessible by public transport. In the bush, a number of hunting, fishing, and wildlife-viewing lodges offer wilderness luxury far from the well-trodden routes. For more information, refer to the detailed listings on pages 242–245.

Hotel Captain Cook in downtown Anchorage *(see p242)*

Seasonal Pricing

While the summer months of June, July, and August offer the year's finest weather, summer prices in Alaska are often two to three times the off-season rates. Between October and April, many of the hostels, hotels, and bed-and-breakfasts located away from urban areas are closed, as are most federal and state campsites. In larger cities, winter hotel rates for luxury rooms may be a true bargain. Exceptions are the Alyeska Ski Resort and those hotels in the Interior that cater to visitors wishing to see the aurora borealis. Here high season can last all year. During the Fur Rondy and the Iditarod Trail Sled Dog Race *(see p49)* in February and March, prices in Anchorage and some other places along the race route may be higher than the usual winter discount rates.

Generally, Alaska has two shoulder seasons, in May and September. Hoteliers may offer discounts of up to 25 percent during these months.

Choosing a Hotel and Getting There

In nearly every town, hotels compete for visiting business travelers by offering convention facilities and wireless Internet connections. Fairbanks, Juneau, Ketchikan, and Anchorage have the most expensive business hotels. Most towns also have comfortable motels providing decent, relatively inexpensive accommodation, as well as historic and independent hotels filled with period furnishings and run with meticulous attention to detail. Virtually all historic Alaska hotels are non-smoking. In addition, a selection of mid-range and budget choices offer travelers a simple bed, a hot shower, and basic amenities.

Some of the better hotels have free telephone links in the baggage claim areas at Anchorage, Fairbanks, and Juneau, as well as at many Alaska Marine Highway terminals. Travelers can use these to arrange rooms or free shuttle transport from the airport or ferry terminal to the hotel. Most cruise ship passengers will have pre-booked rooms in finer establishments near tourist sites.

Most bed-and-breakfasts within a few minutes' drive of a ferry terminal or airport are happy to provide transport for booked guests. Hikers and backpackers hoping to stay in hostels or campsites will have to rely on rental cars or taxis.

Hostels

Alaska has a network of more than 25 official **Alaska Hostel Association** hostels scattered around the state. Largely offering no-frills amenities, these inexpensive options provide a basic place to sleep, most often in a shared dormitory setting with toilets and showers down the hall, as well as communal cooking facilities. Dorms are usually single sex, although, if requested, a private room may

Dating from 1916, the Historic Anchorage Hotel *(see p242)* with its old-time ambiance

◀ Fishing adventure by floatplane, with Mt McKinley in the background

Kenai Princess Wilderness Lodge *(see p242)* in Cooper Landing on the Kenai Peninsula

occasionally be arranged for couples traveling together. While hostels usually provide basic bedding and linen, travelers often bring their own sheets or sleeping bags.

Most hostels offer lockers where luggage or valuables can be stored, as well as a games or television room and laundry facilities. In several places guests are locked out between 9am and 5pm. For this inconvenience, hostelers can expect to pay less than 50 percent of the price of a bed in an inexpensive hotel.

RV Parks

Driving through Alaska in a recreational vehicle or RV *(see pp288–9)* is an extremely popular way of seeing the state. While most RVs can be accommodated at "pull-through" sites in public campgrounds, only private RV parks offer such amenities as hook-ups and dump stations. The better RV parks also provide hot showers, bathrooms, and laundromats. Some even have cable TV and Wi-Fi access. Full hook-up facilities can cost up to $80 per night. Normally, even those not staying at the site can use the showers for a small fee. RV parks are found in most cities and towns along the highway system, as well as in most Marine Highway ports in Southeast and Southcentral Alaska.

Hotel Chains

Anchorage and other large cities have many hotel chains, including **Sheraton Hotels**, **Hilton**, **Hawthorn Suites**, **Embassy Suites**, **Extended Stay**, **Hampton Inn**, **Super 8 Hotels**, **Best Western**, **Marriott Inns**, and **Holiday Inn**. There is little to differentiate one from the other, apart from desired price and location. Many of the newer hotels have large rooms, Wi-Fi access, buffet breakfasts, small fridges and microwaves, and king-size beds. Shuttle services to and from the airport are often available. For cruise ship passengers and visitors looking for a lavish wilderness experience, **Princess Lodges** offer interesting architecture and comfortable accommodation in and around major tourist sites.

Bed-and-Breakfasts

While the bed-and-breakfast idea is relatively new to Alaska, it has rapidly become popular. B&Bs come in many shapes and sizes, but unlike their European counterparts, they are not a budget option. Guests should be prepared to pay at least what they would for an average mid-range hotel room.

The advantage offered by B&Bs is the chance to meet friendly locals and fellow guests while staying in cozy, comfortable homes rather than in impersonal hotels. Many of these places are lovingly tended by people who take pride in their gardening and culinary skills, and who treat their guests not only to excellent breakfasts but often to memorable experiences. Some of the best B&Bs are in quiet neighborhoods or idyllic rural areas, while the more convenient ones in town centers tend to be functional places.

For those who have not pre-booked, a good way to find a B&B is via the brochures stacked in every airport, ferry terminal, and tourist office. Many, but not all B&Bs, are members of the **Bed and Breakfast Association of Alaska**, which can help in finding and booking a room. Some of the best choices are included in the listings on pp242–5.

The facade of the Historic Anchorage Hotel *(see p242)*

Talon Lodge, on a private island, offers superb views of the Sitka shoreline

Campgrounds

Alaska has two main types of campgrounds – public and private. Generally, public campgrounds occupy scenic sites in national and state parks, wildlife refuges, forests, recreation areas, and game sanctuaries. The **Alaska Public Lands Information Centers (APLIC)** provide details on public campgrounds, most of which are not reservable. **Lifetime Adventures** makes reservations for some **Alaska State Park** campgrounds. **Reserve Denali** takes bookings for that popular park. It is worth arriving early on summer weekends to find a good camping spot.

While public campgrounds offer few amenities, they do provide spacious individual campsites and easy access to scenic outdoor attractions. Sites located in government campgrounds along the road system will offer parking spaces, picnic tables, and a basic barbecue pit. Communal facilities usually include outhouses and public water pumps.

A few of the campgrounds administered by the **Chugach National Forest** or **Tongass National Forest** may be used free of charge. However, most of the state and nationally administered sites charge nightly fees for pitching a tent or parking an RV. Some campgrounds include pre-cut firewood in the price of the site. Most of these places are open from mid- or late May to early September. Those that stay open through the winter generally shut down the water supply in early September.

Public Use Cabins

In the Chugach and Tongass National Forests, as well as in several state parks and recreation areas, more than 200 cabins are available for overnight use. Most of these public use cabins are in remote areas or along hiking trails. Access to these isolated cabins is almost always on foot, by boat, or by floatplane.

Many cabins have wood stoves and ranger-provided firewood. They usually contain bunks for eight or more people. Mattresses are not provided and travelers need to bring their own ground pads and sleeping bags. Alaskan public use cabins require pre-booking, and with few exceptions, are available to only one party at a time. Because they get booked up quickly between June and August, reserve in advance, especially in popular locations such as Chugach State Park, Nancy Lake State Recreation Area, and in the Chugach National Forest. National forest cabins may be booked up to six months in advance at **www.recreation.gov**, while state park cabins can be booked with **Alaska State Parks Public Use Cabins**.

Private cabin, Kachemak Bay State Park

Wilderness Lodges

Dotted around the wildest parts of Alaska, wilderness lodges offer accommodation in remote areas off the road system. Usually accessed by boat or bush plane, most have their own dock, airstrip, or floatplane landing facility. While many are hunting or angling lodges, several cater to visitors interested in photography, wildlife viewing, and hiking. Their prices reflect not only the undeniable beauty of the sites, but also the exclusivity of the lodge, the quality of the experience, and the difficulties of accessing and supplying such remote locations. In the most expensive places, prices include accommodation, meals, activities, guides, and local boat or plane transport. Many fishing lodges also provide fishing equipment and freezer space. In the mid-priced lodges, guests can expect to pay a set rate for accommodation, as well as a substantial charge for a bush flight or boat transport and additional charges for meals and activities. While those

The comfortable House of the Rock B&B in Valdez

willing to share rooms or cabins with other guests may be able to get a discount, the tariff will still be two or three times what a traveler would usually pay at a hotel in town. Details of some of the best lodges are included in the listings (see pp242–5).

Recommended Hotels

The hotels on the pages that follow have been carefully selected to cover a variety of accommodation options, from historic city hotels, extended

stay and bed-and-breakfast places, to the most modern high-rises and luxury wilderness lodges. The list also includes youth hostels, camp-grounds for backpackers and RV guests and lodging for travelers on a budget. Entries labelled as DK Choice highlight places that stand out in some way; this might be for their exceptional surroundings, historic architecture, excellent service, friendly hosts, or fine on-site restaurants. For map references to Anchorage see pp68–9.

DIRECTORY

Hostels

Alaska Hostel Association
w alaskahostel association.org

Hotel Chains

Best Western
Tel (800) 780-7234.
w bestwesternalaska. com

Embassy Suites
Tel (800) 362-2779.
w embassysuites.com

Extended Stay
Tel (800) 804-3724.
w extendedstay america.com

Hampton Inn
Tel (800) 426-7866.
w hamptoninn.com

Hawthorn Suites
Tel (800) 337-0202.
w hawthorn.com

Hilton
Tel (800) 445-8667.
w hilton.com

Holiday Inn
Tel (888) 465-4329.
w holidayinn.com

Marriott Inns
Tel (888) 236-2427.
w marriott.com

Princess Lodges
Tel (800) 426-0500.
w princesslodges.com

Sheraton Hotels
Tel (800) 325-3535.
w starwoodhotels.com

Super 8 Hotels
Tel (800) 8454-2313.
w super8.com

Bed-and-Breakfasts

Bed and Breakfast Association of Alaska
w alaskabba.com

Campgrounds

Alaska Public Lands Information Center
Anchorage
605 W 4th Ave, Suite 105.
Tel 644-3661.
w alaskacenters.gov
Fairbanks
101 Dunkel St.
Tel 459-3730.
w alaskacenters.gov
Ketchikan
50 Main St. Tel 228-6220.
Tok
Mile 1314 Alaska Hwy.
Tel 883-5667.
w alaskacenters.gov

Alaska State Parks
Tel 269-8400.
w alaskastateparks.org

Chugach National Forest
161 East 1st Ave, Door #8,
Anchorage.
Tel 743-9500. w fs.usda.
gov/chugach

Lifetime Adventures
Tel (800) 952-8624.
w lifetimeadventures.
net

Reserve Denali
Mile 237 George Parks
Highway No. 3.
Tel (866) 761-6629.
w reservedenali.com

Tongass National Forest
648 Mission St, Ketchikan.
Tel 225-3101. w fs.usda.
gov/tongass

Public Use Cabins

Alaska State Parks Public Use Cabins
550 W 7th Ave, Suite 1260,
Anchorage. Tel 269-8400.
w dnr.alaska.gov/
parks/cabins

Recreation.gov
Tel (877) 444-6777.
w recreation.gov

Where to Stay

Anchorage

Downtown

Anchorage Downtown Hotel $
Boutique   Map C5
826 K St, 99501
Tel *866-258-7669*
🅦 theanchoragedowntownhotel.
com
Convenient for the ocean, shops
and galleries, and the green space
of Delany Park. Rooms have comfy
beds, free Wi-Fi, coffee maker,
microwave, and fridge. There's an
airport shuttle in summer.

Anchorage Grand Hotel $$
Modern   Map C4
505 W 2nd Ave, 99501
Tel *907-929-8888*
🅦 anchoragegrand.com
Comfortable downtown suites
with full kitchens, plus a business
center. Near the 5th St. Mall and
two blocks from the Coastal Trail.

Copper Whale Inn B&B $$
B&B   Map B5
440 L St, 99501
Tel *866-258-7999*
🅦 copperwhale.com
In a historic building with pretty
gardens just a block from the
Coastal Trail. The 15 rooms, some
en suite, are small but clean and
charming, with views across Cook
Inlet. There's one two-room suite.

Historic Anchorage Hotel $$
Boutique   Map D4
330 E St, 99501
Tel *907-272-4553*
🅦 historicanchoragehotel.com
Opened in 1916 and fully
restored in 1989; convenient for
shopping, the 5th Avenue Mall
and Coastal Trail. Free Wi-Fi,
breakfast, fitness center, business
center. Helpful staff include a 24-hr
concierge. Rooms are spacious
and clean, if a bit dated in décor.

DK Choice

Hotel Captain Cook $$$
Luxury   Map B5
939 W 5th Ave, 99501
Tel *907-276-6000*
🅦 captaincook.com
Downtown high-rise with gym,
pool and spa, business center,
beauty salon, barber shop, and
four restaurants. Many rooms
have spectacular views over
Cook Inlet. Suites on the top
floors of one of the hotel's
towers enjoy a lounge offering
free breakfast and refreshments.

**Sheraton Anchorage
Hotel & Spa** $$$
Luxury   Map F5
401 E 6th Ave, 99501
Tel *907-276-8700*
🅦 sheratonanchorage.com
Rooms are large, with big flat-
screen TVs and fridges. The
business and fitness centers are
open 24 hours; the Ice Spa is a
highlight, with treatment rooms
overlooking the Cook Inlet.

Greater Anchorage

Spenard Hostel International $
Hostel   Map E1
2845 W 42nd Ave, 99517
Tel *907-248-5036*
🅦 alaskahostel.org
Clean, basic bunks with linens
provided; three kitchens and
common areas, book exchange
and travel library, yard with
barbecue and off-street parking.

11th Avenue Bed & Breakfast $$
B&B   Map E1
334 W 11th Ave, 99501
Tel *855-446-1410*
🅦 11thavenue.net
In a quiet historic area; rooms
are simply furnished, with private
bath and premium bedding.
Full breakfast and 24-hour
snack service.

Oscar Gill House $$
B&B   Map E1
1344 W 10th Ave, 99501
Tel *907-279-1344*
🅦 oscargill.com
Three clean, unassuming rooms
in a charming restored 1913
home, situated in a quiet
neighborhood bordering Cook
Inlet, but close to downtown and
the Coastal Trail. Two rooms have
a shared bathroom.

The Historic Anchorage Hotel offers comfort
and traditional décor

Price Guide

Prices are based on one night's stay in
high season for a standard double room,
linclusive of service charges and taxes.

$	up to $100
$$	$100 to 250
$$$	over $250

Dimond Center Hotel $$$
Luxury   Map E2
700 E Dimond Blvd, 99515
Tel *907-770-5000*
🅦 dimondcenterhotel.com
Sleek architecture, and art from
the Kachemak Bay region. The
large, modern rooms have
oversized tubs. Airport shuttle,
fitness center, free breakfast
buffet, and business center.

Embassy Suites Anchorage $$$
Modern   Map F1
600 E Benson Blvd, 99503
Tel *907-332-7000*
🅦 embassysuitesanchorage.com
Well-equipped suites midtown,
with lots of amenities and extras,
from a pool and spacious hot tub
to complimentary full breakfast
cooked to order. Good service.

The Kenai Peninsula

**COOPER LANDING: Kenai
Princess Wilderness Lodge** $$
Wilderness Lodge   Map B3
17245 Frontier Circle, 99572
Tel *907-595-1425* **Closed** *Oct–Mar*
🅦 princesslodges.com
Bungalow-style rooms have
vaulted ceilings, sitting areas with
wood-burning stoves and private
porches. Central to the main
lodge is a massive fireplace and
deck overlooking the Kenai River.

KENAI: Quality Inn $
Modern   Map A3
10352 Kenai Spur Hwy, 99611
Tel *907-283-6060*
🅦 qualityinn.com
An indoor pool, hot tub, fitness
center, Wi-Fi, and business center;
the basic, clean rooms have fridge,
coffee maker and microwave.
Buffet breakfast. Restaurants and
fishing charters are nearby.

KENAI: Diamond M Ranch $$
Wilderness Lodge   Map A3
48500 Diamond M Ranch Rd, 99611
Tel *907-283-9424*
🅦 diamondmranchresort.com
Bunkhouse rooms, cabins, or suites
in the main lodge; good amenities,
a fish-cleaning station, and free
Wi-Fi. Organized potluck and
campfire socials are a highlight.

KENAI: Grouchy Old Woman B&B $$
B&B   Map A3
48570 N Earl Dr, 99611
Tel *907-776-8775*
w grouchyoldwoman.homestead.com
Located on Daniels Lake a short drive from Kenai, with flower gardens and a rural setting. Refrigerator space and laundry service available. The downstairs apartment opens to the deck. Other rooms have shared baths. Full cooked breakfast.

DK Choice

KENAI: Hi-Lo Charters and Riverside Lodge $$$
Wilderness Lodge   Map A3
1105 Angler Dr, 99611
Tel *907-398-4162*
w hilofishing.com
Here at Beaver Hole on the lower Kenai River, a top fishing location, lodging consists of suites, each with two bedrooms, one bath, a full kitchen, and an outdoor deck or patio. Social activities include picnicking, horseshoes, and evening cocktails.

SOLDOTNA: Best Western King Salmon Motel $$
Modern   Map A3
35546A Kenai Spur Hwy, 99669
Tel *907-262-5857*
w bestwestern.com
Laundry facilities, restaurant on site. Rooms are basic and clean, with coffee maker, fridge and microwave. Fitness center, ample parking, free Wi-Fi and breakfast.

Prince William Sound

VALDEZ: Best Western Valdez Harbor Inn $$
Modern   Map E4
100 N Harbor Dr, 99686
Tel *907-835-3434*
w bestwestern.com
Standard décor, but large comfortable beds. Rooms and suites have lots of amenities and free Wi-Fi. Restaurant and bar on site; breakfast is complimentary.

VALDEZ: House on the Rock B&B $$
B&B   Map E4
613 S Moraine Dr, 99686
Tel *907-831-9027*
w houseontherockbandb.com
In town close to the docks, shops and trail. Rooms are "rustic Alaska" but with private baths, free Wi-Fi and flat-screen TVs. Common areas

include kitchen and diner, laundry, and a popular massage chair.

VALDEZ: Wild Roses by the Sea B&B $$
B&B   Map E4
629 Fiddlehead Ln, 99686
Tel *907-835-2930*
w alaskabytheseabnb.com
Close to the beach, trails, and town, with wide ocean views. Free Wi-Fi, full breakfast. Private bath, whirlpool tub in king room. Clean, Asian-style furnishings.

Southeast Alaska

JUNEAU: Alaskan Hotel & Bar $$
Boutique   Map F4
167 S Franklin St, 99801
Tel *907-586-1000*
w thealaskanhotel.com
The oldest hotel in downtown Juneau, built in 1913, this is on the National Register of Historic Places. Choose a room with shared or private bath or a suite. Décor is dated but clean.

DK Choice

JUNEAU: Alaska's Capital Inn $$
B&B   Map F4
113 5th Street, 99801
Tel *907-586-6507*
w alaskacapitalinn.com
This 1906 Arts & Crafts mansion sits in a quiet residential neighborhood overlooking the waterfront, and is an easy walk to downtown. The large rooms feature period furnishings; some have whirlpool tubs and fireplaces. Lush garden with a covered hot tub, and a lavish cooked breakfast.

JUNEAU: Historic Silverbow Inn $$
B&B   Map F4
120 2nd St, 99801
Tel *907-586-4146*
w silverbowinn.com
In a convenient downtown location, with free Wi-Fi, full breakfast, and on-site restaurant and wine bar. Rooftop deck with hot tub. Rooms are spacious, simply furnished, with private baths. One has a whirlpool tub.

JUNEAU: Westmark Baranof $$$
Luxury   Map F4
127 N Franklin St, 99801
Tel *907-586-2660*
w westmarkhotels.com
The harbor, museums, shopping, and restaurants are nearby this Art Deco-era hotel, a favorite of

The Historic Silverbow Inn with its rooftop hot tub

business travelers. Clean, simple rooms have standard modern furnishings and free Wi-Fi. Fitness center, lounge, two restaurants.

KETCHIKAN: Cape Fox Lodge $$
Wilderness Lodge   Map F5
800 Venetia Way, 99901
Tel *866-225-8001*
w capefoxlodge.com
Ski lodge-style hotel with Native art, restaurant, comfortable lounge and views of the surrounding Tongass National Forest. Rooms are spacious.

KETCHIKAN: Inn at Creek Street and New York Hotel $$
Boutique   Map F5
207 Stedman St, 99901
Tel *907-225-0246*
w thenewyorkhotel.com
Historic building overlooking the Thomas Basin and Inside Passage. Accommodations range from modern loft units, rooms with period furnishings in a former brothel on the waterfront, and apartment-size suites with full kitchens. Flat-screen TVs, free Wi-Fi, on-site restaurant.

DK Choice

KETCHIKAN: Silverking Lodge $$$
Wilderness Lodge   Map F5
Grant Island, 20 miles NW of Ketchikan, 99901
Tel *800-813-4363*
w silverkingalaska.com
A family-run, all-inclusive lodge enviably situated on a private island with a boardwalk built over the water. On your return from your fishing trips, basic but comfortable rooms with hot showers and a welcoming lounge with open fire await you.

For more information on types of hotels *see pp238–41*

SITKA:
Sitka International Hostel $
Hostel   Map E5
109 Jeff Davis St, 99835
Tel *907-747-8661*
W sitkahostel.org
Quiet, clean and a cut above
most hostels, this offers complete
bedding, morning coffee, a
location just blocks from downtown and one block to the sea.
Laundry room, entertainment
room with library, and kitchen.

SITKA: Alaska Ocean
View Bed & Breakfast $$
B&B   Map E5
1101 Edgecumbe Dr, 99835
Tel *907-747-8310*
W sitka-alaska-lodging.com
Three rooms with lovely down
comforters on the beds and
excellent amenities. Free organic
breakfast, outdoor barbecue, hot
tub, and croquet. Business center.

SITKA: Cascade Inn $$
Boutique   Map E5
2035 Halibut Point Rd, 99835
Tel *907-747-6804*
W cascadeinnsitka.com
On the waterfront, near the only
sandy beach and close to
downtown. Plain, clean rooms
with private balconies; some with
kitchenettes. The cedar deck
overlooks the ocean and has a
barbecue and cedar sauna. Wi-Fi.
Sportfishing charters available.

DK Choice

SITKA: Talon Lodge & Spa $$$
Wilderness Lodge   Map E5
Private island, Sitka, 99835
Tel *1-800-536-1864*
W talonlodge.com
A short boat trip from Sitka,
with unspoiled views of the
Inside Passage and the ocean.
Private and multi-room
accommodations are offered.
Gourmet meals are prepared
each night. Package prices
include local transport, guides,
boats, and equipment.

SITKA: Wild Strawberry Lodge
$$$
Wilderness Lodge   Map E5
724 Siginaka Way, 99835
Tel *907-747-3232*
W wildstrawberrylodge.com
Here, anglers can enjoy guided,
multi- or single-day salmon and
halibut fishing excursions, with
chefs preparing the catch; meals,
fishing gear, and fish-cleaning are
included. Accommodations on
offer are suites, cabins, or a three-
bedroom house. Free Wi-Fi and
airport shuttle.

Cabin-style accommodation at Mount
Aurora Lodge

SKAGWAY: Chilkoot Trail
Outpost $$
B&B   Map E4
7 miles W of Skagway, across from
National Park campgrounds
Tel *907-983-3799*
W chilkoottrailoutpost.com
Get away from it all in individual,
well-equipped log cabins, one
off site. There's a campfire pit, a
nearby waterfall, and a retreat
center. Breakfast included.

Western Interior

FAIRBANKS: Ah, Rose Marie
Downtown Bed & Breakfast $
B&B   Map E2
302 Cowles St, 99701
Tel *907-456-2040*
W ahrosemarie.com
Two quaint 1930s historic homes
an easy walk to downtown.
Accommodating hosts offer rooms
furnished with antiques with
private baths and full breakfasts.

FAIRBANKS: Billie's
Backpackers Hostel $
Campground/Hostels   Map E2
2895 Mack Blvd, 99709
Tel *907-479-2034*
W alaskahostel.com
Good for aurora viewing on a
budget: stay in a dorm, private
room, gazebo, or tent. Free linens,
storage, bike use, Wi-Fi, phone,
coffee/tea, showers. No curfew.

FAIRBANKS: Aurora Borealis
Chalet & Lodge $$
Modern   Map E2
1906 Ridge Run Rd, 99707
Tel *907-389-2812*
W auroracabin.com
Twenty miles north of Fairbanks,
in an ideal spot for aurora viewing
(the two-bedroom chalet has a
viewing platform) and tours.
Rooms are spacious, staff helpful.

DK Choice

FAIRBANKS: Aurora Express
Bed & Breakfast $$
B&B   Map E2
1550 Chena Ridge Rd, 99708
Tel *907-474-0949*
W fairbanksalaskabedand
breakfast.com
Fabulously quirky, memorable
accommodations in authentic
railroad cars refitted Victorian-
style, on tracks overlooking the
Tanana Valley. Breakfast is served
– where else – in the dining car.

FAIRBANKS: Mount Aurora
Lodge $$
Modern   Map E2
2320 Fairbank Creek Rd, 99712
Tel *907-389-2000*
W mountauroralodge.com
A former gold miner bunkhouse
and mess hall remade as cabin-
style rooms. Spacious lounge, full
breakfast. Near skiing and town.

FAIRBANKS: SpringHill Suites
Fairbanks $$$
Modern   Map E2
575 1st Ave, 99701
Tel *907-451-6552*
W marriott.com
Downtown suites with premium
bedding, microwave, fridge, work
area, free Wi-Fi. Fitness center,
indoor pool, free airport shuttle,
and breakfast. On-site restaurant.

TALKEETNA: Denali Fireside
Cabins & Suites $$
Modern   Map E3
22647 Talkeetna Spur Rd, 99676
Tel *907-733-2600*
W denalifireside.com
Suites and cabins, furnished in
rustic Alaskan style, have gas
fireplaces, private baths and
kitchenettes, private decks with
scenic views, and free Wi-Fi.

TALKEETNA: Talkeetna Chalet
Bed & Breakfast $$
B&B   Map E3
26344 S Wolf Track Rd, 99676
Tel *907-733-4734*
W talkeetnachalet.com
Three rooms and two cabins with
premium bedding, private baths,
and Alaskan-style décor. Hot tub,
gourmet breakfast, TV, and Wi-Fi.

TALKEETNA: Denali Overlook
Inn $$$
Modern   Map E3
29198 Talkeetna Spur Rd, 99676
Tel *907-733-3555*
W denalioverlookinn.com
Spectacularly situated, with views
of Mount McKinley. The spacious
rooms, suites and one cabin have
free Wi-Fi. Full cooked breakfasts.

Eastern Interior

COPPER CENTER: Copper River Princess Wilderness Lodge $
Wilderness Lodge   **Map** E3
1 Brenwick Craig Rd, 99573
Tel *907-822-4000*
W princesslodges.com
Ski lodge-style, with forest or mountain views. Basic rooms, free Wi-Fi, restaurant, bar, and coffee shop. Wilderness excursions arranged. Daily shuttle service to Wrangell-St. Elias National Park visitor center.

DK Choice

KENNICOTT: Kennicott Glacier Lodge $$$
Wilderness Lodge   **Map** F3
15 Kennicott Millsite, 99588
Tel *907-258-2350*
W kennicottlodge.com
An exceptional location amid glorious scenery. Rooms in the main lodge share bathrooms and are small but clean; the newer south wing rooms have private baths but no phones, TVs, or other amenities. The restaurant serves breakfast, lunch, and family-style dinner.

TOK: Golden Bear Motel & RV Park $
Modern   **Map** F3
Milepost 124.3 Tok Cutoff, 99780
Tel *866-830-0810*
W alaskagoldenbear.com
Welcoming, pet-friendly, family-run, with free Wi-Fi, a coffee shop, and restaurant. Rooms are clean, with private baths; the large guest den has a big-screen TV.

TOK: Burnt Paw Cabins $$
B&B   **Map** F3
Mile 1314.3 Alaska Hwy, 99780
Tel *907-883-4121*
W burntpawcabins.com
Rustic log cabin rentals with breakfast, private bath, satellite TV, microwave, fridge, and Wi-Fi. Dog team equipment on show, as are puppies when available.

Southwest Alaska

DILLINGHAM: Beaver Creek B&B $$
B&B   **Map** C4
1800 Birch Cir, 99576
Tel *907-842-7335*
W dillinghamalaska.com
Rooms in the main house and large cottages and cabins. Full kitchens, phones, TV, Internet access, laundry facilities.

KING SALMON: Antlers Inn $$
Modern   **Map** D4
471 Alaska Peninsula Hwy, 99613
Tel *907-246-8525*
W antlersinnak.com
A small, basic but clean family hotel, handy for downtown. Rooms have free Wi-Fi and a fridge and microwave, while the suites have full kitchens.

DK Choice

KING SALMON: Alagnak Lodge $$$
Wilderness Lodge   **Map** D4
By floatplane from King Salmon
Tel *800-877-9903*
W alagnaklodge.com
A dream vacation spot for anglers, poised on a bluff overlooking the Alagnak River and Bristol Bay watershed. Guides, boats, and all meals provided; the cooking is of a high order, the rooms clean and comfy, and the ambiance conducive to tale-telling and story-swapping.

KODIAK: Best Western Kodiak Inn and Convention Center $$
Modern   **Map** D4
236 W Rezanof Drive, 99615
Tel *907-486-5712*
W bestwestern.com
Standardized décor, as you might expect, but great on amenities, with a fitness center and hot tub, restaurant, bar, free cooked breakfast, self-service laundry, airport shuttle, and business facilities. Rooms are spacious, with TV, coffee maker, fridge and microwave.

KODIAK: Afognak Wilderness Lodge $$$
Wilderness Lodge   **Map** D4
Afognak Island, 99697
Tel *360-799-3250*
W afognaklodge.com
The only lodging on Afognak Island State Park, and perfect for photography, fishing, and wildlife viewing. The main lodge rooms have Wi-Fi and phone; log cabins have private baths. Meals are served family-style in the main lodge.

KODIAK: Katmai Wilderness Lodge $$$
Wilderness Lodge   **Map** D4
Katmai National Park, 99615
Tel *907-486-8767*
W katmai-wilderness.com
On a private oceanfront site at Kukak Bay, and specializing in guided wildlife adventures. Cabins have all modern amenities; meals are prepared family style.

Arctic & Western Alaska

DK Choice

BARROW: Top of the World Hotel $$$
Modern   **Map** D1
3060 Eben Hopson St, 99723
Tel *907-852-3900*
W tundratoursinc.com
Exceptional rooms for the area, with clean modern furnishings, coffee maker, free Wi-Fi, and ocean views. 24-hour front desk, ATM, fitness room, coin laundry, kitchen facilities, on-site restaurant where you can sample traditional Native foods.

NOME: Dredge No. 7 Inn $$
Modern   **Map** C2
1700 Nome-Teller Hwy, 99762
Tel *907-304-1270*
W dredge7inn.com
In a private location near to town. Free Wi-Fi and clean rooms with historic ambiance. Private baths, TV, fridge, microwave.

NOME: Nome Nugget Inn $$
Modern   **Map** C2
315 Front St, 99762
Tel *877-443-2323*
W nomenuggetinnhotel.com
Expect the usual mod cons here: private bath, free Wi-Fi, fridge, microwave, on-site bar. Ocean-view rooms tend to be quieter.

PRUDHOE BAY: Prudhoe Bay Hotel $
Modern   **Map** E1
100 Main St, 99734
Tel *907-659-2449*
W prudhoebayhotel.com
Walking distance from the airport and geared to local works and visitors. Excellent wildlife viewing. Restaurants, gift shop, Internet access. Shared or private baths.

Looking out to sea at the ocean-facing Katmai Wilderness Lodge

For more information on types of hotels *see pp238–41*

WHERE TO EAT AND DRINK

Most of the larger cities in Alaska have a variety of eateries serving better-than-average fare that spans a range of cuisines reflecting the many immigrant communities that are part of the Alaskan population. Anchorage provides the widest selection, including Indian, Japanese, Vietnamese, and Greek restaurants. Fairbanks, Juneau, Homer, and some of the smaller towns also present a number of fine choices. Nearly all mid-sized communities have Chinese, Mexican, and fast food restaurants, and even the smallest bush community will usually have a basic eatery, a coffee shop, supermarket, food stalls, or a cannery canteen. Mobile or static lunch wagons provide welcome pitstops in many remote areas. Alaskan cuisine includes hearty, filling dishes, featuring well-prepared steak and a range of seafood. Portions are generous and may come with large starters, and as many baskets of bread or tortilla chips as are requested by the diners.

Types of Restaurants

The most expensive options are the true gourmet restaurants, which are found only around Anchorage or in larger towns, but many mid-range restaurants in other areas offer dishes that approximate gourmet standards.

The majority of Alaskan restaurants are individual and family-run and range from satisfying to superb. In small highway towns and along the road system, roadhouses provide excellent breakfasts, lunches with homemade soups, and a variety of filling dinners. The larger hotels usually have their own restaurants, which in wilderness areas may be the only places to eat in the vicinity. The larger towns have chain restaurants that offer decent food at good prices and in very generous portions that few people can finish. The assumption is that most diners will pack up the leftovers in a doggy bag to eat later. Many supermarkets have bakeries, delis, noodle bars, sushi bars, and cafés for quick and filling fare.

Towns of all sizes have at least one fast food chain serving up the usual range of burgers, fried chicken, sub sandwiches, pizzas, or tacos.

Reservations and Dress Codes

While dining in Alaska is most often casual and informal, advance dinner reservations are recommended for upscale places, and in the case of popular restaurants that don't accept bookings, it pays to arrive as early as possible. When it comes to dress, Alaska is possibly the most relaxed state in the country, and only a few of the finest restaurants request jackets and ties.

When to Eat

In Alaska, breakfast is served early – often beginning at 6am – to allow guests to eat and get a good start on the day's

The Exit Glacier Salmon Bake in Seward knows how to reel in a crowd

activities. The first meal of the day can be anything from fruit, toast, and coffee to a hearty spread that includes juice, eggs cooked to order, ham, steak, bacon, or sausage. Fried potatoes, biscuits and gravy, pancakes, and several Mexican possibilities involving beans, vegetables, salsa, tortillas, and cheese may also be on the menu.

Lunch, therefore, can often be a lighter meal than breakfast, especially when daylight hours need to be made the most of. Staples include appetizing soups – often fish chowder – and salads, burgers, or sandwiches.

Dinner is the main meal of the day, and is usually eaten between 5 and 9pm. In the long daylight hours of summer, Alaskans tend to eat late, after recreational activities are finished for the day, and outdoor evening barbecues are very popular. Dinner usually includes fish or meat – beef, pork, chicken, and occasionally moose or even reindeer – as well as a vegetable dish, a salad, and potatoes.

A converted railway tram car houses Smoke Shack in Seward

Pleasant outdoor seating at a restaurant on Homer Spit

What to Eat

Alaskan cuisine *(see pp248–9)* is hearty, as befits its heritage as an adventurous, outdoorsy state, and has some of the world's finest fish and game. In urban restaurants, meals range from the usual Alaskan meat-and-potatoes fare to international options such as Italian, Greek, Mexican, Thai, Chinese, Korean, and Japanese food.

Above all, Alaska has access to superlative seafood, from plump, cold-water Kachemak Bay oysters and Alaska king crab to halibut and, of course, wild Alaska salmon, one of the most popular products of the state. In the summer, restaurants and tourist-oriented businesses in many towns organize salmon bakes – often served in an all-you-can-eat style – with freshly caught wild salmon.

Prices and Tipping

Despite the fact that shipping distances dictate higher prices than those found in the Lower 48, visitors will find that restaurant meals in Alaska generally represent good value. In fact, in hotels, locally run places, and sit-down chain restaurants, generous portions of tasty, filling food will cost only a bit more than if you prepared them yourself. What the food might lack in sophistication, it amply makes up for in quantity and taste. Even fine-dining restaurants are reasonably priced and provide value for money.

As with any restaurant in the country, tipping is essential. Restaurant employees are typically paid low wages under the assumption that customers will liberally tip the servers and bus staff. Tips are usually determined by the quality of the service received, with the average being around 15–20 percent. A tip of 10 percent will make it clear that the service was lacking, while 20 percent will indicate an appreciation of outstanding service.

Vegetarian Choices

Despite the local fondness for fish and game, vegetarians will be happy to find that most Alaskan restaurants cater to a wide variety of preferences, and that Anchorage, Juneau, and Fairbanks have some excellent places specializing in vegetarian cuisine. In small towns, Asian places are usually the best bet for vegetarian meals, and wilderness lodges offer buffets with both vegetarian and meat-oriented selections. Visitors on cruises or organized tours will also find that their culinary preferences are almost universally accommodated.

Children

Most Alaskan restaurants cater to children with simple meals that include hot dogs, French fries, burgers, and other items that appeal to the younger set. These will typically cost around half the price of an adult meal. In addition, many places provide high chairs, play areas, coloring books, and crayons to keep kids busy while they wait for their meals.

Accessibility

The US is perhaps one of the world's most progressive countries in terms of providing easy access to public buildings for guests with mobility challenges, and new buildings are designed with accessibility in mind. Still, many restaurants in Alaska's small towns are in older buildings that date from the Gold Rush era and have not been modernized. In remoter areas where dining options are limited, it might be wise to check online or call ahead.

Recommended Restaurants

The best way to find a decent meal is to ask locals, including hotel staff and taxi drivers, who are usually pleased to promote their favorite spots. Tourist offices can provide listings but may not make recommendations.

The restaurants on pp250–55 offer options for every region to suit every budget and taste. The DK Choice heading highlights establishments that offer terrific food, exceptional service, or perhaps occupy an unrivalled location; they may simply be the locals' favorite for brunch or a great steak and beer, or elevate food from the mediocre to the sublime with innovative use of ingredients, often sourced locally from nearby fisheries and gardens. Whatever the reason, they will offer a memorable dining experience.

For map references to Anchorage see pp68–9.

Ketchikan's popular Bar Harbor Restaurant *(see p253)*

The Flavors of Alaska

From Alaska's cold waters, commercial deep-sea fishermen harvest some of the world's best wild salmon, halibut, and cod, as well as three species of crab and other shellfish. Seafood is served grilled, baked, or broiled, or preserved by smoking, drying, or canning. Hunters bring in game meat such as Dall sheep, moose, caribou, and black-tailed deer, which are prepared in a variety of creative ways. A range of local produce, including potatoes, carrots, and other "winter" vegetables, is grown commercially in the Mat-Su Valley; some of these grow to gargantuan proportions in the long daylight hours of the Alaskan summer *(see p88)*.

Alaskan crowberries and lowbush cranberries

Commercial crab fisherman off Juneau in Southeast Alaska

Alaskan Food

Alaska's cuisine reflects the variety of people who have come to the state from all over the US and other parts of the world. However, most ethnic foods have been adapted to local tastes. Local specialties include pizzas made with reindeer sausage, bolognaise sauces made with moose meat, and taco fillings that include carrots and halibut. Fresh vegetables play less of a role than they do in the Lower 48. Instead, most Alaskans favor hearty fare that is heavy on meat and fish. In the summer, barbecued meat or grilled fish is accompanied by sourdough bread, salads, light soups, and local vegetables, while in the winter, a typical meal would include a bowl of warming chili or beef, game, or chicken stew, along with potato dishes and vegetable casseroles topped with cheese and breadcrumbs.

The most reliable places to find authentic Alaskan "home cooking" are wilderness lodges and roadhouses along the highway system, which serve up hearty, filling fare that usually features meat, potatoes, and cold-weather vegetables.

Salmon filet

Salmon steak

Halibut filet

Trout

Shrimp

Scallops

A selection of fresh seafood available in Alaska

Alaskan Dishes and Specialties

Alaskan sourdough

Most fine Alaskan restaurants serve local seafood using various creative recipes for wild salmon and halibut, as well as king, Dungeness, and snow crab. Available in season, these are most often served as a pile of legs and claws, accompanied by a selection of dipping sauces. Game meat is also a staple and a few restaurants offer options such as reindeer sausage. Potatoes figure prominently in most meals, and the most popular vegetables used are hardy varieties that can be grown in cold climates. Meals may also feature Alaskan sourdough bread, which was popularized during the Gold Rush. It is made with a starter, which contains a yeast that causes the dough to rise. The periodic addition of sugar keeps the yeast growing and some starters in use today date from the early 1900s. Desserts include pies, tarts, or cobblers made from local wild berries.

Salmon, an iconic Alaskan dish, is served grilled, baked, or alder-smoked with lemon, dill, and melted butter. Alaska has five species of Pacific salmon.

Sampling beer at the Alaskan Brewing Company *(see p144)* in Juneau

Vegetables and Fruits

Alaska's main agricultural area, the Matanuska Valley, produces a wide range of cold-climate vegetables such as carrots, squash, zucchini (courgettes), potatoes, kohlrabi, rutabagas (swede), cauliflower, broccoli, and turnips. These are usually used in stews, baked into casseroles, or eaten as stand-alone dishes after being baked, boiled, or mashed. The climate of Anchorage, the Kenai Peninsula, and the Mat-Su is also suitable for growing orchard fruits such as apples and cherries, although not in commercial quantities. Rhubarb and a wide variety of berries grow well through much of the southern half of the state. Most are cultivated in gardens and canned, made into jams and jellies, or baked into delicious pies.

Beer and Wine

The state has seen a growth of microbreweries in the larger towns, where many pubs and brewhouses will offer a selection of craft ales. Alaska's only fully fledged brewery is the Alaskan Brewing Company in Juneau. Its range of award-winning beers include stout, amber, pale ale, and both summer and winter ales, which are available all over Alaska, as well as in the western states.

Alaska's climate is too cold for growing wine grapes, but that does not stop a few enterprising winemakers producing refreshing wines, either from imported grape must or from local flowers, fruits, and other produce – birch sap, honey, and even potatoes, onions, and carrots. In Homer, Bear Creek Winery produces rhubarb, blueberry, and raspberry wines. Anchorage's Denali Winery imports grapes to produce palatable vintages.

Native Foods

Akutaq "Eskimo ice cream" is made by the Inuit from seal oil, whipped berries, and snow.

Caribou, moose, black-tailed deer Hunted by Alaska Natives in Southeast, Interior, and Arctic Alaska, wild game meat is dried, frozen, or eaten in any meat-based recipe.

Dried fish Fish are preserved by drying them on large racks.

Smoked fish Fish are smoked in a wood-fired smoker, usually using alder wood, which adds a fine flavor.

Whale This beef-like meat is a favored part of the local diet. Inupiat villages are allowed to catch small numbers of whales.

Muktuk Whale blubber, the fatty layer beneath the outer skin, is chewed raw or softened by boiling or pickling.

Berries Historically, berries such as salmonberries, elderberries, and blueberries were the main source of sugar in the Native diet.

Crab legs and claws are steamed or boiled and served with a variety of sauces. Diners need a crab-cracker to extract the meat from the shell.

Reindeer sausage pizza is a thick crust pizza spread with marinara sauce and cheese, topped with reindeer sausage, roasted peppers, and onions.

Wild blueberry pies are made by baking berries with sugar, cornstarch, and lemon juice in a pie shell. They are served with whipped cream.

Where to Eat and Drink

Anchorage

Downtown

Alaska's Gourmet Sub   **$**
Café   Map D5
601 W 7th Ave, 99501
Tel *907-297-7827*   **Closed** *Sun*
A favorite with local workers for a
quick lunch such as submarine
sandwiches. A good choice of
breads, dressings, and fillings,
including several veggie options.
Also serves gyros, wraps, pizzas,
and a daily lunch special.

Brown Bag Sandwich Co.   **$**
Pub   Map D4
400 D St, 99501
Tel *907-277-0202*
Hearty sandwiches are good
value at $10. A favorite is grilled
spicy roast beef made with
London broil, cheddar, Dijon
mustard, and horseradish on
marble rye. Local beers.

Midnight Sun Café   **$**
Café   Map E4
245 W 5th Ave, 99501
Tel *907-743-0572*
Breakfast bagels, croissants,
muffins, and scones. For lunch, deli
and grilled sandwiches, paninis,
salads, smoothies. Lots of teas and
fresh-roasted specialty coffee.

Snow Goose Restaurant   **$**
Pub   Map D4
717 W 3rd Ave, 99501
Tel *907-277-7727*   **Closed** *Sun &
Mon in winter*
Great views across Cook Inlet
and a menu of nachos, salmon
sliders, salads, chowders, burgers,
meatloaf. Award-winning craft
beers and ales from their own
brewery, the Sleeping Lady.

**Humpy's Great Alaskan
Alehouse**   **$$**
Pub   Map D5
610 W 6th Ave, 99501
Tel *907-276-2337*
Steamer clams, chowder, wings,
salads, burgers, sandwiches, and
fresh seafood. The selection of
craft beers is outstanding. There's
live music through the week, and
an outdoor patio.

White Spot Café   **$$**
Café   Map E4
109 W 4th Ave, 99501
Tel *907-279-3954*
No-frills diner serving breakfast
and lunch with super-fast service
– a good spot for quick family
meals. Breakfast is the favorite,
especially biscuits and gravy.

Club Paris   **$$$**
Steak   Map D5
417 W 5th Ave, 99501
Tel *907-277-6332*
Cozy and unpretentious, often
voted Anchorage's best steak
house. Sandwich meats are
smoked or roasted in-house.
Steaks include filet mignon, New
York, rib eye, and prime rib;
there's also fresh Alaskan seafood,
combos of meat and fish, a few
simple salads and sides, and
desserts such as tart key lime pie
and chocolate sweet potato pie.
Limited wine list, big beer list.

Crush Wine Bar & Bistro   **$$$**
Café   Map D5
343 W 6th Ave, 99501
Tel *907-865-9198*   **Closed** *Sun*
More than 40 wines by the glass
and a wide choice of beers. Salads,
soups, desserts, and light dishes
change daily and are offered
with wine pairings. Hip, cozy
atmosphere. Wine shop upstairs.

Ginger   **$$$**
Asian   Map D5
425 W 5th Ave, 99501
Tel *907-929-3680*
Pacific Rim-style food such as
tamarind-cashew shrimp, spring
rolls, spicy ahi tuna and Korean
BBQ ribs. Lots of salads and
vegetarian options; separate bar
menu. Sleek, stylish interior.

DK Choice

Glacier Brewhouse   **$$$**
Pub   Map D5
737 W 5th Ave Ste 110, 99501
Tel *907-274-2739*
This is a popular local gathering
spot and is busy most evenings.
It has a big, rowdy, rustic wood
dining room, serving up fresh
seafood, wood-grilled steaks,
ribs and chicken, pastas, pizzas,
sandwiches, and salads. Kids'
and gluten-free options for
lunch, dinner, and dessert. Huge
selection of craft beers on tap.

Sacks Café and Restaurant   **$$$**
Seafood   Map D4
328 G St, 99501
Tel *907-274-4022*
Contemporary diner-style décor
at this friendly place serving
lunch and dinner, with brunch
too on Saturday and Sunday.
Menu selections include seafood,
pastas, risottos, pork, lamb, duck,
and chicken, imaginatively
prepared. Daily home-made
soup and salads. Good wine list.

Price Guide

The price ranges cover a main dish with
sides, taxes, and service charges, but
exclude alcoholic beverages.

$	up to $25
$$	$25 to $50
$$$	over $50

Sullivan's Steakhouse   **$$$**
Steak   Map D5
320 W 5th Ave, 99501
Tel *907-258-2882*
This upscale chain features hefty
steaks, from an 8-oz filet to a
26-oz rib eye. Live music in the
evening, specialty cocktails, and
a large wine list.

DK Choice

The Marx Bros Café   **$$$**
Seafood   Map D4
627 W 3rd Ave, 99501
Tel *907-278-2133*   **Closed** *Sun &
Mon*
Fine dining in a simple, quiet
dining room. The limited
seating makes reservations a
necessity. Appetizers include
seared foie gras, fresh Alaska
oysters, and Neapolitan seafood
mousse. Favorite entrées are
wild-caught salmon, braised
rabbit, tea-smoked duck, and
grilled scallops. Desserts are
elegant and there's a huge
wine selection.

Greater Anchorage

Great Harvest Bread Co.   **$**
Café   Map F1
570 E Benson Blvd, 99503
Tel *907-274-3331*   **Closed** *Sun*
Different fresh-baked breads,
cookies, scones and pound
cakes daily. Permanent treats
include chocolate chip oatmeal
cookies, blueberry scones, and
tasty ham and cheese rolls.

The popular Glacier Brewhouse with its big
rustic dining room

Dami Japanese Restaurant $$
Japanese Map E1
642 E 5th Ave, 99501
Tel *907-274-5211*
Traditional Japanese sushi,
teriyaki, and tempura. The bento
bowls and volcano rolls are
popular, and the green tea ice
cream is a must. Friendly service.

Doriola's $$
Café Map E2
510 W Tudor Rd, 99503
Tel *907-375-0494* **Closed** *Sat &
Sun in winter*
Cold deli and grill-pressed
sandwiches, quiches and salads
are lunch favorites. A variety of
coffees, smoothies, and sodas.
Waiting list for monthly summer
Saturday dinners.

Gumbo House $$
Cajun/Creole Map E1
611 W 9th Ave, 99501
Tel *907-222-2930*
Cajun and Creole specialties
including red beans and rice,
jambalaya and the daily po'boy
and gumbo with plenty of spice.
Authentic cuisine in big portions.

Moose's Tooth Pub & Pizzeria $$
Pizzeria Map F1
3300 Old Seward Hwy, 99503
Tel *907-258-2537*
Legendary pizza place with a
huge and inventive selection of
toppings, plus succulent chicken
wings, wide choice of local beers,
and brewed root beer. Come
early or prepare for a wait.

Samurai Sushi Garden $$
Japanese Map F1
1265 Muldoon Rd, 99504
Tel *907-332-1020*
Classic, very fresh Japanese sushi
rolls, California rolls, bento boxes,
tempura, and soups. Children's
menu. A good selection of sake
and beer; fast service.

Snow City Café $$
Café Map E1
1034 W 4th Ave, 99501
Tel *907-272-2489*
Popular for all-day breakfast and
brunch, with omelets, breakfast
sandwiches, biscuits and gravy,
and eggs Benedict. Vegan and
gluten-free options.

Spenard Roadhouse $$
Café Map E1
1049 Northern Lights Blvd, 99503
Tel *907-770-7623*
A clean, modern dining spot with
a varied menu, including Thai
curry, jambalaya, flatiron steak,
fish and chips, soups, salads, and
sandwiches. Local beers and
small-batch bourbon.

The Kingfisher Roadhouse in its enviable position in the Kenai Peninsula

The Red Chair Café $$
Café Map E1
337 E 4th Ave, 99501
Tel *907-270-7780*
Slick urban atmosphere. Lots of
vegetarian and vegan options,
as well as burgers, steaks, and
sandwiches, omelets and other
breakfast dishes. Beer and wine.

Campobello Bistro $$$
Mediterranean Map E1
601 W 36th Ave, 99503
Tel *907-563-2040*
Mediterranean dishes, showcasing
seafood, pasta, fresh Alaskan
salmon and halibut, plus chops,
steaks, and duck. Big wine list and
attentive staff.

DK Choice

Jen's Restaurant $$$
Seafood Map F1
701 W 36th Ave, 99503
Tel *907-561-5367* **Closed** *Sun*
In the Olympic Center, a strip
mall, Jen's boasts an elegant
dining room with paintings by
local artists. The wonderful,
ever-changing Alaskan/Danish
menu features fresh-caught
oysters, salmon, rockfish, and
scallops, as well as farm-raised
duck, pork, lamb, and beef
specialties. House-made pastas
and salads. Big wine list.

Kincaid Grill & Wine Bar $$$
Seafood Map E2
6700 Jewell Lake Blvd, 99502
Tel *907-243-0507* **Closed** *Sun &
Mon*
Fine dining on Alaskan game and
seafood, and steaks. Try the
roasted beet salad with goat
cheese frittata, salmon with
chimichurri, tomato bacon jam
and grilled asparagus, then
chocolate bourbon soufflé. Large
wine list, boutique coffees, and
attentive service. Dinner only.

Kinley's Restaurant & Bar $$$
Seafood Map F1
3230 Seward Hwy, 99503
Tel *907-644-8953* **Closed** *Sun*
Varied menu featuring fresh
seafood, pastas, salads, home-
made soups, burgers, and steaks.
Good vegetarian and gluten-free
options, wide wine list.

DK Choice

Villa Nova Restaurant $$$
Seafood Map E2
5121 Arctic Blvd 1, 99503
Tel *907-561-1660* **Closed** *Sun-
Mon*
Sicilian Chef Giorgio makes
everything from scratch, and
the menu features fresh seafood
choices that change daily with
the catch. Count on classics
such as veal parmigiano, chicken
piccata, home-made pastas and
sauces, and tiramisu. Good wine
list; quaint Italian décor.

The Kenai Peninsula

**COOPER LANDING: Sackett's
Kenai Grill** $$
Café Map B3
Mile 50.4 Sterling Hwy, 99572
Tel *907-595-1827*
Combination pizzeria, barbecue
joint, and bakery. Smoked prime
rib sandwich for lunch is popular.
Draft beer. Casual dining on
picnic tables in good weather.

**COOPER LANDING: Kingfisher
Roadhouse** $$$
Seafood Map B3
Mile 47.4 Sterling Hwy, 99572
Tel *907-595-2861*
Daily specials feature salmon,
steak, and huge burgers. Many
dishes include local, organic
ingredients. A deck overlooks the
river; there's live music most nights.

For more information on types of restaurants *see pp246–7*

DK Choice

HALIBUT COVE: Saltry Restaurant $$$
Seafood   Map A4
1 W Ismilof, 99603
Tel *907-226-2424*
Seafood is caught the same day and prepared with care here, where the words local, home-made, fresh, and organic feature heavily on the menu. Oysters or chowder for starters are especially good, enjoyed in a dining room that has wide ocean views. The friendly, knowledgeable waitstaff are helpful when it comes to pairing food with the extensive selection of wines and beers.

HOMER: Captain Pattie's Fish House $$$
Seafood   Map A4
4241 Homer Spit Rd, 99603
Tel *907-235-5135*   **Closed** *Mon*
Fresh local salmon and halibut, as well as king crab, oysters, and scallops are the best choice. The menu also offers steak, pastas and chicken, burgers, salads, and soups. Come early or make a reservation.

HOMER: Chart Room Restaurant $$$
Seafood   Map A4
4876 Homer Spit Rd, 99603
Tel *907-235-0400*
A sweeping view of the bay, with an outdoor deck for good weather dining. Baked halibut topped with crab is the signature dish. Fish specials according to the catch. Experienced waitstaff, full bar, and good wine list.

HOMER: Wasabi's $$$
Seafood   Map A4
59217 East End Rd, 99603
Tel *907-226-3663*   **Closed** *Sun–Tue in winter*
Expertly prepared Japanese-style fresh sushi and seafood as well as steaks and specialties such as mac and cheese and potstickers. Reserve a table by the window for the ocean view.

KENAI: Burger Bus $
Café   Map A3
409 Overland Ave, 99611
Tel *907-283-9611*   **Closed** *Sun*
Known for the biggest and best burgers in town, with the Kenai King a favorite – a succulent beef patty with bacon, jalapeno, cheese, onion, tomato, and home-made fries. Service is from a converted school bus, to eat or takeout; there are picnic tables for good weather.

KENAI: Playa Azul $
Mexican   Map A3
104 Haller St, 99611
Tel *907-283-2010*
Ignore the exterior and come for the Mexican favorites, including fresh fish tacos, carne asada, chimichangas and salsa bar.

KENAI: Veronica's Coffee House $
Café   Map A3
604 Peterson Way, 99611
Tel *907-283-2725*
Home-made soups, salads, sandwiches, quiches, and desserts. Specialty teas and coffees. Try the cinnamon apple pie with ice cream. Live entertainment Fri–Sat.

KENAI: Louie's Steak & Seafood $$
Seafood   Map A3
47 Spur View Dr, 99611
Tel *907-283-3660*
Stuffed wildlife and old Alaska artifacts in a lodge-style dining room. Portions of stroganoff, steamers, salmon, chowder, and halibut are huge, and the service is efficient and friendly.

KENAI: Paradiso's Restaurant $$
International   Map A3
811 Main St, 99611
Tel *907-283-2222*
Longtime favorite serving a mix of cuisines: Italian chicken Parmesan, Mexican enchiladas, Greek pizzas and gyros, American steaks, and seafood. Will deliver.

SEWARD: Nature's Nectars $
Café   Map B4
1313 4th Ave, 99664
Tel *907-422-0688*
Small, friendly takeout stand with specialty coffees, plus fruit and veggie smoothies made to order from fresh local ingredients.

Saltry Restaurant, perched above the water in Halibut Cove

SEWARD: Le Barn Appetit $$
Café   Map B4
11786 Old Exit Glacier Rd, 99664
Tel *907-224-8706*
Specializing in crepes and Belgian waffles; a favorite is the reindeer sausage with spinach and egg. Portions are huge, but seating limited (just 21 covers), so there are often long lines.

SEWARD: Smoke Shack $$
Steak   Map B4
411 Port Ave, 99664
Tel *907-224-7427*
A fun venue with limited seating in a converted railway train car. Expect long lines for breakfast and take-out barbecue. Snow crab eggs Benedict, spicy breakfast burritos, French toast, biscuits and gravy, and hash are the specialties.

SOLDOTNA: Firehouse BBQ $
Steak   Map A3
43837 K-Beach, 99669
Tel *907-252-7747*
All types of barbecue, such as pulled pork sandwiches, brisket and ribs, with beans and slaw. Stuffed potatoes are favorites. Dine in, drive-up to order for takeout, or eat at picnic tables in good weather.

SOLDOTNA: Odie's Deli $
Café   Map A3
35228 Kenai Spur Hwy, 99669
Tel *907-260-3255*
A local institution, with a new second location at Kenai Airport. Home-made soups change daily. Sandwiches are prepared with breads baked on the premises. Fresh salads, local beer on tap.

SOLDOTNA: The Moose is Loose $
Café   Map A3
44278 Sterling Hwy, 99669
Tel *907-260-3036* **Closed** *Sun & Mon*
Doughnuts and other baked goods are the draw here, from cinnamon rolls to cookies and breads. The champagne cake doughnuts are a favorite. Lots of moose-themed trinkets and gifts in the adjoining gift shop.

SOLDOTNA: St. Elias Brewing Company $$
Pub   Map A3
434 Sharkathmi Ave, 99669
Tel *907-260-7837*   **Closed** *Mon*
Fresh pizzas, salads, sandwiches, and desserts served in a simple, bar-style setting, with outdoor seating for summer. As many as 11 ales are available on tap from the on-site brewhouse, as well as a large wine list with some Alaskan labels.

Prince William Sound

VALDEZ: Old Town Burgers $
Café **Map** E4
E Pioneer Dr, 99686
Tel *907-831-0999*
Huge omelets and chicken-fried steak are breakfast favorites. Double cheeseburger is enough for two and fish and chips are top rated. Simple diner style with picnic tables for good weather.

VALDEZ: A Rogue's Garden $
Café **Map** E4
354 Fairbanks Dr, 99686
Tel *907-835-5880* **Closed** *Sun*
A natural foods store and café with organic espresso and smoothie bar, fresh baked pastries, and home-made soups, salads, and sandwiches.

VALDEZ: Alaska Halibut House $$
Seafood **Map** E4
208 Meals Ave, 99686
Tel *907-835-2788*
Fried halibut and shrimp platters with home-made waffle fries are to die for. Fresh and plentiful portions in a modest setting.

VALDEZ: Fat Mermaid $$
Pizzeria **Map** E4
143 N Harbor Dr, 99686
Tel *907-835-3000*
Huge salads, burgers, and bar food such as quesadillas and nachos, and a wide selection of pizzas. Gluten-free options. Local beers on tap. Lively atmosphere.

VALDEZ: Totem Inn Restaurant $$
Café **Map** E4
144 Egan Ave, 99686
Tel *907-835-4443*
All types of fish and burgers, huge breakfasts with the chili cheese omelet a favorite. Busy, diner-type ambiance. Fast, efficient service.

Southeast Alaska

JUNEAU: Alaskan Crepe Escape $
Café **Map** F4
350 S Franklin St, 99802
Tel *907-586-1846* **Closed** *winter*
Big variety of sweet and savory crepes. Try the Gastineau with salmon, cream cheese, spinach, lemon, and herbs. Good sandwiches and smoothies too.

JUNEAU: Island Pub $$
Pizzeria **Map** F4
1102 2nd St, 99824
Tel *907-364-1595*
In a newly refurnished historic building on Douglas Island,

Shops and restaurants lining Front St, Ketchikan

offering soups and salads, chicken skewers, wraps and wood-fired pizzas; the pizza dough and focaccias are made on site daily.

JUNEAU: Randy's Rib Shack $$
Steak **Map** F4
356 S Franklin St, 99801
Tel *907-957-1294*
Fabulous barbecue from a trailer hidden behind the town library: tender smoked ribs, pulled pork and chicken sandwiches, juicy brisket, and home-made sauce.

JUNEAU: The Rookery Café $$
Café **Map** F4
111 Seward St, 99801
Tel *907-463-3013* **Closed** *Sun*
Fresh baked goods, burgers, sandwiches, and salads during the day; a more refined menu for dinner, prepared by an award-winning chef.

JUNEAU: Sandpiper Café $$
Café **Map** F4
429 W Willoughby Ave, 99801
Tel *907-586-3150*
A favorite breakfast and brunch spot; opt for French toast with mounds of fresh fruit, eggs Benedict, burritos, or a smoked salmon omelet. Ample seating; sleek, contemporary décor.

DK Choice

JUNEAU: Tracy's King Crab Shack $$
Seafood **Map** F4
406 S Franklin St, 99802
Tel *907-723-1811*
On the pier right next to the cruise ship dock. Feast on succulent Bristol Bay king crab legs fresh from the sea, king crab bisque, and spicy crab cakes or rolls; plus snow crab, scallops, shrimp, and Dungeness crab in the summer. The only sides are garlic rolls, rice, and slaw.

KETCHIKAN: Burger Queen $
Café **Map** F5
518 Water St, 99901
Tel *907-225-6060* **Closed** *Sun*
Surprisingly good, juicy burgers, chicken, fish and chips, and thick milkshakes in a plain little diner with just four tables. Will also deliver to all local areas.

KETCHIKAN: Sweet Mermaids $
Café **Map** F5
340 Front St, 99901
Tel *907-225-3287* **Closed** *Sun & Mon in winter*
Specialty coffees and a good variety of pastries, including cakes, cookies, croissants, and pies. Fresh chowder, sandwiches, and salads too, plus free Wi-Fi, make this a local favorite.

KETCHIKAN: Bar Harbor Restaurant $$$
Steak **Map** F5
2813 Tongass Ave, 99901
Tel *907-225-2813*
Attentive service and a varied menu that includes juicy pot roast, fresh seafood, steaks, salads, pastas, and home-made breads and desserts.

SITKA: Highliner Coffee $
Café **Map** E5
327 Seward St, 99835
Tel *907-747-4924* **Closed** *Sat & Sun*
Drive-through and café with house-roasted gourmet coffees, teas, and fresh-baked pastries. Wi-Fi and a selection of gifts in the comfortable café; a popular local hangout.

SITKA: Homeport Eatery $
Café **Map** E5
209 Lincoln St, 99835
Tel *907-966-2336* **Closed** *Mon*
Rustic old cable house with ocean views. Hot and cold sandwiches, coffees and pastries, chowder, big brunch selection. Live music on weekends.

DK Choice

SITKA: Ludvig's Bistro $$
Mediterranean   **Map** E5
256 Katlian St, 99835
Tel 907-966-3663   Closed Sun
and Oct–Jan
Famous for its service and its cuisine: rustic Mediterranean specialties featuring local seafood and local produce. Try the Alaskan rockfish, grilled lamb chops with lentils, bistro steak or fresh halibut. Be sure to book as there's limited seating, but there's also a wine bar and gallery with an outdoor deck.

SITKA: Channel Club $$$
Steak   **Map** E5
2906 Halibut Point Rd, 99835
Tel 907-747-7440
Elegant dining with a view of Mt Edgecumbe. Attentive service. Salmon and halibut specials, prime rib and steaks cooked over wood fires. Full wine list.

SKAGWAY: Bites on Broadway $
Café   **Map** E4
648 Broadway, 99840
Tel 907-983-2166
Friendly owners and service. Breakfast sausage or bacon and cheese biscuits are huge and fresh; try chili or chowder for lunch. Desserts include German chocolate cake or red velvet cake.

SKAGWAY: Sugar Mama's $
Café   **Map** E4
382 5th Ave, 99840
Tel 907-983-2288
Huge, moist cupcakes are baked fresh daily. Choices include rhubarb, cherry, cheesecake, red velvet, chocolate peanut butter, double vanilla. Gluten-free options.

Western Interior

FAIRBANKS: Alaska Coffee Roasting Co. $
Café   **Map** E2
4001 Geist Rd, Ste 2, 99709
Tel 907-457-5282
Fresh-roasted coffee and fresh-baked goods such as cinnamon and pecan rolls. Savory flatbreads, sandwiches and soups. Biscuits and gravy on the weekends.

FAIRBANKS: The Crepery $
Café   **Map** E2
535 2nd Ave, 99701
Tel 907-450-9192
Fresh, filling and inventive crepes such as savory smoked salmon or brie and cranberry, and dessert crepes such as crème brûlée,

cheesecake with fresh berries, and banana and Nutella. Specialty coffees and outstanding service. Limited seating but free Wi-Fi and a pleasant atmosphere.

FAIRBANKS: Fudge Pot $
Café   **Map** E2
515 1st Ave, 99701
Tel 907-456-3834
Specializing in desserts, including home-made fudge in 30 different flavors; blueberry and cranberry are made from Alaska berries.

FAIRBANKS: McCafferty's, A Coffee House, Etc $
Café   **Map** E2
408 Cushman St, 99701
Tel 907-456-6853   Closed Mon
Cozy, with simple furnishings and a stage for live music on weekends. Coffee roasted in house and always fresh; fresh-baked cookies and pastries. Top marks for the friendly baristas.

FAIRBANKS: Pita Place $
Middle Eastern   **Map** E2
3300 College Rd, 99709
Tel 907-687-2456   Closed Sun, Mon, and winter
Perfectly spiced falafel and huge pitas with sauces and veggies to eat at picnic tables or take away. Authentic Turkish coffee.

FAIRBANKS: Bad 2 da Bone BBQ $$
Grill   **Map** E2
80 5th St, 99701
Tel 907-699-2663
Authentic pit barbecue ribs, pulled pork, juicy brisket, chicken, tri-tip beef, and home-made sauces from a little place attached to a gas station, and in summer from a roving mobile food truck. Go early to get your choice.

Try an Alaskan favorite, juicy steak, at one of the region's steak houses

FAIRBANKS: The Cookie Jar $$
Café   **Map** E2
1006 Cadillac Ct, 99701
Tel 907-479-8319
Breakfast all day, with fresh baked goods, whole-bean coffee and large portions of eggs, meats, and potatoes. Pastas, salads, soups, and burgers for lunch; steaks and seafood at dinner.

FAIRBANKS: Thai House Restaurant $$
Thai   **Map** E2
412 5th Ave, 99701
Tel 907-452-6123   Closed Sun
Traditionally garbed servers tend a small, clean dining room. Favorites from the large menu include classic pad Thai, drunken noodles, shrimp fried rice, and red curry vegetables.

FAIRBANKS: Wasabi Bay $$
Seafood   **Map** E2
1448 S Cushman St, 99701
Tel 907-452-0521
Traditional and American-style sushi with fresh-caught fish. Try the salmon and white tuna, the Caterpillar, Cherry Blossom, or Dragon, all menu favorites.

DK Choice

FAIRBANKS: Lavelle's Bistro $$$
Steak   **Map** E2
575 1st Ave, 99701
Tel 907-450-0555
Friendly staff and excellent wine list, with seating in the bar or romantic main room. Menu options include prime rib, filet, halibut, rack of lamb, lobster cakes, red prawn curry, fresh local vegetables, and classic Caesar salad. Crème brûlée and double chocolate mousse cake are popular desserts. Reservations recommended.

TALKEETNA: Flying Squirrel Bakery Café $
Café   **Map** E3
Mile 11, Talkeetna Spur Rd, 99676
Tel 907-733-6887   Closed Mon-Tue
Home-made soups served with artisan bread, breakfast pastries, desserts, deli salads, sandwiches, and wraps. Wood-fired pizzas on weekends. Eat in or take out.

TALKEETNA: Spinach Bread $
Café   **Map** E3
Main St, 99676
Addictive toasted bread topped with spinach, garlic, and cheese served from a silver Airstream trailer. Try the limeade, chipotle hot chocolate, and veggie bowls too. Gluten-free options.

**TALKEETNA: Mountain High
Pizza Pie** $$
Pizza **Map** E3
22165 C St, 99676
Tel *907-733-1234*
Crispy pizzas with more than 30
toppings, as well as salads and
salmon mac and cheese. Jaunty
décor, local beers on tap, and live
music most summer evenings.

DK Choice

**TALKEETNA: Talkeetna
Roadhouse** $$
Café **Map** E3
13550 E Main St, 99676
Tel *907-733-1351*
Huge meals served family-style
in an historic frontier roadhouse
more than 100 years old. Soups,
breads, and pastries are all made
from scratch. The sourdough
hotcakes, Granny's chocolate
potato cake, cream cheese
brownies, and gingersnaps are
favorites. Try the Roadhouse
Standard breakfast: eggs, home
fries, and thick peppered bacon.

Eastern Interior

**COPPER CENTER: Tonsina River
Lodge Restaurant** $$$
Russian **Map** E3
Mile 79 Richardson Hwy, 99573
Tel *907-822-3000*
Try Russian classics like borscht,
meat or veggie *blinchiki* (crepes),
or stick with grilled steak or fish,
or home-made soups. Family-
style dining room and bar area.

**DELTA JUNCTION: Taste of
Europe Restaurant** $$$
European **Map** F3
1205 Richardson Hwy, 99737
Tel *907-895-9880* **Closed** *Sun*
Ring the changes with Eastern-
European style dumplings,
gnocchi, Russian meatballs
over fettucine, kabobs, pizzas,
and other traditional dishes from
Uzbekistan, Ukraine, and Italy.

KENNICOTT: The Pizza Bus $$
Pizza **Map** F3
*Lot 9, Mile 59 Edgerton Hwy,
Wrangell-St Elias National Park, 99588*
Tel *907-554-2324*
Friendly diner in a converted bus
near the mine, with terrific views.
Fresh salads and local veggies,
pizzas, noodle bowls, and wraps.

TOK: Fast Eddy's Restaurant $$
Café **Map** F3
Mile 1313 Alaska Hwy, 99780
Tel *907-883-4411*
Solid American fare – burgers,

Enjoy Russian classics at Tonsina River Lodge

curly fries, milkshakes, hefty
breakfasts with eggs, biscuits,
and gravy, very fresh salad
bar. Crowded and at times
pretty boisterous, this is a
local favorite.

Southwest Alaska

DILLINGHAM: Bayside Diner $$
Café **Map** C4
Bristol Inn, 104 Main St, 99576
Tel *907-842-1013*
Fresh salads, sandwiches, and
crab and shrimp dinners.
Breakfasts are hearty and meat-
centric, with bacon, ham, or
reindeer sausage and fresh eggs.

**KING SALMON:
Eddie's Fireplace Inn** $
Pub **Map** D4
1 Main St, 99613
Tel *907-246-3435*
A fair option in this remote spot
for burgers, pizzas, chicken
strips, fish and chips, and
sandwiches. Pizza served in the
bar after the restaurant is closed.
Breakfasts are huge, with
specialty coffees.

KODIAK: Java Flats $
Café **Map** D4
11206 Rezanof Dr, 99619
Tel *907-487-2622* **Closed** *Mon*
The huge and heavenly fresh-
baked cookies are the stars, but
the plentiful light-meal options
here are just as good, and made
with fresh local produce.

**KODIAK: Rendezvous
Bar & Grill** $$
Pub **Map** D4
11652 Rezanof Dr W, 99615
Tel *907-487-2233*
A local favorite watering hole;
good choices include the clam
chowder, fish tacos, Sicilian
chicken sandwich. Good wine
list and wide beer selection.

Arctic and Western
Alaska

BARROW: Sam & Lee's $$
Asian/American **Map** D1
1052 Kogiak St, 99713
Tel *907-852-5556*
The menu includes kimchi, pizza,
egg drop soup, chicken-fried
rice, and more Japanese,
Chinese, and Korean dishes,
plus American favorites such
as breakfast pancakes.

**KOTZEBUE:
Bayside Restaurant** $
Café **Map** C2
303 Shore Ave, 99752
Tel *907-442-3600*
Famous for its extensive and
eclectic menu, from sushi to
cheeseburgers. Try the home-
made strawberry lemonade. The
Wi-Fi is free and fast.

NOME: Airport Pizza $$
Pizza **Map** C2
406 Bering St, 99762
Tel *907-443-7992*
Try the giant breakfast burrito,
spicy pepper pizza, or Philly-style
cheese steak. Dozens of
combinations for pizzas and
meals throughout the day. Some
veggie options; free Wi-Fi.

DK Choice

**NOME: Pingo Bakery-Seafood
House** $$
Café **Map** C2
308 Bering St, 99762
Tel *907-387-0654* **Closed** *Mon &
Tue*
In a turn-of-the-century Gold
Rush house, offering fresh
baked breads and pastries,
freshly caught local seafood,
and home-made desserts, all to
eat in or take out. Seafood
omelets are favorites, as are the
chocolate chip cookies to go.

CRUISING IN ALASKA

Wildlife sightings on land and sea, tide-water glaciers and snowcapped peaks, and the cultural heritage of Alaska's indigenous peoples provide the big draw for cruising the Inside Passage *(see pp38–9)* and the Gulf of Alaska *(see pp40–41)*. For many travelers, an Alaskan cruise is a once-in-a-lifetime experience, providing a luxurious way to see some of the wildest places on earth. Rates vary greatly depending upon the cruise line, the season, and national economic conditions. Cruise lines like to appeal to as wide a market as possible, offering numerous itineraries on various classes of ship, resort-style amenities, and a range of shore excursions. All travelers need to be prepared for Alaska's unpredictable weather. While the parkas may end up packed away the entire time, so may the swimsuit and sandals.

Best Times to Go

While weekly cruises to tropical islands operate all year round, the Alaska cruise season lasts less than five months, typically from mid-May to mid-September. Sun worshippers can aim for cruises that depart at the end of June and through July. With a decrease in the likelihood of storms, this is considered peak season, and cruise lines charge accordingly. Also, as the summer solstice nears, the northern latitudes make for exceptionally long days. This translates into late evenings and technicolor sunsets almost at midnight.

If price matters more than the weather, it is best to hunt for deals in the September and May shoulder seasons *(see p270)*. Generally, the later in the season that travelers depart, the greater the likelihood of damp weather. However, passengers need to be prepared at all times for Alaska's erratic weather.

Choosing a Cruise Line and Ship

Budget may be the most important factor in influencing the choice of a cruise. Also, it is essential to decide which is more important – the ship or the itinerary. For some, cruising is all about low fares, fresh air, and the destination itself. For others, imaginative itineraries and creature comforts matter more.

Cruise lines rate themselves according to a star system that is, however, fast losing definition. Six-star lines offer smaller, more intimate ships, the best cuisine, superior accommodation, and services to match. Naturally, such luxury comes at a price, but travelers may be able to find fares that include round-trip air travel, onboard expenses, and excursions. Mass market ships advertise the lowest rates. No line with less than four or five stars will mention their rating, while others may exaggerate their status. Be sure to research the ship's age and when it began to sail under its current name. Lastly, do not judge a ship by the cruise line. Even mass-market cruise lines offer new ships with design features and amenities that approach luxury.

Choosing an Itinerary

Consult cruise route maps *(see pp38–41)* to get your bearings. The Inside Passage has the largest concentration of accessible towns, glaciers, fjords, and forests. Popular stops include Glacier Bay, Haines, Hoonah, Juneau, Skagway, Sitka, Ketchikan, and Misty Fiords. The Gulf of Alaska has fewer ports of call, but benefits include the glaciers, deep fjords, and marine life of Hubbard Glacier and Prince William Sound.

Week-long round-trip cruises between Juneau and Seattle, San Francisco, and Vancouver in Canada take in the Inside Passage and are especially

Multi-level cruise ship moored in Juneau's Gastineau Channel

Cruise ship with a large decktop swimming pool

popular. As the route heads north from Canada or the US to Juneau, Seward, or Whittier, signs of modern civilization recede gradually with each passing day. Another popular itinerary goes across the Gulf of Alaska between Seward or Whittier and Juneau, and includes points of interest both in the Gulf and in the Inside Passage as far south as Misty Fiords National Monument.

Planning and Research

To ensure a great vacation, it would be wise to devote some time to planning and research. The Internet offers extensive information on cruise lines and is a fast and efficient way to compare the best deals. **Alaska Cruising Report, Cruise Critic, Cruise Reviews, and Cruise Mates** all maintain websites with comprehensive, insightful reviews and information on how to book a cruise. For proprietary cruise information, browse through the websites of cruise companies.

Travel bookstores are also an invaluable resource, as are travel-related websites such as **Expedia Travel**. For the latest deals, consult the travel sections of leading newspapers in early spring.

Major Cruise Lines

Most major cruise lines have in their fleet at least two or more ships that are large enough to carry hundreds or even thousands of passengers. Common facilities on board include restaurants and buffets, health spas and salons, theaters, themed lounges, bars, dance clubs, swimming pools and hot tubs, and children's clubs.

Large and midsized cruise ships are offered by **Regent Seven Seas Cruises, Celebrity Cruises, Holland America Line, Princess Cruise Line, Royal Caribbean Line, Norwegian Cruise Line, Disney Cruise Line, Silversea Cruises,** and **Carnival Cruise Lines**. Silversea vessels are among the best in Alaskan waters, while Holland America and Princess Cruises have tied up with Alaska Railroad to offer train tours (see pp284–7).

Small Ships

The only way to sail into secluded villages and hidden coves that large ships cannot approach is to book a cruise with small-ship operators or off-the-beaten-track adventure specialists. There's often a high standard of comfort and good food on these trips, but the glitzier cruise entertainments are traded for on-board experts in subjects such as marine biology and photography, and shore excursions may range from informal encounters with local culture to two-day forest hikes. **Alaskan Dream Cruises, Discovery Voyages, Un-Cruise Adventures,** and **Lindblad Expeditions** are excellent choices for this type of cruise.

What's Included

Fares on all mass market cruise ships include meals, snacks, shows, and complimentary drinks at a "Captain's Meet and Greet" cocktail party. Passengers have some control over the amount of gratuities, but more and more lines include a nominal fee for wait staff and room stewards on the final bill. Luxury ships may offer complimentary alcoholic beverages or wine during meals, while other upscale lines stock cabins with bottles of liquor. Economy ships charge for everything at every turn. All purchases made on board are added to the final bill.

Special Deals

Promotional fares are easily available in the weeks just before the peak season. The first and last weeks of the season have the cheapest fares. All major lines also offer air add-ons and hotel stays, and in Alaska, that can mean extended rail tours to Denali and other points of interest in the Interior.

Look out for special deals offered on the websites of cruise lines and travel agencies. Travel clubs, academic societies, and other membership associations organize charters to take advantage of group rates. Large cruise lines sponsor themed cruises and these might occasionally offer a good bargain.

Traveling Solo

Fares are always based on double occupancy unless stated otherwise. However, a single traveler can find deals that waive or reduce what is called the single supplement – an additional fee added to single fares that can sometimes equal another full fare. When such deals are not available travel agents can help book cabins to be shared by single travelers of the same gender. Most large cruise lines also arrange onboard events and parties meant for singles.

Cabin Types

Experienced cruisers have two opposing views on how to choose cabins. One opinion holds that as most passengers merely sleep, bathe, and dress in their cabins, it makes little sense to reserve a deluxe stateroom with all possible amenities. However, under certain conditions, comfortable cabins can make all the difference. Travelers should consider booking either an inexpensive inside cabin or an outside one with portholes (or windows that increase in size with every category upgrade). Cabins with balconies are ideal for romantic and restful settings and usually sell first, despite being considerably more expensive. However, many cruisers argue that the same views are available for free from the public decks.

Deluxe cabins may include mini-suites with sitting areas or apartment-style penthouses with separate rooms that can sleep four. Some modern ships have taken this category to new heights, creating opulent spaces for six people, complete with conference facilities, butlers, private hot tubs, and large secluded patios on the ship's top deck.

Cabin Facilities

While all standard cabins include a bathroom, beds for two, sufficient storage, a room safe, television, cabin phone,

Atrium bar offering a chic sitting area on a cruise ship

toiletries, and most importantly, lifejackets, all facilities improve with higher fares. Amenities can include a refrigerator, wider and thicker mattresses, softer pillows, and plush comforters. Bathrooms in high-priced cabins offer superior quality toiletries.

Location Within the Ship

The websites of all cruise lines provide the deck plans of each ship and a layout showing cabin locations. Cabins can be situated aft, forward, or amidships. Depending on the quality of the ship, lower aft cabins can be subject to muted engine noise, vibrations, and heat. In rough seas, lower forward cabins experience the maximum vibrations from wave impact. Even so, if wind and wave height create heavy sway, those subject to sea-sickness would do well to book a lower cabin amidships, as motion intensifies the higher one goes. However, for some, watching waves splash against their portholes can cause anxiety – such travelers may prefer an upper cabin. It is wise to select a cabin near an elevator

if the ship has over a dozen decks. With an upper outside cabin, check that a lifeboat does not obstruct the view.

Restaurants and bars can be located anywhere on the ship, while buffets are generally higher up near the pools.

Public Areas

Framed art and sculpture line the stairways and hallways of virtually every ship. While the art can range from sedate to postmodern and whimsical, travelers will almost always find some vestiges of the classic Art Deco era – the

Ship library providing a quiet retreat

glory era of cruise ships – whether in the details of the handrail design or in themed restaurants. Towering atriums are *de rigueur*, and passengers with vertigo should steer clear of the overlooks. Most include comfortable bars and lounges on the periphery, or generic sitting areas with splendid views out to sea.

Large ships stage Vegas- and Broadway-themed shows in plush theaters, full of glitz and glamor. More sophisticated ship theaters come complete with multiple stage lifts, large orchestras, and a huge revue staff of singers and dancers. Other cruise lines, while well funded, choose to economize by investing little or nothing in stage musicians, using pre-recorded soundtracks instead.

Quiet libraries and card rooms are common, especially in cruise lines popular with the retired set. Most lines have Internet facilities, and some offer Wi-Fi to those with their own laptop computers.

The luxurious lobby of an onboard spa and salon

Spa, Fitness, and Beauty Salons

Every large or midsized ship boasts a spa and salon with trained staff who pamper passengers with spa treatments and massages. Onboard spas reduce their rates when the ship is in port and as the cruise proceeds, but only for more expensive packages.

To maintain your at-home fitness regimen, exercise rooms of large ships have a range of equipment, including climbers and treadmills. They almost always offer hot tubs, some provide saunas, and a few offer steam baths. Fitness centers often remain open round the clock, while salons keep long hours. Fitness programs can include yoga, Pilates, and personal training.

To prepare for formal or gala nights, salons will generally offer passengers total makeovers, as well as hair styling and facials.

Medical Facilities

All cruise ships will have a licensed medical professional on board to deal with illness, emergencies, and patient evacuations. If travelers have special needs or require specific medical equipment, it is best to check before making your reservations. While no cruise ship pretends to be a floating hospital, some do advertise such equipment as dialysis machines. Costs can vary from ship to ship, but in general the fee for visits and medication is significantly higher than on land.

DIRECTORY

Planning and Research

Alaska Cruising Report
w alaskacruisingreport.com

Cruise Critic
w cruisecritic.com

Cruise Mates
w cruisemates.com

Cruise Reviews
w cruisereviews.com

Expedia Travel
w expedia.com

Major Cruise Lines

Carnival Cruise Lines
Tel (800) 764-7419.
w carnival.com

Celebrity Cruises
Tel (800) 647-2251.
w celebrity.com

Disney Cruise Line
Tel (800) 951-3532.
w disneycruise.com

Holland America Line
Tel (877) 724-5425, (877) 932-4259.
w hollandamerica.com

Norwegian Cruise Line
Tel (800) 327-7030.
w ncl.com

Princess Cruise Line
Tel (800) 774-6237.
w princess.com

Regent Seven Seas Cruises
Tel (800) 784-0022.
w regentcruises.com

Royal Caribbean Line
Tel (866) 562-7625.
w royalcaribbean.com

Silversea Cruises
Tel (877) 215-9986.
w silversea.com

Small Ships

Alaskan Dream Cruises
Tel (855) 747-8100.
w alaskandreamcruises.com

Discovery Voyages
Tel (907) 653-1957, (800) 324-7602.
w discoveryvoyages.com

Lindblad Expeditions
Tel (800) 397-3348.
w expeditions.com

Un-Cruise Adventures
Tel (888) 862-8881.
w un-cruise.com

Life on Board

The day-to-day goings on of a cruise to Alaska mirror life on board any other cruise, but with a few major exceptions – there is unlikely to be a white sand beach for tanning, and there may be more hiking boots than sandals on deck. Likewise, ship staff never try to re-create tropical themes, leaving the grandeur of Alaska to speak for itself with every passing seascape, fjord, and glacier-topped peak. However, it is still a cruise, and passengers can expect levity, dancing, late-night parties, theater productions, and casino action, as they would on a cruise anywhere in the world.

Enjoying sunshine and a wide-ranging view from the deck

Entertainment and Activities

Ship theaters on the larger lines boast professionally lit stages with state-of-the-art audio, and draw full-house crowds for events on each night of the cruise. Talent and musicianship vary among cruise lines, and the Vegas- and Broadway-style productions alternate with stand-up comics. Some of the latter have content older than the ocean, while others present risqué humor. Bigger ships often maintain a separate venue for game shows hosted by cruise directors who urge audiences to participate.

A good ship will also have country singers, jazz crooners, string trios and quartets, and classical pianists to entertain lounge patrons, atrium visitors, and strollers on the ship's interior promenades.

Art shows represent an outlet for buyers interested in originals or numbered prints signed by the artist. Onboard art auctions usually manage to bring in a large crowd of cruisers.

Given the variable climate, Alaskan lines make none of the promises that tropical operators do. Ships shy away from planning too many outdoor activities that could suffer cancellations due to bad weather. However, deck parties do take place, along with midnight fiestas, usually with a Mexican theme.

Glitzy stage show providing live onboard entertainment

Casinos

After shopping and sunning on deck, spending time and money in the casino is one of the popular cruise pastimes, despite poor odds of winning.

Gambling options depend on the cruise line and the class of the ship and can range from craps, roulette, and simple slot machines to blackjack, poker, and baccarat. Most ship casinos also offer video poker machines. Ship casinos have a vested interest in educating their clients, so the house often offers classes on how to play some of the more esoteric games.

A shipboard casino is more or less like a land-based one, but with a few differences. It is open only while the ship is actually sailing in international waters. Only passengers over 21 years of age are allowed to play, although anyone may pass through when it is closed to take pictures. It would be considered unusual, and possibly an infringement of casino rules, to photograph ongoing games or people gambling. While every ship has a bar that exclusively serves the casino, patrons are usually not offered free drinks, except at occasional promotional events, such as when the casino first opens.

Shopping

Those interested in buying luxury items such as tobacco, spirits, designer clothing and cosmetics, digital cameras, and jewelry will find them at excellent prices, all tax- and duty-free. Usually designed to resemble upscale shopping malls, onboard arcades can sprawl over two decks, or simply consist of a string of interconnected shops. All through the cruise, selected merchandise is also sold at slashed prices in hallways or outside on the upper deck, and liquor tastings are also common. Passengers should note that they cannot take possession of their alcohol purchases until their last night on board the ship.

Crew members preparing a buffet barbecue

Meals

For many travelers, cruising is all about the cuisine. In addition to three heavy meals a day, served in the main dining rooms, hot and cold buffets, snack bars, cafés, and deckside grills cater to the huge demand.

Large ships manage the rush by establishing at least two main seatings for dinner and assigning tables for the duration of the cruise. Dinner typically begins at 6pm and 8:30pm. Passengers who are dissatisfied with their seating or table may consult the ship's *maître d'* after the first night to ask for a change, but there is no guarantee of one. Tables for two may not be easy to find, even if passengers make the request prior to booking. Many ships now have more flexible dining programs and a range of onboard restaurants that require no bookings.

The tradition of dining with the captain is mostly historical, and not a common practice. A good alternative is attending the captain's cocktail party to meet him and his senior officers.

Expenses

Costs mount rapidly during a cruise. Onboard purchases, beverages, and casino expenses can reach unimaginable heights. The need for ready cash almost disappears on a ship, as passengers have the convenience of paying with a swipe of a key card. Many generous passengers do dole out bills as tips to room stewards and other crew members. Note that all cruise lines assert that tipping is optional while stating clearly their policy of adding a basic rate of gratuity for services rendered during the cruise. Passengers are free to accept, raise, or lower that amount at the Purser's Desk.

Dress Code

Check the ticket packet for details of the ship's dress code for the main dining room. Most disallow jeans, sleeveless T-shirts, shorts, or tennis shoes for dinner, but relax the rules for other meals and buffet restaurants. Dress rules and styles change all the time, but even aboard luxury ships the trend towards casual lifestyles has prevailed. Still, the classic cruise tradition of formal nights persists for at least one night of the week. Black tie dinners are solely in the province of six-star ships.

For formal nights, men can wear suits; tuxedos are in the minority on most ships. Women wear cocktail dresses or gowns. Semi-formal nights require sports coats and tie and slacks for men, and cocktail dresses for women. Resort casuals such as cotton dresses for women and khaki pants and button-up shirts for men apply on other nights. Except on the most sophisticated ships, restaurant staff rarely turn away inappropriately dressed passengers.

Traveling with Children

Virtually all ships have relaxed their restrictions in recent years and allow children of all ages. Most cruise ships come equipped with facilities exclusively for children. Activities range from crafts and treasure hunts for young kids, to teen discos, talent shows, and karaoke events for older children. Baby-sitting fees are incurred for child care when the formal programs end, usually after 10pm. Many programs do not accept children under two or three years of age unless accompanied by a parent. Famous for its family cruises, Disney Cruise Line now visits Alaska's Inside Passage.

What to Pack

On average, cruise lines provide four baggage tags per person. To carry anything beyond that, passengers must check with the cruise line. Essentials for an Alaskan cruise include:
- Cell phone and charger
- Rain shell, hat, and warm sweater
- Comfortable walking or hiking boots
- Toiletries and cosmetics
- Medication and first aid, including sunscreen
- Passport, travel insurance, cruise documents
- Camera, memory card, and batteries
- Formal, semi-formal, and resort casual wear
- Shorts, swimwear, sunglasses and sandals
- Laptop computer
- Portable music player
- Books and magazines
- Spare luggage for purchased items

Hiking boots for excursions

Shore Excursions

While not all the tourists who flock to Alaska each year travel via cruise ships, the ones who do often consider shore excursions to be the main event. Tours emphasize Alaska's geological wonders such as tidewater glaciers and vast temperate rainforests, while nature sightseeing focuses on wildlife. Historical tours, on the other hand, offer engaging presentations of human history from the earliest Native American settlements to the first Europeans. No cruise passenger has the time or opportunity to try each tour, but with careful planning, visitors can return home with a deeper understanding of what makes Alaska magical.

Small pleasure craft moored next to a giant cruise ship in Whittier

What's Included

Ticket packets, cruise line websites, and flyers placed at the shore excursion desk on board the ship give brief descriptions of each excursion along with the duration and degree of physical stamina required. Usually, all that passengers need are sun or rain protection, water if none is provided, and a willingness to share the experience with fellow passengers. It always helps to ask a few questions before signing up about the chances of cancellation, how large the group will be, and whether food or water will be provided during the excursion.

Booking

More and more cruise lines allow online bookings for the dozens of shore excursions offered during week-long cruises. Online booking saves passengers the trouble of filling out forms soon after boarding, which is the recommended time to make choices before tours fill up. Most ships also have drop boxes for filled-out registration forms, to eliminate waiting in line. However, most travelers still prefer to sign up in person, which ensures a face to face meeting with shore tour staffers.

Sometimes a shore operator may cancel the tour if too few people register, or the weather is unfavorable. Always check for postings that identify cancellations, and conversely, if any new tours have been added to the inventory.

Excursion Prices

The fee per person per tour varies widely from one cruise line to another. A walking tour around historic neighborhoods may cost less than $40, and kayaking less than $100. Tours that involve dog sledding, glacier travel, flightseeing by floatplane to remote areas, or heli-skiing can cost hundreds of dollars per person. Depending on the location, luxury cruise lines offer upscale tour programs that can cost over $10,000.

Cancellation policies vary, but in general, there is a 24-hour window before the tour in which visitors can change their minds. After the excursion, refunds are rare, although shore tour staff can reduce or waive the entire fee if a passenger can justify being completely dissatisfied.

Grizzly bear with cubs at Denali National Park

Creek Street, part of a Ketchikan walking tour, a popular shore excursion

Going Ashore

Information printed on tour tickets tells passengers where and when to meet, either on the ship or the pier. Private shore tour operators usually hold up boards clearly marked with the tour's name making it easy for passengers to spot where they need to be. Passengers taking tours enjoy priority status once the gangway opens. Some ports cannot handle large ships at the pier, so small launches bring dozens of cruisers ashore, starting with the passengers taking tours.

Independent Travel

Cruise lines have made it easier for passengers to book tours with the introduction of online billing systems, among other innovations, and tend to mark up tour costs because tourists usually pay willingly for the convenience.

However, some travelers prefer to arrange hotel stays, rail journeys, and tours entirely on their own. Before taking such matters into your own hands, it is wise to consider all the factors. Research the company and find out about the level of experience of the staff and how long the operator has been in business,

and if it makes customer testimonials available. Remember also that you will be without a tour representative, and will have to get to the tour start point alone. No matter how you book, additional expenses will arise, gratuities, food, and drink among them.

Getting back to the ship after a tour poses other challenges. While ships usually depart promptly at a well-publicized time, they will wait a few minutes for stray passengers after courteous public announcements. The only exception to this rule, and one that will certainly delay a departure, is if a shore excursion group booked via the shore desk is delayed.

Being completely alone may appeal to the adventurous, but travelers need to plan very carefully and stay well-informed.

Safety on Shore

Alaskan life in small seaside towns is slow and steady, with few residents and not much bustle. Even in the larger cities along the coast, personal safety poses no real concern. However, while most locals will be glad to help you navigate to where you want to go, as with any travel away from home, keep your valuables protected.

Best Shore Excursions

Providing shore excursions for their passengers has become a gigantic industry for cruise lines. Holland America Line and Princess Cruise Line, for example, offer hundreds of tours in Alaska and are specialists in the field. Among the interesting shore excursions visitors can expect to find are:
• Halibut and salmon fishing charters from Ninilchik and Deep Creek (see p110)
• Walking Creek Street in Ketchikan (see pp128–9)
• Visiting Saxman Totem Park near Ketchikan (see p129)
• Flightseeing in Misty Fiords National Monument (see p130)
• Riding the Mount Roberts tramway above Juneau (see pp142–3)
• Helicopter tours to the Juneau Icefield (see p145)
• Riding the White Pass and Yukon Route Railroad in Skagway (see pp150–53)
• Brown bear watching in Denali National Park (see pp166–9)
• Alaska Railroad trips to Denali (see pp166–9) or Seward (see pp102–3)

Helicopter readying for a flight at Skagway's heliport

Floatplane taking off from the serene waters of a lake

OUTDOOR ACTIVITIES

Known around the world as a premier wilderness and adventure holiday destination, Alaska offers visitors a diverse range of outdoor activities. In the summer, visitors can go sportfishing *(see pp44–5)*, hiking, mountaineering, canoeing, and whitewater rafting, while the winter brings opportunities for snowmachining, dog sledding *(see pp42–3)*, and skiing. The daring can even try heli-skiing. Operators usually organize transport, food, and equipment, and even provide guides. For those with the proper equipment, camping, hiking, backpacking, canoeing, and Nordic skiing can be inexpensive and spectacular. However, anything that involves bush travel or motorized vehicles such as snowmachines and ATVs will require extensive planning and cost considerably more. For a price, operators will provide equipment and handle all the logistics.

Hikers on a trail in Girdwood on the outskirts of Anchorage

Hiking

Alaska is a hiker's paradise, and Southcentral, Southeast, and Interior Alaska boast numerous picturesque hiking and trekking trails. The possibilities range from short 2-mile (3-km) strolls to all-day hikes, multi-day backpacking trips, and cross-country wilderness expeditions.

In Southeast Alaska, nearly every city and town lies within easy reach of scenic hiking trails that lead up through lush forest and muskeg to points offering great views. The most popular long-distance route here is the historic Chilkoot Trail *(see pp152–3)*, which requires stamina as well as preparation. **Gastineau Guiding** offers the best excursions around the Juneau area.

Most of the popular trails in Interior Alaska, such as those in Denali State Park *(see p164)* and Wrangell-St. Elias National Park *(see pp192–3)*, are longer, often unmarked routes that demand at least some hiking experience. Even in popular Denali National Park *(see pp166–9)*, there are few marked trails. Here, most hiking is cross-country, and needs back-country permits, orientation skills, and the ability to ford unbridged rivers. **Denali Trekking Company** organizes customized trips for visitors.

Even on the outskirts of Anchorage, it is possible to hike one of the many trails in Chugach State Park or around Girdwood. On the Kenai Peninsula, many routes through the spectacular state parks and the Chugach National Forest, including the popular Resurrection Pass Trail *(see p105)*, make excellent introductions to multi-day hiking. **Arctic Wild** adventure guide service offers a range of specialty ecotours.

In Southwest, Arctic, and Western Alaska, hiking is limited to cross-country wilderness routes that can be accessed only by bush plane. **Kodiak Treks** conducts low-impact bear-viewing trips.

Bush Travel

Due to Alaska's limited road and ferry systems, transport around the state is quite different from other parts of the US. Access to the bush – any place off the highway or Marine Highway systems – requires a helicopter, a boat or water taxi, or a bush plane on wheels, floats, or skis.

Bush flights, which carry residents and supplies to remote homesteads and fly anglers and rafters to uncrowded streams also provide access to rural villages and bush lodges. **Rust's Flying Service**, **Wrangell Mountain Air** and **Brooks Range Aviation** are some of the better operators that arrange trips for tourists. Clients must pay not only for the flight out, but also for the pilot's return trip. The rates differ according to the type of plane, the number of passengers, and the duration of the flight. Client luggage is always limited to the amount of gear that the plane can safely carry. Anyone who wants to haul a boat or camping gear

Floatplane taking off for the bush, Lake Hood, Anchorage

Cross-country skiing in an Anchorage park, against the backdrop of the Chugach Mountains

and supplies for the length of the trip may have to pay for more than one run to the drop-off location.

Usually, a pre-arranged pick-up is scheduled, but travelers need to be flexible, and it is always necessary to carry extra supplies. Note that once the water taxi or bush plane has dropped off its passengers and is out of view, people are on their own until the pick-up date. Remote areas are ruled by the weather, and clouds, wildfires, storms, snow, and wind can make travel impossible, so it is important not to embark on a bush trip without a fair amount of cushion time.

Snowmachining

In the winter, rivers and lakes in the Interior freeze, becoming transport routes and opening up much of the state to relatively easy access. These routes were historically nego-tiated by dog sled, but today, sleds have been replaced by snowmachines (or snowmo-biles). They not only provide access to places off the road system, but also serve as rec-reational vehicles that allow adrenaline-pumping runs. Snowmachines range from 550cc to 700cc models, and only those who are confident of their riding and navigation skills should consider renting one. Rentals require a hefty security

deposit, and tax and fuel may be extra. **Alaska Snow Safaris** and **Glacier City Snowmobile Tours** offer rentals and a range of guided trips, including short introductory runs, half-day backcountry trips, and full- and multi-day tours.

Mountaineering

Mountaineering is extremely popular in Alaska and Mount McKinley is the destination of most climbers. While it can be scaled without a guide, guided expeditions must use one of the six accredited outfits listed on the **Denali National Park** web-site, including the recommen-ded **Alaska Mountaineering School**. All climbers, guided or not, must register with the **Talkeetna Ranger Station** (see p162) 60 days before the trip and pay a Mountaineering Special Use Fee of $200.

Alaska is one of the few places in the world that still offers summits that are as yet unclimbed and even unnamed. Most serious climbers arrive either with a pre-organized expedition or come months in advance to seek out appealing peaks and prepare for the ascent. Guiding companies such as **St. Elias Alpine Guides**, **Alaska Mountain Guides and Climbing School**, and **Kennicott Wilderness Guides** accept prospective mountaineers of all levels.

Skiing

Alaska's only world class downhill ski resort is Alyeska, at Girdwood, 40 miles (60 km) south of Anchorage. There are also smaller resorts at Alpenglow and Hilltop in Anchorage, Eaglecrest in Juneau, Cleary Summit near Fairbanks, and Mount Eyak near Cordova.

Heli-skiing – downhill skiing on mountains and glaciers accessed by helicopter – is rapidly gaining in popularity, especially around Valdez and Haines. **Valdez Heli-Ski Guides** offers coaching and individual packages, and **Valdez Heli Camps** organizes luxury and adventure trips. In the summer, Ruth Glacier, in Denali National Park, and the Juneau and Harding Icefields become ski fields. Note, however, that glacier skiing is only for experienced skiers with safety training and equipment.

Nordic or cross-country skiing is widely available, and snowmachine tracks all over the state double as ski trails. Cross-country skiing and noisy snowmachines are not fully compatible, but the fine groomed trails around Anchorage and Fairbanks are reserved for skiing. In the Mat-Su, Hatcher Pass (see p91) offers excellent wilderness trails. The Fairbanks area has good trails both in town and at Chena Hot Springs (see p177).

Cycling and Mountain Biking

In the summer, cycling and mountain biking are popular activities, but cyclists must be prepared to encounter animals, traffic, and narrow shoulders on most paved highways. The Copper River Highway *(see p123)*, the Denali Highway *(see p165)*, the extensive routes on Prince of Wales Island *(see pp132–3)*, and the Edgerton Highway/McCarthy Road *(see p187)* are among the best, most scenic routes. Biking is allowed on most trails in the Chugach and Tongass National Forests and on limited routes in the state parks. **Alaskabike, Alaska Backcountry Bike Tours**, and **Backroads** offer guided cycling tours all over Alaska. Anchorage's **Downtown Bicycle Rentals** and **Pablo's Bicycle Rentals** hire out bicycles. The **Arctic Bicycle Club** offers information on cycling, mountain biking, and organized rides.

Rafting and Canoeing

For most people, the appeal of a whitewater trip lies in running the rapids. Rapids are graded Class I to V, but anything above Class III will need good whitewater skills, while Class V will need an expert guide. The most popular rivers, and the easiest to access, include the Nenana River *(see p172)* and the Chulitna River near Denali National Park, the upper Kenai River *(see p100)*, the Matanuska River, the Eagle River near Anchorage, and Six Mile Creek south of Anchorage. **Nova River**

Rafting on the Chilkoot River near Skagway

Rafters and **Chilkat Guides** are among Alaska's oldest adventure companies, offering statewide packages. **Talkeetna River Guides** rafts rivers in the Interior, while **Arctic Wild** runs rivers in the Brooks Range.

For a more contemplative, secluded experience, canoe trips of a day or more are possible on many of Alaska's lake and river systems, such as the Lynx Lake Loop *(see p160)* north of Anchorage and the Kenai Peninsula's Swan Lakes Loop *(see p109)*.

Ocean Kayaking

One of the best ways to see Alaska's sheltered coastal areas is by kayak, providing easy access to remote beaches in Southeast Alaska, Prince William Sound, the Kenai Fjords, and other well-sheltered waterways. On fine days, the scenery is spectacular, and there is a chance of spotting marine wildlife. Thorough preparation is essential, and a number of companies hire out

gear and offer instruction, kayak transport, and guides. **Anadyr Adventures** and **Prince William Sound Kayak Center** offer trips around Prince William Sound, while **Alaska Canoe and Campground** and **True North Kayak Adventures** operate on the Kenai Peninsula. The Southeast has several good agencies offering comparable packages. These include **Glacier Bay Sea Kayaks** in Gustavus, **Sitka Sound Ocean Adventures**, and **Southeast Sea Kayaks** in Ketchikan.

Tours

Visitors who prefer organized activities can select from a range of operators. In the Southeast, **Alaska Waters** organizes a variety of tours, **Breakaway Adventures** offers jet boat rides, **Allen Marine Tours** and **Orca Enterprises** arrange whale-watching tours, **Coastal Helicopters** sets up glacier tours, and **Chilkoot Charters and Tours** runs fishing trips. **Phillips Cruises and Tours** *(see p118)* and **Glacier Wildlife Cruises** offer tours in Prince William Sound, while **Glacier Bay Tours** explores Glacier Bay National Park. **Katmailand** runs freshwater sportfishing trips and **Kenai Fjords Tours** offers wildlife cruises. **K2 Aviation** has flightseeing tours to McKinley, and the **Northern Alaska Tour Company** offers visits to the Arctic. **St. Paul Island Tours** and **Wilderness Birding Adventures** lead native trips in western Alaska.

Kayakers preparing to set off, Whittier

DIRECTORY

Hiking

Arctic Wild
Fairbanks. **Tel** 577-8203, (888) 577-8203.
W arcticwild.com

Denali Trekking Company
PO Box 93, Talkeetna.
Tel 733-2566.
W alaskahiking.com

Gastineau Guiding
Juneau. **Tel** 586-8231.
W stepintoalaska.com

Kodiak Treks
11754 S Russian Creek Rd, Kodiak. **Tel** 487-2122.
W kodiaktreks.com

Bush Travel

Brooks Range Aviation
PO Box 10, Bettles. **Tel** 692-5444, (800) 692-5443.
W brooksrange.com

Rust's Flying Service
Anchorage. **Tel** 243-1595, (800) 544-2299.
W flyrusts.com

Wrangell Mountain Air
McCarthy. **Tel** 554-4411, (800) 478-1160.
W wrangellmountain air.com

Snowmachining

Alaska Snow Safaris
Palmer. **Tel** (888) 414-7669. **W** snowmobile-alaska.com

Glacier City Snowmobile Tours
Box 1018, Girdwood.
Tel 783-5566.
W snowtours.net

Mountaineering

Alaska Mountain Guides and Climbing School
PO Box 1081, Haines.
Tel 766-3396. **W** alaska mountainguides.com

Alaska Mountain-eering School
PO Box 566, 3rd St, Talkeetna. **Tel** 733-1016.
W climbalaska.org

Denali National Park
W nps.gov/dena

Kennicott Wilderness Guides
PO Box 1 MXY, Glennallen.
Tel (800) 664-4537, 554-4444 (summer), 554-1070 (winter).
W kennicottguides.com

National Outdoor Leadership School (N.O.L.S)
Tel 745-4047, (800) 710-6657. **W** nols.edu

St. Elias Alpine Guides
Tel 554-4445, (888)933-5427. **W** steliasguides.com

Skiing

Valdez Heli Camps
Valdez. **Tel** 783-3243.
W valdezhelicamps.com

Valdez Heli-Ski Guides
Valdez. **Tel** 835-4528.
W valdezheliskiguides.com

Cycling and Mountain Biking

Alaska Backcountry Bike Tours
Box 4260, Palmer.
Tel 746-5018, 376-6262.
W mountainbike alaska.com

Alaskabike
2720 Lexington Circle, Anchorage. **Tel** 245-2175.
W alaskabike.com

Arctic Bicycle Club
W arcticbike.org

Backroads
Berkeley, CA.
Tel (800) 462-2848.
W backroads.com

Downtown Bicycle Rentals
333 W 4th Ave, Anchorage. **Tel** 279-5293.
W alaska-bike-rentals.com

Pablo's Bicycle Rentals
501 L St, Anchorage.
Tel 250-2871.
W pablobicycle rentals.com

Rafting and Canoeing

Arctic Wild
See Hiking.

Chilkat Guides
PO Box 170, Haines.
Tel 766-2491.
W raftalaska.com

Nova River Rafters
Chickaloon.
W novalaska.com

Talkeetna River Guides
Main St, Talkeetna.
Tel (800) 353-2677.
W talkeetnariver guides.com

Ocean Kayaking

Alaska Canoe and Campground
Sterling. **Tel** 262-2331.
W alaskacanoetrips.com

Anadyr Adventures
Valdez. **Tel** 835-2814.
W anadyradventures.com

Glacier Bay Sea Kayaks
PO Box 26, Gustavus.
Tel 697-2257. **W** glacier bayseakayaks.com

Prince William Sound Kayak Center
PO Box 622, Whittier.
Tel 472-2452.
W pwskayakcenter.com

Sitka Sound Ocean Adventures
112 Tovio Circle, Sitka.
Tel 752-0660.
W kayaksitka.com

Southeast Sea Kayaks
1007 Water St, Ketchikan.
Tel 225-1258, (800) 287-1607.
W kayakketchikan.com

True North Kayak Adventures
Homer Spit, Homer.
Tel 235-0708.
W truenorthkayak.com

Tours

Alaska Waters
PO Box 1978, Wrangell.
Tel (800) 347-4462.
W alaskawaters.com

Allen Marine Tours
Juneau **Tel** (888) 289-0081; Ketchikan **Tel** (877) 686-8100; Sitka **Tel** (888) 747-8101. **W** allen marinetours.com

Breakaway Adventures
PO Box 2107, Wrangell.
Tel 874-2488.
W breakawayadven tures.com

Chilkoot Charters and Tours
PO Box 1336, Skagway.
Tel (877) 983-3400.
W chilkootcharters.com

Coastal Helicopters
8995 Yandukin Dr, Juneau Airport, Juneau. **Tel** (800) 789-5610. **W** coastal helicopters.com

Glacier Bay Tours
241 W Ship Creek Ave, Anchorage.
Tel (888) 229-8687.
W visitglacierbay.com

Glacier Wildlife Cruises
Valdez. **Tel** (800) 4110090.
W lulubelletours.com

K2 Aviation
Box 545B, Talkeetna.
Tel (800) 764-2291.
W flyk2.com

Katmailand
4125 Aircraft Dr, Anchorage.
W katmailand.com

Kenai Fjords Tours
Seward Waterfront, Seward. **Tel** (877) 777-4051.
W kenaifjords.com

Northern Alaska Tour Company
PO Box 82991, Fairbanks.
Tel (800) 474-1986.
W northernalaska.com

Orca Enterprises
495 S Franklin St, Juneau.
Tel (888) 733-6722.
W orcaenterprises.com

St. Paul Island Tours
Tel (877) 424-5637.
W alaskabirding.com

Wilderness Birding Adventures
40208 Alpenglow Circle, Homer. **Tel** (907)299-3937.
W wildernessbirding.com

SURVIVAL
GUIDE

PRACTICAL INFORMATION

Thanks to its unparalleled natural beauty, abundant wildlife, and rich cultural history, Alaska attracts a growing number of visitors from all over the world each year. The state's tourist infrastructure is fairly well developed, offering a range of accommodation and restaurant options. A large number of local tour operators can also organize just about any sort of adventure a visitor may want to undertake. Road and rail systems link numerous sites of interest, but even places away from the highways can be readily accessed via the extensive air transport and ferry routes. Visitor information centers, even in small towns, are plentiful and go out of their way to provide information and assistance. The following pages include tips on a range of practical matters that will assist visitors in getting the most out of their visit to this sprawling, majestic state.

When to Go

The finest weather in Alaska usually occurs from mid-May to mid-July, when most of the state, except for the Southeast and the Aleutians, experiences almost perpetual daylight. This is the time when all parks and services are open and the state is geared up for visitors.

Rainfall is common all year round in Southeast Alaska, while the Arctic receives little rain. In most parts of Alaska, however, the annual "rainy season" begins in mid-July, ending in early September, when most national park facilities close. However, there are plenty of reasons to visit in the off-season. As nights become colder, the chances of seeing the aurora borealis increase. From December to April, there are outdoor activities *(see pp264–7)* and the entertaining winter festivals *(see pp48–9)* to enjoy. The May and September shoulder seasons are also pleasant, avoiding the bad weather and minimal facilities of the off-season, and the prices and crowds of the high season.

Visa Regulations

Citizens of Canada, Australia, New Zealand, the UK, and most European Union nations can visit the US without a visa, but need a passport that is valid for at least six months after their trip, an onward or return ticket, and a completed Electronic System for Travel Authorization (ESTA) form, available online at https://esta.cbp.dhs.gov/esta. Canadians need to show their passport to enter the US. Visitors from nations that require visas must apply to a US embassy and may be asked for proof of financial solvency and intention to return home.

Visitor Information

Most tourist offices in Alaska are known for the quality of their information. All offer free maps, brochures, and hotel and restaurant listings, and local staff can answer most travel-related queries. The **Alaska Public Lands Information Centers** and the **Alaska Travel Industry Association** are also good information sources. National parks have their own visitors' centers, with rangers and volunteer staff who help with planning and organizing the necessary permits. The **Alaska Department of Fish and Game** issues hunting and fishing licenses. Most visitor centers are open long hours in the summer, but winter hours are limited. Throughout this guide, details of visitor information centers in major towns are provided.

Rainforest around Ward Lake, Ketchikan

◀ Challenging driving conditions near Nome, just south of the Arctic Circle

Taxes and Tipping

While Alaska does not have a state sales tax, most cities and boroughs impose local sales taxes. These can be up to 8 percent of the purchase price, added to the total at the checkout. A host of taxes are imposed on goods and services that apply mainly to tourists. A bed tax applies to B&Bs, hotels, hostels, lodges, and some campsites. A statewide $40 per head tax is applied to all cruise ship passengers. Rental cars are also subject to tax, and drivers renting vehicles from airport rental desks may have to pay up to 29 percent extra to cover airport maintenance.

Service is not included on restaurant checks, and the tip is usually 15 percent (see pp246–7). Taxi drivers will expect $2–5, depending on the fare. At hotels, tip $2 per bag and $1 per day for the room maid. In wilderness lodges, the tip is given to the desk clerk, to be divided among the staff. While tour guides get about $10 per day, depending on the service, fishing guides often get a sum commensurate with the success of the trip.

Smoking

As in the rest of America, Alaska's attitude toward smoking has changed dramatically and more and more towns are moving to restrict where smoking is permitted. Smoking is banned in all public buildings, shops, and public transport vehicles. Most accommodation options are also smoke-free, although a few may offer specific rooms where smoking is allowed.

In Anchorage, Haines, Juneau, and Unalaska, all restaurants and bars are smoke-free by local ordinance.

DIRECTORY

Visitor Information

Alaska Department of Fish and Game
Tel 465-4100.
W adfg.alaska.gov

Alaska Public Lands Information Centers
605 W 4th Ave, Anchorage.
Tel 644-3661.
W alaskacenters.gov

Alaska Travel Industry Association
2600 Cordova St,
Suite 201, Anchorage.
Tel 929-2200.
W travelalaska.com

Anchorage

Anchorage Convention and Visitors' Bureau
524 W 4th Ave,
Anchorage. Tel 274-3531.
W anchorage.net

Chugach State Park Eagle River Nature Center
Tel 694-2108. W ernc.org

Mat-Su Convention and Visitors' Bureau
Tel 746-5000.
W alaskavisit.com

Palmer Chamber of Commerce
Tel 745-2880.
W palmerchamber.org

The Kenai Peninsula

Alaska Maritime National Wildlife Refuge
95 Sterling Hwy, Homer.
Tel 235-6961.
W islandsandocean.org

Homer Chamber of Commerce Visitors' Center
Tel 235-7740.
W homeralaska.org

Kenai Fjords National Park Visitors' Center
Tel 422-0500.
W nps.gov/kefj

Seward Convention and Visitors Bureau
Tel 224-8051.
W seward.com

Prince William Sound

Cordova Chamber of Commerce
Tel 424-7260.
W cordovachamber.com

Valdez Convention and Visitors' Bureau
Tel 835-4636.
W valdezalaska.org

Southeast Alaska

Haines Convention and Visitors' Bureau
Tel 766-2234.
W haines.ak.us

Juneau Convention and Visitors' Bureau
Tel 586-2201.
W traveljuneau.com

Ketchikan Visitor Information Center
Tel 225-6166.
W visit-ketchikan.com

Petersburg Visitor Information Center
Tel 772-4636.
W petersburg.org

Sitka Convention and Visitors' Bureau
Tel 747-5940.
W sitka.org

Skagway Convention and Visitors' Bureau
Tel 983-2854.
W skagway.com

Western Interior Alaska

Denali National Park Visitor Access Center
Tel 683-2294.
W nps.gov/dena

Fairbanks Convention and Visitors' Bureau
Tel 456-5774.
W explorefairbanks.com

Eastern Interior Alaska

Dawson City Visitors' Center
Tel (867) 993-5575.
W dawsoncity.ca

Eagle Historical Society
Tel 547-2325. W eaglehistoricalsociety.org

Wrangell-St. Elias National Park Visitors' Center
Tel 822-5234.
W nps.gov/wrst

Southwest Alaska

Kodiak Island Convention and Visitors' Bureau
Tel 486-4782.
W kodiak.org

Unalaska/Dutch Harbor Convention and Visitors' Bureau
Tel 581-2612.
W unalaska.info

Arctic and Western Alaska

Inupiat Heritage Center
Barrow. Tel 852-0422.
W nps.gov/inup

Nome Visitors' Center
Tel 443-6555.
W visitnomealaska.com

Northwest Arctic Heritage Center
Kotzebue.
Tel 442-3890.
W nps.gov/kova/parknews/nwahc.htm

Strolling down Anchorage's 4th Avenue

Traveling with Children

With its great opportunities to see wildlife and get outdoors, Alaska is excellent for children. Many towns, especially Anchorage, have attractions that were built with children in mind, such as the H2Oasis water park and the Alaska Zoo. Most museums offer free or discounted admission for children, with the cut-off age ranging from 3 to 17 years. Many Alaska National Parks offer **Junior Ranger programs** for kids, and the majority of hotels and restaurants are child-friendly. Some hotels offer parents discounted or free accommodation for children in their booking.

Many tour companies welcome children, but some wilderness lodges, upscale restaurants, and adventure tours, such as helicopter tours or kayaking, may have a minimum age limit.

Anyone organizing a family driving trip through Alaska should bear in mind that distances are long, especially if the trip starts in the Lower 48. Renting an RV *(see pp288–9)* can make the journey easier. There are plenty of parks and highway pull-offs where families can stop for picnics or where kids can take a short walk with a field guide to identify plants, birds, and animals. **Pamela Lanier's Family Travel** is a useful resource for general information about traveling with children.

Senior Travelers

Although the age defining a senior citizen is usually 65, discounts are sometimes accessible to those over 55 or 60 as well. While many senior travelers in Alaska opt for all-inclusive cruises and package tours, many prefer to travel independently in private vehicles, especially RVs. However, it is worth noting that most car and RV rental firms have an upper age limit.

Several national institutions give senior concessions. The

National Park Service offers Senior Passes that reduce the cost of entry, camping, and services in national parks. **Road Scholar** (formerly Elderhostel) has educational trips for travelers over 55, which may include inexpensive accommodation, lectures, and meals. For around $16, seniors can join the **American Association of Retired Persons (AARP)**, which issues cards that make available a host of travel discounts.

Student Travelers

Students receive few special considerations in Alaska apart from discounts on some cultural programs and museum admissions. However, it never hurts to ask. Proof of student status will be needed, such as a current student body card from a specific school or university or an **International Student Identification Card** (ISIC). Inexpensive tickets can be arranged by **Student Travel Association** (STA) branches.

Travelers with Disabilities

While the Alaskan back-country can be quite challenging for travelers with limited mobility or other disabilities or health problems, the state does offer a large number of accessible

Travelers aboard a tour boat in Rudyard Bay in Misty Fiords National Monument

options. As in the rest of the country, Alaska has regulations requiring government offices, businesses, public transport, and taxis to be designed to accommodate wheelchairs, while road crossings in cities have dropped curbs to enable easier access. In addition, most car parks, public toilets, hotels, and supermarkets offer special arrangements for the wheelchair-bound. Service animals, such as guide dogs, are allowed on public transport and in public buildings.

Frontcountry areas of most national and state parks often have paved or graded trails and viewing platforms that are wheelchair accessible. The National Park Service also offers an America the Beautiful Access Pass, which grants disabled individuals free entry to all national parks.

Cruise ships, tour buses, and railway cars all cater to disabled travelers, and many adventure tour companies do their best to accommodate clients with disabilities. **Access Alaska** can assist in finding accommodations and services for disabled travelers.

In the winter, the challenges can be greater, as snow renders streets and sidewalks difficult for wheelchair users and absorbs many of the acoustics that assist navigation for the blind. More information, from how to rent a specially adapted car to qualifying for parking permits, is offered by the **Access-Able Travel Source** and the **Society for Accessible Travel and Hospitality**, who promote awareness and accessibility for travelers with special needs.

Etiquette

In general, Alaskans are polite, friendly, and helpful, although they may appear to be a bit more outspoken than other Americans. Visitors from across the world are welcomed, but are also expected to respect local ways, especially when visiting Native villages. It is illegal to bring alcohol into some areas and it is always wise to ask before taking photographs, especially of ceremonies, homes, or dances. Dress-wise, Alaska is one of the most relaxed states in the US. Attire tends to be informal, climate-dependent, and practical. Casual clothes such as jeans, T-shirts, flip-flops, and light woolens can be worn even for public performances or in upscale restaurants. Many Alaskans do not allow smoking in their homes or cars and it is considered courteous to check with your hosts if you may smoke (see p271).

Electricity

Across the US, the electrical current is 110 volts at 60 hertz. Visitors from abroad need an adaptor plug for the two-prong sockets and a voltage converter to operate 220-volt appliances, such as hairdryers and rechargers for cell phones and laptop computers (unless they have a built-in adaptor). However, bear in mind that most hotel rooms have hairdryers and dedicated sockets for electric shavers.

Conversion Chart

One US pint (0.5 liter) is smaller than one UK pint (0.6 liter). One Imperial gallon is the equivalent of five US quarts. To convert from degrees Celsius to degrees Fahrenheit, multiply by 1.8 and then add 32. From degrees Fahrenheit to degrees Celsius, subtract 32 and divide by 1.8.

US Standard to Metric
1 inch = 2.54 centimeters
1 foot = 30 centimeters
1 yard = 0.91 meters
1 mile = 1.6 kilometers
1 ounce = 28 grams
1 pound = 454 grams
1 US quart = 0.947 liters
1 US gallon = 3.79 liters

Metric to US Standard
1 centimeter = 0.4 inches
1 meter = 3 feet 3 inches
1 kilometer = 0.6 miles
1 gram = 0.04 ounces
1 kilogram = 2.2 pounds
1 liter = 1.1 US quarts

(see p271)

DIRECTORY

Traveling with Children

Junior Ranger Program
W nps.gov/kids/jrRangers.cfm

Pamela Lanier's Family Travel
W pamelalanier.com

Senior Travelers

American Association of Retired Persons (AARP)
601 E St NW, Washington, DC 20049. **Tel** (888) 687-2277.
W aarp.org

National Park Service
Tel (888) 275-8747.
W nps.gov/fees_passes.htm

Road Scholar
11 Avenue de Lafayette, Boston, MA 02111-1746.
Tel (800) 454-5768.
W roadscholar.org

Student Travelers

International Student Identification Card
W isic.org

Student Travel Association
W statravel.com

Travelers with Disabilities

Access-Able Travel Source
PO Box 1796, Wheat Ridge, CO 80034.
Tel (303) 232-2979.
W access-able.com

Access Alaska
1217 East 10th Ave, Anchorage.
Tel 248-4777.
W accessalaska.org

Society for Accessible Travel and Hospitality (SATH)
347 5th Ave, Suite 610, New York, NY 10016. **Tel** (212) 447-7284.
W sath.org

Personal Security and Health

In contrast to much of the US, Alaska has no really large cities, and while Anchorage has some gang and drug-related violence, it is not usually directed at visitors. On the whole, Alaska is a relatively safe place to visit, but even in small towns, it is wise to be alert and learn which areas are unsafe, especially at night. For visitors on adventure holidays *(see pp264–7)*, safety is paramount in the wilds of Alaska. Carry maps and follow the advice of rangers or visitors' centers – they can offer invaluable information on wilderness survival and basic safety procedures. Those on organized tours or cruises should follow the instructions provided by crew or tour leaders. Before setting out, it is a good idea to check local newspapers and television and radio channels for weather reports.

Police patrol car

Personal Safety

Surprisingly, Alaska possesses one of the country's higher crime rates, although most tourist hubs are relatively non-threatening. Nevertheless, visitors should observe a few basic rules. Never carry large amounts of cash. Wallets kept in back pockets will tempt pickpockets. It is best to wear handbags and cameras over the shoulder, strapped firmly across the chest, and to keep passports separate from cash and traveler's checks. Drivers should try to keep valuables locked in the trunk of their car when parked at trailheads, especially those around Anchorage – they are known for break-ins. Large towns can be unsafe at night, so avoid walking around alone and try to stay away from areas that are known to be risky. Avoid panhandlers or anyone visibly intoxicated.

In Alaska, law enforcement in cities, towns, and certain boroughs is handled by local police departments. The **Alaska State Troopers** cover the rest of the state. In national parks, some park rangers are additionally in charge of law enforcement.

Lost Property

It is necessary to report all lost and stolen property to the police in order to make an insurance claim, even though it is unlikely that small items will be recovered. Victims should telephone the **Police Non-Emergency Line** and report the incident. They will subsequently be issued a police report, which can be used to file the claim.

Stolen and lost credit cards and traveler's checks should be reported to the issuer immediately to avoid misuse. Most card companies have toll-free numbers *(see p277)*. Visitors who have kept a record of the check numbers will find replacement a fairly painless experience – new ones are usually issued within 24 hours.

Foreign visitors who have lost their passport should contact their nearest embassy or consulate, which will probably be in San Francisco or Seattle. Normally, the consulate will issue a temporary replacement. In order to speed up the replacement process, visitors might find it useful to keep photocopies of their driver's license, birth certificate, and passport.

Medical Concerns

Hospitals in Alaska's largest cities are very well-equipped, but small towns usually only have health clinics, while rural villages often have just a public health nurse. Bear in mind that a range of drugs, such as codeine-based painkillers, may need prescriptions in the US. Prescription medication in the US is expensive, so those with prescriptions should carry extra supplies. All pharmacies sell prescription drugs, but only hospital pharmacies are open 24 hours a day. Local brand names can be confusing, so keep a list of the generic names of drugs you may need and seek assistance in a drugstore if you are having difficulty finding the drug. Supermarkets such as Carrs stock non-prescription drugs and are open 24 hours.

Denali National Park ranger guiding visitors, Toklat Ranger Station

Medical care in the US can be expensive. Even with medical insurance, you may still have to pay upfront and claim reimbursement from your insurance company later, so ask for all forms and receipts.

Travel Insurance

Partly due to the high cost of medical care in the US, visitors are strongly urged to purchase travel health insurance for the duration of their stay. The package should cover death or dismemberment, dental and medical care, flight delays and cancellations, and lost or stolen baggage.

Emergencies

For emergencies that require medical, fire, or police services, dial 911. Contact numbers of ambulance services, the Coast Guard, Rescue Services for stranded hikers or campers, Fire Departments, and the Poison Control Center are given in telephone directory Blue Pages.

All hospitals in Alaska are equipped with emergency rooms, and their numbers are listed in the telephone book. Although critical emergency cases cannot be turned away by hospitals, evidence of the ability to pay may be required before treatment in non-emergency cases.

Hotel personnel will usually be able to call a doctor or a dentist and recommend a hospital on request. **Fairbanks Memorial Hospital** in Fairbanks and Anchorage's **Providence Alaska Medical Center** offer general medical care and critical care services. **Alaska Regional Hospital** also offers a Physician Referral Service. **Bartlett Regional Hospital** in Juneau has an acute care and emergency department, while **Central Peninsula General Hospital** in Soldotna has a shock trauma center.

Outdoor Hazards

Alaska's weather can be extreme and volatile, and without proper clothing and shelter, even in the summer, hypothermia is a risk on wet, windy days. The layering method works best, and must include layers for warmth and insulation, as well as an outer waterproof shell.

At higher elevations, the summer sun can be surprisingly strong. It is wise to use an effective sunscreen, wear a hat, and carry sufficient water. Filtering any water taken from natural sources is vital, as Alaskan streams and lakes harbor the giardia parasite.

In the summer, wildfires and thunderstorms are perpetual risks, especially in the Interior. It is important to watch

Classic Smokey Bear fire prevention sign, Dawson City, Canada

campfires closely and to extinguish cigarettes carefully. Visitors who see a developing forest fire, especially near populated areas, should move away and report it to the authorities. During lightning storms, avoid ridges or open areas, and do not stand or camp beneath tall trees.

Earthquake and tsunami warnings are issued by the **Alaska Tsunami Warning Center**, but the chances of these occuring during a visit are remote. While most people are concerned about bear encounters, following a few simple guidelines *(see p111)* will almost eliminate the possibility of harm.

DIRECTORY

Banking and Currency

Visitors will generally not encounter any problems with financial transactions in Alaska. Banks are plentiful and foreign currency exchanges are available in larger cities, but it is best to verify opening hours before visiting banks or exchange bureaus. Automated teller machines (ATMs), which enable visitors to make cash withdrawals with debit or credit cards, are available all over Alaska, even in small towns and some villages. Found in most banks, supermarkets, and general stores, these are open 24 hours a day. Some banks even have drive-up ATMs. Credit cards are commonly used for making payments, especially at hotels and car rental companies.

widely used cards are VISA and **MasterCard**, but most places also accept American Express, **Diner's Club**, and **Discover Card**.

ATMs offer better foreign exchange rates than banks, and all credit, charge, and debit cards can be used to withdraw cash from ATMs, with a bank transaction fee of $2 to $3, in addition to the credit card company's charges. The most common international systems are Cirrus and Plus. Before you leave home, it is best to ask your bank or credit card company which ATM system your card can access.

ATMs can dispense cash, enact account transfers, and show bank balances

Banks and Foreign Currency Exchange

Alaskan banks are generally open from 9 or 10am to 4:30, 5, or 6pm on weekdays, and often on Saturdays from 10am to 2 or 3pm, but these hours can vary across the state. Banks will convert traveler's checks to US dollars, and for a substantial commission, some **Wells Fargo** banks in Anchorage, Fairbanks, and Juneau will also change foreign currency traveler's checks and cash.

Traveler's Checks

Traveler's checks are safer than cash as they can be replaced if lost or stolen. It is important to keep the checks separate from the list of check numbers, which are required if checks have to be replaced in case of loss or theft. Foreign currency traveler's checks may be cashed at Wells Fargo banks in Juneau,

Anchorage, and Fairbanks, but they are otherwise of little use in Alaska. To avoid extra charges, it is best to carry **American Express** or **VISA** traveler's checks in US dollars. These are always accepted as cash, without fees, in hotels, restaurants, shops, gas stations, and other businesses across Alaska, except in some of the smallest rural villages. Often, some form of photo ID, such as a passport or driver's license, is required as identification when using traveler's checks.

Credit, Debit, and Charge Cards

Credit and charge cards are practically essential when traveling in the US. The cards are usually required as a guarantee when renting a car or RV (see pp288–9), and are used to book tours, airline tickets, and tickets for most forms of entertainment. The most

Wiring Money

Money can be wired to Alaska from more than 100 countries. Money transfers can usually be sent and received within 15 minutes, but in some cases, it may take as much as a full day or even up to a week. The fastest and most popular service is **Western Union**, which is found all over Alaska, but banks also offer wire services, albeit slower. Thanks to the number of foreign crew members on cruise ships, other businesses offering wire services can usually be found near the cruise ship docks.

Currency

US currency is based on the decimal system, and the standard unit is the US dollar, divided into 100 cents. Bills, or bank notes, are all of similar size and greenish in color (newer bills have subtle color backgrounds), so it is wise to always check the denomination and count change carefully. In villages and remote areas, smaller bills are preferred, and in some places, $50 and $100 bills are not accepted at night. Similarly, some liquor stores will not change $50 or $100 bills unless the purchase is over half the amount of the bill. The quarter (25-cent piece) is useful for public telephones. It is also best to carry cash for small transactions and tips, and for use on public transport and in taxis.

Coins

US coins come in $1, 50-, 25-, 10-, 5-, and 1-cent pieces. Each coin has a popular name: 1-cent coins are pennies, 5-cent coins are nickels, 10-cent coins are dimes, and 25-cent coins are quarters. State quarters are in circulation, as are goldtone Sacagawea dollars. The Susan B. Anthony and Eisenhower dollars are uncommon, as is the John F. Kennedy 50-cent coin, which is now a collector's item.

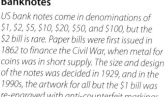

25-cent coin (a quarter)

10-cent coin
(a dime)

5-cent coin (a nickel)

1-cent coin (a penny)

1-dollar coin (a buck)

Banknotes

US bank notes come in denominations of $1, $2, $5, $10, $20, $50, and $100, but the $2 bill is rare. Paper bills were first issued in 1862 to finance the Civil War, when metal for coins was in short supply. The size and design of the notes was decided in 1929, and in the 1990s, the artwork for all but the $1 bill was re-engraved with anti-counterfeit markings.

DIRECTORY

American Express
Tel (800) 926-9400 (Moneygram US only), (800) 221-7282 (check replacement), (800) 992-3404 (stolen cards).

Diner's Club
Tel (800) 234-6377.

Discover Card
Tel (800) 347-2683.

MasterCard
Tel (800) 627-8372.

Thomas Cook/MasterCard UK
Tel (800) 223-7373.

VISA
Tel (800) 227-6811 (check replacement), (800) 847-2911 (stolen cards).

Wells Fargo
Anchorage Tel 265-2523.
Fairbanks Tel 459-4300.
Juneau Tel 586-3324.
W wellsfargo.com

Western Union
Tel (800) 325-6000 (wiring money US), (800) 833833 (wiring money UK).
W westernunion.com

1-dollar bill ($1)

5-dollar bill ($5)

10-dollar bill ($10)

20-dollar bill ($20)

50-dollar bill ($50)

100-dollar bill ($100)

Communications and Media

The United States has some of the most sophisticated communications systems in the world. Postal, telephone, and Internet services are all widely available, providing fast and efficient services to destinations both in-state and worldwide. Public card phones and pay phones are found in most parts of Alaska in cafés, bars, gas stations, supermarkets, hotels, and public buildings. However, in the more remote regions, pay phones and mailboxes are found only in towns and cell phone coverage is usually quite limited.

Telephones

All local telephone numbers have seven digits. The cost of a local call is 25 to 35 cents, which is usually good for any length of call. Alaska's area code is 907. This is required when calling long-distance, even in-state. Long-distance calls to any number outside the local area (especially in-state calls) cost considerably more, but are cheaper when dialled direct or at off-peak times, usually in the evenings and on weekends. Calls made on hotel phones will usually be charged at much higher rates.

Pay phones are becoming increasingly rare as cell phones replace landlines. They can be used for international calls, but callers will need a stack of change to dial direct and will be interrupted by an operator

Phone cards for long-distance calls

when more money is needed. A phone card is easier, but it is advisable to use only reputable companies such as AT&T. Cards can be purchased at supermarkets, convenience stores, and hotels for values between $5 and $50, and operate by providing a series of numbers to punch into the phone, which then accesses the account and announces how much time remains on that card. Each card has clear usage instructions printed on it.

If you are having difficulty getting through or a collect (reverse charge) call is needed, call the operator and ask to be connected manually (this costs more than a direct-dial call).

Toll-free numbers are widely used in the US for contacting hotels, car rental companies, tour operators, and even some tourist offices. While most toll-free numbers are not accessible when calling from outside the US, in some cases they may occasionally be connected through an operator and charged at the regular toll rate.

Cell Phones, Internet, and Fax Services

Many travelers bring their own cell (mobile) phones, but service varies among operators, so check if your service provider provides coverage in Alaska. Coverage is usually good in towns, and even, surprisingly, in many remote areas, but may be erratic outside towns.

Internet cafés are common, and an increasing number of establishments offer Wi-Fi access, often free, to patrons with their own laptop computers. Most hotels offer Internet access to their guests. Virtually all libraries also have free Internet access. Faxes can often be sent from larger hotels and copy centers. Many places in rural Alaska have only dial-up Internet or no access at all.

Mail Services

In the US, all domestic mail is First Class unless otherwise requested, and generally takes between three and five days to arrive. First Class mail costs only about 20 percent more than parcel post (surface mail), which is also available. International mail sent by air takes between five and ten days to arrive, but surface parcels

Typical US mailbox

may take over four weeks. Special parcel services are also offered by the **US Postal Service**. Priority Mail delivers faster than normal First Class and costs only marginally more. Express Mail guarantees next day delivery within the Lower 48 states, and a day or two more to Hawaii. International Express Mail

---

Useful Dialing Codes

- To make a direct-dial long-distance call within Alaska, the rest of the US, or Canada, dial **1** (the country code) followed by the area code and local number. Useful area codes: Alaska **907**, Yukon Territory **867**, British Columbia (and Hyder in Alaska) **250**.
- For international direct-dial calls, dial **011** followed by the desired country code. Then dial the area or town code (omitting the first 0 or 1), and the local number.
- To make an international call via the operator, dial **01** and follow the same procedure as detailed above.

- For international operator assistance, dial **01**.
- For local operator assistance, dial **0**.
- For international directory inquiries, dial **00**.
- For local directory inquiries, dial **411**.
- For inquiries in another US or Canadian area code, dial **1** followed by the desired area code and **555-1212**.
- For emergency police, fire, and ambulance services, dial **911**.
- Dial **844** for temperature, weather, and time.
- **1-800**, **866**, **877**, and **888** indicate toll-free numbers.

Newspaper vending machines on 4th Avenue, downtown Anchorage

DIRECTORY

Mail services

DHL
Tel (800) 225-5345.
Ⓦ dhl.com

Federal Express (FedEx)
Tel (800) 463-3339.
Ⓦ fedex.com

UPS
Tel (800) 742-5877.
Ⓦ ups.com

US Postal Service
Tel (800) 275-8777.
Ⓦ usps.com

guarantees to deliver in five working days. Several private international couriers offer next-day delivery for foreign mail, the best known being **DHL**, **Federal Express**, and **UPS**.

All Alaskan towns have at least one post office. Small packages and letters may be dropped into mailboxes, but all parcels will need to be inspected at the post office counter. Contract post offices in shops and small towns often have shorter queues, but don't accept international parcels.

Newspapers, Radio, and Television

The major daily newspaper in Alaska is the weekly *Anchorage Daily News*. Other major papers are the *Fairbanks New-Miner*, *Juneau Empire*, and the *Mat-Su Frontiersman*. Bestselling national daily papers such as the *Wall Street Journal*, the *New York Times*, and *USA Today* are also available, although a few days late, at large bookshops and newsstands in major airports. Some visitors' centers and shops offer free papers listing local weather, events, and news. The most popular of these is the *Anchorage Press*.

The Alaska Public Radio Network has stations in all major cities and towns. Anchorage's 91.1 FM is the most popular; 650 and 700 AM have news and talk. In Fairbanks, 970 AM has the news, while 104.7 FM plays rock. 630 AM in Juneau has the news. Most hotels offer a range of cable and satellite TV channels.

Alaskan Lexicon

Baleen – strips of fibrous tissue from the mouths of baleen whales, used to filter plankton from the sea.
Breakup – wet and muddy period when the ice melts in April.
Bush – the part of Alaska that is off the highway and ferry systems.
Cache – hut built on stilts and used to store items out of reach of animals.
Camai – an Athabaskan greeting (pronounced "cha-MAI") that is the Alaskan equivalent of "Aloha."
Cheechako – a newcomer who has been in Alaska less than about 20 years.
Chinook – warm wind from the Southeast that can melt the snow, even in midwinter.
Igloo – a variation of the Inupiat word *illu*, which means "house." The ice block variety is used only as an emergency shelter.

Lower 48 – all US states except Alaska and Hawaii.
Mukluks – moosehide or sealskin boots.
Muktuk – whale or seal blubber favored by Native Alaskans.
Mushing – driving a dog sled, also Alaska's state sport.
Native – spelled with an uppercase "N," it refers to an indigenous Alaskan. Spelled with a lowercase "n," it refers to anyone born in Alaska.
Outhouse – outdoor toilet consisting of a hole in the ground covered by a shelter.
Permafrost – permanently frozen ground overlain by topsoil or muskeg.
Potlatch – Southeast Alaska Native feast in which the host distributes numerous possessions.
Scrimshaw – Native designs etched onto walrus ivory.
Skookum – anything that's strong, great, or wonderful.
Slough – stagnant backwater formed by old river channels (pronounced "slew").

Snowbirds – older people who live in Alaska but winter in the Lower 48.
Snowmachine – what other North Americans would call a snowmobile or ski-doo.
Sourdough – an old-time prospector or any long-time Alaskan, usually those who have been in Alaska for at least two decades. The word is derived from the bread made with sourdough starter (see p248).
Taiga – Russian for "little sticks," referring to black spruce. Much of Alaska's muskeg and boreal forest consists of taiga vegetation.
Tundra – derived from the Finnish word for "treeless plain," it refers to areas of miniature plants in Alaska's northern and alpine areas.
Ulu – a crescent-shaped knife used by Natives for cleaning and skinning animal skins and cutting meat.
Xtra Tufs – high-top rubber boots used throughout Alaska.

TRAVEL INFORMATION

The majority of overseas visitors to Alaska land in Anchorage, the state's main gateway. Those coming from the Lower 48 can fly from Seattle directly to Ketchikan or Juneau. Bus services link the Lower 48 and Canada with Anchorage and Fairbanks, but many visitors journey overland by car on the Alaska Highway, or sail on an Alaska Marine Highway vehicle ferry from Bellingham, Washington, through the Inside Passage to Southeast Alaska. There, travelers can transfer to ferries bound for the Kenai Peninsula, Southwest Alaska, and Prince William Sound, where it is possible to connect to the Alaska Railroad. Within Alaska, rental vehicles are a good alternative to the limited public transport systems and provide maximum freedom. Sites off the highways can be accessed by an extensive network of scheduled or chartered flights.

Arriving by Air

All major cities and towns in Alaska have an airport, while remote towns and villages have airstrips for transport planes and bush traffic. The state's biggest airport – and the one most visitors are likely to see first – is Ted Stevens International Airport in Anchorage, which receives all international flights from Europe and Asia and the greatest number of flights from the Lower 48.

As the only non-stop intercontinental flights to Alaska are from Frankfurt and East Asia, most overseas visitors arrive via Seattle. There are also non-stop flights from select US cities, including Minneapolis, Salt Lake City, Maui, Honolulu, Los Angeles, Dallas, Portland, Phoenix, Chicago, and Denver.

Alaska's major airline, **Alaska Airlines**, is based in Seattle and connects a host of cities across the US and Mexico to a wide variety of Alaskan destinations such as Anchorage and Fairbanks, several towns in the Southeast including Juneau, Sitka, and Ketchikan, Cordova in Prince William Sound, Nome and Kotzebue in the western Arctic, Barrow in the far north, and Dutch Harbor in the Aleutians.

Scheduled flights into Anchorage are also offered by **Condor**, **American Airlines**, **Air Canada**, **US Airways**, **Iceland Air**, **Delta**, **Frontier**, **China Airlines**, and **United Airlines**. They fly to cities around the US, and to international destinations.

International Arrivals

Overseas visitors arriving in the US must present a passport and, if necessary, a visa to immigration officials before claiming their baggage. Those catching connecting flights must collect their luggage at the first point of entry into the US and take it through US Customs before checking it on to their final destination.

Non-resident adults are allowed to bring in a limited amount of duty-free items. These include 0.2 gallons (1 liter) of alcohol, 50 non-Cuban cigars, 200 cigarettes, and up to $100 worth of gifts. There is no legal limit on the amount of money that can be brought into the US, but cash amounts over $10,000 should be declared to US Customs. Completed customs declaration forms must be submitted to a US Customs officer while exiting the Customs hall.

Most major airports offer a wide range of services such as newsstands, car rental companies, shuttle buses, and taxi services. Most terminals also offer facilities for the disabled.

Specially painted Alaska Airlines aircraft underscoring the carrier's role in transporting Alaskan seafood

Floatplane taking off to tour remote corners of Alaska

Internal Flights

In addition to the numerous Alaska Airlines services, several domestic airlines offer convenient, if occasionally somewhat expensive, services. **Ravn Alaska** (formed by a merger between Era Alaska and Arctic Circle Air) flies throughout the state, including from Anchorage and Fairbanks to Prince William Sound, Kenai, Peninsula, Kodiak, and Western Alaska. **PenAir** flies to a host of destinations on the Alaska Peninsula and the Aleutian Islands, including the Pribilof Islands. **Bering Air** accesses tiny places in Western Alaska from Nome and Kotzebue, and also operates charter flights to the Russian Far East. **Grant Aviation** does daily runs between Southwest Alaska, Anchorage, Homer, and Bethel. **Wings of Alaska** serves the Southeast, and **Warbelow's Air Ventures** links many far-flung areas of the state.

Alaska also has a host of charter airlines which can take passengers to just about any airport or airstrip in the state, as well as bush airlines *(see p264)* that land fly-in hunters, anglers, river runners, or hikers on remote lakes, rivers, glaciers, or gravel bars.

Air Fares

There is a vast array of fare types and prices available for travel to and around Alaska. Airlines compete with each other, and it pays to compare and book early to get the cheapest fares, especially during the busy summer. Although several websites do offer bargains on last-minute bookings, direct flights to the US and Alaska usually need to be booked in advance.

It is usually less expensive to book an APEX (Advance Purchase Excursion) fare, which must be bought no less than seven or 14 days in advance. However, these tickets impose such restrictions as minimum (usually seven days) and maximum (three to six months) lengths of stay. It can be difficult or expensive to alter APEX flight dates after purchase, so it is wise to include compensation for delays or cancellations on a travel insurance policy. A fly-drive deal, where the cost of the ticket includes car rental, is also a lower-priced option that may be worth taking.

Travel agents are useful sources of information on the latest bargains. They may also be able to offer special deals to visitors who book rental cars, accommodation, and domestic flights in addition to their international ticket.

Baggage Restrictions

Most airlines now charge for checked bags, but allow carry-ons consisting of one piece of hand luggage and a small handbag. On smaller domestic airlines, flightseeing trips, and bush flights, only one piece of hand luggage is accepted and the weight of checked baggage may be limited to as little as 20 lb (9 kg) per person.

DIRECTORY

Airline Carriers

Air Canada
Tel (888) 247-2262.
w aircanada.com

Alaska Airlines
Tel (800) 252-7522.
w alaskaair.com

American Airlines
Tel (800) 433-7300.
w aa.com

Bering Air
Tel (800) 478-5422.
w beringair.com

China Airlines
Tel (800) 227-5118.
w china-airlines.com

Condor
Tel (866) 960-7915.
w condor.com

Delta
Tel (800) 221-1212.
w delta.com

Frontier
Tel (800) 432-1359.
w frontierairlines.com

Grant Aviation
Tel (888) 359-4726.
w flygrant.com

Iceland Air
Tel (800) 223-5500.
w icelandair.com

PenAir
Tel (800) 448-4226.
w penair.com

Ravn Alaska
Tel 248-4422, (800) 866-8394.
w flyravn.com

United Airlines
Tel (800) 864-8331.
w united.com

US Airways
Tel (800) 428-4322.
w usairways.com

Warbelow's Air Ventures
Tel 474-0518, (888) 459-6250.
w warbelows.com

Wings of Alaska
Tel 789-0790, (800) 789-9464.
w wingsofalaska.com

Alaska Marine Highway

Often called the "Blue Canoe," the state-run Alaska Marine Highway provides year-round access from Bellingham in Washington state and Prince Rupert in British Columbia, Canada. It also connects the mostly roadless areas of the Southeast, Southwest, and Prince William Sound. The route is so beautiful that it has been officially designated a National Scenic Byway, a term usually reserved for highways. The Marine Highway is also an easy, if expensive, way to transport a vehicle to Alaska, and with advance planning, it is possible to stop off in any of the ports of call along the way. Schedules, however, can often go awry, so it is wise to allow a bit of buffer time.

Routes

The Alaska Marine Highway has three main routes: Southeast, Southcentral, and Southwest. The Southeast route is the longest one, following the spectacular Inside Passage up the west coast of North America from Bellingham in Washington state to Prince Rupert in Canada, and then northward through Southeast Alaska's islands and channels to Haines and Skagway. Ports of call along the way usually include Ketchikan, Wrangell, Petersburg, and Juneau, with some sailings calling in at Sitka. The MV Kennicott does the cross-Gulf run, from Juneau in the Southeast to Whittier in Prince William Sound via Yakutat, Cordova, and Valdez. The Southcentral route connects Whittier to Cordova, Valdez, and Chenega Bay, and also to Kodiak, Port Lions, Homer, and Seldovia. On the Southwestern route, the MV Tustumena (see p215) sails between April and September from Homer to Seldovia, Kodiak, and Port Lions, and down the Alaska Peninsula and the Aleutians to Chignik, Sand Point, King Cove, Cold Bay, and Dutch Harbor.

Access to Hollis on Prince of Wales Island is provided by **Inter-Island Ferries**, while **British Columbia Ferries** sails from the northern tip of Vancouver to Prince Rupert.

Ferries

Eleven different ferries of various sizes regularly ply the Southeast, Southcentral, and Southwest Alaska routes. Traditionally and legally, the vessels in the fleet are named after Alaskan glaciers. The largest of the ferries, the flagship MV Columbia holds 625 passengers and is usually used on runs between Bellingham, WA, and Haines, as is the MV Malaspina. Both ships boast a dining room, gift shop, cocktail lounge, solarium, and observation lounge.

The MV Aurora and the catamaran MV Chenega run shorter routes in the Southeast and also serve Prince William Sound. MVs Kennicott, Taku, Matanuska, LeConte, Lituya and the catamaran MV Fairweather do a variety of runs in the Southeast. The fleet's oldest, sturdiest ship, the MV Tustumena, does the turbulent Aleutian Island run.

Facilities

In general, the long-haul ferries are better equipped than the ones doing day runs. Except for the fast catamarans MV Fairweather and MV Chenega, which have only snack bars, the larger vessels have cafeterias that serve snacks, hot meals, and beverages. The MV Columbia and MV Tustumena also have full-service dining rooms, where both American and Continental breakfasts are available, and lunch and dinner menus usually offer a daily special or choice of main dishes, featuring seafood, salad, and vegetable dishes. Sandwiches and snacks are always available. Mixed drinks are sold only on the MV Columbia and MV Tustumena, but beer and wine are available in the snack bars on the fast ferries.

MVs Columbia, Malaspina, Matanuska, Tustumena, and Taku offer cabins with private bathroom facilities, while the MV Kennicott has a few two-berth unserviced rooms without facilities. The five short-haul ferries do not have cabins. All ferries, however, have public showers.

Marine Highway ferry sailing away from Valdez in Prince William Sound

Under the solarium on the upper deck of a Marine Highway ferry

DIRECTORY

Ferries

Alaska Marine Highway
7559 N Tongass Hwy,
Ketchikan.
Tel 465-3941, (800) 642-0066.
W ferryalaska.com

Inter-Island Ferries
PO Box 495, Craig.
Tel 826-4848, (866) 308-4848.
W interislandferry.com

British Columbia Ferries
Tel (250) 386-3431, (888) 223-3779.
W bcferries.com

Deck passengers on overnight trips can sleep in the indoor recliners, or on reclining plastic deck chairs in the heated solariums on the top decks of the ferries. On all overnight sailings, travelers are allowed to pitch tents on the top deck and fix them with waterproof duct tape. These are usually quite close to the smokestack and noisy engines, so it may be useful to carry some earplugs. All ferries have elevators and wheelchair-accessible facilities, and the larger vessels also offer cabins suitable for disabled passengers.

Life on Board

There are few things more relaxing than sitting in the observation lounge or warm solarium of a ferry and watching the passing scene. While onboard amenities are spartan by most standards, there's always plenty to fill up the time. In addition to watching the undeniably spectacular landscapes along most routes, passengers find they have plenty of time to lean back with a book, take a hot shower, sleep or lounge in the fresh air, and meet people from across the world.

Taking a Vehicle

Book as far in advance as possible in order to transport a vehicle on the Marine Highway, especially between Bellingham, WA, and Haines in the peak season from June to August. Tariffs depend on the size of the vehicle, measured from the front bumper to the end of the back bumper or trailer. Most vessels on the Southeast and Southcentral routes can take vehicles up to 70-ft (20-m) long, but the maximum length on the MV *Tustumena* is 40 ft (12 m). Except in some small ports,

drivers will usually be required to check in two hours before sailing. The crew will direct them to their parking location, where they must set their hand brake, take any possessions needed onboard, and lock the vehicle. The vehicle deck will not be accessible while sailing. However, escorted trips to the vehicle deck are periodically announced by the purser, and there is vehicle access while the vessel is in port. RV propane tanks and firearms must be reported to the purser upon boarding, so they can be sealed by the crew. Boats under 100 lb (45 kg), bicycles, and kayaks incur an extra charge, while larger boats will be charged as vehicles. Except for guide dogs, transporting pets also incurs an extra charge.

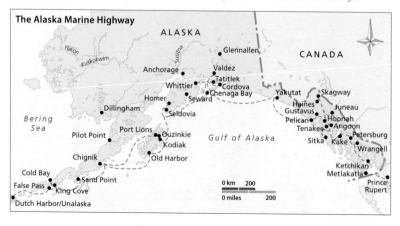

The Alaska Marine Highway

Traveling by Bus and Train

Although slower than car and plane travel, taking a bus or train in Alaska can be an enjoyable way of exploring the region. Long-distance bus services, however limited, are the least expensive way to travel, although some places are served only by costly tour buses. Within the larger cities, local buses are the only form of public transport. Although these tend to focus on daytime services for local commuters, they are also useful to visitors since most centrally placed attractions lie along or near main bus routes. A good option is to buy an Alaska Pass, which allows unlimited bus, train, and ferry travel for a set period on the Alaska Railroad, Alaska Marine Highway, White Pass and Yukon Route Railroad (WP&YR), and Gray Line buses in Alaska.

Alaska Railroad train pulling into Denali National Park station

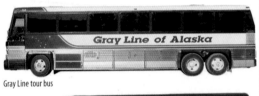

Gray Line tour bus

Skagway's popular yellow tourist bus

Traveling by Bus

In Alaska, only a handful of popular routes are served by long-distance buses, and those services that do exist are generally infrequent. Many services are operated only during the summer.

The best-served routes are those between Anchorage, Fairbanks, and the Kenai Peninsula, and points in between. **Alaska Park Connection** runs from Seward to Denali National Park via Anchorage. **Seward Bus Lines** connects Anchorage with Seward while the **Homer Stage Line** runs between Anchorage, Homer, and Seward. **Alaska-Yukon Trails** has a year-round service between Anchorage and Fairbanks, as well as summer services to Dawson City in Canada. **Interior Alaska Bus Lines** operates services between Anchorage, Fairbanks, and Whitehorse, in Canada's Yukon Territory. **Kennicott Shuttle**

buses run between Glennallen and McCarthy in Wrangell-St. Elias National Park.

To reach Alaska by bus from the Lower 48 states, it is best to take **Greyhound Canada** to Whitehorse, and connect to the Alaska Direct Bus or Alaska/Yukon trails to Anchorage or Fairbanks. **Green Tortoise** is a unique bus touring company with several 10- or 14- day trips each summer. It's an especially popular option with young international travelers.

Traveling by Train

Traveling by train in Alaska means riding the **Alaska Railroad** (see pp286–7) between Seward and Fairbanks or taking the tourist route on the **White Pass and Yukon Route Railroad** (see pp152–3) from Skagway. While rail services are limited and relatively expensive, they're both relaxing and scenic, and most visitors will want to experience at least one rail trip during their stay.

The Alaska Railroad is an extremely popular and convenient way to reach Denali National Park. While there are no overnight trains and, therefore, no sleeper services, all visitor-oriented trains on the main line between Seward and Fairbanks offer onboard dining services. Because so many cruise ships and tour companies use the Alaska Railroad to transport their passengers from Seward and Whittier to Anchorage, Denali National Park, and Fairbanks, many trains have special double-decker domed observation cars owned by

Park shuttle buses lining up for passengers, Denali National Park

White Pass and Yukon Route Railroad depot, Skagway

a day's notice, **Anchor Rides** provides door-to-door transport for disabled or elderly passengers. **Metropolitan Area Commuter System** (MACS) covers the Fairbanks area. **Capital Transit** in Juneau links the downtown area with the Mendenhall Valley and Douglas Island. **The Bus** in Ketchikan connects the downtown area, the North Tongass Highway, and Saxman village.

Princess Cruise Line and Holland America Line *(see pp256–9)*. Accessible only to tour members, these offer onboard guides and other amenities. In addition, the railroad has its own luxurious "Goldstar" railcars with open-air viewing platforms. A number of seasonal day trips are also offered by the **Alaska Railroad** from Anchorage and other cities. Especially popular is the all-day Spencer Glacier float trip. This includes a rail ride to the glacier on the Kenai Peninsula with a gentle raft trip past icebergs on the lake and then down the Placer River.

City Public Transport

Only Anchorage, Juneau, Fairbanks, and Ketchikan have regular public bus services, but Barrow, Kodiak, the Mat-Su region, Sitka, and Skagway have limited services or shuttles. In Anchorage, **People Mover** covers most parts of the city from the Downtown Transit Center. Services run from 6am to 10pm from Monday to Friday, with limited routes on weekends. People Mover will take passengers as far north as Eagle River, where on weekdays the buses connect with **Mat-Su Community Transit** (MASCOT) buses to Palmer or Wasilla. With

Tickets and Bookings

One of the best ways to see the state is to buy an **Alaska Pass** for $749–899. This pass allows unlimited travel for a set period on the Alaska Railroad, Alaska Marine Highway, and WP&YR with credit for a car rental to Fairbanks. For other trains and buses, it is advisable to book tickets well in advance as this ensures availability, confirms the place to meet the bus, and provides assurance that the service is operating – bus lines cancel trips if there is insufficient interest. Buses leave from the bus company's offices or from a centrally located landmark.

DIRECTORY

Bus Companies

Alaska Park Connection
PO Box 22–1011, Anchorage. **Tel** (800) 266-8625.
🆆 alaskacoach.com

Alaska-Yukon Trails
PO Box 84608, Fairbanks. **Tel** (800) 770-7275.
🆆 alaskashuttle.com

Green Tortoise
Tel (415) 956-7500, (800) 867-8647.
🆆 greentortoise.com

Greyhound Canada
877 Greyhound Way SW, Calgary AB T3C 3V8. **Tel** (800) 661-8747.
🆆 greyhound.ca

Homer Stage Line
Homer. **Tel** 235-2252, 868-3914.
🆆 stagelineinhomer.com

Interior Alaska Bus Lines
PO Box 501, Anchorage. **Tel** (800) 770-6652 (Anchorage), (867) 668-4833 (Whitehorse, YT).
🆆 alaskadirectbusline.com

Kennicott Shuttle
PO Box 65, Glennallen. **Tel** 822-5292.
🆆 kennicottshuttle.com

Seward Bus Lines
3333 Fairbanks St, Anchorage. **Tel** (888) 402-7788, 224-3608.
🆆 sewardbuslines.net

Rail Companies

Alaska Railroad
PO Box 107500, Anchorage. **Tel** 265-2494, (800) 544-0522.
🆆 alaskarailroad.com

White Pass and Yukon Route Railroad
231 2nd Ave, Skagway. **Tel** (800) 343-7373.
🆆 whitepassrailroad.com

City Public Transport

Anchor Rides
Anchorage. **Tel** 343-7433.
🆆 peoplemover.org

Capital Transit
Juneau. **Tel** 789-6901.
🆆 juneau.org/capitaltransit

Mat-Su Community Transit
Tel 864-5000.
🆆 matsutransit.com

Metropolitan Area Commuter System
Fairbanks. **Tel** 459-1011.
🆆 co.fairbanks.ak.us/transportation

People Mover
Tel 343-6543.
🆆 peoplemover.org

The Bus
Ketchikan. **Tel** 225-8726, 247-5541.
🆆 borough.ketchikan.ak.us /145/Transit

Tickets and Bookings

Alaska Pass
Tel (800) 248-7598.
🆆 alaskapass.com

The Alaska Railroad

The Alaska Railroad may not be that far off the mark when it claims to offer the best rail trips in the world. Few journeys in the country cross such beautiful and wild terrain as this ribbon of steel that stretches across the landscape between Seward and Fairbanks. The trains allow passengers the best views possible, with all seats facing forward in the 1950s railcars. Travelers on the *Denali Star* can book seats in the domed viewing cars and access outdoor viewing areas from where the best photographs can be taken. Some trains also carry viewing cars owned by cruise companies and reserved exclusively for their clients.

History of the Railroad

The Alaska Railroad had its beginnings in 1903 when the Alaska Central Railway was built northward from Seward. In 1907, after 50 miles (80 km) of track were laid, the company went bankrupt. After the firm was reorganized as the Alaska Northern Railway, another 21 miles (34 km) of track were laid. In 1914, the US Congress sanctioned $35 million for the construction of a complete line between Seward and Fairbanks, and the tent city of Anchorage was designated as a railroad construction camp. The entire 470-mile (756-km) Alaska Railroad line was finally completed in 1917, and was inaugurated by President Warren G. Harding in Nenana in 1923 *(see p173)*.

A branch line to Whittier was laid during World War II by blasting tunnels through the Chugach Range, and the railroad began making a profit by transporting military and civilian supplies. In addition to the $30 million damage caused by the 1964 Good Friday earthquake, the railroad has overcome landslides, heavy snowfalls, derailments, and even chemical spills. The rolling stock was upgraded between 1999 and 2005, and today the scenic lines of the Alaska Railroad rank among the state's most popular tourist attractions.

Baggage tickets issued by the Alaska Railroad

Regular Services

While some regular commuter services on the railroad double as tourist services, other trains cater specially to tourists while also accommodating local passengers. Most of the visitor-oriented trains carry a dining car and railway gift shop, and each summer, guides on the trains interpret the history and wildlife seen along the route.

Between mid-May and mid-September, the daily Coastal Classic runs between Anchorage and Seward. During the same period, the regularly scheduled Glacier Discovery connects Anchorage to Whittier, followed by an optional trip to Spencer Glacier. From the glacier, passengers can either take a raft trip or continue to Grandview Pass for spectacular glacier viewing. The most popular route, however, is the Denali Star, which does the incredibly scenic run between Anchorage and Fairbanks, stopping en route at Denali National Park. The summer Hurricane Turn has Thursday to Sunday services, with extra runs on certain holidays, to serve bush passengers between Talkeetna and Hurricane. This 60-mile (97-km) local route has no food services.

In the winter, the Aurora does a weekend run between Anchorage and Fairbanks, with flag-stop services. From October to May, on the first Thursday of each month, the winter Hurricane Turn does the return day trip between Anchorage and Hurricane, offering wonderful views of the Susitna Valley and the Alaska Range.

The Hurricane Turn rolling across Hurricane Gulch, between Talkeetna and Denali National Park

Flag-stop passengers boarding the Alaska Railroad

Flag-Stop Service

The Alaska Railroad proudly boasts that its summer Hurricane Turn train between Talkeetna and Hurricane is one of the last rail journeys in the world to offer a flag-stop service. Passengers can flag down the train – also called the "Bug Car" due to a profusion of onboard mosquitos in the summer – anywhere along the route, and it will stop to let them board. In the winter, all Alaska Railroad trains offer a flag-stop service. This is important for bush residents who live in remote areas without ready access to the road system. Similarly, travelers can disembark anywhere for a few days of hiking or fishing, and then board the train again wherever they would like to continue with their journey. Note that stove fuel cannot be carried on the train.

Event Trains

During the off-season, the railroad runs many special services between Anchorage and Portage or Seward. Known as Event Trains, these are, in effect, rolling festivities with specific themes. The Alaska Railroad Blues Train runs in September and features local blues bands, a blues concert, a barbecue, and an overnight stay in Seward. In October, the Great Alaska Beer Train offers Alaskan appetizers and microbrews from Anchorage's Glacier Brewhouse (see p250) while traveling between Anchorage and Portage. The popular Fair Train provides a great way to visit the state fair in Palmer. Trains leave Anchorage in the morning, returning in the evening. They operate the last weekend of August and the first weekend of September. For Halloween, the Alyeska Mystery Trail includes a rail trip to "Girdwoodvania" for a haunted murder mystery. The railroad's website has detailed information on tours.

Special Tours

The railroad has teamed up with local operators to offer visitors unique rail-based itineraries and peripheral tours. These include a fabulous ten-day trip covering the entire railbelt, taking in Anchorage, Seward, Denali, Fairbanks, and Whittier. Other options take in sections of these routes, including a Prince William Sound cruise with Phillips Cruises and Tours, a flight to the Arctic Circle offering magnificent views, river trips in Talkeetna with **Mahay's Riverboat Service**, and a Glacier Bay cruise with glacier landings by helicopters. The railroad's website provides timetables and details on special tours.

Tickets and Booking

In the summer, cruise lines and organized tour companies book up large blocks of seats on the Glacier Discovery, Coastal Classic, and Denali Star. While many clients are accommodated on the companies' special private rail cars, other seats get booked up quickly – especially the Alaska Railroad's own domed cars – so it pays to reserve online, or call or mail the railroad as far in advance as possible. For the smaller local trains, such as the summer Hurricane Turn, tickets are available onboard or from railroad reservation counters.

DIRECTORY

Alaska Railroad

Main Office
PO Box 107500, Anchorage.
Tel (800) 554-0552, 265-2494.
W alaskarailroad.com

Anchorage Depot
411 W 1st Ave, Anchorage.
Tel 265-2494.

Denali Park Depot
Mile 1.25, Denali National Park Road.

Fairbanks Depot
1745 Johannsen Expressway, Fairbanks. **Tel** 458-6025.

Seward Depot
410 Port Ave, Seward.

Talkeetna Depot
Mile 13.5, Talkeetna Spur Road, Talkeetna.

Tour Operators

Mahay's Riverboat Service
Tel 733-2223, (800) 736-2210.
W mahaysriverboat.com

Phillips Cruises and Tours
Tel 276-8023, (800) 544-0529.
W 26glaciers.com

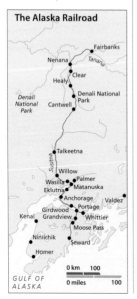

The Alaska Railroad

Fairbanks
Nenana
Tanana
Clear
Healy
Denali National Park
Denali National Park
Cantwell
Talkeetna
Susitna
Willow
Wasilla
Palmer
Eklutna
Matanuska
Anchorage
Valdez
Portage
Girdwood
Grandview
Whittier
Kenal
Moose Pass
Ninilchik
Seward
Homer

0 km 100
0 miles 100

GULF OF ALASKA

Traveling by Car and RV

Although it is possible, with some effort, to travel around Alaska on public transport, nothing compares to the freedom of the open road that comes with using a private or rental vehicle. For both residents and visitors, driving is a necessary part of life and will also be the only means of reaching many sites of interest. The road system may be limited, but where it is possible to drive, few will be disappointed with what is on offer, as the scenery is spectacular throughout the state. In addition, some fabulously scenic routes, such as the Denali Highway, the Elliott Highway, the Steese Highway, and the back roads of Southeast Alaska are accessible only by car.

Renting a Car

Anyone over 20 years of age can rent a vehicle, but some agencies impose a surcharge on people under 25. Overseas visitors need an International Driving License if their home license is not in Roman script. It is also essential to have a credit card to pay rental deposits, as few agencies accept cash. Child seats or cars for disabled drivers must be arranged in advance.

Visitors who rent a car in one city and leave it in another have to pay hefty drop-off fees. Cars must be returned with a full tank of gas.

Collision Damage Waiver (CDW) insurance, covering the car for any visible damage, and state and local taxes can increase the final total by 20 to 30 percent. Discounts may be available for members of the **American Automobile Association** (AAA) or the American Association of Retired Persons *(see p273)*. Most national agencies, such as **Alamo**, **Avis**, **Budget**, **Hertz**, **Thrifty**, and **Enterprise**, have outlets at airports, but charge more than local agencies and may add airport taxes. For inexpensive rentals, try the local **Cheapwheels Rent-a-Car**.

The biggest issue drivers will face is that rental agencies do not allow their non-4WD (four-wheel drive) cars to be taken on unpaved roads or to be driven off-road, and some of Alaska's finest routes are gravelled, including the McCarthy Road and the Taylor, Denali, Elliott, Steese, Dalton, and Top of the

World Highways. Driving any of them in a rental vehicle will invalidate any insurance or maintenance agreements, which means an accident or breakdown could wind up being very costly. However, visitors should be aware that renting a 4WD vehicle will typically double the charge. Only **Denali Car Rental** allows gravel road travel (except on the Dalton Highway north of the Yukon River) in a non-4WD. They require advance booking, especially in the summer peak season.

Gold Rush centenary license plate

Renting an RV

Renting a Recreational Vehicle (RV) can be an excellent, if expensive, way of getting around. Rates are lowest before mid-May and after mid-September. Smaller vehicles start around $185 per day in mid-summer with unlimited miles. Fully equipped motor homes usually include a bathroom, a kitchen, and hideaway beds, sleeping four to eight people and costing as much as $240 per day. National RV rental agencies such as **Cruise America** and local ones such as **ABC Motorhome Rentals**, **Alaska Motorhome Rentals**, and **Clippership Motorhome Rentals** offer a wide range of RVs. **Great Alaskan Holidays** also rents larger RVs with expanding "pop-out" living rooms. Private RV campsites usually provide dump stations and water and electricity hookups. Some rental agreements, especially those for over a week, include unlimited mileage, while others may limit drivers to 50 or 100 miles (80 or 160 km) per day, after which an additional per mile charge applies.

Rules of the Road

Alaska's road systems are not as developed as those in the Lower 48, and there are less than 60 miles (96 km) of freeways. Highway speed limits range from 50 mph (80 kmph) on frost-heaved roads to 65 mph (105 kmph) for open stretches on main roads. The limit on some highways is 65 mph (105 kmph) but most roads are 55 mph (90 kmph). On gravel roads, the limit varies

Traffic on Tudor Road, one of Anchorage's main thoroughfares

Recreational vehicle in Alaska

The Great American RV

Every summer, people from the Lower 48 head north in motor homes equipped with every imaginable amenity, including televisions, satellite dishes, microwaves, gas cans, showers, bicycles, and rowboats. Many pull trailers carrying the family car or a pair of ATVs (all-terrain vehicle). The snail analogy is enhanced by the fact that the slow, heavily loaded RVs cannot reach speeds acceptable to drivers of smaller cars, and winding or busy roads can rapidly become jammed as traffic backs up behind a string of RVs. RV drivers should note that in Alaska, drivers must pull over by law if more than five vehicles are being held up behind their vehicle.

from 30 mph (50 kmph) to 50 mph (80 kmph). Posted limits vary in towns, and during school hours, limits in school zones drop to 20 mph (30 kmph). Local police and the Alaska State Troopers enforce speed limits with particular vigilance in and around Anchorage, Fairbanks, and Juneau.

The blood alcohol content limit in Alaska is 0.08 percent and there are heavy penalties for driving while drunk. Further information on local traffic rules is available from rental agencies or the AAA.

Gas Stations

Fuel is much cheaper in the US than in Europe, but prices do vary, and gas is sold by the gallon, not by the liter. In remote areas, drivers may pay a third more than they would in major cities, and prices may double along the Dalton Highway and other gravel roads. All stations are self-service, and take most major credit cards at the pump. At non-automated stations, drivers may have to pay in advance. The cheapest gas is found at stores such as Fred Meyer, Carrs, and Costco. Those traveling on remote routes should carry extra gas as stations can be few and far between. The longest stretch without fuel is the

244-mile (390-km) leg between Coldfoot and Deadhorse on the Dalton Highway.

Off-Road Driving

While traveling in remote parts of Alaska, it is important to have the latest maps, check the route in advance, and be aware of seasonal dangers. If there is a chance of snowfall, it may be best to change plans, as snow could make an otherwise viable route impassable and few minor roads are maintained in the winter. A 4WD is essential in many areas, especially in the winter and during the spring thaw. Minor routes may have unbridged river crossings that become impassable to low-clearance vehicles after rain, and many forestry roads are little more than parallel ruts meant for logging trucks. Avoid driving off-track, as it damages vegetation and increases the risk of the vehicle bogging.

While information about the weather and routes will be available at tourist offices, local residents should also be able to help. It is wise to inform local tourist offices of your route and return date, and report back to them upon returning. Carry extra water, food, and gas for emergencies.

The Alaska Highway

For many drivers, the Alaska Highway – formerly called the Alcan, short for the Alaska-Canada Highway – is the adventure of a lifetime. Crossing some of the wildest territory in the world, every stretch of this 1,390-mile (2,224-km) road offers breathtaking sights and experiences. Starting in Dawson Creek in Canada's British Columbia, it crosses remote ranges, running through taiga forests and past crystalline lakes into the Yukon Territory. At Haines Junction, drivers can take the Haines Cut-Off *(see p154)* to Southeast Alaska, or continue northwest through Canada's strikingly lovely Kluane National Park. For the next 200 miles (320 km), it crosses scenic mountain country to the US-Canada border, and continues northwest past the Alaskan gateway town of Tok for its final stretch to Fairbanks.

Truck hauling freight over Tok River Bridge east of Tok

History of the Highway

Although an overland route to Alaska was being considered as early as 1930, it was not until the December 7, 1941, attack on Pearl Harbor that it became clear how militarily strategic this route would be. In February 1942, President Franklin D Roosevelt authorized the construction of the Alaska Highway, and soon, an agreement with Canada granted the US right of way and waived taxes, import duties, and immigration requirements.

The first surveyors who marched across the wilderness to locate a route roughly followed a chain of airstrips known as the Northwest Staging Route. Wherever possible, they used existing winter roads, pack trails, and trap lines, often having to divert to avoid muskeg and rough terrain. Construction began in March 1942, with temperatures of -40° C (-40° F), while in the summer, the workers battled mosquitoes, black flies, and the blazing sun.

In June 1942, the Aleutian Islands were invaded by the Japanese army and a sense of urgency arose to complete the road. More than 10,000 troops worked feverishly 16 hours a day, seven days a week, cutting trees, mashing out a road surface, and bridging rivers and streams. The final construction work ended on October 25, 1942. While the military road officially opened in November, civilian traffic was restricted until 1948.

Welcome sign,
Alaska Highway

Driving the Alaska Highway

The Alaska Highway has long had a reputation for challenging road conditions, but over time, the conditions have improved. The entire two-lane highway is now paved or chip-sealed, and is also shorter than it originally was, with at least 35 miles (56 km) of the historical route having been cut off due to rerouting and straightening. It is still a long trip, however, and the roadside scenery is so fabulous that it is worth allowing extra time for sightseeing.

Despite these improvements, some parts of the highway still suffer from serious cracks, frost heaves, and potholes, and every summer, long stretches of the road undergo extensive construction and repair, which can significantly slow drivers' progress. The roughest, most frost-heaved portion is between Canada's Kluane Lake and the Alaskan border, while the most serious grades and turns are found between Dawson Creek and Watson Lake in Canada. Information on highway conditions can be obtained from **Drive British Columbia**, **Yukon Daily Road Report**, and the **Alaska Road Traveler Information Service**.

As far as safety regulations go, drivers in Canada are required to use their headlights at all times and this is also required on some Alaska highways. Drivers should watch out for wildlife on the road. Moose are common everywhere and a collision can destroy both the animal and the vehicle. There are bison in northern British Columbia and the Yukon Territory, and in the winter, caribou stand on the road to lick salt off the surface.

At the US-Canada border, US and Canadian citizens must present a passport. International visitors must show their passports and, if necessary, their visas *(see p270)*.

Alaska Highway passing through the Yukon Territory, Canada

DIRECTORY

Highway Information

Alaska Road Traveler Information Service
Tel 511 or (866) 282-7577.
W http://511.alaska.gov

Drive British Columbia
Tel (800) 550-4997.
W drivebc.ca

Yukon Daily Road Report
Tel (877) 456-7623.
W 511yukon.ca

Alaska Highway Services

Between the 1940s and the early 1980s, fuel was available only every 250 miles (400 km) or so, but as the road became more traveled, more businesses sprang up along the route, and now there are gas stations approximately every 50 miles (80 km). There are also plenty of roadhouses and lodges along the way, where drivers can stop for a meal or a night's rest. The towns of Watson Lake, Whitehorse, Haines Junction, Beaver Creek, and Tok all have breakdown services and shops selling groceries and other supplies. Whitehorse, which is the capital of the Yukon Territory, has the most amenities and services.

The Cassiar Highway

Coming from the US or the Canadian west coast, many drivers opt to take the Cassiar Highway, which is a shorter but equally beautiful and more rugged alternative to the Alaska Highway. The Cassiar Highway is entirely asphalt surfaced, but the stretch between Iskut and Dease Lake in Canada contains several steep and winding sections.

Beginning at the Skeena River Bridge at Kitwanga in the Canadian province of British Columbia, the Cassiar Highway runs north for 450 miles (720 km) before connecting with the Alaska Highway 13 miles (21 km) west of Watson Lake in the Yukon Territory.

The Cassiar is also the access route to Hyder, Alaska (see p130), 40 miles (64 km) west of Meziadin Junction, and to Telegraph Creek on the upper Stikine River (see p135), 70 miles (112 km) on a gravel road west of Canada's Dease Lake.

There are several highlights along the way. The Kitwanga Fort National Historic Site located at Mile 2 is the site of an 18th-century indigenous fortified village and offers excellent views of the Kitwanga River valley. The beautiful Kinaskan Lake Provincial Park at Mile 227 is good for trout fishing. Drivers can see huge jade boulders being cut at Jade City at Mile 375. Boya Lake at Mile 397 is known for its clear aquamarine waters and excellent camping and fishing.

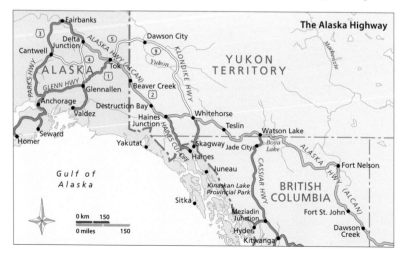

The Alaska Highway

General Index

Acknowledgments

Dorling Kindersley would like to thank the following people whose contributions and assistance have made the preparation of this book possible.

Main Contributor

After graduating from university, Deanna Swaney cast around in search of a career befitting a hopeless travel addict and eventually – following a bout of financial systems programming – she stumbled across travel writing and photography. As a result, over the past 20 years, she has researched and written eight first edition Lonely Planet titles, covering Bolivia; Tonga; Samoa; Iceland, Greenland, and the Faroe Islands; Zimbabwe, Botswana, and Namibia; Norway; The Arctic; and Namibia. She has also collaborated on dozens of Lonely Planet updates on six continents and has contributed text and photographs to numerous newspaper, magazine, and web features. Between trips, she finds time to work on construction projects around Big Lake, Alaska, and seeks out additions to her increasingly burdensome collections of rocks and frogs.

Additional Contributor

Eric Amrine is a freelance writer, photographer, and musician living with his wife and two children in Seattle's Fremont district. His favorite travel assignments include hiking, kayaking, and wildlife, and have taken him through Alaska's Inside Passage via luxury yacht, white-water rafting in Oregon's Rogue River wilderness, and expedition cruising to the pristine beaches and remote islands of the Sea of Cortez in Mexico. Eric is passionate about the Caribbean, having reviewed the cruise ships that regularly sail there.

Fact Checkers Don Pitcher, Claus Vogel
Proofreader Vandana Bhagra
Indexer Jyoti Dhar

Design and Editorial

Publisher Douglas Amrine
Publishing Managers Jane Ewart, Scarlett O'Hara
Senior Editor Kathryn Lane
Senior Designer Paul Jackson
Senior Cartographic Editor Casper Morris
Senior DTP Designer Jason Little
DTP Designer Natasha Lu
Picture Researcher Ellen Root

Editorial and Design Revisions

Louise Abbott, Claire Baranowski, Mariana Evmolpidou, Emer FitzGerald, Anna Freiberger, Camilla Gersh, Julia Harris-Voss, Mohammad Hassan, Christine Heilman, McKibben Jackinsky, Bharti Karakoti, Phoebe Lowndes, Hayley Maher, Alison McGill, Sonal Modha, George Nimmo, Carolyn Patten, Helen Peters, Marianne Petrou, Don Pitcher, Rada Radojicic, Ellen Root, Neil Simpson, Susana Smith, Joanna Stenlake, Conrad Van Dyk

DK Picture Library Romaine Werblow
Production Controller Linda Dare

Additional Photography

Geoff Brightling, Eric Crichton, Peter Gathercole, Frank Greenaway, Andrew Holligan, Ellen Howdon, Dave King, Ian O'Leary, Kim Taylor.

Cartography DK Cartography, London

Special Assistance

Dorling Kindersley would like to thank the following for their kind permission to photograph at their establishments: Alaska Aviation Heritage Museum, Alaska Native Heritage Center, Jason Wettstein and the Alaska SeaLife Center, Alaska State Museum, Alaska State Trooper Museum, Janet Asaro and the Anchorage Museum of History and Art, Baranov Museum, Hammer Museum, Isabel Miller Museum, Petroglyph Beach State Historic Site, Pioneer Park Air Museum, Pratt Museum, Saxman Totem Park, Sheldon Jackson Museum, Sheldon Museum, Sitka National Historical Park, Soldotna Historical Society Museum, Southeast Alaska Discovery Center, Totem Heritage Center, Town Docks Museum, Hull, Valdez Museum, Wrangell Museum.

Picture Credits

Key: a-above; b-below/bottom; c-centre; f-far; l-left; r-right; t-top

Works of art have been reproduced with the permission of the following copyright holders: *Crystal Lattice* © Robert Pfitzenmeier Front Endpaper Ltl, 66; *Raven the Creator* © John Hoover 76tr.

The publisher would like to thank the following for their kind permission to reproduce their photographs:

Alamy Images: Accent Alaska.com 10cl, 13tl, 180; Ace Stock Limited 85br; Alaska Stock LLC 24tr, 24bl, 44cl, 44br, 45tl, 45cr, 84tr, 82tr, 82bl, 118bl, 182cl 184t, 231br, 262b; Alaska Stock LLC/Design Pics Inc 237-236; Alaska Stock/Design Pics Inc/Patrick Endres 170-1, 218; Wally Bauman 161c; Walter Bibikow 38br; Steve Bly 23tr, 44tr; David Boag 119tr; Chris Boswell 14tc; Bill Brooks 41tl, 154bl; Bryan & Cherry Alexander Photography 51tr, 60b, 224tl; Loetscher Chlaus 179cl, 189tl, 219b, 220tr, 224br, 225crb; Gary Cook 183tr, 199cra, 199crb, 199bl; Danita Delimont 48t, 139cl, 166cl, 204cl, 261tl; Danita Delimont Agent/Dave Bartruff 254bc; David Sanger Photography 22t, 27bl, 36-37c; Design Pics Inc 11tr; Design Pics Inc / Mike Criss 86-87; Design Pics Inc / Michael DeYoung 2-3; Design Pics Inc /Matt Hage 250br; Robert Destefano 38tr; Douglas Peebles Photography 240tc; DY Riess MD 41cr; Dennis Frates 248tr; Lee Foster 66; Jeff Greenberg 248cl; Blaine Harrington III 62-63; Bill Heinsohn 15tl; Imagebroker 90cl, 91c, 150cr, 153tl; Jon Arnold Images

57bl, 57br, 79cr, 90tr, 188cl, 193bl; Jon Arnold Images/Walter Bibikow 40cl; Steven J. Kazlowski 137br; Terrance Klassen 21b; Dennis MacDonald 74tl; Medioimages 30tr, 136t; Ron Niebrugge 20t, 21tr, 22bl, 23b, 31tl, 38clb, 47bc, 48br, 65tr, 106cla, 106clb, 165bc, 183cr, 188tr, 193tl, 198cl, 220cl, 222cl, 223crb, 223b, 252bc; Luc Novovitch 37tr; Purcell Team 36clb; RGB Ventures/SuperStock 10bc, 36br; Kevin Schafer 203b, 214bc; John Schwieder 147tl, 158cl, 194br; Steve Bloom Images 210cl; Allen Thornton 165cl; Mireille Vautier 230tc; Visions of America, LLC 109cb; Westend61 GmbH /Erich Kuchling 207crb; Doug Wilson 44bl; Richard Wong 11br; WorldFoto 39bl.

Alaska Airlines: Alaska Airlines 280b.

Alaska Photographics.com: 89bl, 156; Patrick J. Endres 20bl, 25tl, 33crb, 37cr, 40tr, 40br, 41bl, 42-43c, 43ca, 43bl, 47tc, 49cc, 49br, 88, 115b, 163b, 173bl, 176cr, 181b, 188bl, 189cr, 193cr, 197tl, 198tl, 199tl, 210tr, 210bl, 222tr, 222br, 223tl, 226b.

Alaska Public Lands Information Centers/NPS: 70cla.

Courtesy of the Alaska Railroad Corporation: Calvin Hall 286b, 287tl.

Alaska Volcano Observatory: Alaska Division of Geological and Geophysical Surveys/C Nye 29tl, 211cr, C.Neal 211br; U.S. Park Service/ B Cella 192cl; Image Analysis Laboratory, NASA Johnson Space Center 28cl, 28cr; U.S. Geological Survey 29bl, Game McGimsey 29tr.

Alaska Wild Berry Products: 80tl.

Photos courtesy of Anchorage Museum of History and Art: 71cr, 73cb.

Autographs and Ogden Photography: © 2005 Doug Ogden 185tr.

Bridgeman Art Library: Jamestown-Yorktown Educational Trust, VA, USA Alaska, Purchased from Russia in 1867 (tapestry), Mabelle Linnea Holmes (1894-1987) 8-9.

Corbis: 56br, 58bc, 151br; Dave Bartruff 25tr; Tom Bean 26crb, 31cra, 207t, 209tl; Peter Beck 44-45c; Joel Bennett 26cl, 208bc; Bettmann 52, 55br, 57tr, 58cb, 59tr, 60tl; Gary Braasch 121bl; Tom Brakefield 33b; Brandon D. Cole 84br, 131bc; Richard A. Cooke 205b; Roy Corral 211tl; Richard Cummins 257tl; Design Pics/Michael DeYoung 13br; Michael DeYoung 157b, 190-191, 265t; Kevin Fleming 46cl, 133br, 159b; Natalie Fobes 61tl, 202, 214cl; Werner Forman 25bl; D. Robert/Lorri Franz 34br; H.S. Graves 58t; Gunter Marx Photography 59br, 290cl; Peter Guttman 27crb; Carol Havens 175br; Historical Picture Archive 54t; Eric and David Hosking 113tr, 240br; Rob Howard 155bl; JAI / Walter Bibikow 135-134; Ann Johansson 24br, 235b; Mark A. Johnson 146bl; Wolfgang Kaehler 39cra; Karen Kasmauski

186cl; Steve Kaufman 35cr, 169tr, 195cr, 209b; Blake Kent 197tr; Kit Kittle 139tr; Bob Krist 81br, 91tr 126; Dan Lamont 26bl, 133tl; Jacques Langevin 36tr; Danny Lehman 166bl; George D. Lepp 232cl; W. Wayne Lockwood, M.D 32cr; Charles Mauzy 161ca; Michael Maslan Historic Photographs 36cla; Arthur Morris 233tc; David Muench 30cla; Museum of History and Industry 56cl; Pat O'Hara 24-5c, 33cl, 42cla, 231tl, 235tl; Charles O'Rear 36bl; Papilio / Bjorn Backe 195cb; Douglas Peebles 39tl, 43cb; PEMCO - Webster & Stevens Collection/ Museum of History and Industry, Seattle 42tr; Greg Probst 31bl, 129tr; Progressive Image/Bob Rowan 25cra, 27tr; Lynda Richardson 84cl; David Samuel Robbins 249bl; Joel W. Rogers 34tr, 107tl; Galen Rowell 34-35c, 64tr, 88br, 226tl, 227cr; Galen Rowell 221t; Kevin Smith 12bl; Richard Hamilton Smith 169br; Scott T. Smith 33cr; Paul A. Souders 32bc, 33bl, 42bl, 64bl, 75tl, 89t, 131br, 162bl, 186bl, 233bl; Vince Streano 39crb, 151tl, 174cl, 187br; Tim Thompson 132cl, 147cr, 151cr, 216cl; Visuals Unlimited/Hugh Rose 225cra; Kennan Ward 35br, 111cr; Karl Weatherly 137tr; Stuart Westmorland 167tl, 217br; Staffan Widstrand 27cla, 225bl; Yogi, Inc. 168b; Zefa/Frank Krahmer 225br, /Elisabeth Sauer 164bc; Zuma / US Airforce/Joshua Strang 176b.

Dreamstime.com: Hasan Can Balcioglu 15br; Cecoffman 114; Karrapavan 14bc; Kenneth Mellott 18; Lawrence Weslowski Jr 253tr.

Ben Moeller-Gaa: 246bl.

Getty Images: Michael Cogliantry 268-9; Digital Vision 176cl; John Elk 246cra; Gerry Ellis 225cl; Kim Heacox 30-1c; David Madison 228-9; National Geographic Image Collection/Joseph Baylor Roberts 213t; Photographer's Choice 230b.

The Granger Collection, New York: 53bl, 54bl, 56-7c.

Historic Anchorage Hotel: 238br, 239br, 242bc.

Holland America Line: 33clb, 258tr, 258br, 259tr; Andy Newman 260bc.

House on the Rock B&B: 241tr.

Juneau Convention and Visitors Bureau: 32tr.

Mary Evans Picture Library: 55tc, 56bl, 57cr.

Masterfile: Andrew Wenzel 42br.

Perry and Angela Mollan: 245br.

Mount Aurora Lodge: 244tc.

Courtesy of National Park Service Digital Image Archives: 212tl, 212b.

National Oceanic and Atmospheric Administration: Central Library 29crb.

North Wind Picture Archives: 55clb.

Photolibrary: Index Stock Imagery, Inc /Mark Gibson 46bc.

Anuranjan Roy: 251tr.

SeaLife Center: Clark James 104cl; Jason Wettstein 104clb, 105tl, 105cra.

Silverbow Inn Bakery and Catering: 243tr.

Deanna Swaney: 82clb, 83cr.

Kevin Turinsky: 255tr.

University of Washington Libraries, Special Collections: Negative Nummber UW9069 57tl.

US Fish and Wildlife Service, Alaska Image Library: 33tc, 33br, 161bc, 213br, 232tr; Steve Amstrup 111br; Bob Angell 217bl; Kate Banish 32br; Connie Barclay 227tl; Vernon Byrd 216br; David Cline 33tr; Donna Dewhurst 161cl, 161crb 217tc; Steve Hillebrand 32bl, 111cl; Dean Kildaw 217cl; John Sarvis 161br; Art Sowls 217tr, 217cr.

USDA Forest Service, Tongass National Forest: 31crb

Harry M Walker: 70br, 234b.

Front Endpapers: Alamy Images: Accent Alaska Rtr, Alaska Stock/Design Pics Inc / Patrick Endres Rtl; Lee Foster Lcla; Alaska Photographics.com: Patrick J. Endres Rcr; Corbis: Bob Krist Lcra; Natalie Fobes Rbc; Dreamstime.com: Cecoffman Lcrb.

Jacket images: Front and Spine: AWL Images: Danita Delimont.

All other images © Dorling Kindersley
For further information see: www.dkimages.com

Transport Map of Alaska

Arctic Ocean

ALASKA
CANADA

Kenai Peninsula

SE Alaska

Chukchi Sea

RUSSIA

Bering Sea

Point Lay

Point Hope

Kivalina
Noatak
Cape Krusenstern NM
Noatak

Kotzebue

Shishmaref

Bering Land Bridge National Preserve
Deering

Wales

Teller
Kougarok
Council

Nome
Ha

Gambell
Savoonga

St. Lawrence Island

Shaktoolik

Stebbins

Kotlik

Sheldon Point
Yukon
Anvik
Holy Cross

Mountain Village

Hooper Bay

Newtok
Kusko

The Kenai Peninsula

Anchorage
Chugach State Park
Hope
College Fjord
Whittier
Resurrection Pass Trail
Blackstone Bay
Captain Cook State Recreation Area
Kenai National Wildlife Refuge
Kenai
Sterling
Moose Pass
Kenai
Cooper Landing
Chugach National Forest
Soldotna
Chenega
Clam Gulch
Seward
Ninilchik
Nikolaevsk
STERLING HWY
SEWARD HWY
Anchor Point
Kenai National Wildlife Refuge
Homer
Halibut Cove
Kenai Fjords National Park
Seldovia

0 km 50
0 miles 50

Kasigluk

Kipnuk
Kwigillingok
Wood-Sta
Quinhagak
Kuskokwim Bay
Platinum
Togiak
Alek
Walrus Islands State Game Sanctuary
Dilling

Bristo Bay

St. Paul
Pribilof Islands

St. George

Port Heiden
Chi

Port Moller

Cold Bay
Izembek NWR
Sand Point
False Pass
King Cove

Dutch Harbor
Akutan
Unalaska
Islands
Aleutian

Pac

Key

- ✈ International airport
- ✈ Domestic airport/airstrip
- ⛴ Ferry port
- Alaska Highway
- Major road
- ⋯ Minor road
- Alaska Railroad
- Alaska Marine Highway
- International border